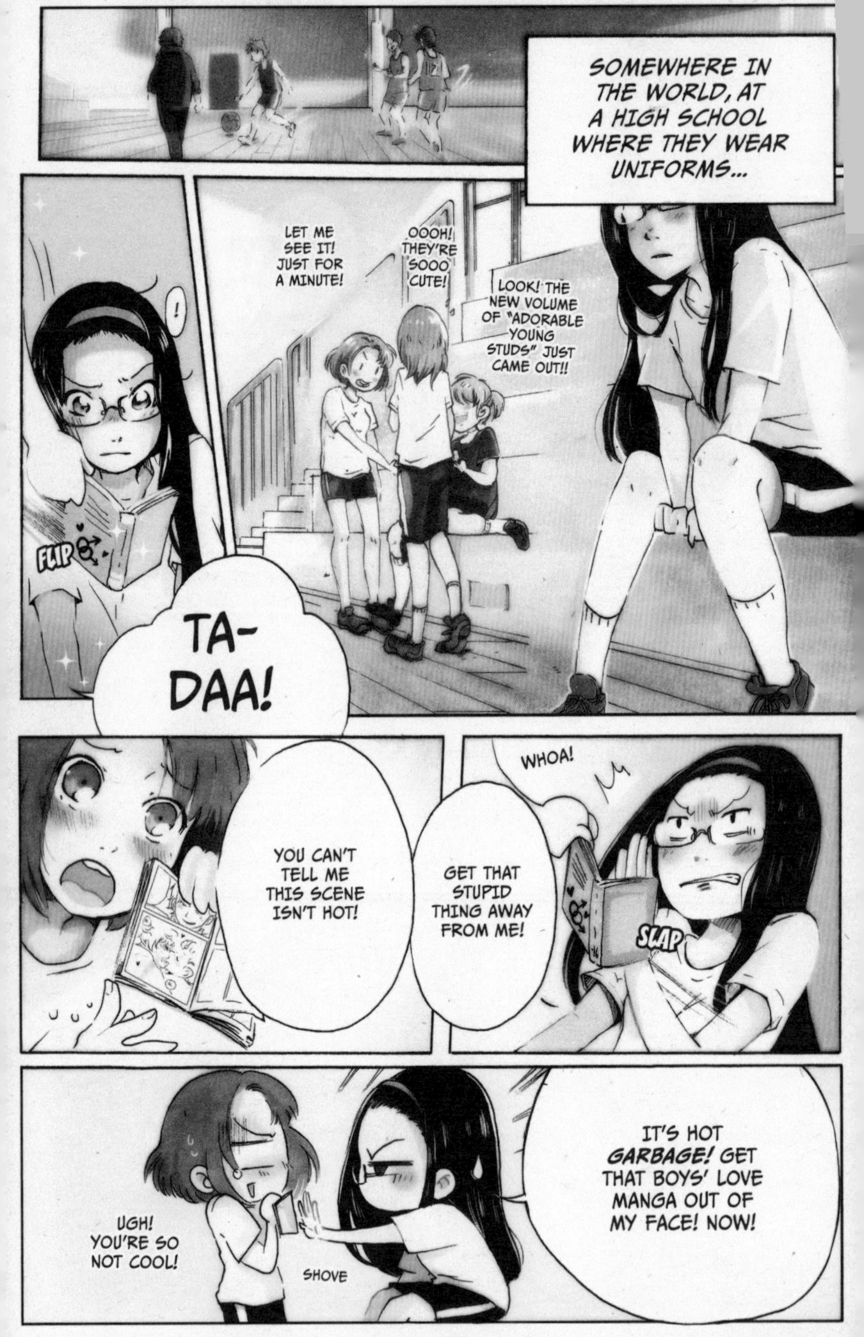
SOMEWHERE IN THE WORLD, AT A HIGH SCHOOL WHERE THEY WEAR UNIFORMS...
LOOK! THE NEW VOLUME OF "ADORABLE YOUNG STUDS" JUST CAME OUT!!
OOOH! THEY'RE SOOO CUTE!
LET ME SEE IT! JUST FOR A MINUTE!
!
FLIP
TA-DAA!
WHOA!
GET THAT STUPID THING AWAY FROM ME!
SLAP
YOU CAN'T TELL ME THIS SCENE ISN'T HOT!
IT'S HOT *GARBAGE!* GET THAT BOYS' LOVE MANGA OUT OF MY FACE! NOW!
SHOVE
UGH! YOU'RE SO NOT COOL!

Table of Contents

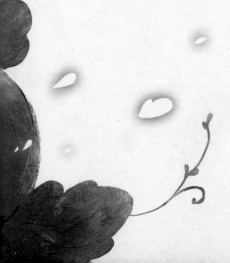

Chapter 1
Blooming

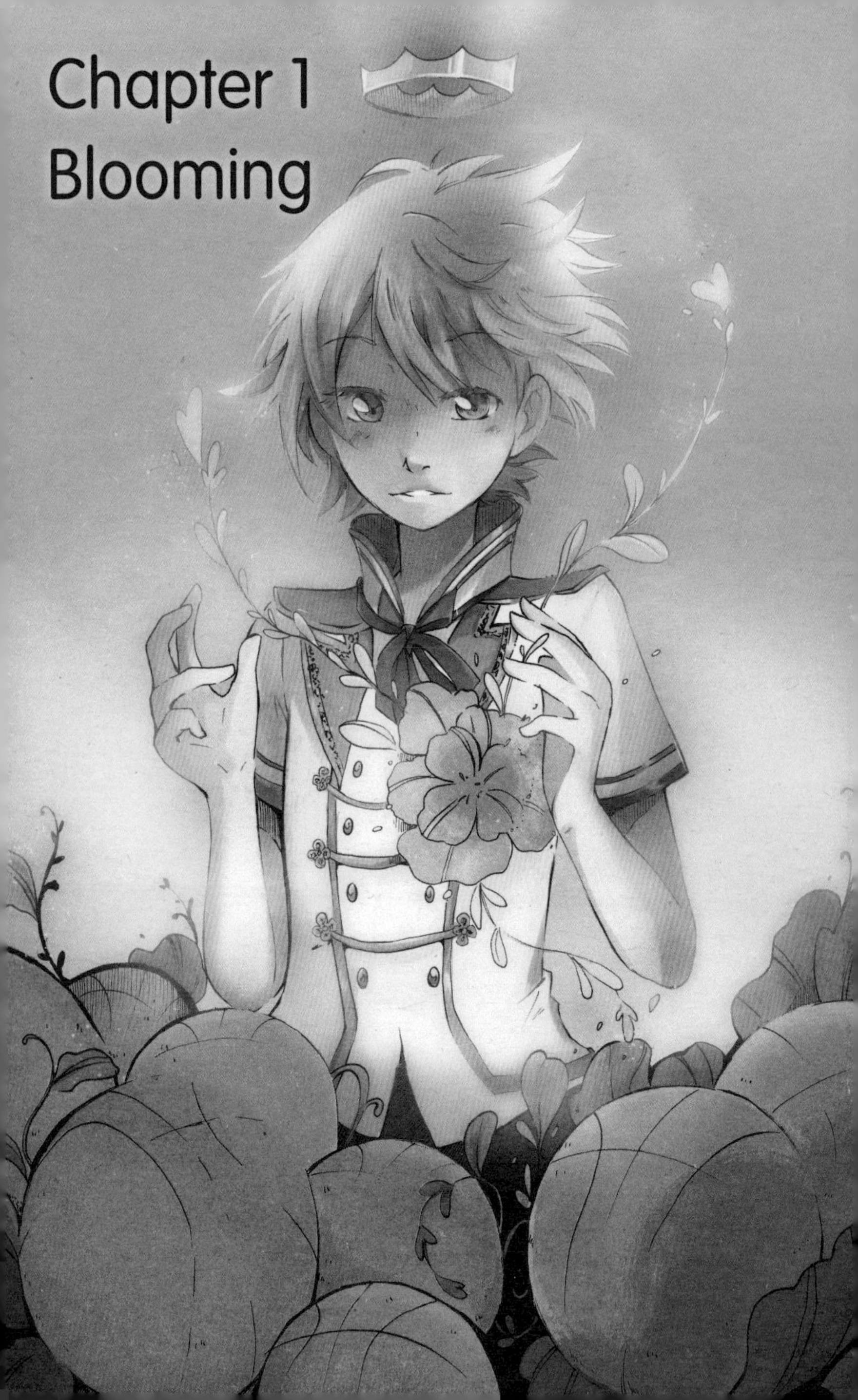

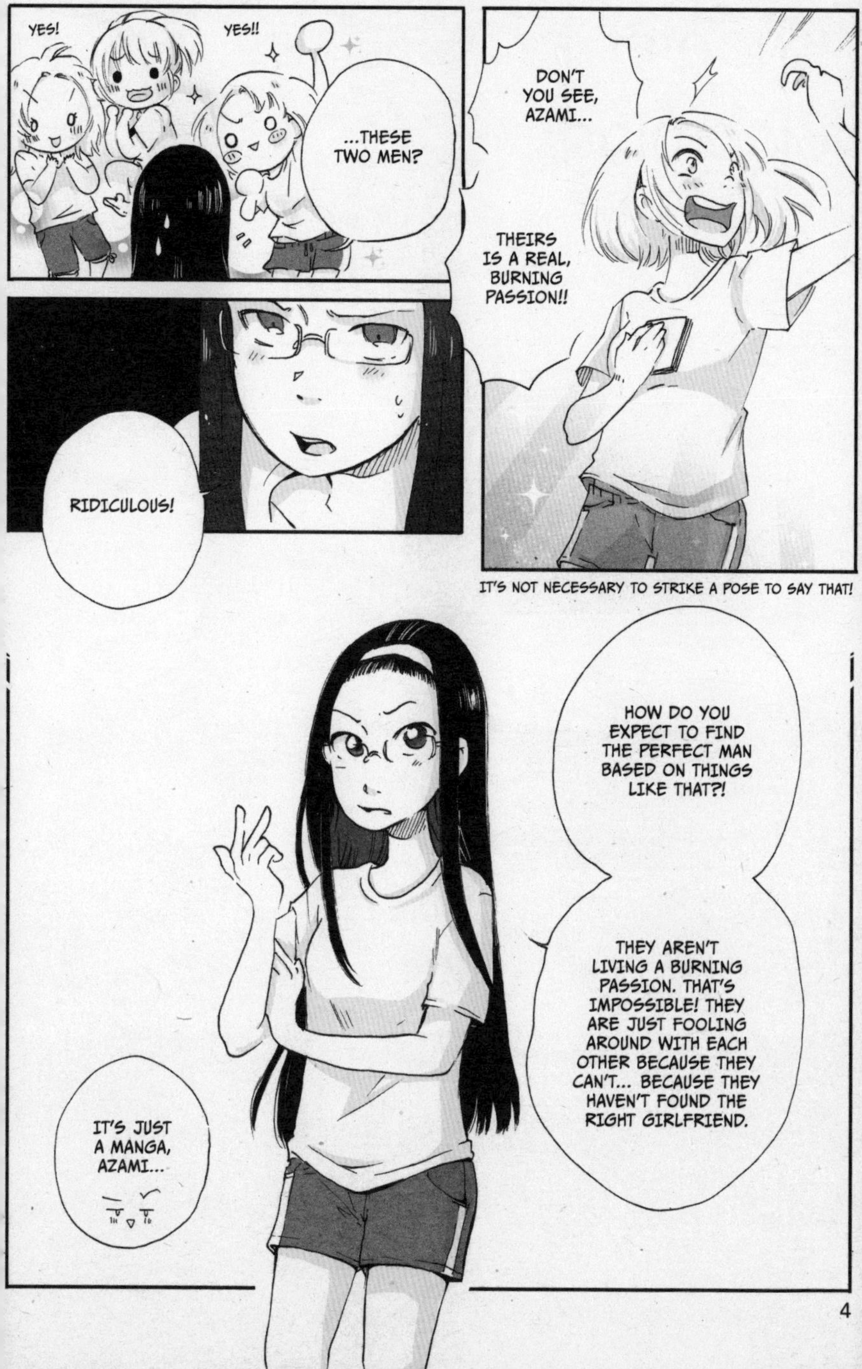
DON'T YOU SEE, AZAMI...
THEIRS IS A REAL, BURNING PASSION!!
...THESE TWO MEN?
YES!!
YES!
RIDICULOUS!
IT'S NOT NECESSARY TO STRIKE A POSE TO SAY THAT!
HOW DO YOU EXPECT TO FIND THE PERFECT MAN BASED ON THINGS LIKE THAT?!
THEY AREN'T LIVING A BURNING PASSION. THAT'S IMPOSSIBLE! THEY ARE JUST FOOLING AROUND WITH EACH OTHER BECAUSE THEY CAN'T... BECAUSE THEY HAVEN'T FOUND THE RIGHT GIRLFRIEND.
IT'S JUST A MANGA, AZAMI...

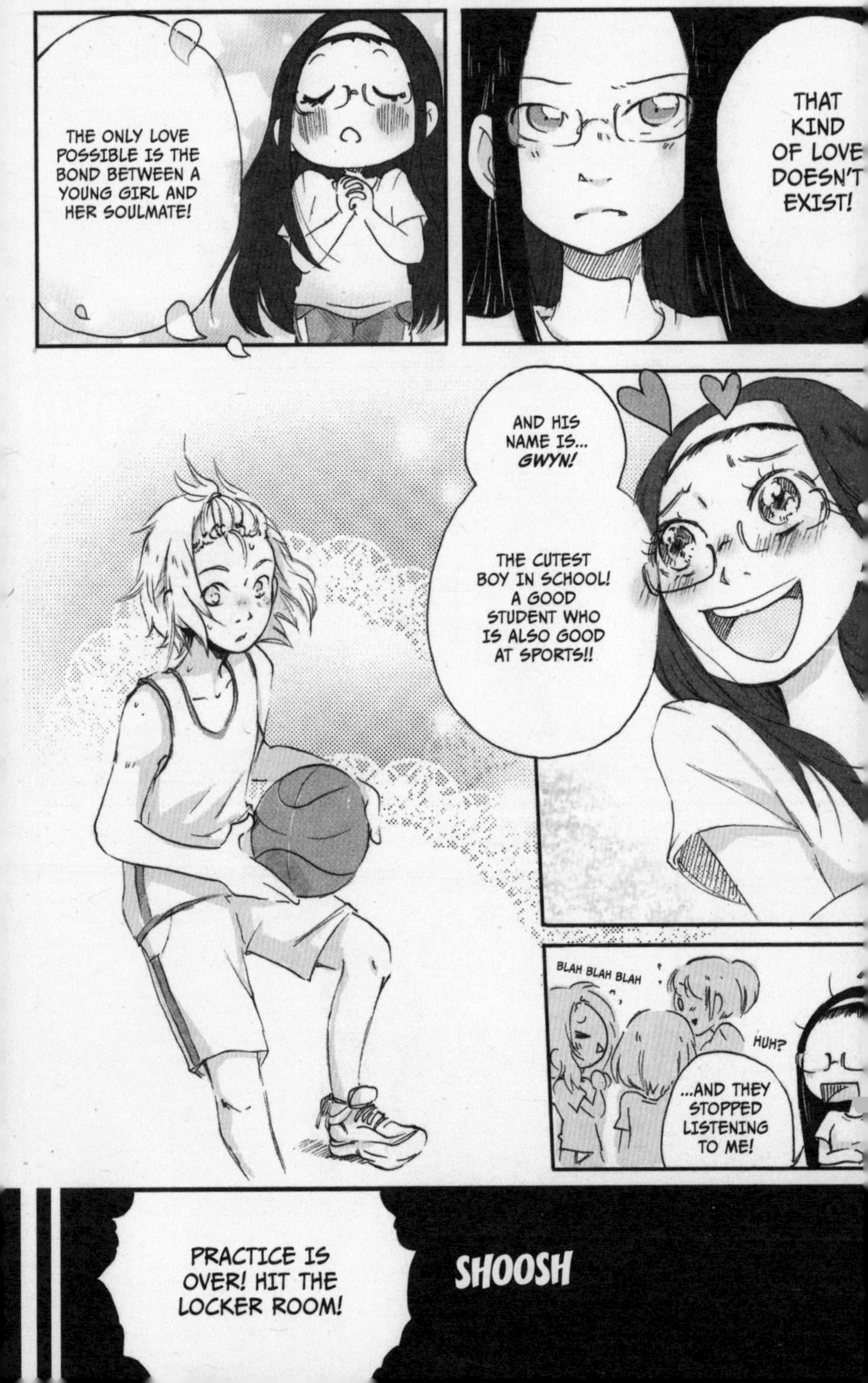
THAT KIND OF LOVE DOESN'T EXIST!
THE ONLY LOVE POSSIBLE IS THE BOND BETWEEN A YOUNG GIRL AND HER SOULMATE!
AND HIS NAME IS... GWYN!
THE CUTEST BOY IN SCHOOL! A GOOD STUDENT WHO IS ALSO GOOD AT SPORTS!!
HUH?
BLAH BLAH BLAH
...AND THEY STOPPED LISTENING TO ME!
SHOOSH
PRACTICE IS OVER! HIT THE LOCKER ROOM!

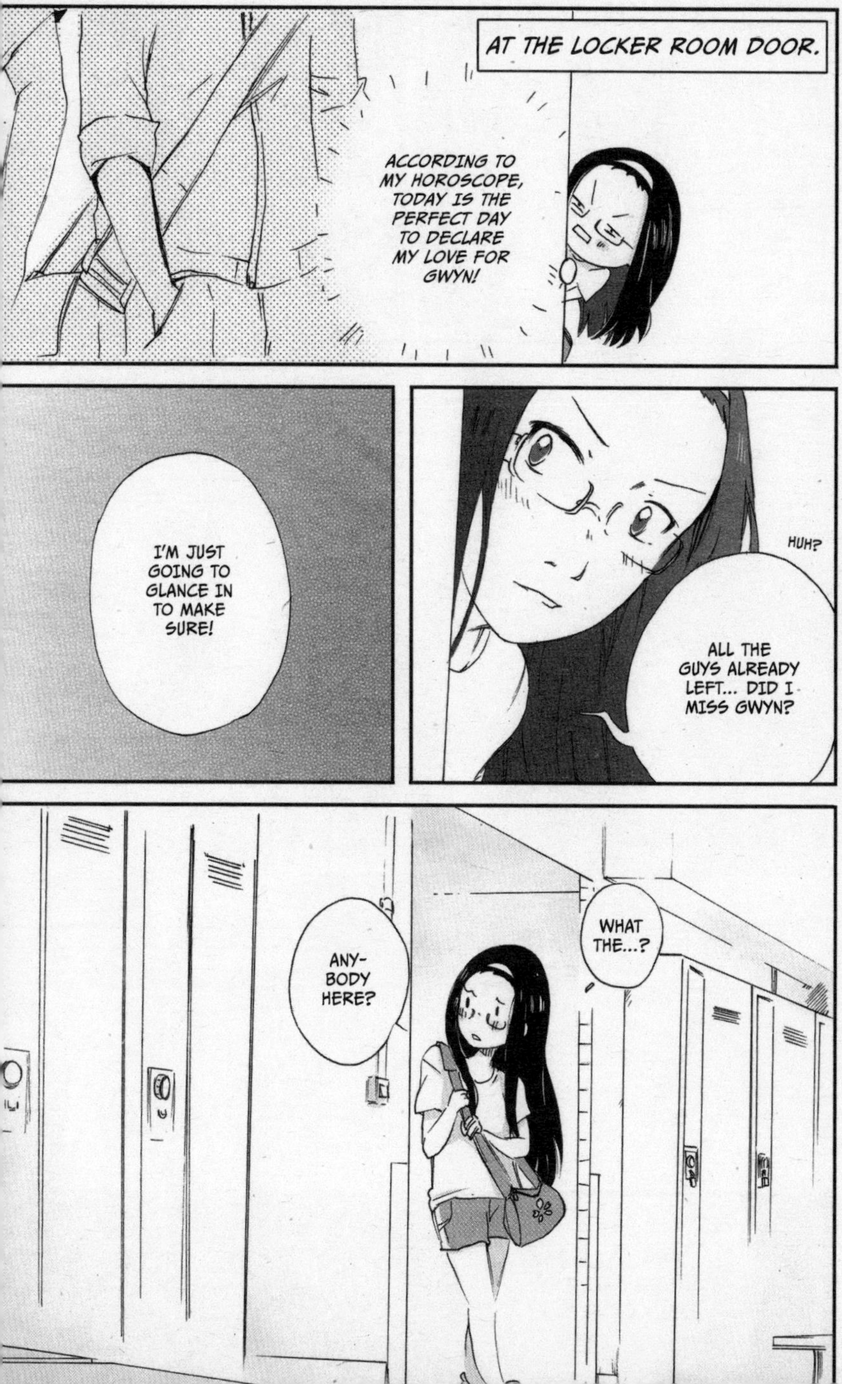
AT THE LOCKER ROOM DOOR.
ACCORDING TO MY HOROSCOPE, TODAY IS THE PERFECT DAY TO DECLARE MY LOVE FOR GWYN!
HUH?
ALL THE GUYS ALREADY LEFT... DID I MISS GWYN?
I'M JUST GOING TO GLANCE IN TO MAKE SURE!
WHAT THE...?
ANY-BODY HERE?

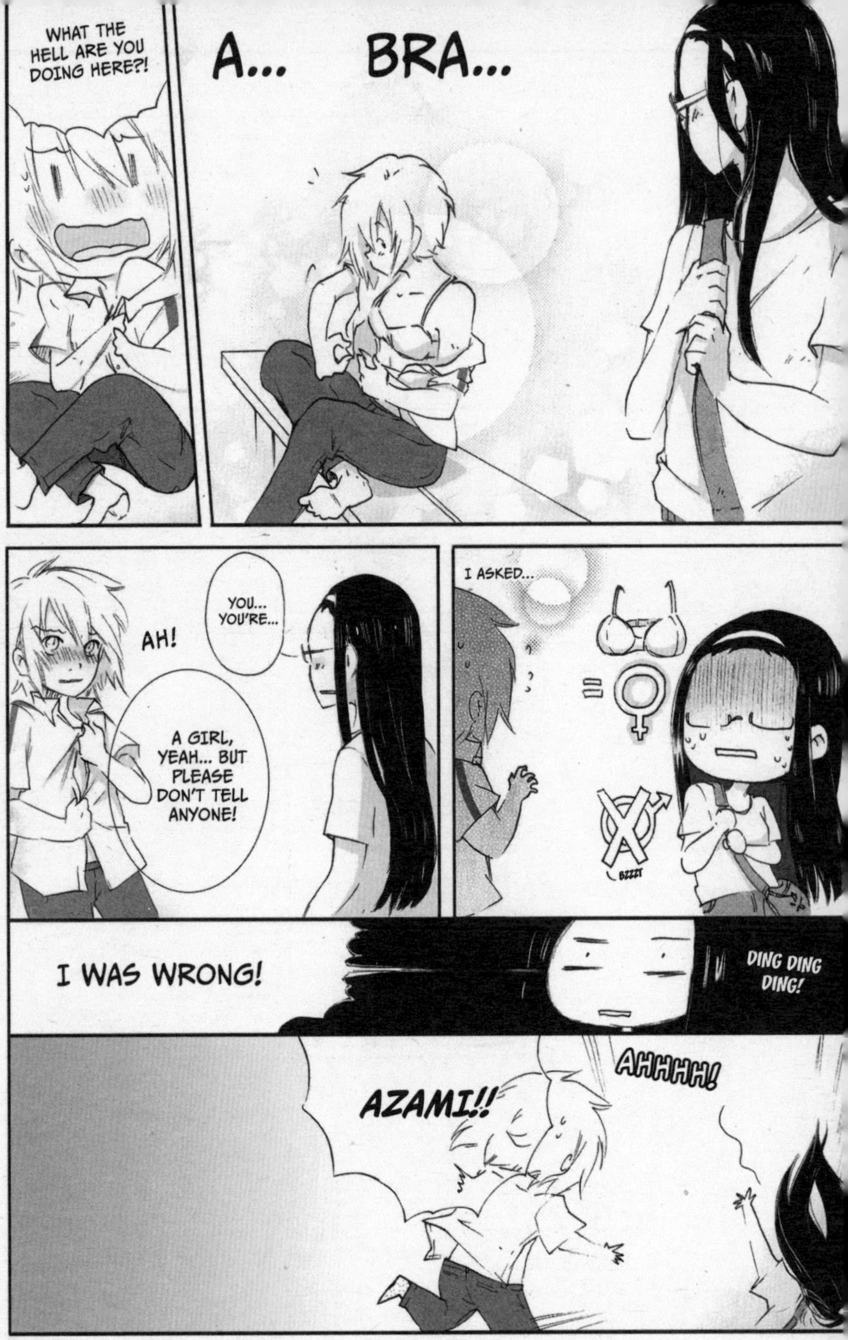
A... BRA...
WHAT THE HELL ARE YOU DOING HERE?!
I ASKED...
BZZZT
YOU... YOU'RE...
AH!
A GIRL, YEAH... BUT PLEASE DON'T TELL ANYONE!
DING DING DING!
I WAS WRONG!
AHHHH!
AZAMI!!

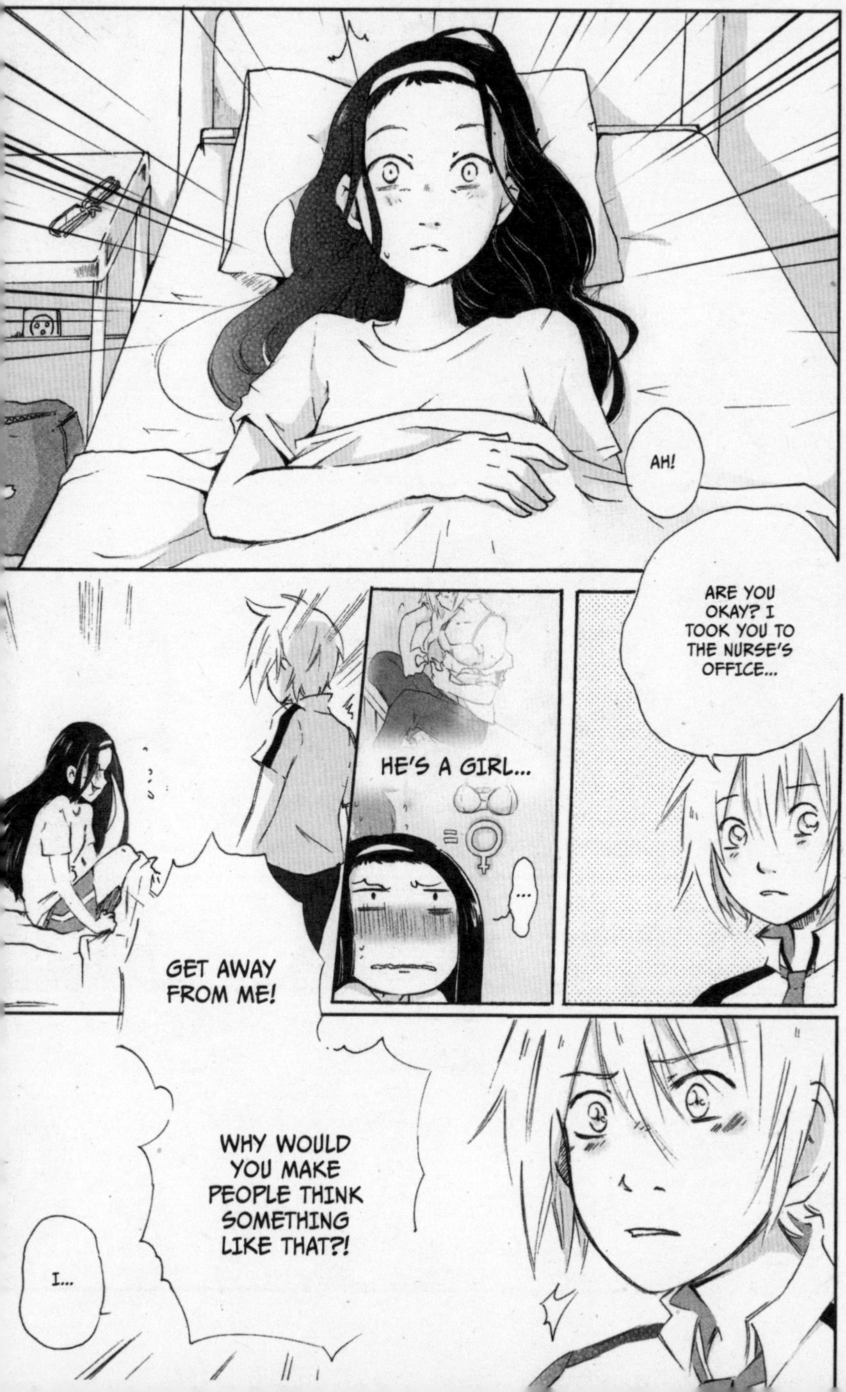
AH!
ARE YOU OKAY? I TOOK YOU TO THE NURSE'S OFFICE...
HE'S A GIRL...
...
GET AWAY FROM ME!
WHY WOULD YOU MAKE PEOPLE THINK SOMETHING LIKE THAT?!
I...

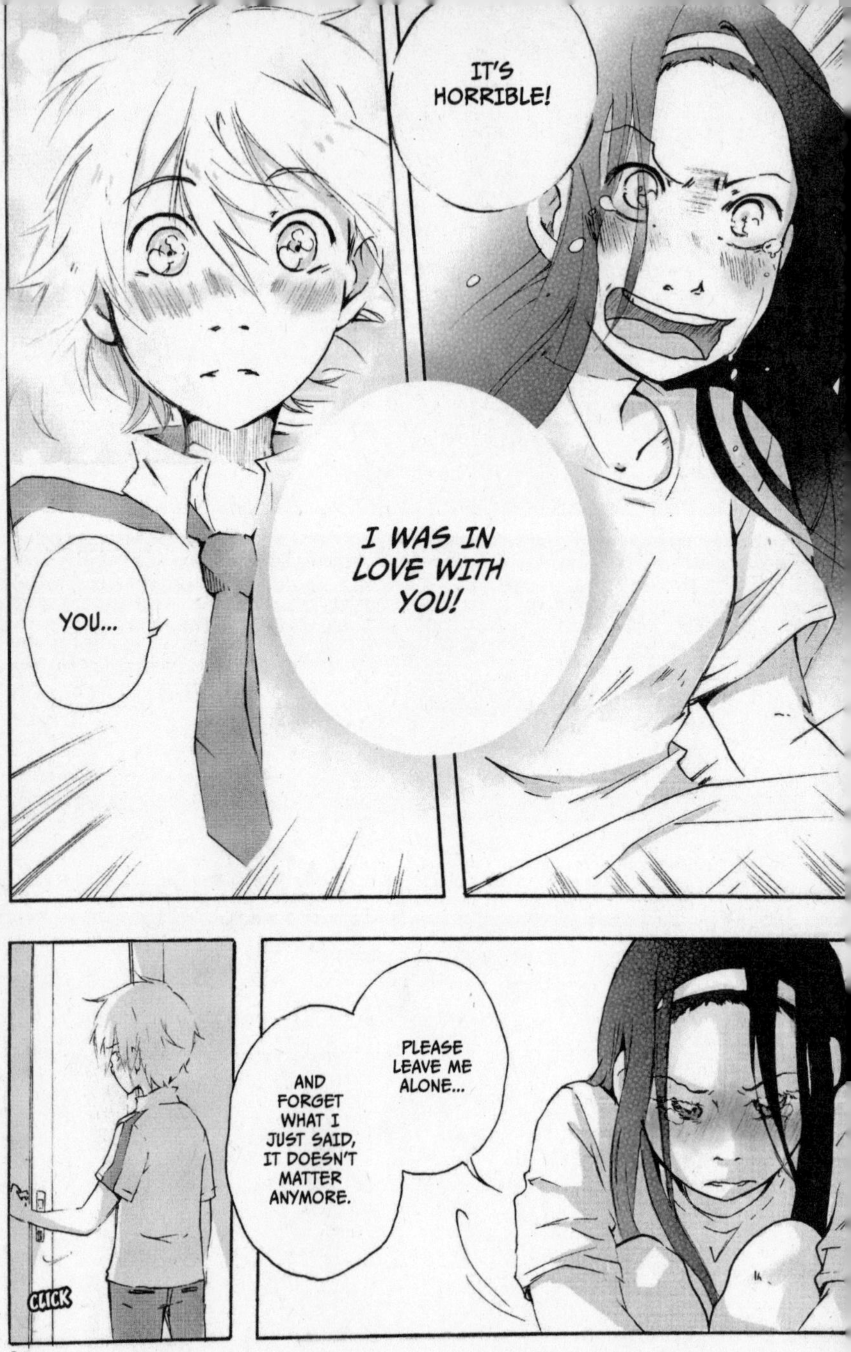
IT'S HORRIBLE!
I WAS IN LOVE WITH YOU!
YOU...
PLEASE LEAVE ME ALONE...
AND FORGET WHAT I JUST SAID, IT DOESN'T MATTER ANYMORE.
CLICK

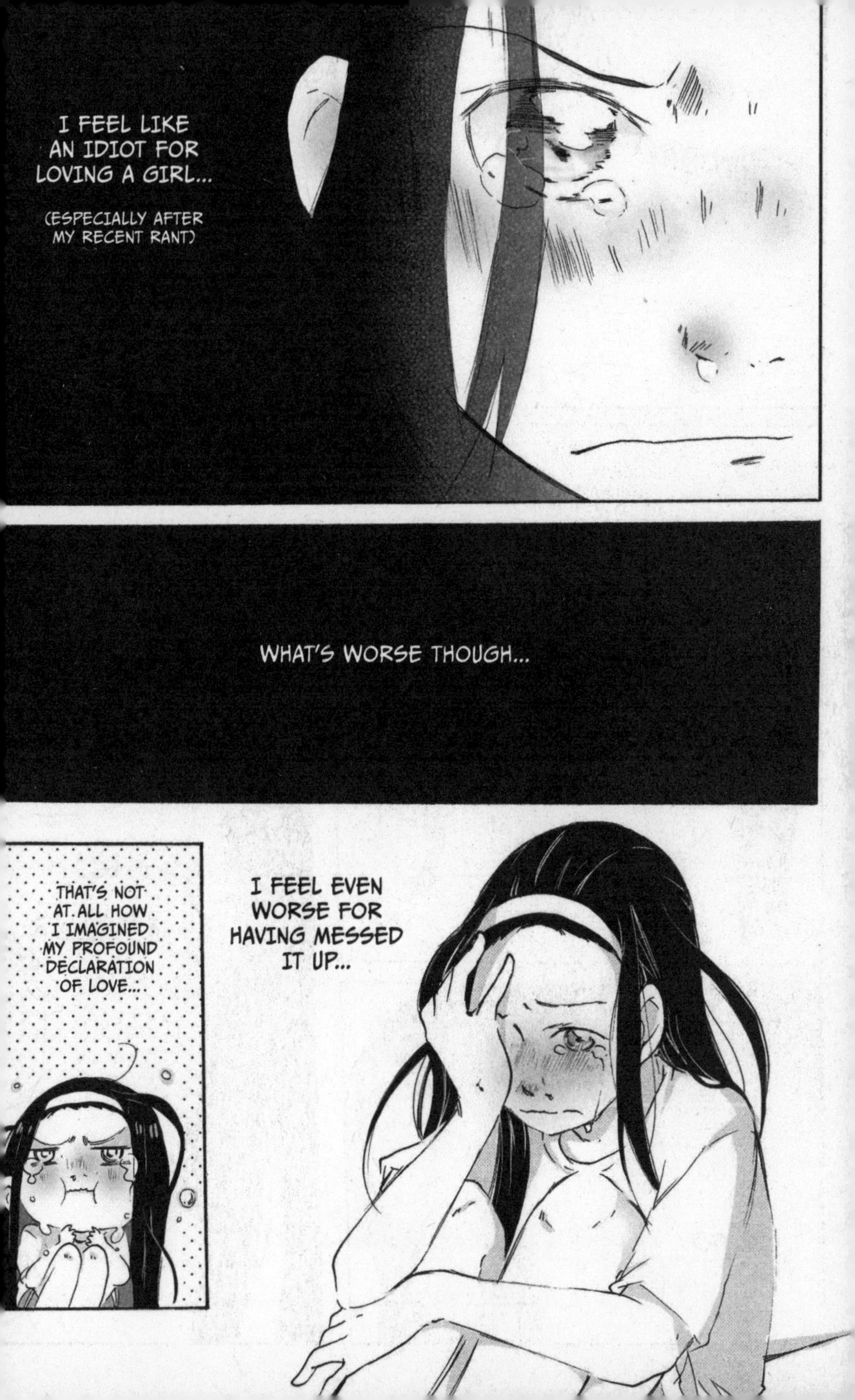
I FEEL LIKE AN IDIOT FOR LOVING A GIRL...
(ESPECIALLY AFTER MY RECENT RANT)
WHAT'S WORSE THOUGH...
I FEEL EVEN WORSE FOR HAVING MESSED IT UP...
THAT'S NOT AT ALL HOW I IMAGINED MY PROFOUND DECLARATION OF LOVE...

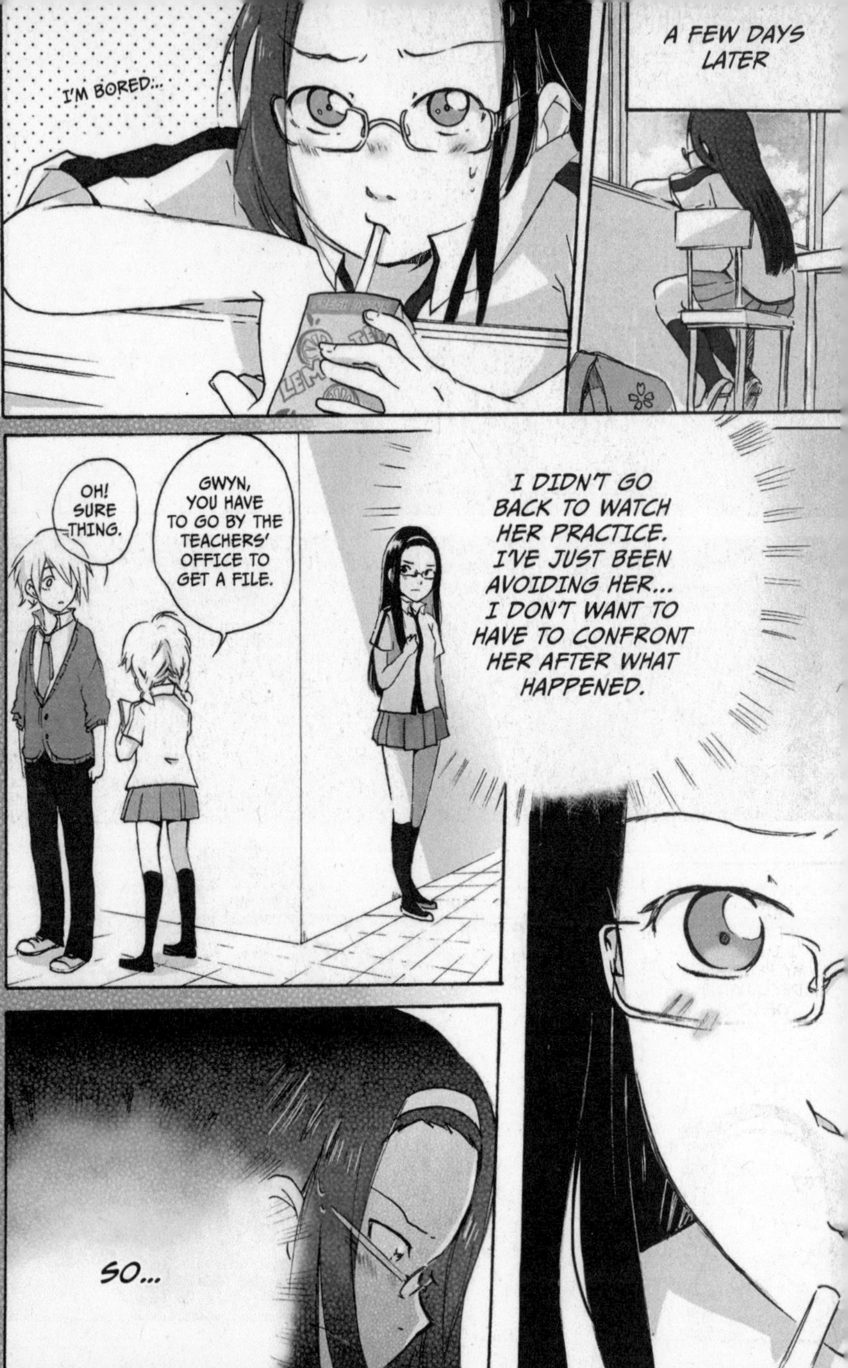
A FEW DAYS LATER
I'M BORED...
I DIDN'T GO BACK TO WATCH HER PRACTICE. I'VE JUST BEEN AVOIDING HER... I DON'T WANT TO HAVE TO CONFRONT HER AFTER WHAT HAPPENED.
GWYN, YOU HAVE TO GO BY THE TEACHERS' OFFICE TO GET A FILE.
OH! SURE THING.
SO...

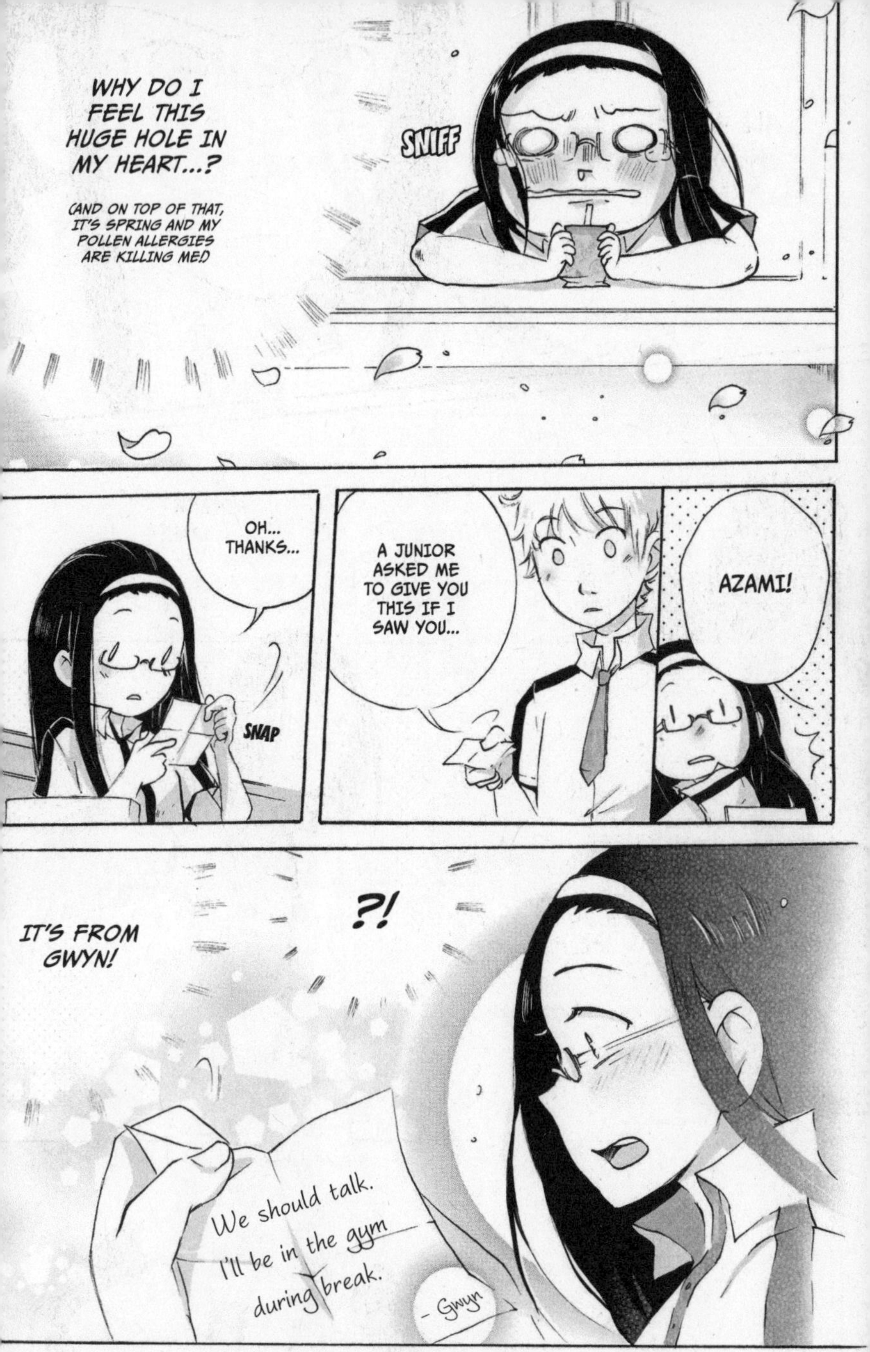
WHY DO I FEEL THIS HUGE HOLE IN MY HEART...?
(AND ON TOP OF THAT, IT'S SPRING AND MY POLLEN ALLERGIES ARE KILLING ME!)
SNIFF
AZAMI!
A JUNIOR ASKED ME TO GIVE YOU THIS IF I SAW YOU...
OH... THANKS...
SNAP
?!
IT'S FROM GWYN!
We should talk. I'll be in the gym during break.
- Gwyn

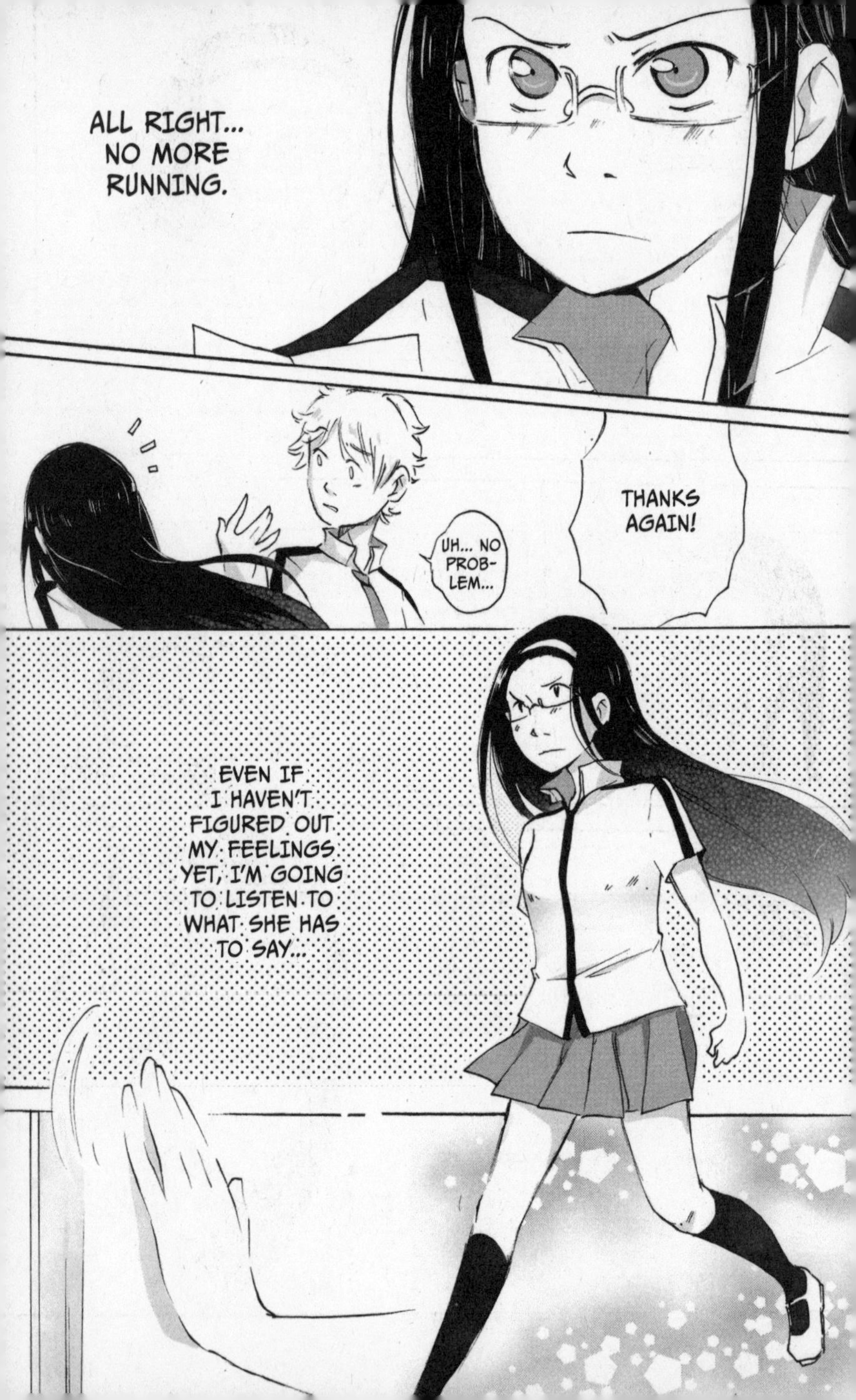
ALL RIGHT... NO MORE RUNNING.
THANKS AGAIN!
UH... NO PROB-LEM...
EVEN IF I HAVEN'T FIGURED OUT MY FEELINGS YET, I'M GOING TO LISTEN TO WHAT SHE HAS TO SAY...

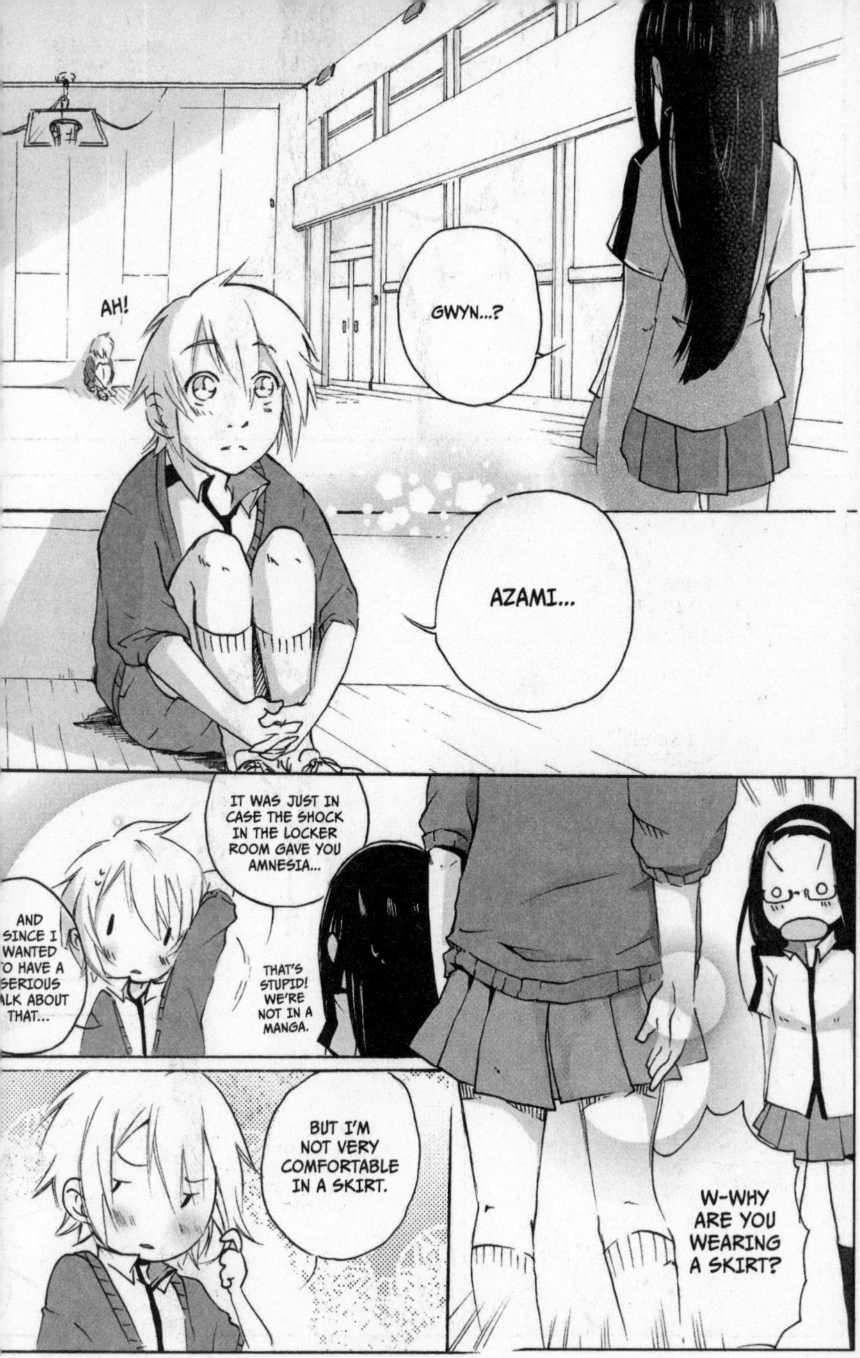
GWYN...?
AH!
AZAMI...
W-WHY ARE YOU WEARING A SKIRT?
IT WAS JUST IN CASE THE SHOCK IN THE LOCKER ROOM GAVE YOU AMNESIA...
THAT'S STUPID! WE'RE NOT IN A MANGA.
AND SINCE I WANTED O HAVE A ERIOUS ALK ABOUT THAT...
BUT I'M NOT VERY COMFORTABLE IN A SKIRT.

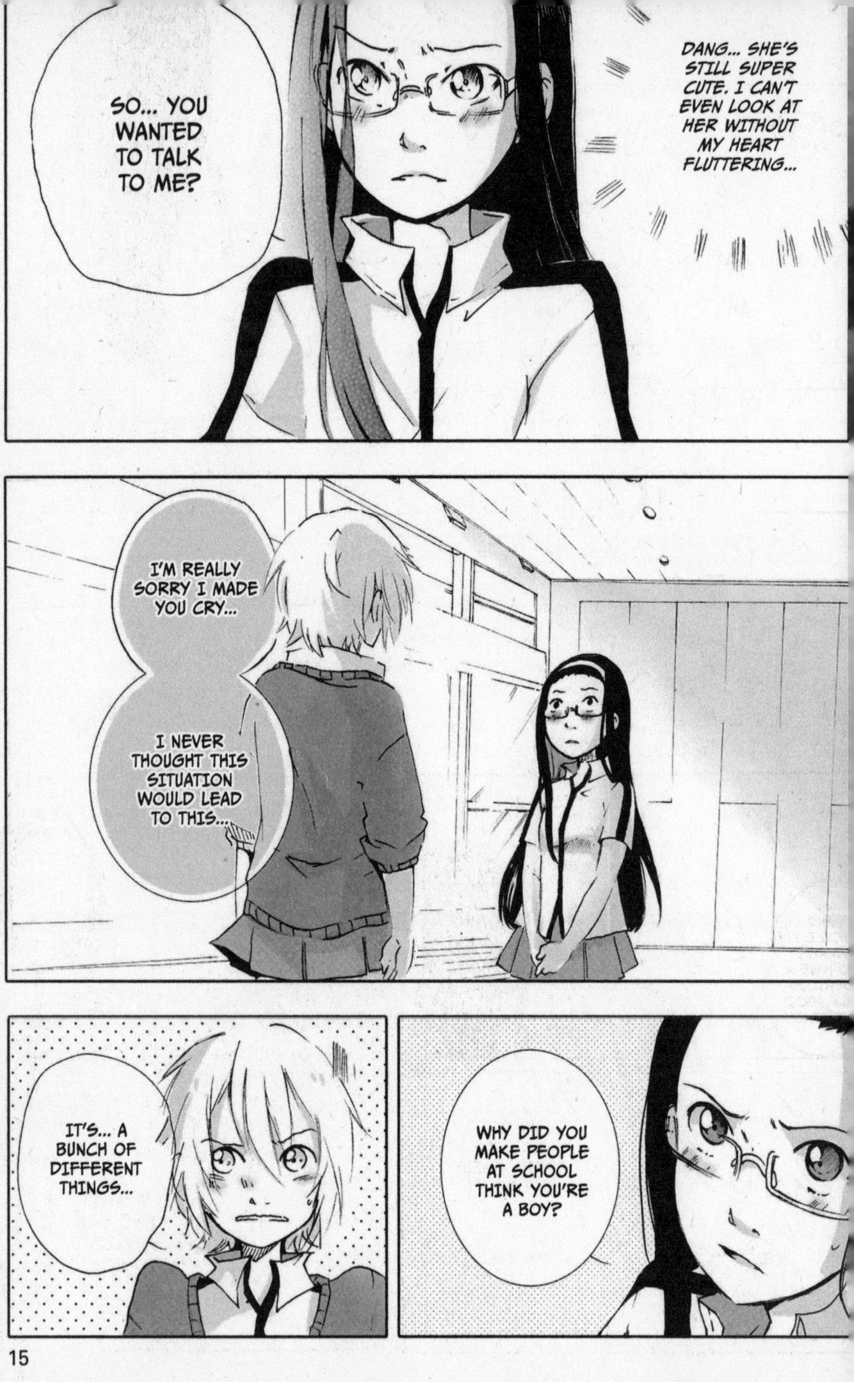
DANG... SHE'S STILL SUPER CUTE. I CAN'T EVEN LOOK AT HER WITHOUT MY HEART FLUTTERING...
SO... YOU WANTED TO TALK TO ME?
I'M REALLY SORRY I MADE YOU CRY...
I NEVER THOUGHT THIS SITUATION WOULD LEAD TO THIS...
WHY DID YOU MAKE PEOPLE AT SCHOOL THINK YOU'RE A BOY?
IT'S... A BUNCH OF DIFFERENT THINGS...

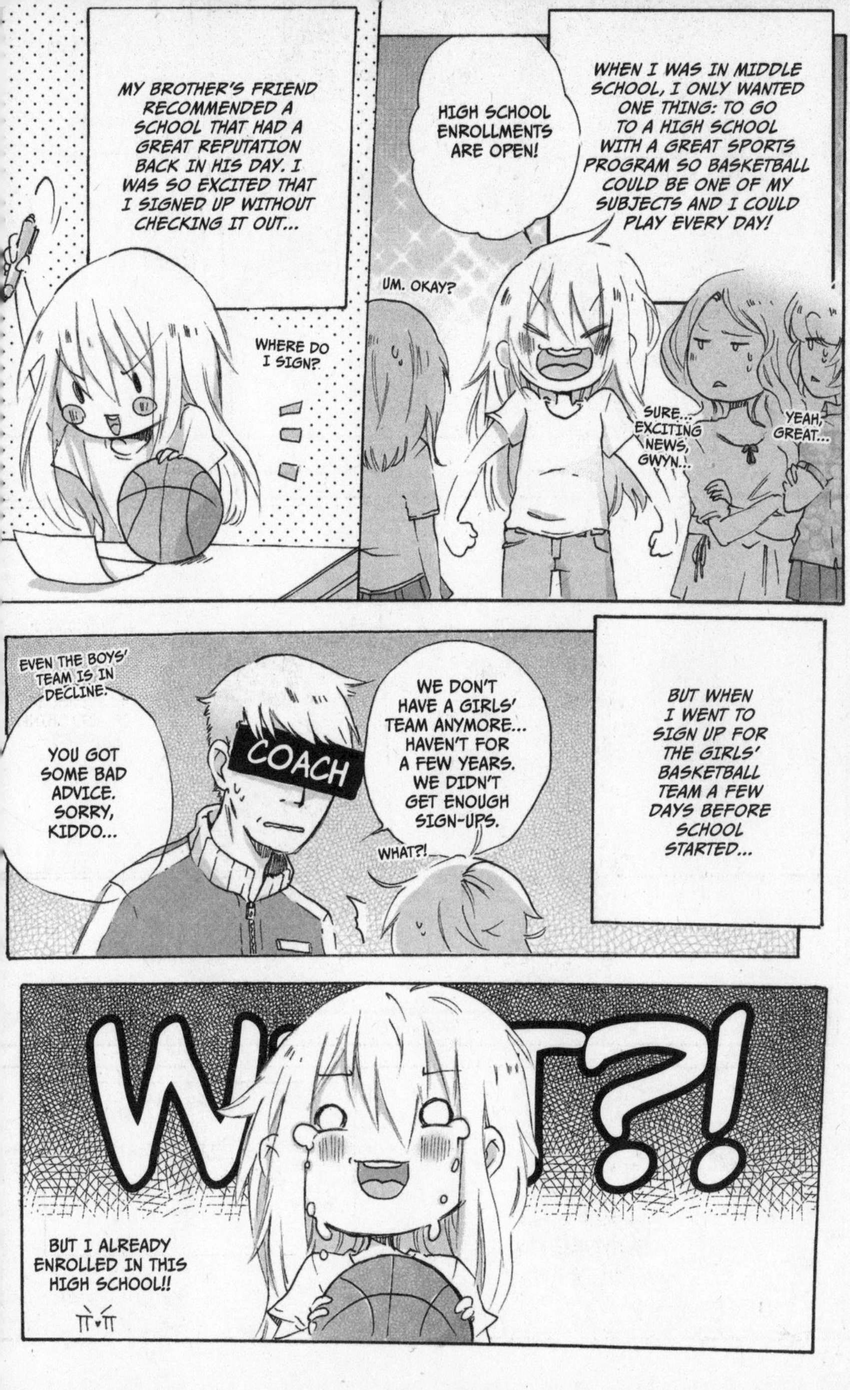

WHEN I WAS IN MIDDLE SCHOOL, I ONLY WANTED ONE THING: TO GO TO A HIGH SCHOOL WITH A GREAT SPORTS PROGRAM SO BASKETBALL COULD BE ONE OF MY SUBJECTS AND I COULD PLAY EVERY DAY!
HIGH SCHOOL ENROLLMENTS ARE OPEN!
YEAH, GREAT...
SURE... EXCITING NEWS, GWYN...
UM. OKAY?
MY BROTHER'S FRIEND RECOMMENDED A SCHOOL THAT HAD A GREAT REPUTATION BACK IN HIS DAY. I WAS SO EXCITED THAT I SIGNED UP WITHOUT CHECKING IT OUT...
WHERE DO I SIGN?
BUT WHEN I WENT TO SIGN UP FOR THE GIRLS' BASKETBALL TEAM A FEW DAYS BEFORE SCHOOL STARTED...
WE DON'T HAVE A GIRLS' TEAM ANYMORE... HAVEN'T FOR A FEW YEARS. WE DIDN'T GET ENOUGH SIGN-UPS.
WHAT?!
COACH
EVEN THE BOYS' TEAM IS IN DECLINE.
YOU GOT SOME BAD ADVICE. SORRY, KIDDO...
BUT I ALREADY ENROLLED IN THIS HIGH SCHOOL!!

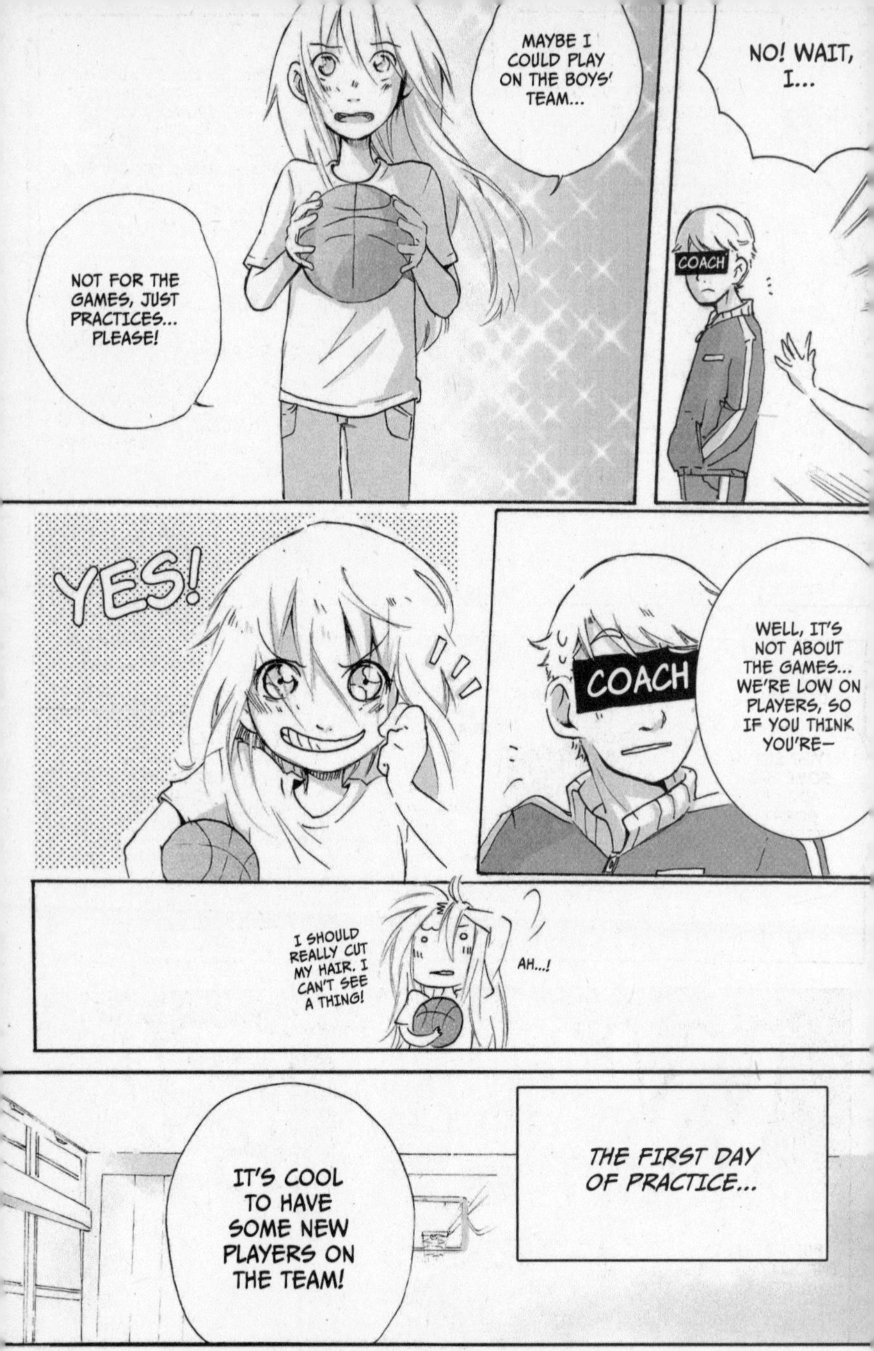
NO! WAIT, I...
COACH
MAYBE I COULD PLAY ON THE BOYS' TEAM...
NOT FOR THE GAMES, JUST PRACTICES... PLEASE!
COACH
WELL, IT'S NOT ABOUT THE GAMES... WE'RE LOW ON PLAYERS, SO IF YOU THINK YOU'RE—
YES!
AH...!
I SHOULD REALLY CUT MY HAIR. I CAN'T SEE A THING!
THE FIRST DAY OF PRACTICE...
IT'S COOL TO HAVE SOME NEW PLAYERS ON THE TEAM!

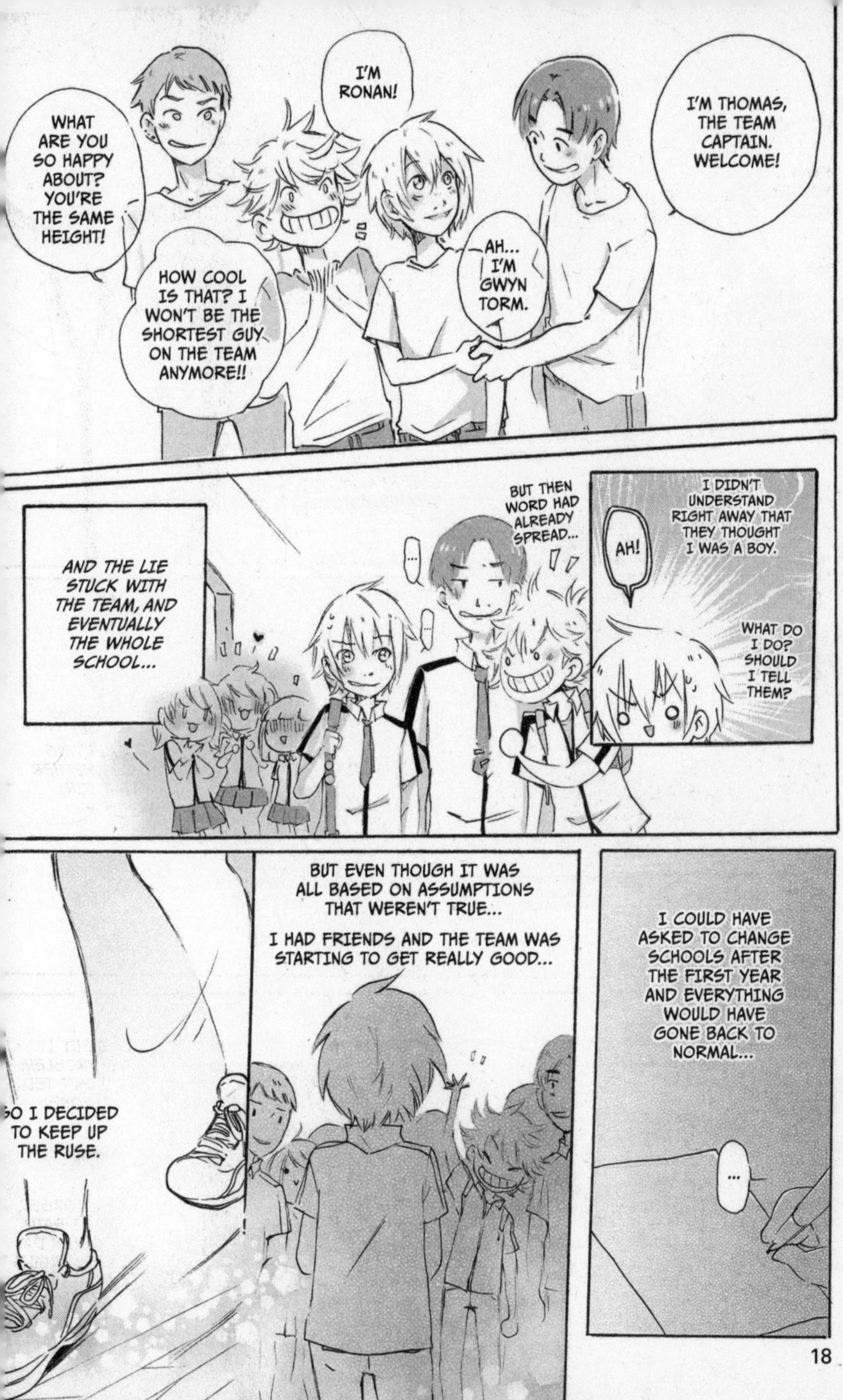
I'M THOMAS, THE TEAM CAPTAIN. WELCOME!
AH... I'M GWYN TORM.
I'M RONAN!
HOW COOL IS THAT? I WON'T BE THE SHORTEST GUY ON THE TEAM ANYMORE!!
WHAT ARE YOU SO HAPPY ABOUT? YOU'RE THE SAME HEIGHT!
I DIDN'T UNDERSTAND RIGHT AWAY THAT THEY THOUGHT I WAS A BOY.
AH!
WHAT DO I DO? SHOULD I TELL THEM?
BUT THEN WORD HAD ALREADY SPREAD...
...
...
AND THE LIE STUCK WITH THE TEAM, AND EVENTUALLY THE WHOLE SCHOOL...
I COULD HAVE ASKED TO CHANGE SCHOOLS AFTER THE FIRST YEAR AND EVERYTHING WOULD HAVE GONE BACK TO NORMAL...
...
BUT EVEN THOUGH IT WAS ALL BASED ON ASSUMPTIONS THAT WEREN'T TRUE...
I HAD FRIENDS AND THE TEAM WAS STARTING TO GET REALLY GOOD...
SO I DECIDED TO KEEP UP THE RUSE.

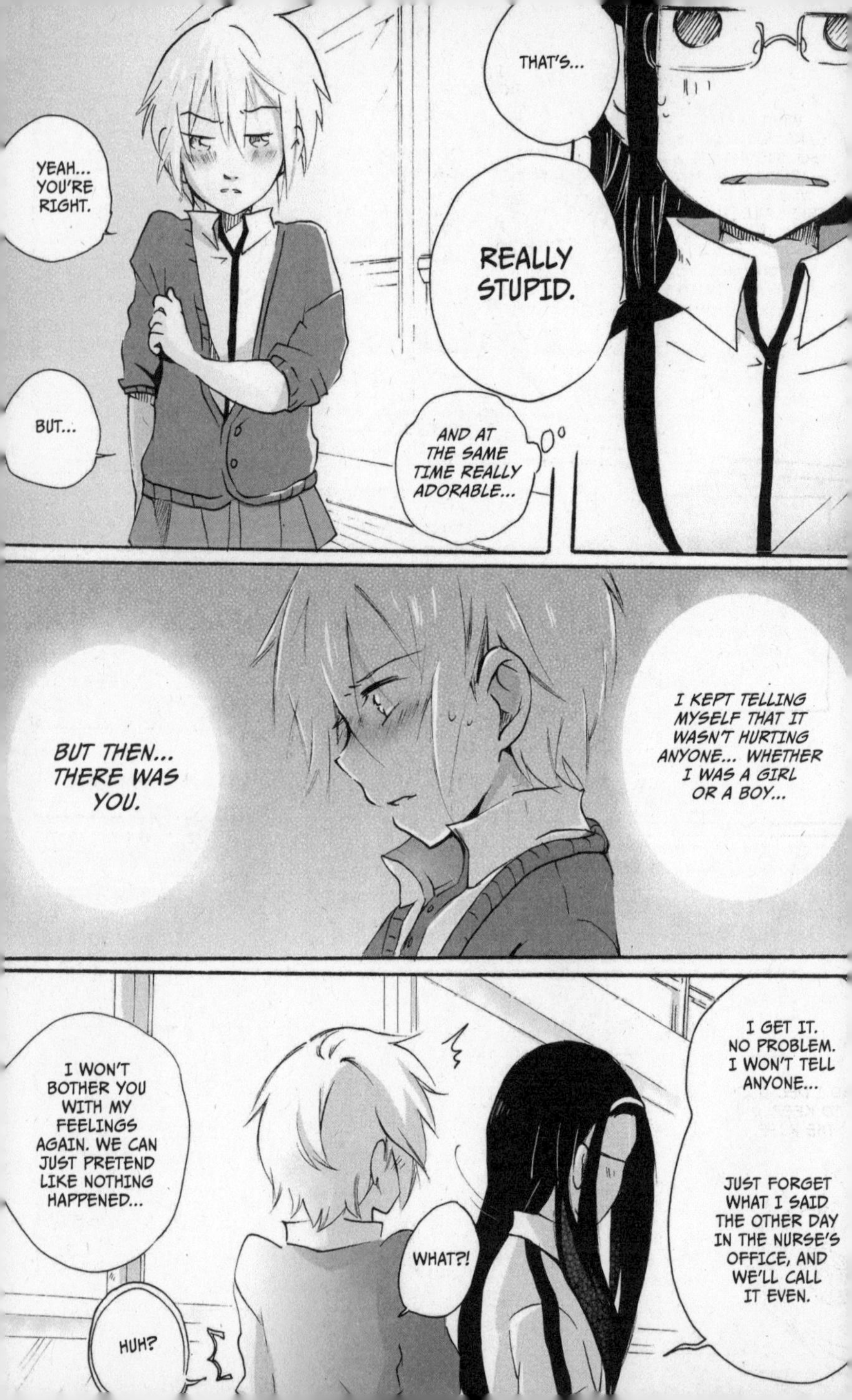

THAT'S...
REALLY STUPID.
AND AT THE SAME TIME REALLY ADORABLE...
YEAH... YOU'RE RIGHT.
BUT...
I KEPT TELLING MYSELF THAT IT WASN'T HURTING ANYONE... WHETHER I WAS A GIRL OR A BOY...
BUT THEN... THERE WAS YOU.
I GET IT. NO PROBLEM. I WON'T TELL ANYONE...
I WON'T BOTHER YOU WITH MY FEELINGS AGAIN. WE CAN JUST PRETEND LIKE NOTHING HAPPENED...
JUST FORGET WHAT I SAID THE OTHER DAY IN THE NURSE'S OFFICE, AND WE'LL CALL IT EVEN.
WHAT?!
HUH?

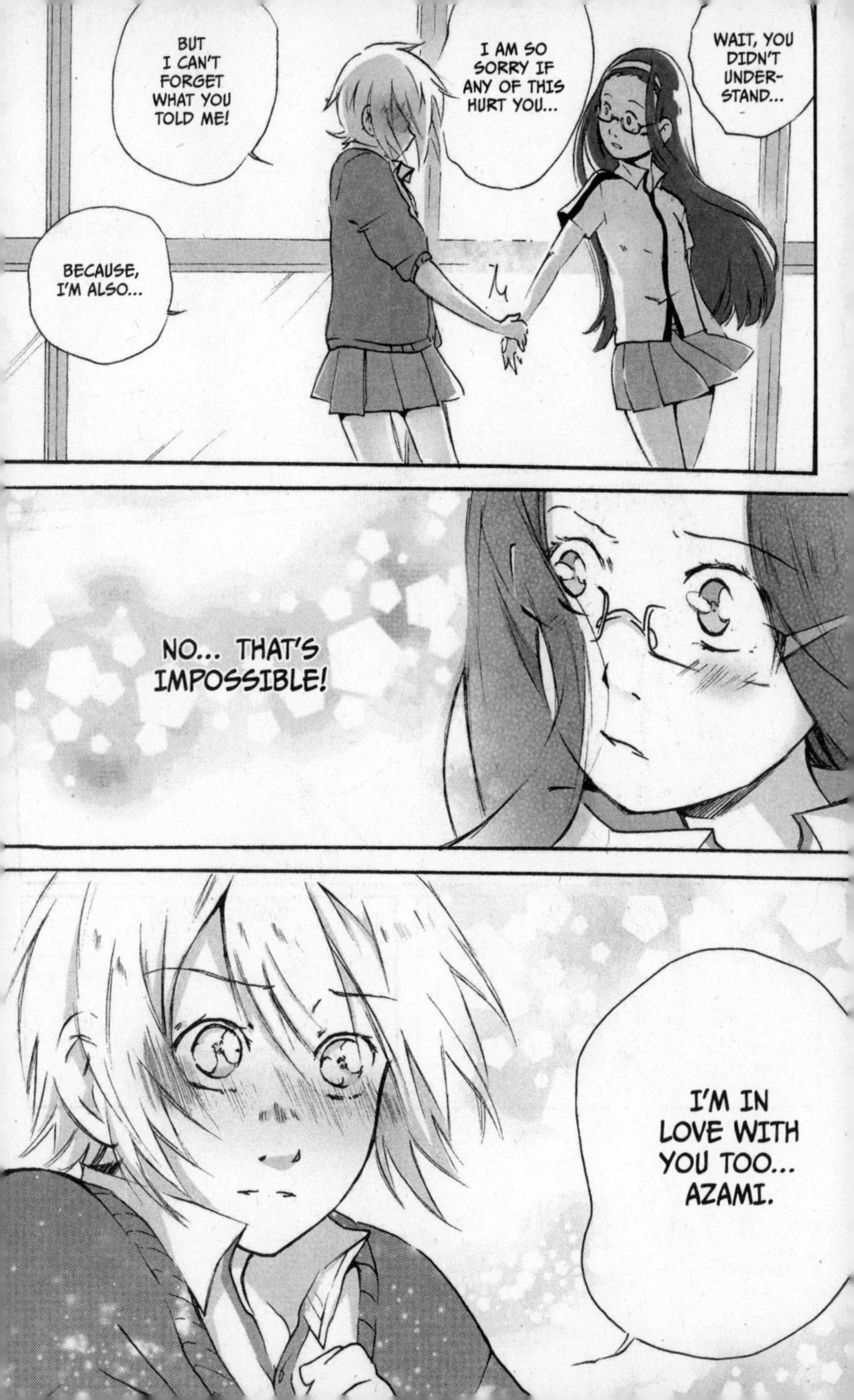
WAIT, YOU DIDN'T UNDER-STAND...
I AM SO SORRY IF ANY OF THIS HURT YOU...
BUT I CAN'T FORGET WHAT YOU TOLD ME!
BECAUSE, I'M ALSO...
NO... THAT'S IMPOSSIBLE!
I'M IN LOVE WITH YOU TOO... AZAMI.

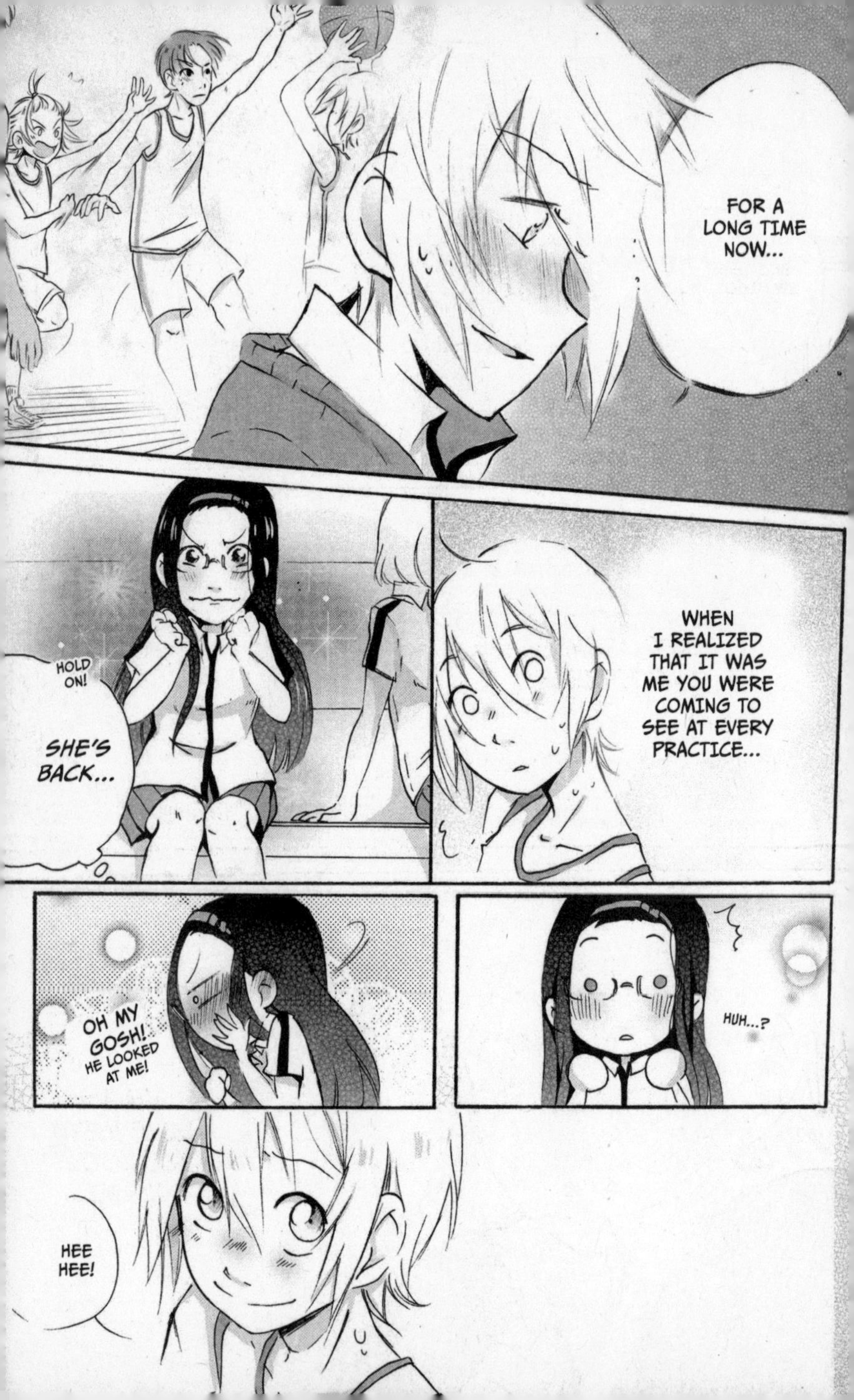
FOR A LONG TIME NOW...
WHEN I REALIZED THAT IT WAS ME YOU WERE COMING TO SEE AT EVERY PRACTICE...
HOLD ON!
SHE'S BACK...
HUH...?
OH MY GOSH! HE LOOKED AT ME!
HEE HEE!

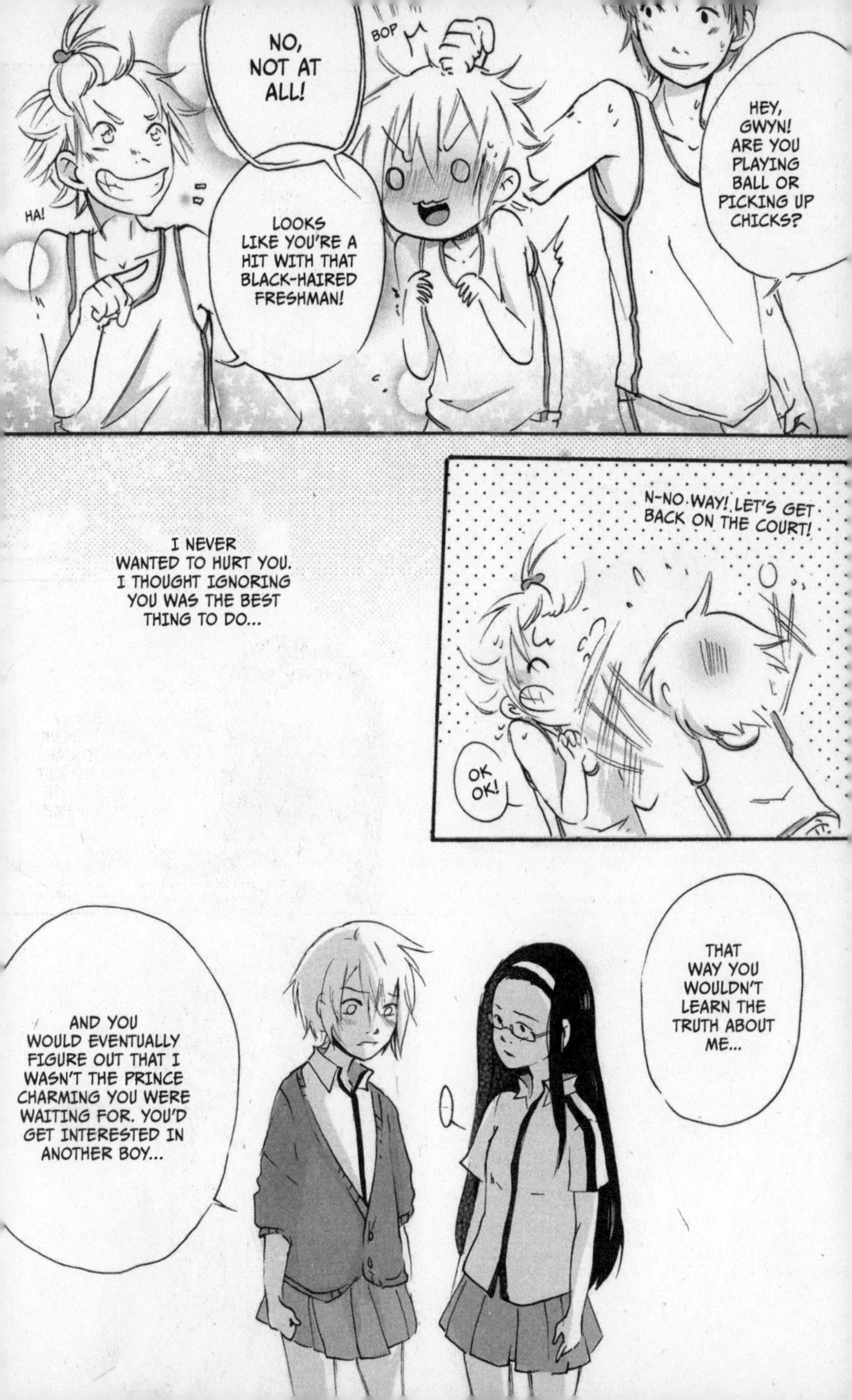
HEY, GWYN! ARE YOU PLAYING BALL OR PICKING UP CHICKS?
BOP
NO, NOT AT ALL!
LOOKS LIKE YOU'RE A HIT WITH THAT BLACK-HAIRED FRESHMAN!
HA!
N-NO WAY! LET'S GET BACK ON THE COURT!
OK OK!
I NEVER WANTED TO HURT YOU. I THOUGHT IGNORING YOU WAS THE BEST THING TO DO...
THAT WAY YOU WOULDN'T LEARN THE TRUTH ABOUT ME...
AND YOU WOULD EVENTUALLY FIGURE OUT THAT I WASN'T THE PRINCE CHARMING YOU WERE WAITING FOR. YOU'D GET INTERESTED IN ANOTHER BOY...

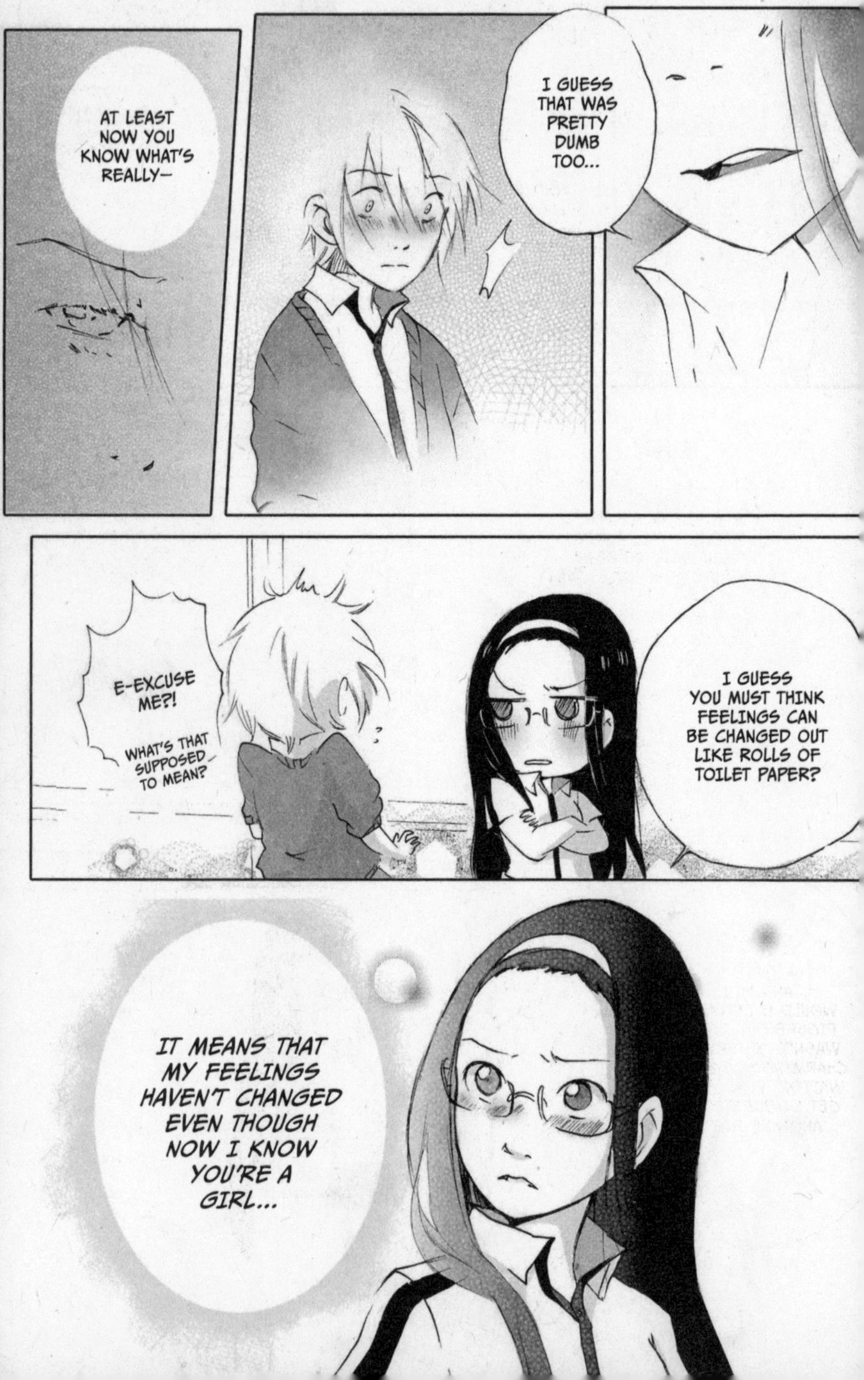
I GUESS THAT WAS PRETTY DUMB TOO...
AT LEAST NOW YOU KNOW WHAT'S REALLY—
I GUESS YOU MUST THINK FEELINGS CAN BE CHANGED OUT LIKE ROLLS OF TOILET PAPER?
E-EXCUSE ME?!
WHAT'S THAT SUPPOSED TO MEAN?
IT MEANS THAT MY FEELINGS HAVEN'T CHANGED EVEN THOUGH NOW I KNOW YOU'RE A GIRL...

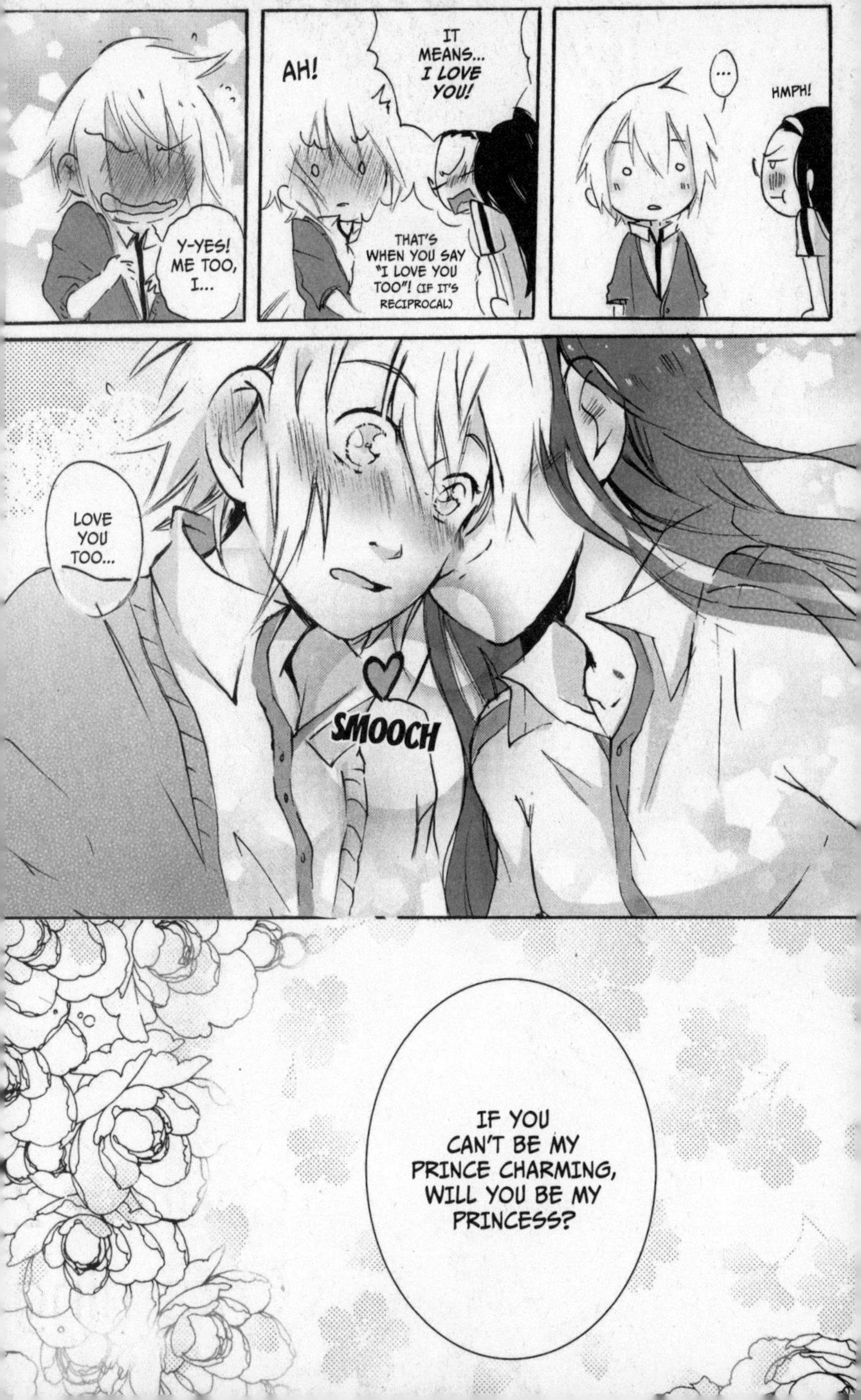
HMPH!
...
IT MEANS... I LOVE YOU!
AH!
THAT'S WHEN YOU SAY "I LOVE YOU TOO"! (IF IT'S RECIPROCAL)
Y-YES! ME TOO, I...
LOVE YOU TOO...
SMOOCH
IF YOU CAN'T BE MY PRINCE CHARMING, WILL YOU BE MY PRINCESS?

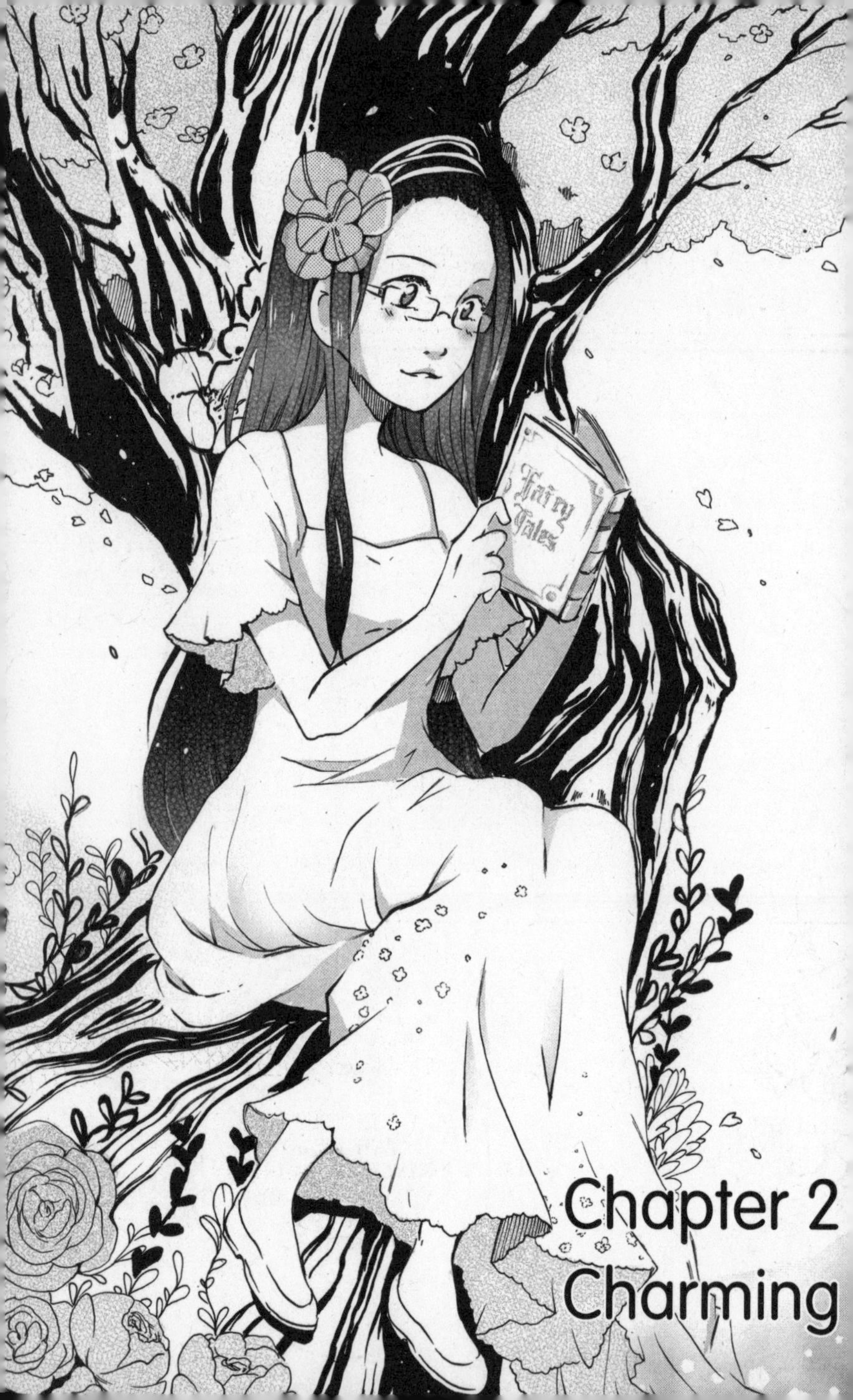
Fairy Tales
Chapter 2
Charming

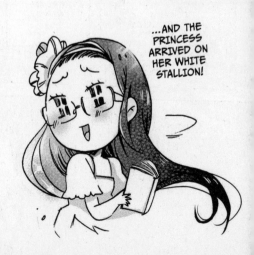

...AND THE PRINCESS ARRIVED ON HER WHITE STALLION!

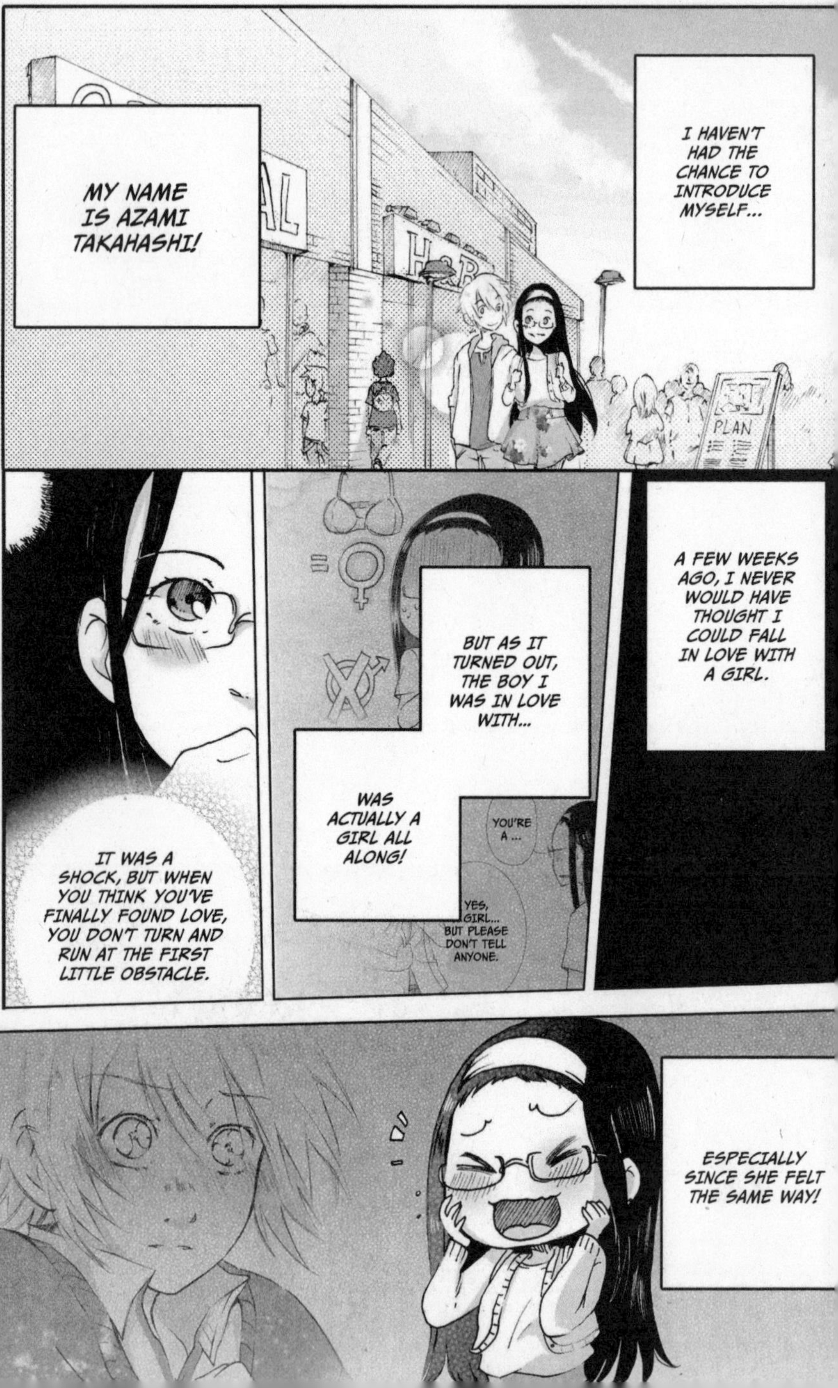
I HAVEN'T HAD THE CHANCE TO INTRODUCE MYSELF...
MY NAME IS AZAMI TAKAHASHI!
PLAN
A FEW WEEKS AGO, I NEVER WOULD HAVE THOUGHT I COULD FALL IN LOVE WITH A GIRL.
BUT AS IT TURNED OUT, THE BOY I WAS IN LOVE WITH...
WAS ACTUALLY A GIRL ALL ALONG!
YOU'RE A ...
YES, GIRL... BUT PLEASE DON'T TELL ANYONE.
IT WAS A SHOCK, BUT WHEN YOU THINK YOU'VE FINALLY FOUND LOVE, YOU DON'T TURN AND RUN AT THE FIRST LITTLE OBSTACLE.
ESPECIALLY SINCE SHE FELT THE SAME WAY!

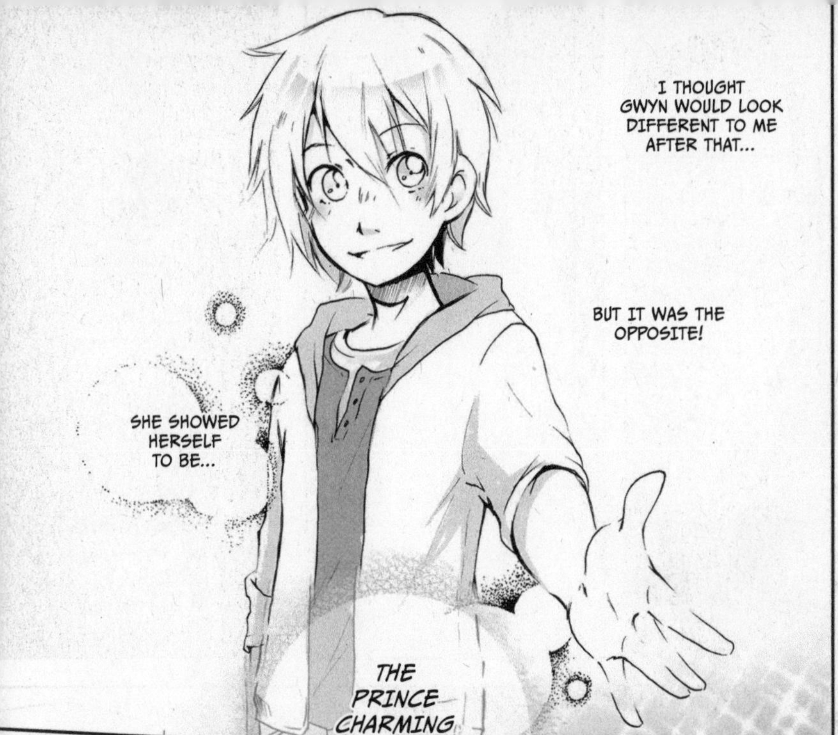
I THOUGHT GWYN WOULD LOOK DIFFERENT TO ME AFTER THAT...
BUT IT WAS THE OPPOSITE!
SHE SHOWED HERSELF TO BE...
THE PRINCE CHARMING I'VE ALWAYS IMAGINED!
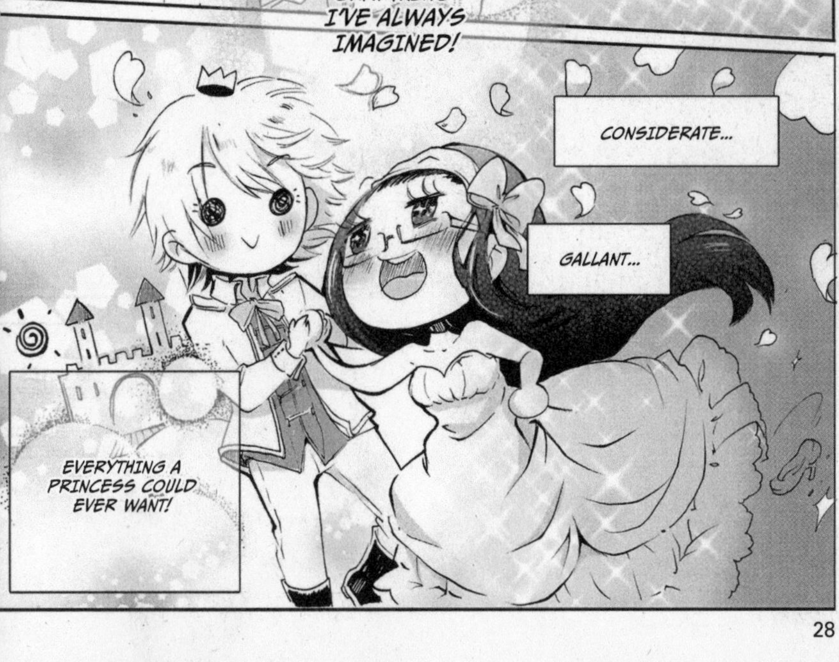
CONSIDERATE...
GALLANT...
EVERYTHING A PRINCESS COULD EVER WANT!

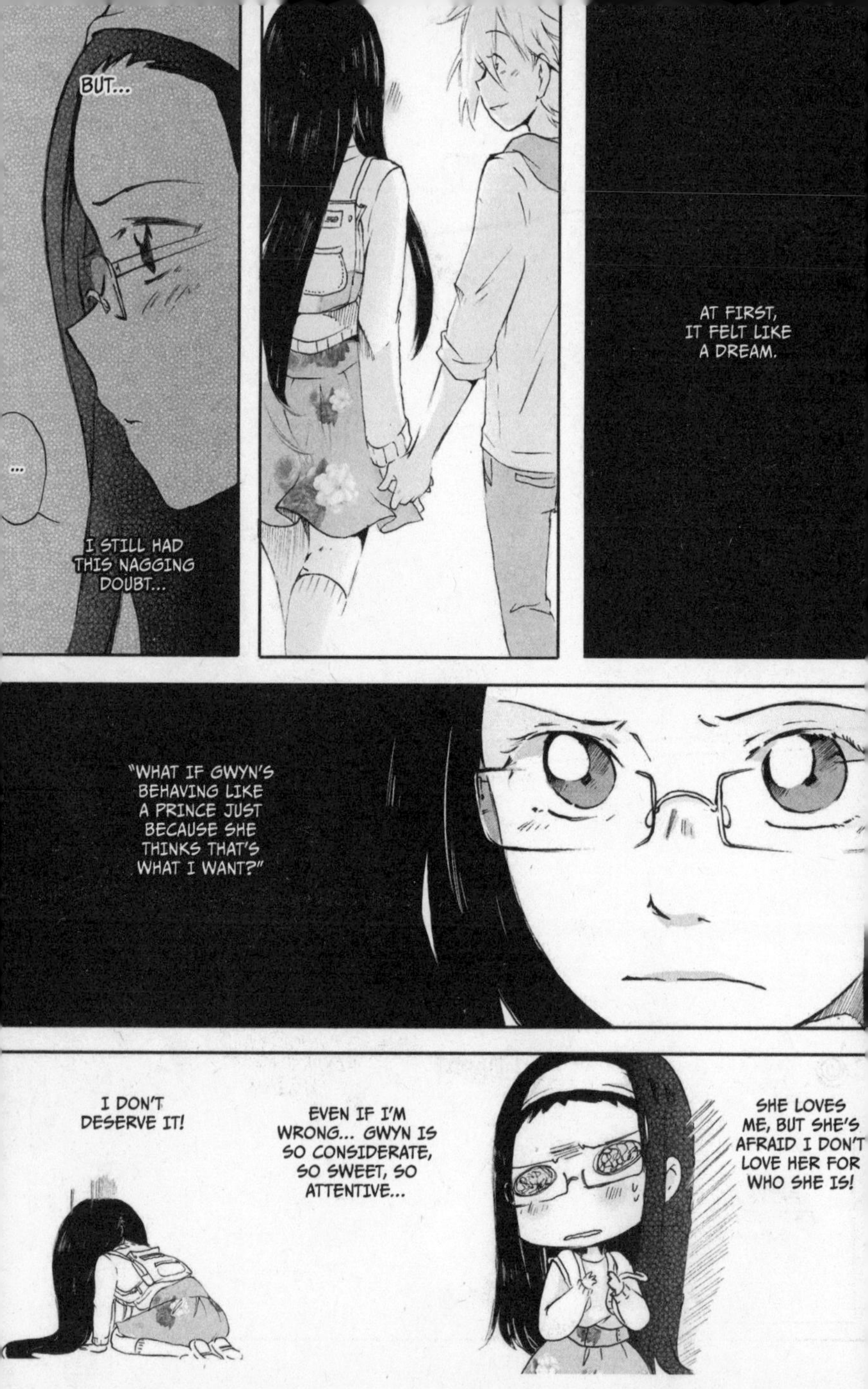
AT FIRST, IT FELT LIKE A DREAM.
BUT...
...
I STILL HAD THIS NAGGING DOUBT...
"WHAT IF GWYN'S BEHAVING LIKE A PRINCE JUST BECAUSE SHE THINKS THAT'S WHAT I WANT?"
SHE LOVES ME, BUT SHE'S AFRAID I DON'T LOVE HER FOR WHO SHE IS!
EVEN IF I'M WRONG... GWYN IS SO CONSIDERATE, SO SWEET, SO ATTENTIVE...
I DON'T DESERVE IT!

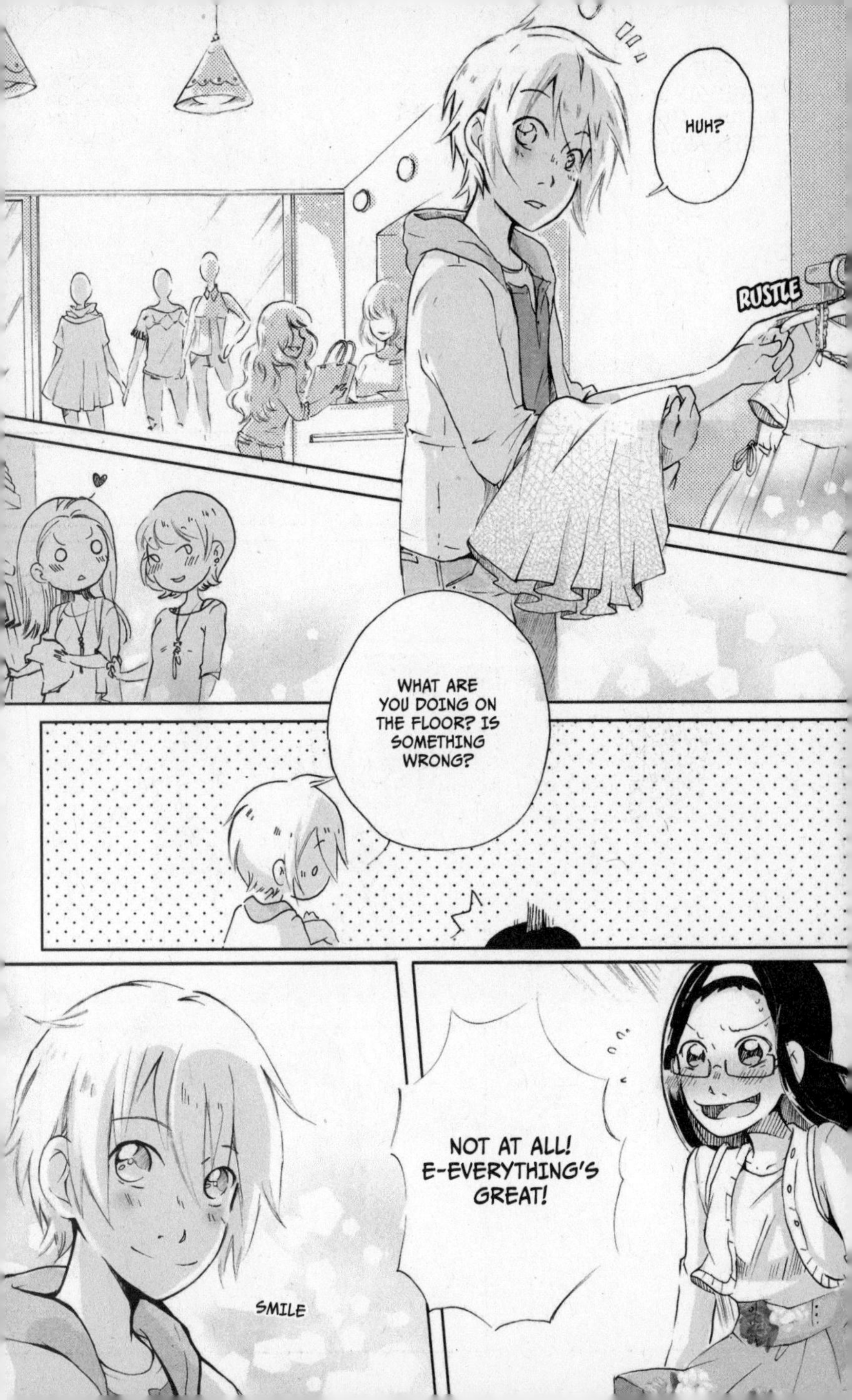
HUH?
RUSTLE
WHAT ARE YOU DOING ON THE FLOOR? IS SOMETHING WRONG?
NOT AT ALL! E-EVERYTHING'S GREAT!
SMILE

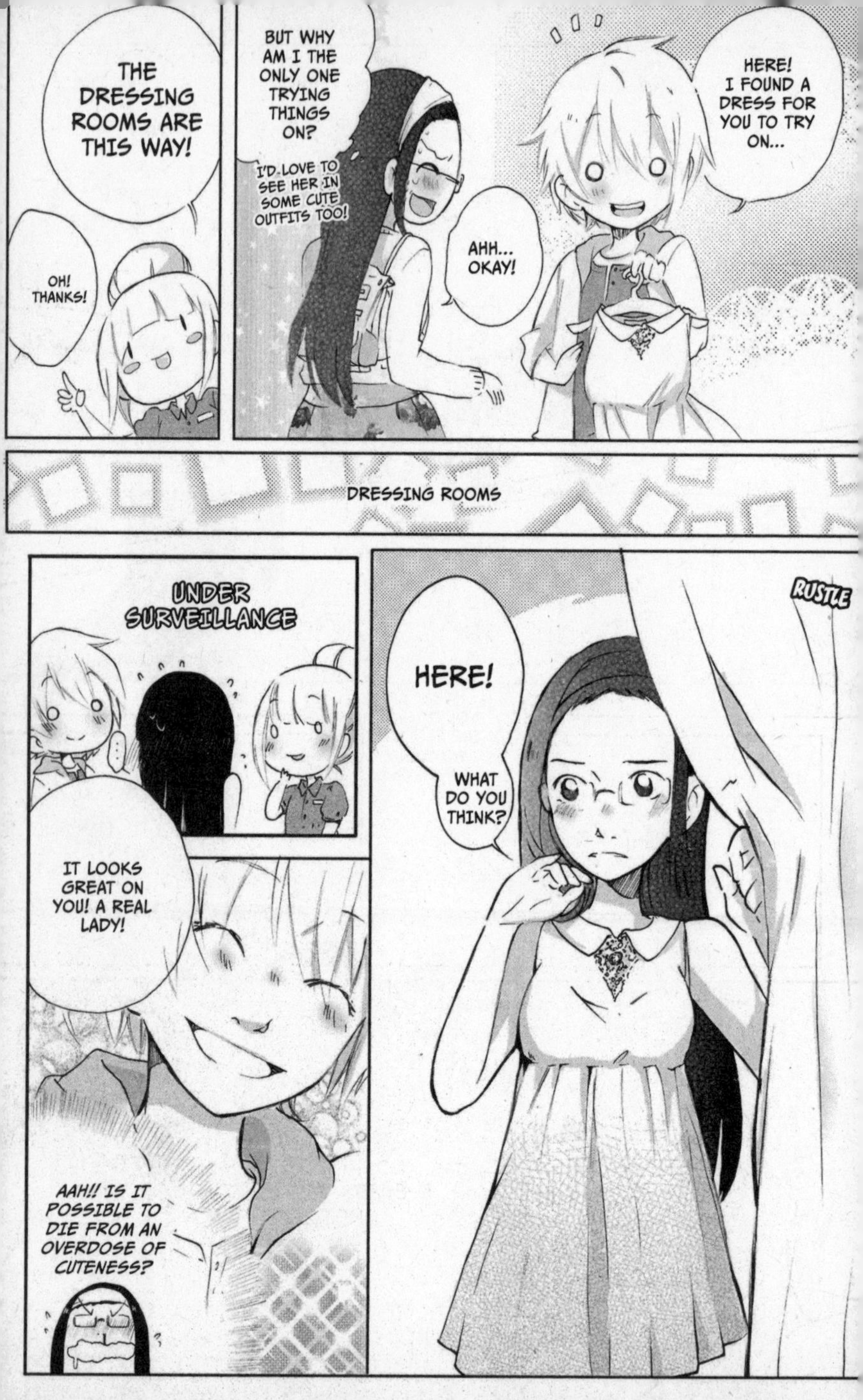
HERE! I FOUND A DRESS FOR YOU TO TRY ON...
AHH... OKAY!
BUT WHY AM I THE ONLY ONE TRYING THINGS ON?
I'D LOVE TO SEE HER IN SOME CUTE OUTFITS TOO!
THE DRESSING ROOMS ARE THIS WAY!
OH! THANKS!
DRESSING ROOMS
RUSTLE
HERE!
WHAT DO YOU THINK?
UNDER SURVEILLANCE
...
IT LOOKS GREAT ON YOU! A REAL LADY!
AAH!! IS IT POSSIBLE TO DIE FROM AN OVERDOSE OF CUTENESS?

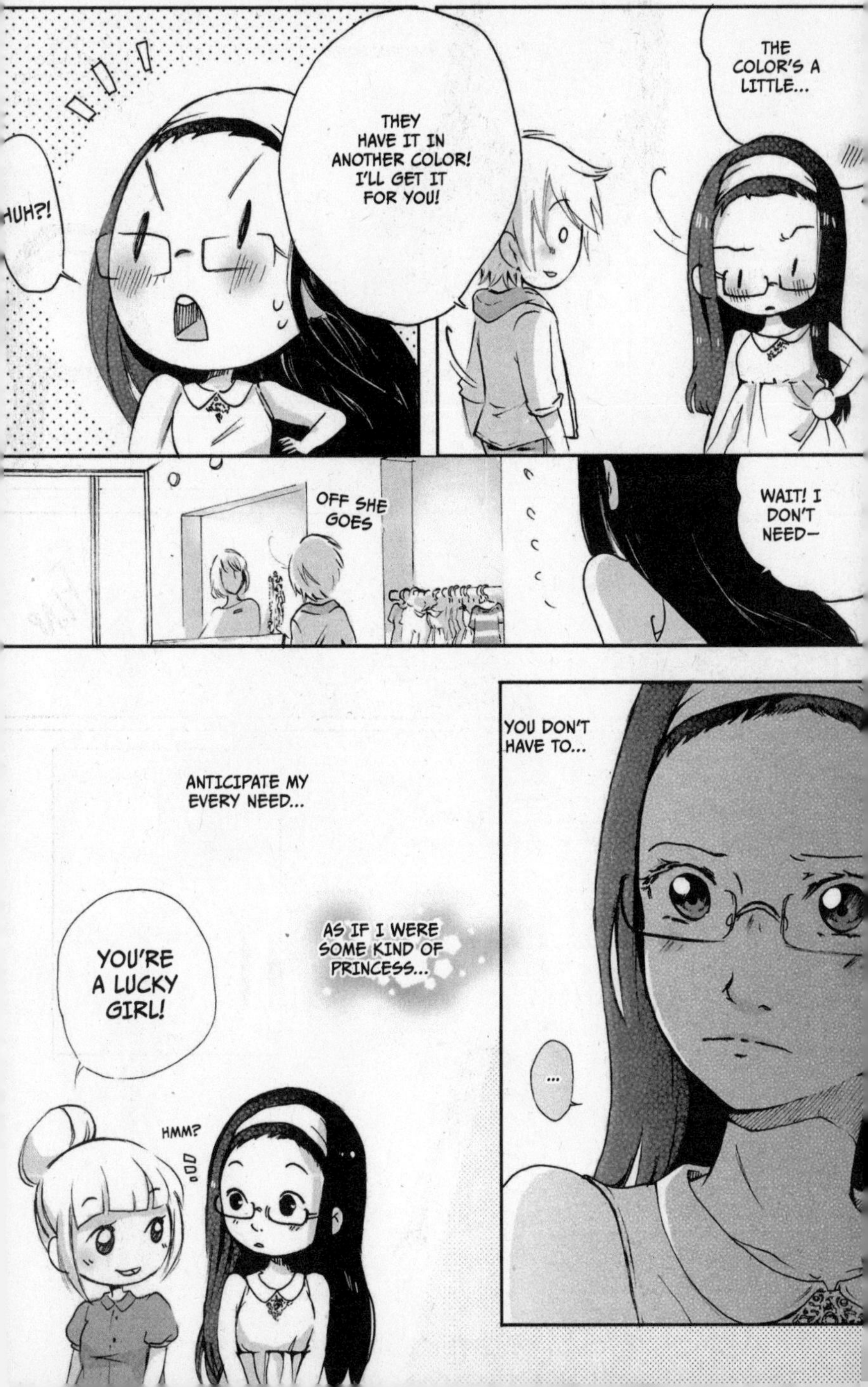
THE COLOR'S A LITTLE...
THEY HAVE IT IN ANOTHER COLOR! I'LL GET IT FOR YOU!
HUH?!
WAIT! I DON'T NEED—
OFF SHE GOES
YOU DON'T HAVE TO...
...
ANTICIPATE MY EVERY NEED...
AS IF I WERE SOME KIND OF PRINCESS...
YOU'RE A LUCKY GIRL!
HMM?

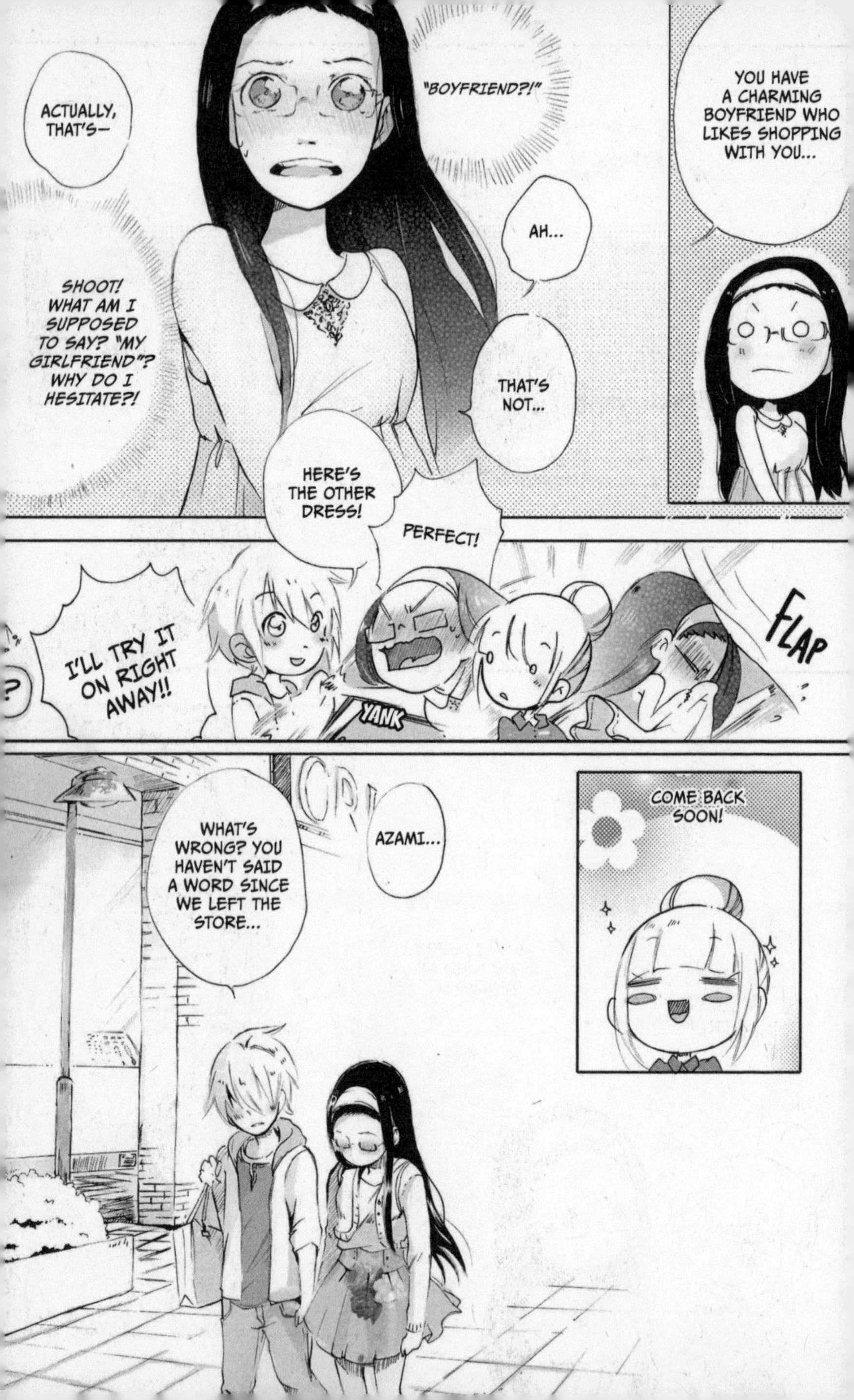
YOU HAVE A CHARMING BOYFRIEND WHO LIKES SHOPPING WITH YOU...
"BOYFRIEND?!"
AH...
THAT'S NOT...
ACTUALLY, THAT'S—
SHOOT! WHAT AM I SUPPOSED TO SAY? "MY GIRLFRIEND"? WHY DO I HESITATE?!
HERE'S THE OTHER DRESS!
FLAP
PERFECT!
YANK
I'LL TRY IT ON RIGHT AWAY!!
COME BACK SOON!
AZAMI...
WHAT'S WRONG? YOU HAVEN'T SAID A WORD SINCE WE LEFT THE STORE...

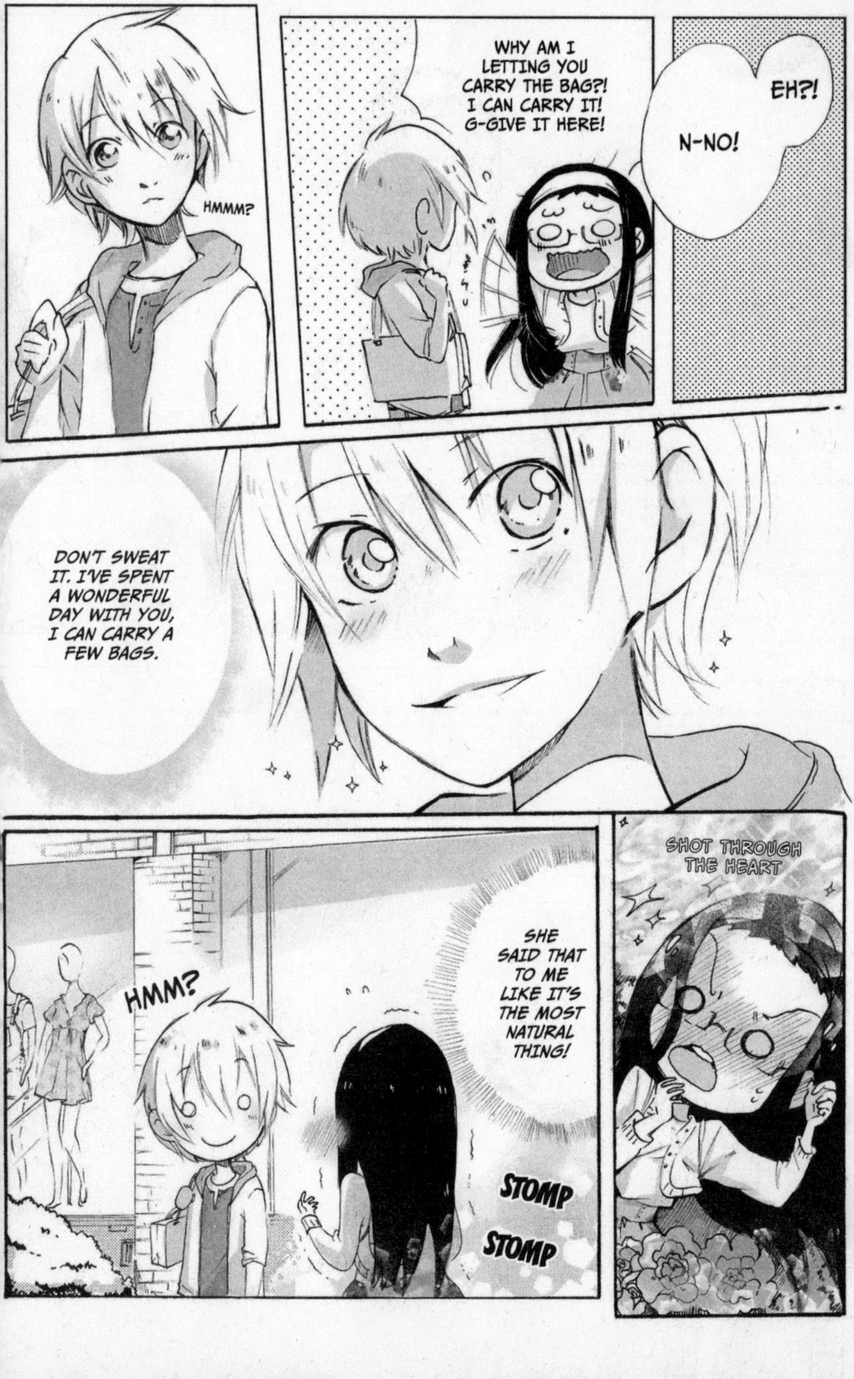
EH?!
N-NO!
WHY AM I LETTING YOU CARRY THE BAG?! I CAN CARRY IT! G-GIVE IT HERE!
HMMM?
DON'T SWEAT IT. I'VE SPENT A WONDERFUL DAY WITH YOU, I CAN CARRY A FEW BAGS.
SHOT THROUGH THE HEART
SHE SAID THAT TO ME LIKE IT'S THE MOST NATURAL THING!
HMM?
STOMP
STOMP

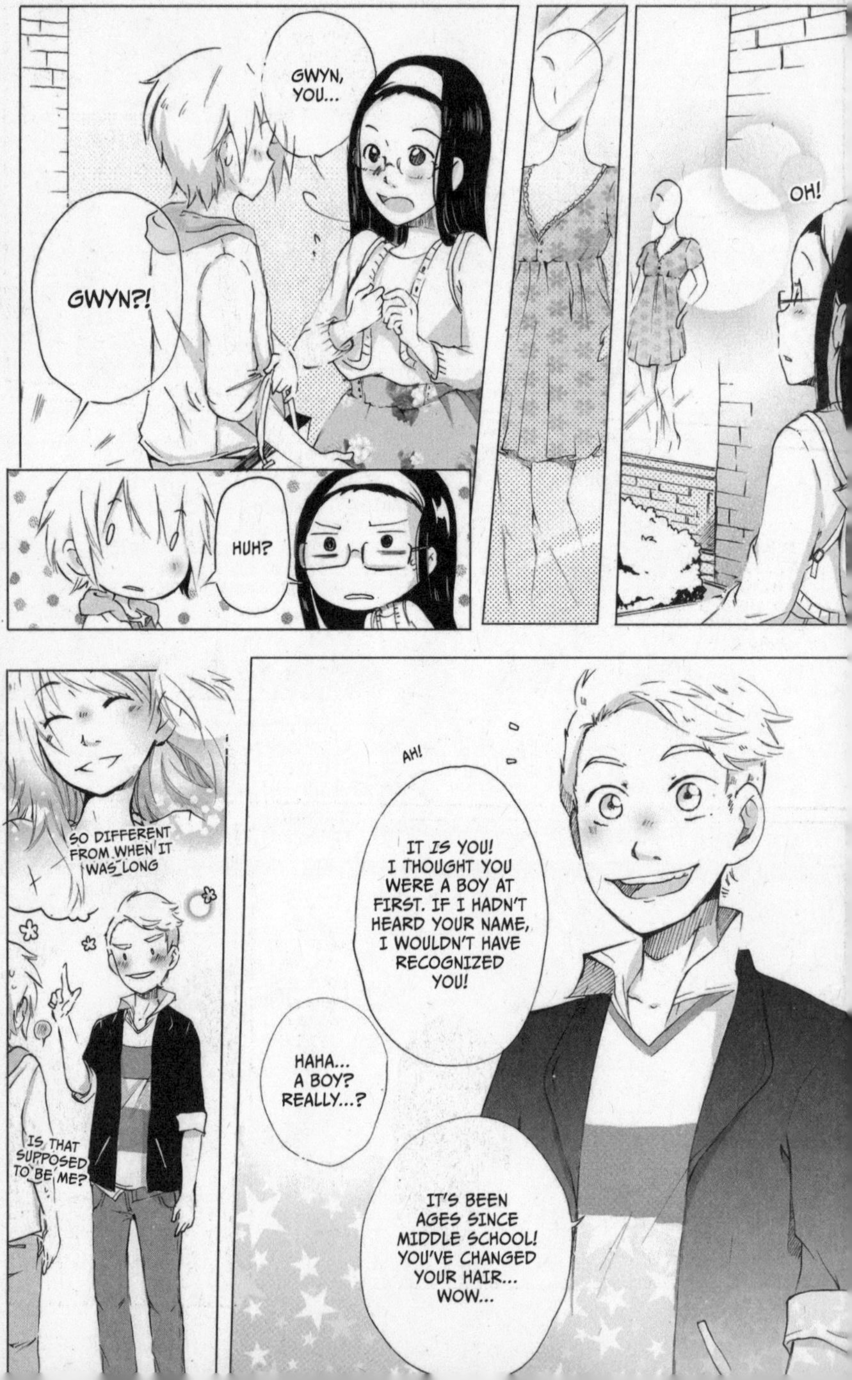
OH!
GWYN, YOU...
GWYN?!
HUH?
AH!
IT *IS* YOU! I THOUGHT YOU WERE A BOY AT FIRST. IF I HADN'T HEARD YOUR NAME, I WOULDN'T HAVE RECOGNIZED YOU!
HAHA... A BOY? REALLY...?
IT'S BEEN AGES SINCE MIDDLE SCHOOL! YOU'VE CHANGED YOUR HAIR... WOW...
SO DIFFERENT FROM WHEN IT WAS LONG
IS THAT SUPPOSED TO BE ME?

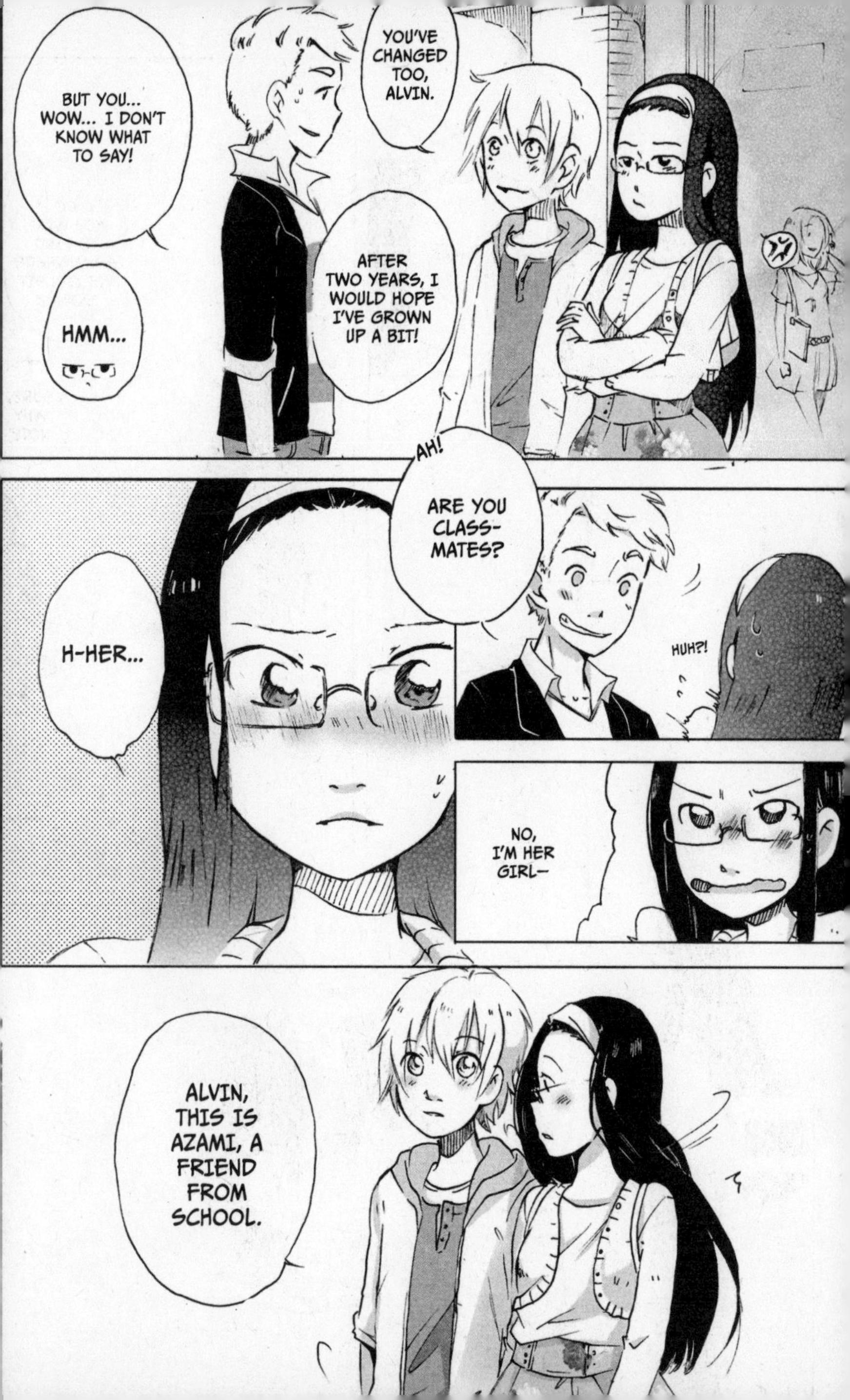
YOU'VE CHANGED TOO, ALVIN.
BUT YOU... WOW... I DON'T KNOW WHAT TO SAY!
AFTER TWO YEARS, I WOULD HOPE I'VE GROWN UP A BIT!
HMM...
AH!
ARE YOU CLASS-MATES?
HUH?!
NO, I'M HER GIRL–
H-HER...
ALVIN, THIS IS AZAMI, A FRIEND FROM SCHOOL.

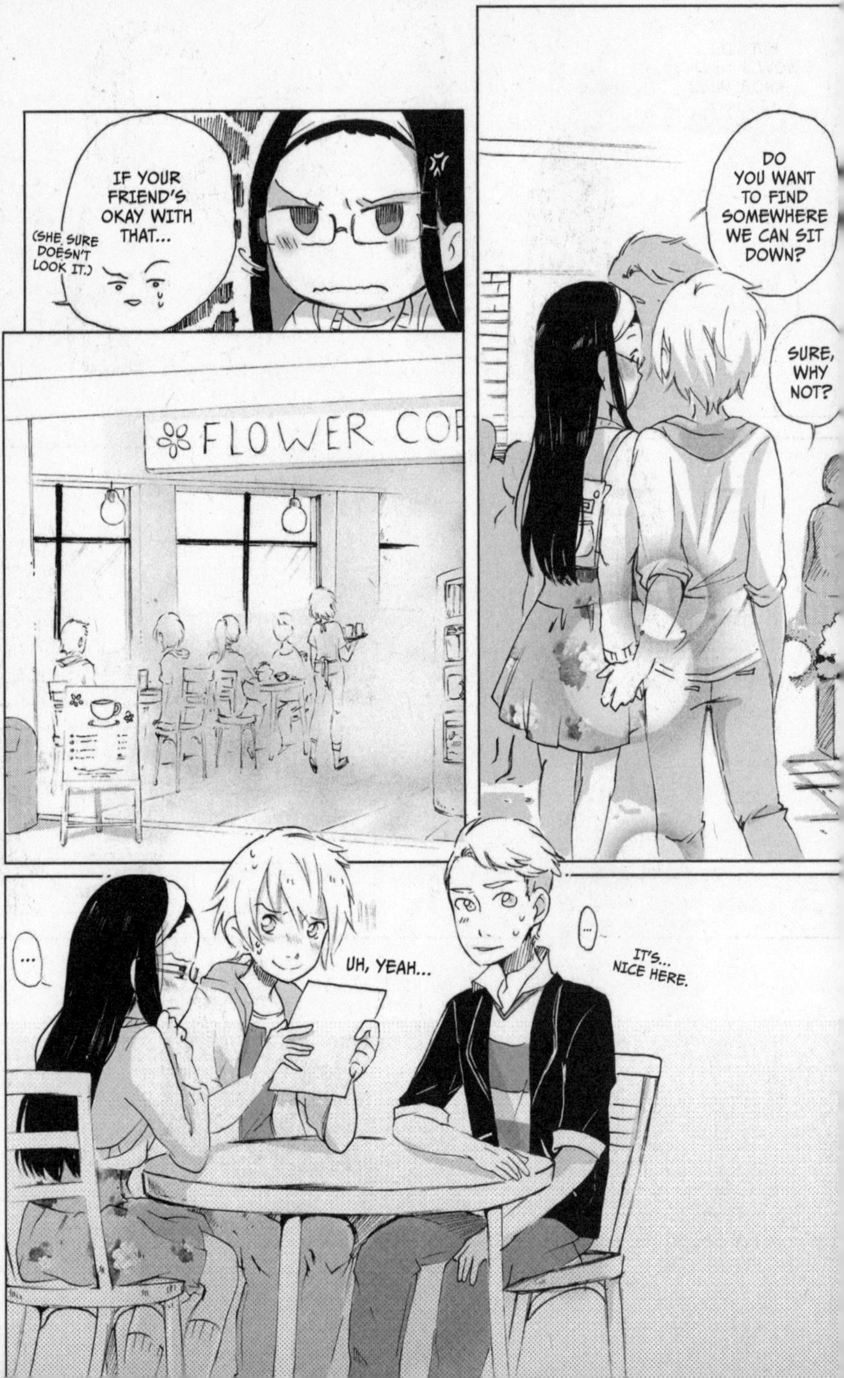
DO YOU WANT TO FIND SOMEWHERE WE CAN SIT DOWN?
SURE, WHY NOT?
IF YOUR FRIEND'S OKAY WITH THAT...
(SHE SURE DOESN'T LOOK IT.)
FLOWER CO
...
IT'S... NICE HERE.
UH, YEAH...
...

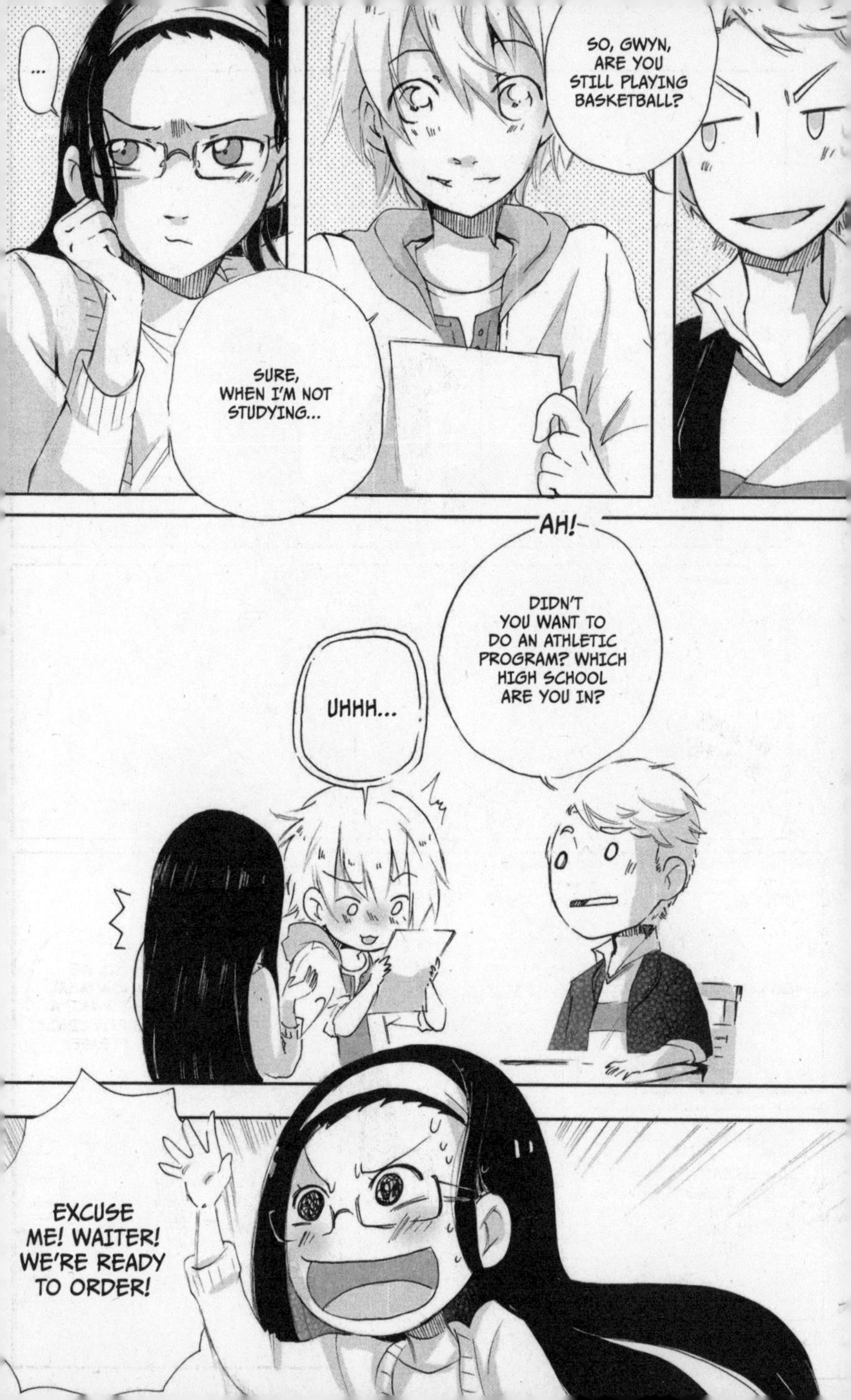
SO, GWYN, ARE YOU STILL PLAYING BASKETBALL?
SURE, WHEN I'M NOT STUDYING...
...
AH!
DIDN'T YOU WANT TO DO AN ATHLETIC PROGRAM? WHICH HIGH SCHOOL ARE YOU IN?
UHHH...
EXCUSE ME! WAITER! WE'RE READY TO ORDER!

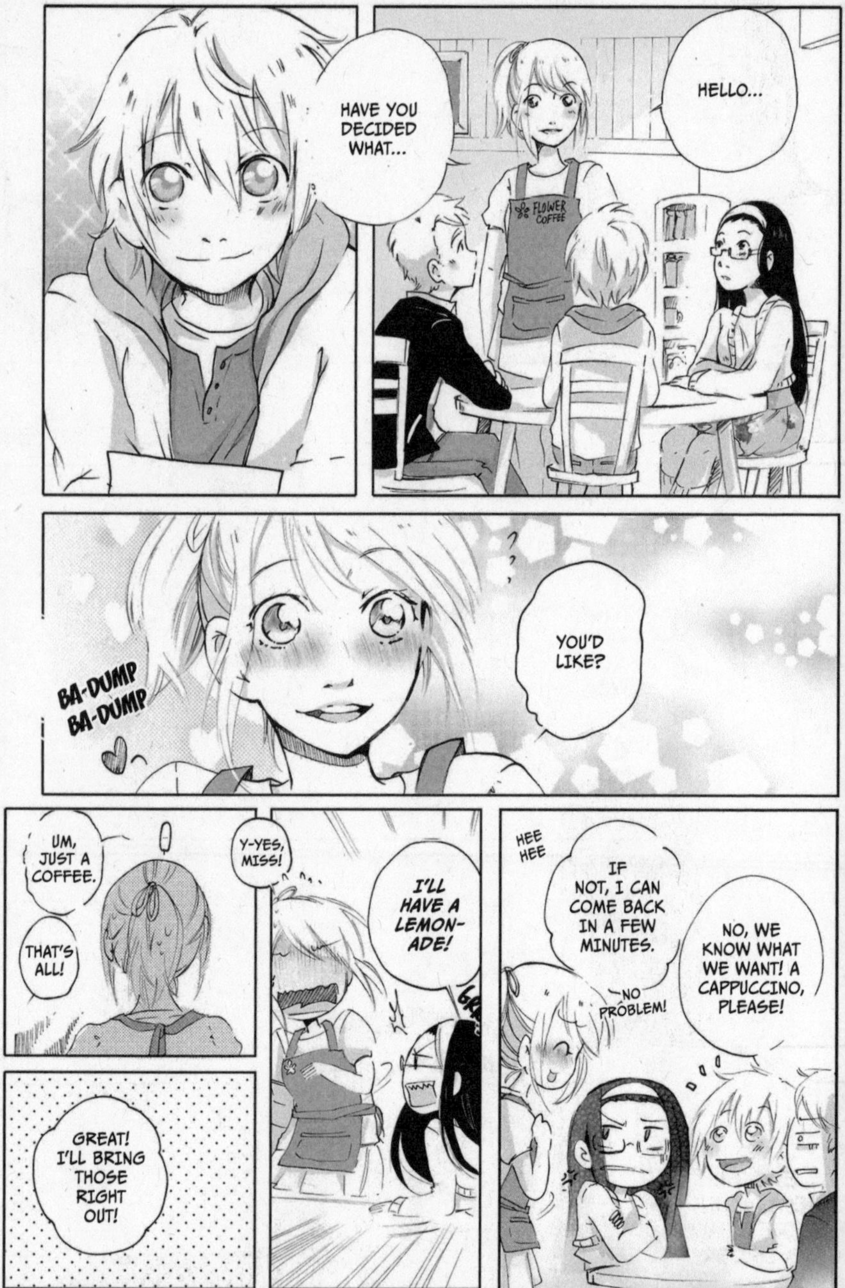
HELLO...
HAVE YOU DECIDED WHAT...
YOU'D LIKE?
BA-DUMP BA-DUMP
HEE HEE
IF NOT, I CAN COME BACK IN A FEW MINUTES.
NO, WE KNOW WHAT WE WANT! A CAPPUCCINO, PLEASE!
NO PROBLEM!
Y-YES, MISS!
I'LL HAVE A LEMONADE!
UM, JUST A COFFEE.
THAT'S ALL!
GREAT! I'LL BRING THOSE RIGHT OUT!

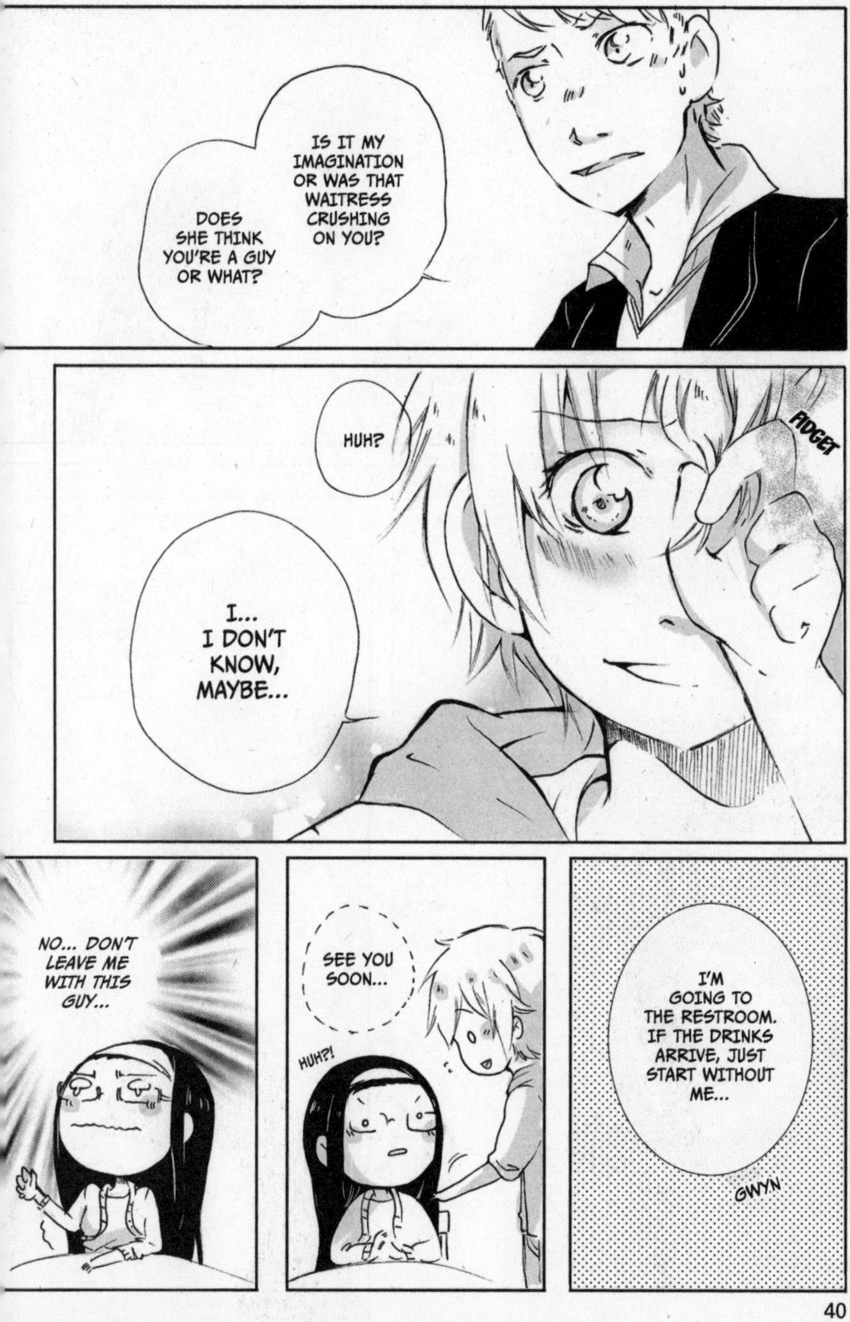
IS IT MY IMAGINATION OR WAS THAT WAITRESS CRUSHING ON YOU?
DOES SHE THINK YOU'RE A GUY OR WHAT?
FIDGET
HUH?
I... I DON'T KNOW, MAYBE...
I'M GOING TO THE RESTROOM. IF THE DRINKS ARRIVE, JUST START WITHOUT ME...
GWYN
SEE YOU SOON...
HUH?!
NO... DON'T LEAVE ME WITH THIS GUY...

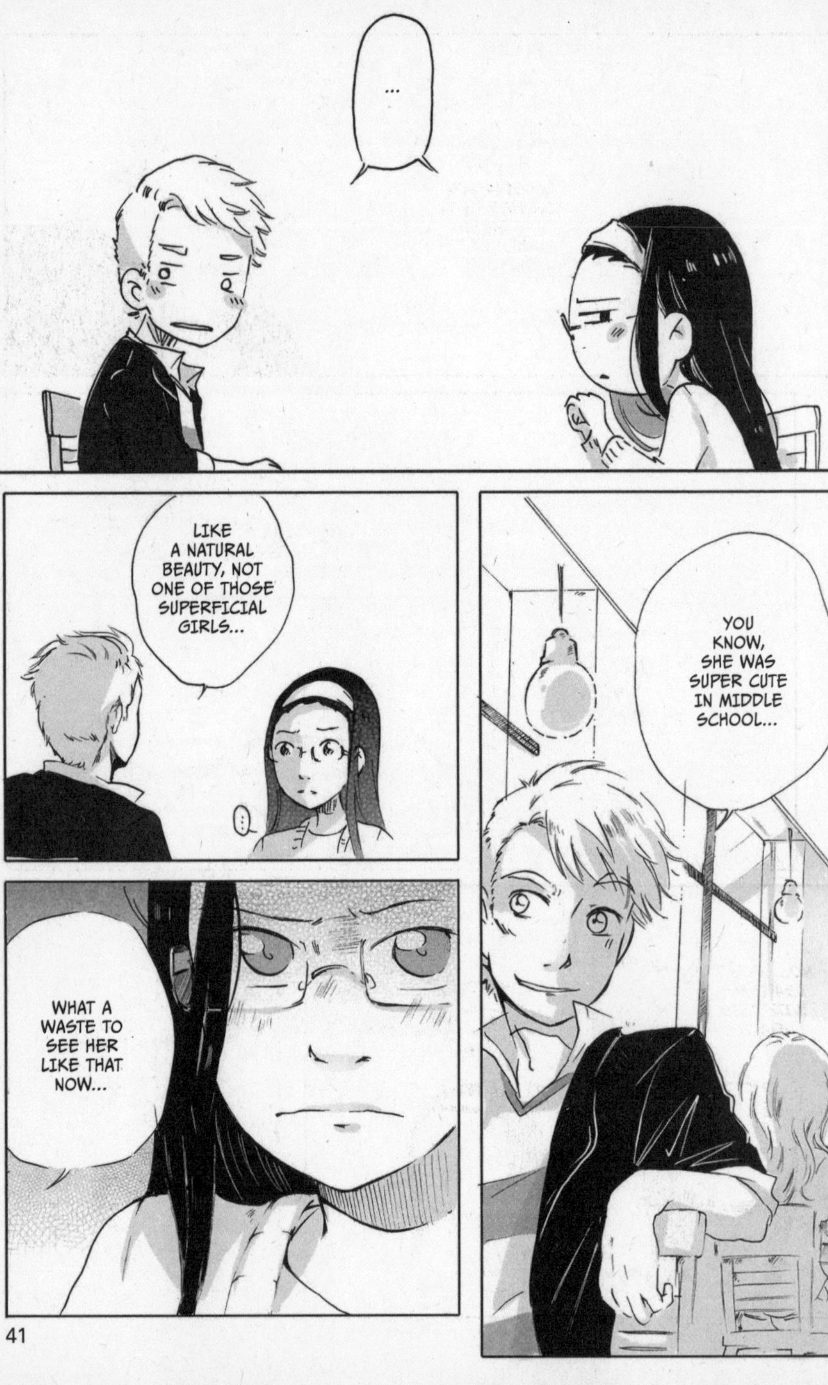
...
YOU KNOW, SHE WAS SUPER CUTE IN MIDDLE SCHOOL...
LIKE A NATURAL BEAUTY, NOT ONE OF THOSE SUPERFICIAL GIRLS...
...
WHAT A WASTE TO SEE HER LIKE THAT NOW...

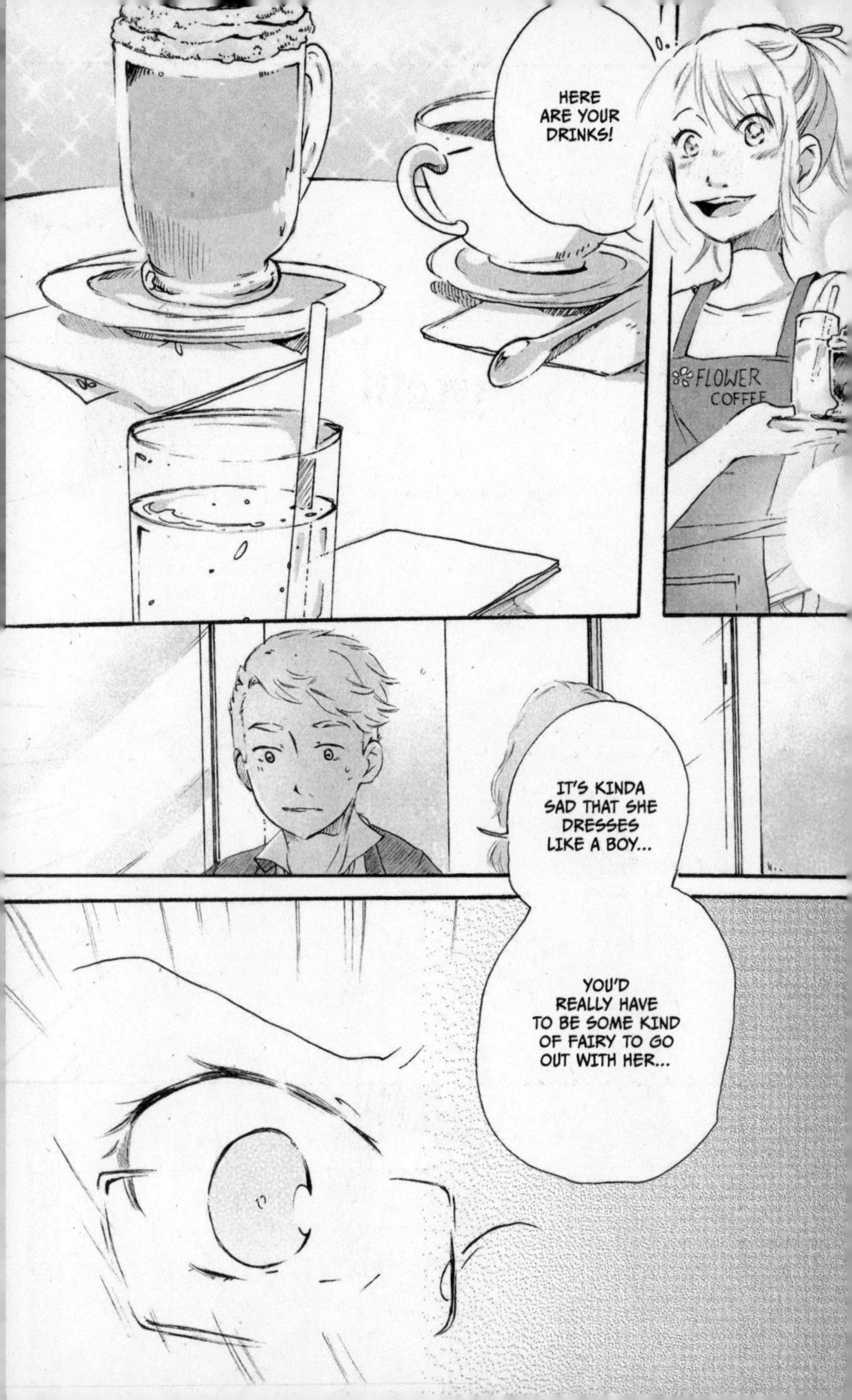
HERE ARE YOUR DRINKS!
FLOWER COFFEE
IT'S KINDA SAD THAT SHE DRESSES LIKE A BOY...
YOU'D REALLY HAVE TO BE SOME KIND OF FAIRY TO GO OUT WITH HER...

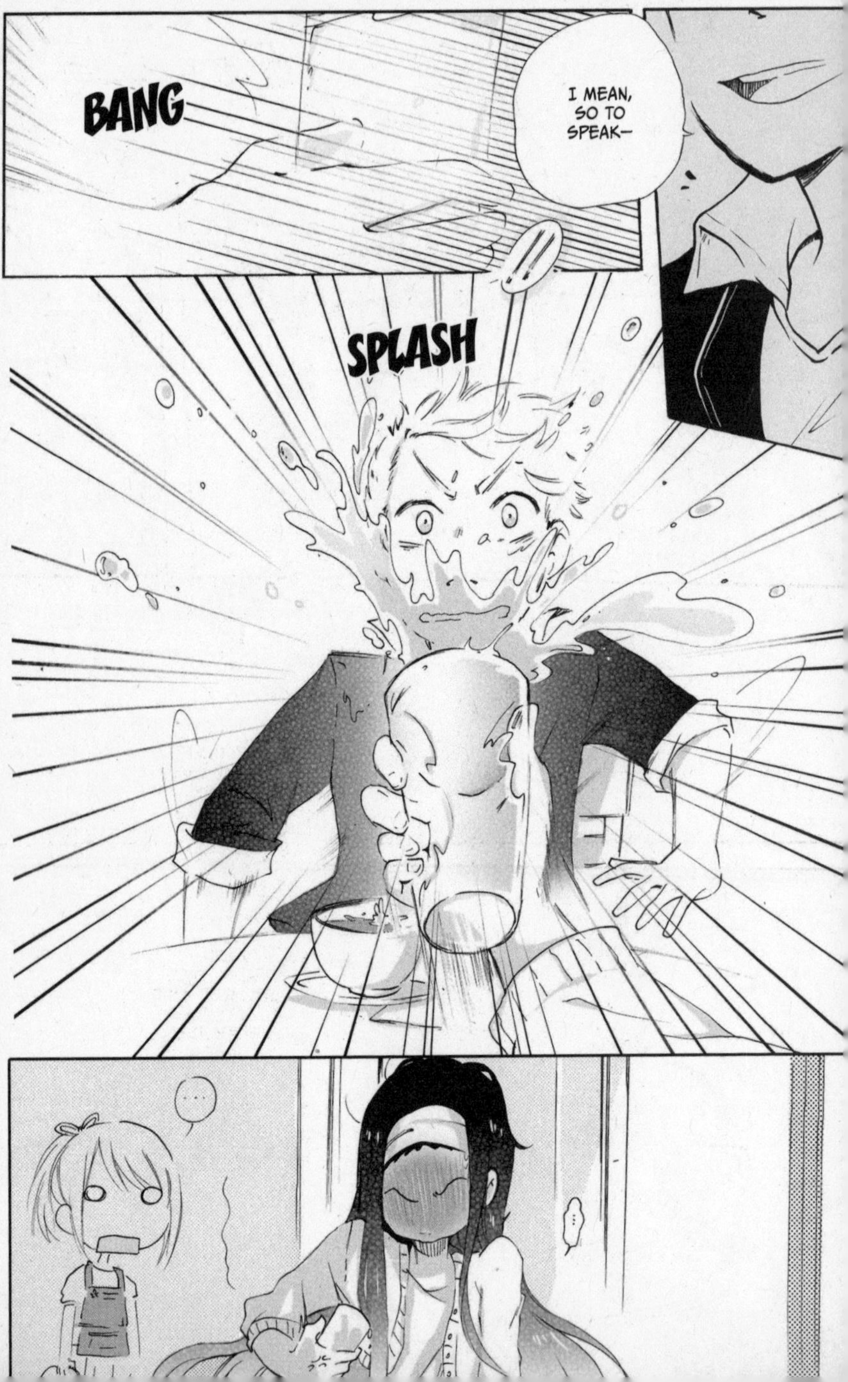
I MEAN, SO TO SPEAK—
BANG
SPLASH
...
...

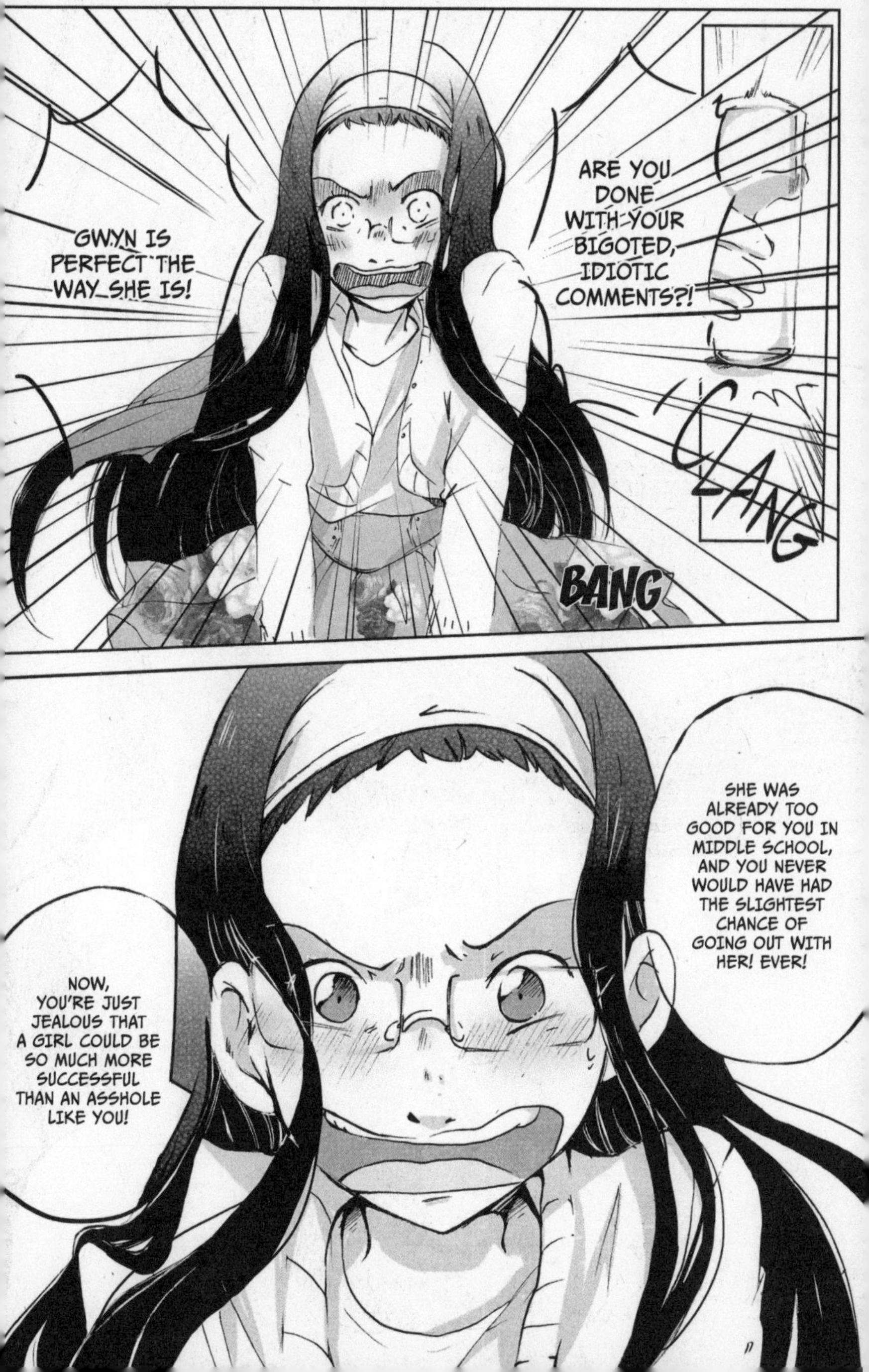
ARE YOU DONE WITH YOUR BIGOTED, IDIOTIC COMMENTS?!
GWYN IS PERFECT THE WAY SHE IS!
CLANG
BANG
SHE WAS ALREADY TOO GOOD FOR YOU IN MIDDLE SCHOOL, AND YOU NEVER WOULD HAVE HAD THE SLIGHTEST CHANCE OF GOING OUT WITH HER! EVER!
NOW, YOU'RE JUST JEALOUS THAT A GIRL COULD BE SO MUCH MORE SUCCESSFUL THAN AN ASSHOLE LIKE YOU!

Chapter 3
Talking over

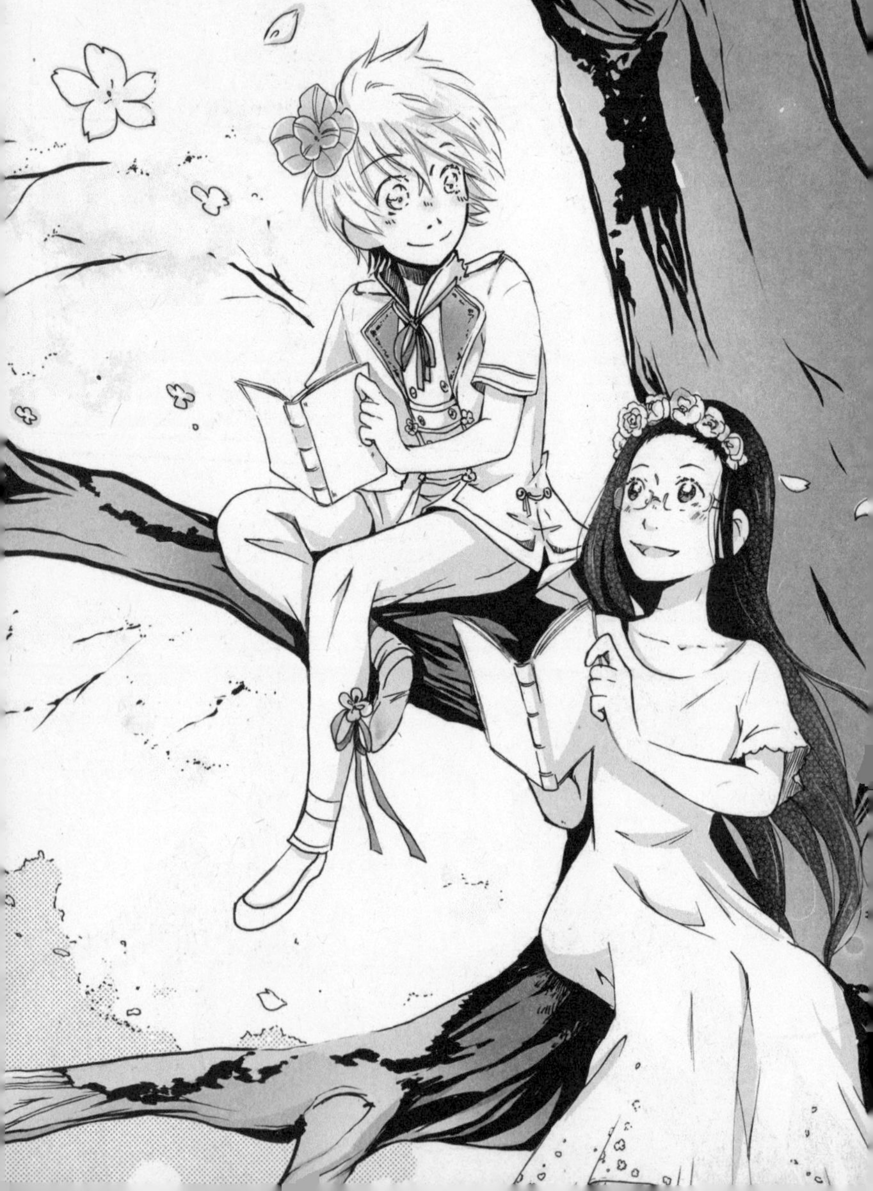

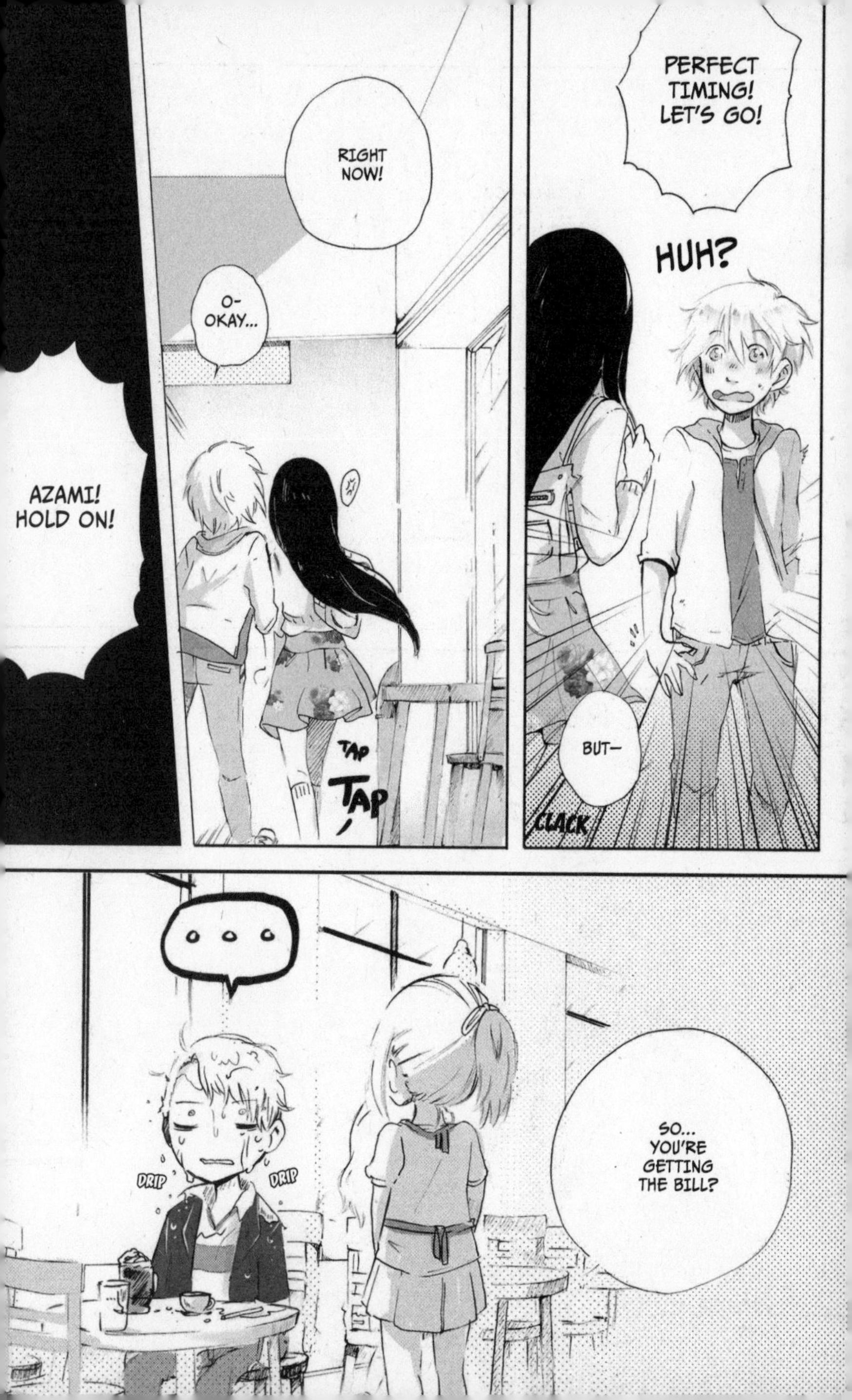
PERFECT TIMING! LET'S GO!
HUH?
BUT—
CLACK
RIGHT NOW!
O-OKAY...
TAP
TAP
AZAMI! HOLD ON!
SO... YOU'RE GETTING THE BILL?
...
DRIP
DRIP

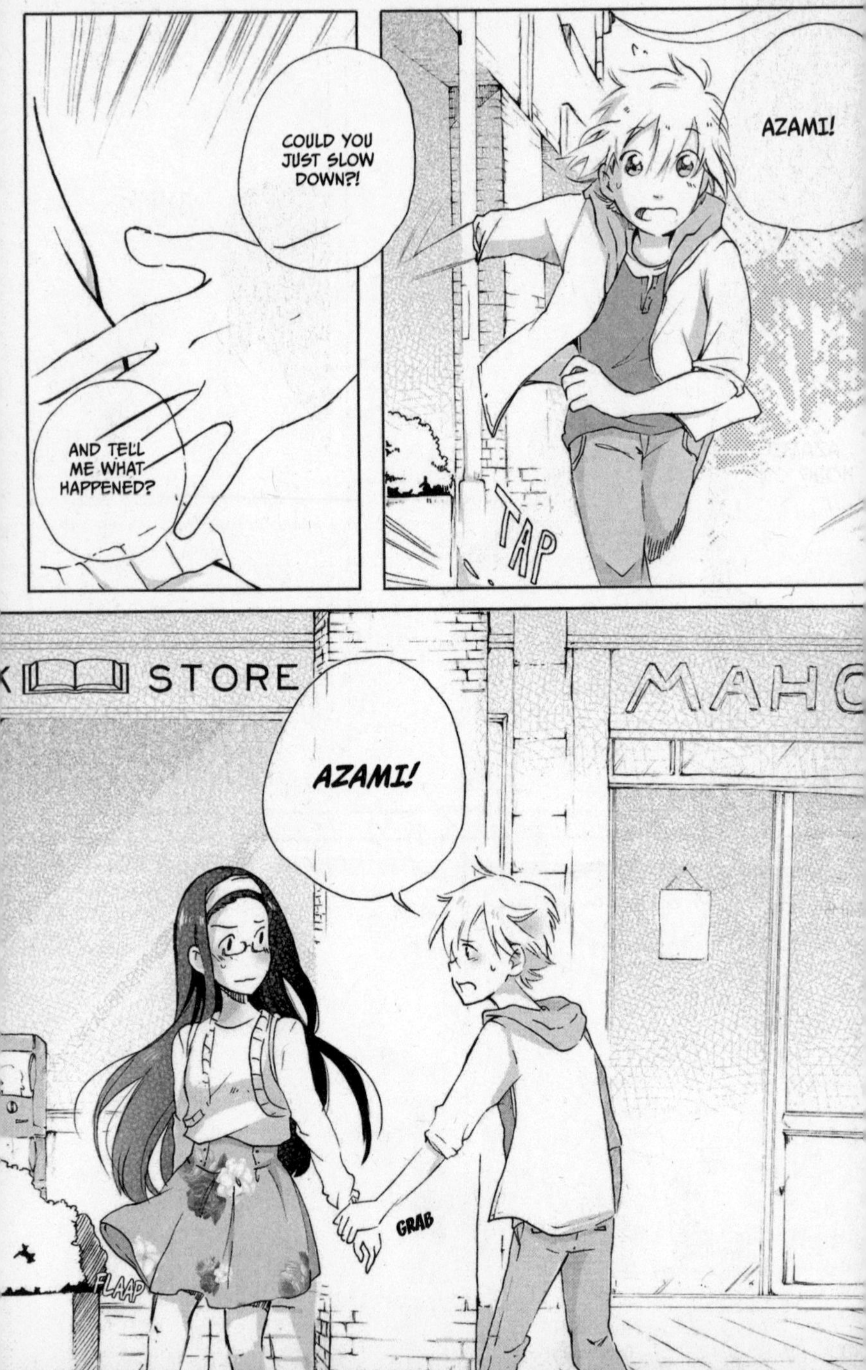
AZAMI!
TAP
COULD YOU JUST SLOW DOWN?!
AND TELL ME WHAT HAPPENED?
MAHO
STORE
AZAMI!
GRAB
FLAAP

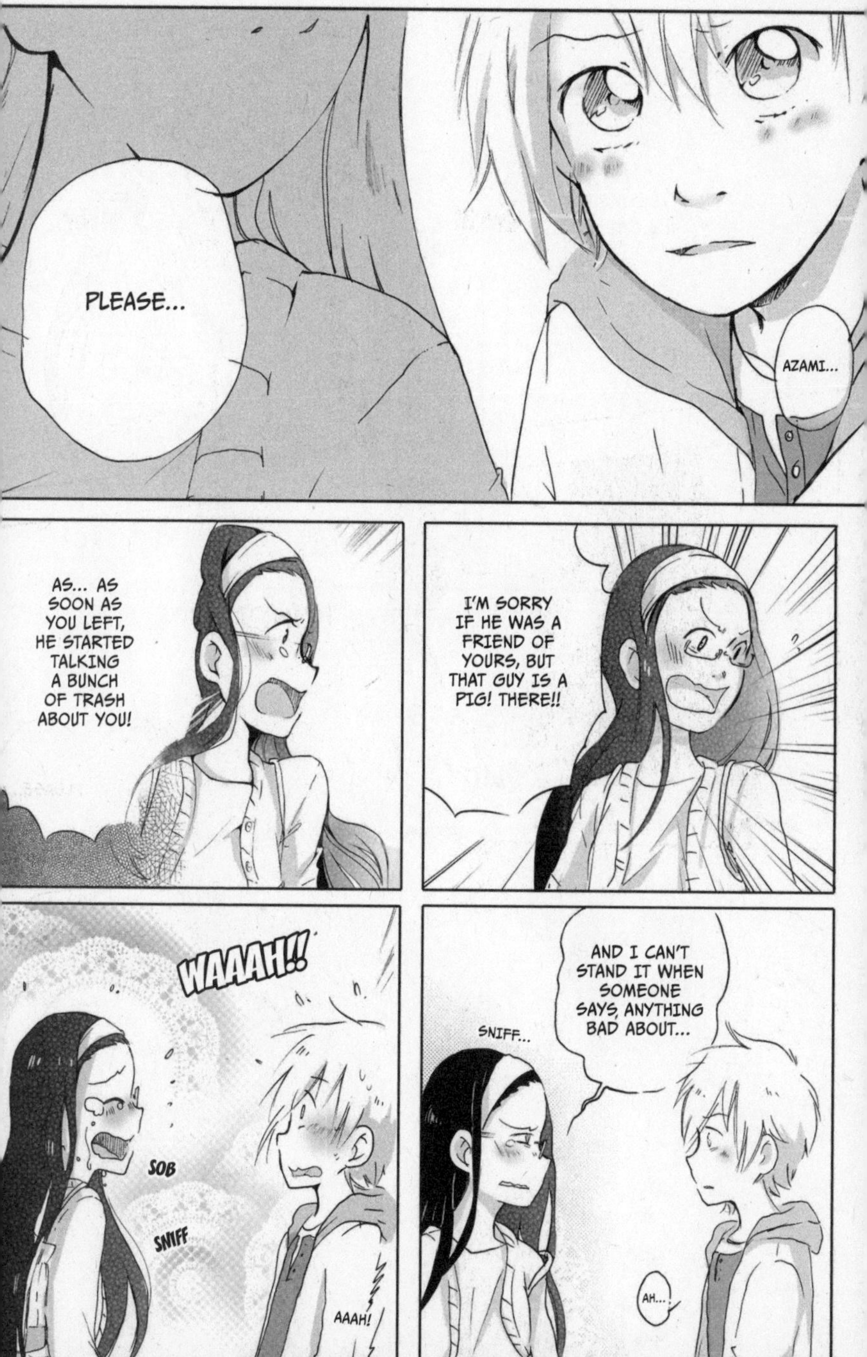
AZAMI...
PLEASE...
I'M SORRY IF HE WAS A FRIEND OF YOURS, BUT THAT GUY IS A PIG! THERE!!
AS... AS SOON AS YOU LEFT, HE STARTED TALKING A BUNCH OF TRASH ABOUT YOU!
AND I CAN'T STAND IT WHEN SOMEONE SAYS, ANYTHING BAD ABOUT...
SNIFF...
AH...
WAAAH!!
SOB
SNIFF
AAAH!

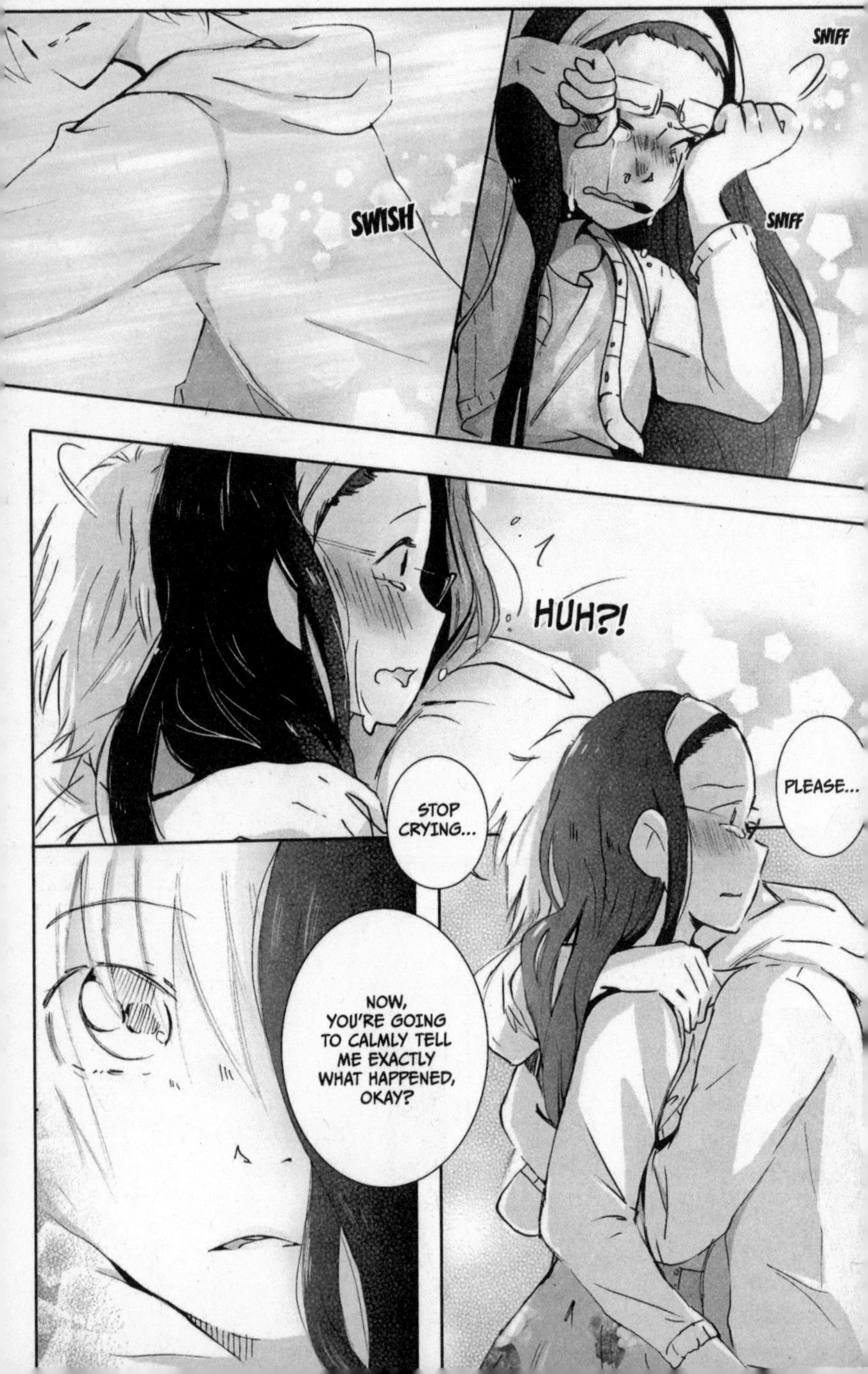
SNIFF
SNIFF
SWISH
HUH?!
STOP CRYING...
PLEASE...
NOW, YOU'RE GOING TO CALMLY TELL ME EXACTLY WHAT HAPPENED, OKAY?

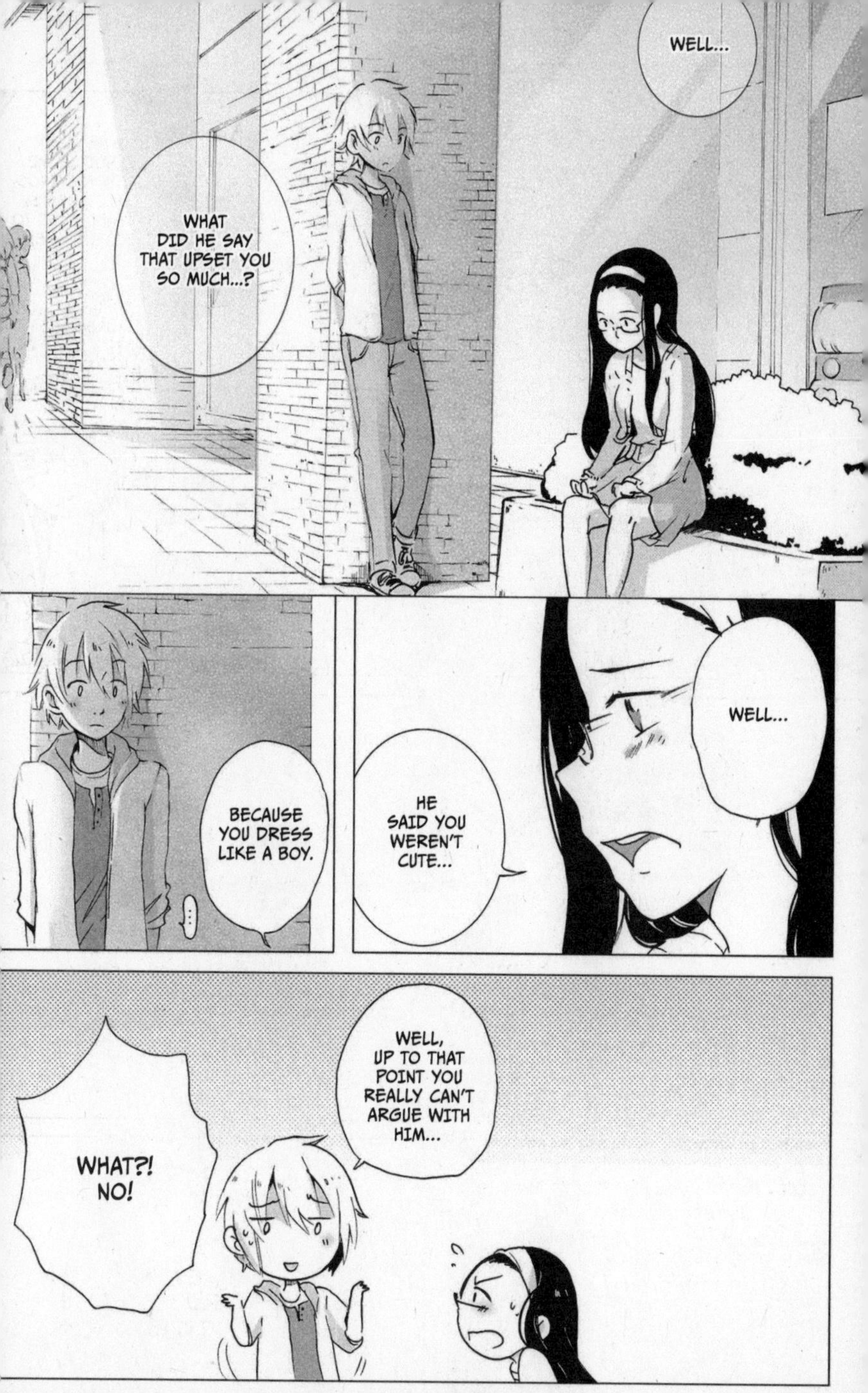
WELL...
WHAT DID HE SAY THAT UPSET YOU SO MUCH...?
WELL...
HE SAID YOU WEREN'T CUTE...
BECAUSE YOU DRESS LIKE A BOY.
...
WELL, UP TO THAT POINT YOU REALLY CAN'T ARGUE WITH HIM...
WHAT?! NO!

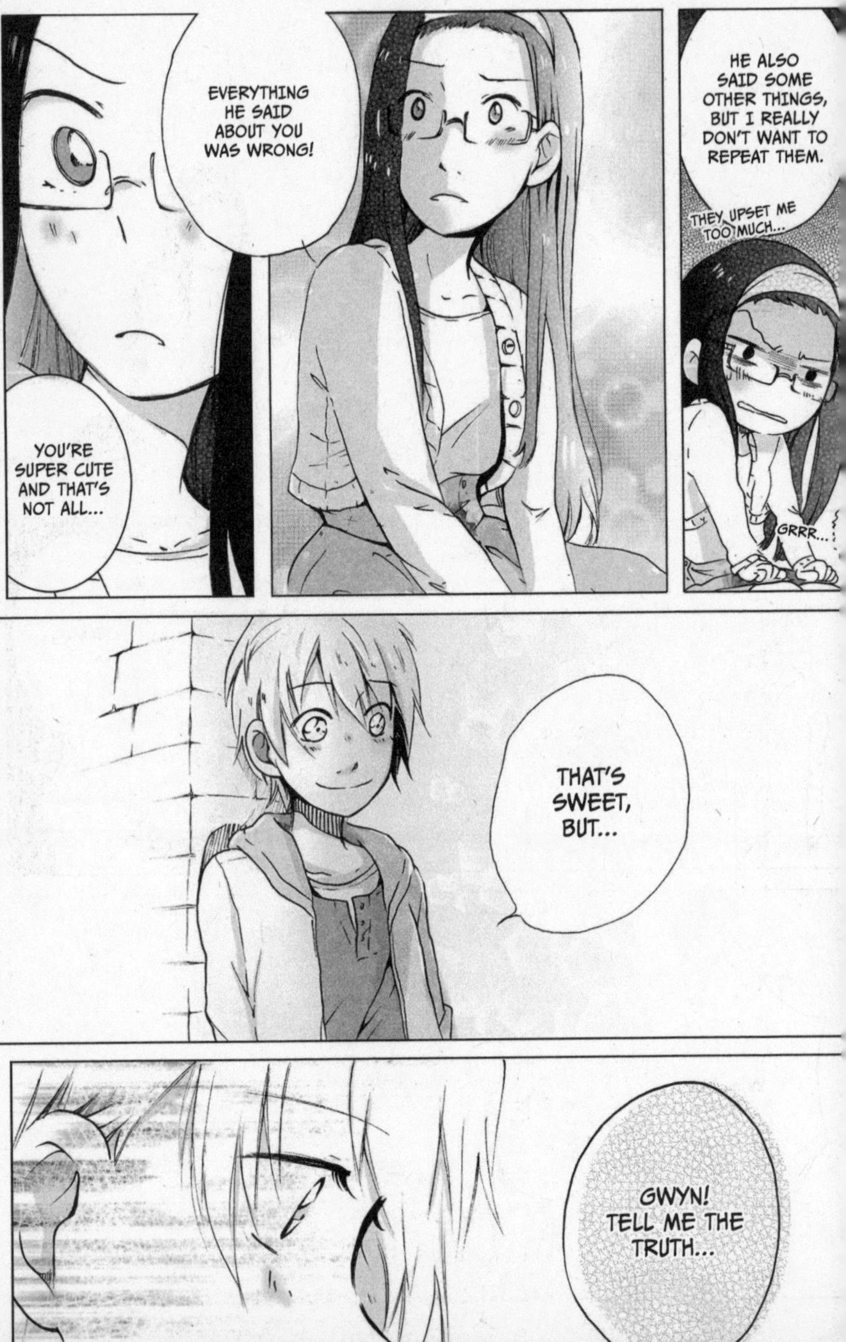
HE ALSO SAID SOME OTHER THINGS, BUT I REALLY DON'T WANT TO REPEAT THEM.
THEY UPSET ME TOO MUCH...
GRRR...
EVERYTHING HE SAID ABOUT YOU WAS WRONG!
YOU'RE SUPER CUTE AND THAT'S NOT ALL...
THAT'S SWEET, BUT...
GWYN! TELL ME THE TRUTH...

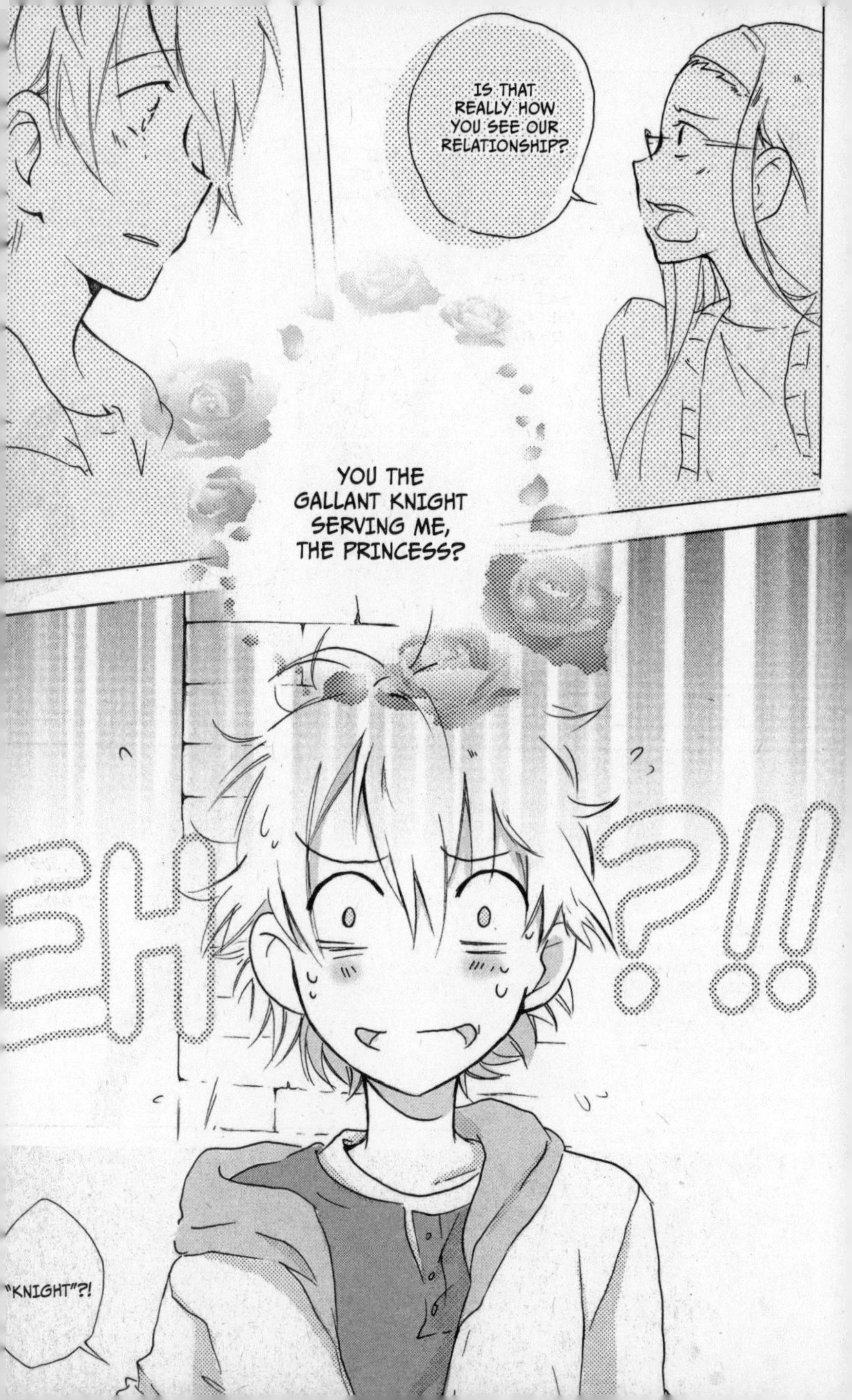
IS THAT REALLY HOW YOU SEE OUR RELATIONSHIP?
YOU THE GALLANT KNIGHT SERVING ME, THE PRINCESS?
EH?!!
"KNIGHT"?!

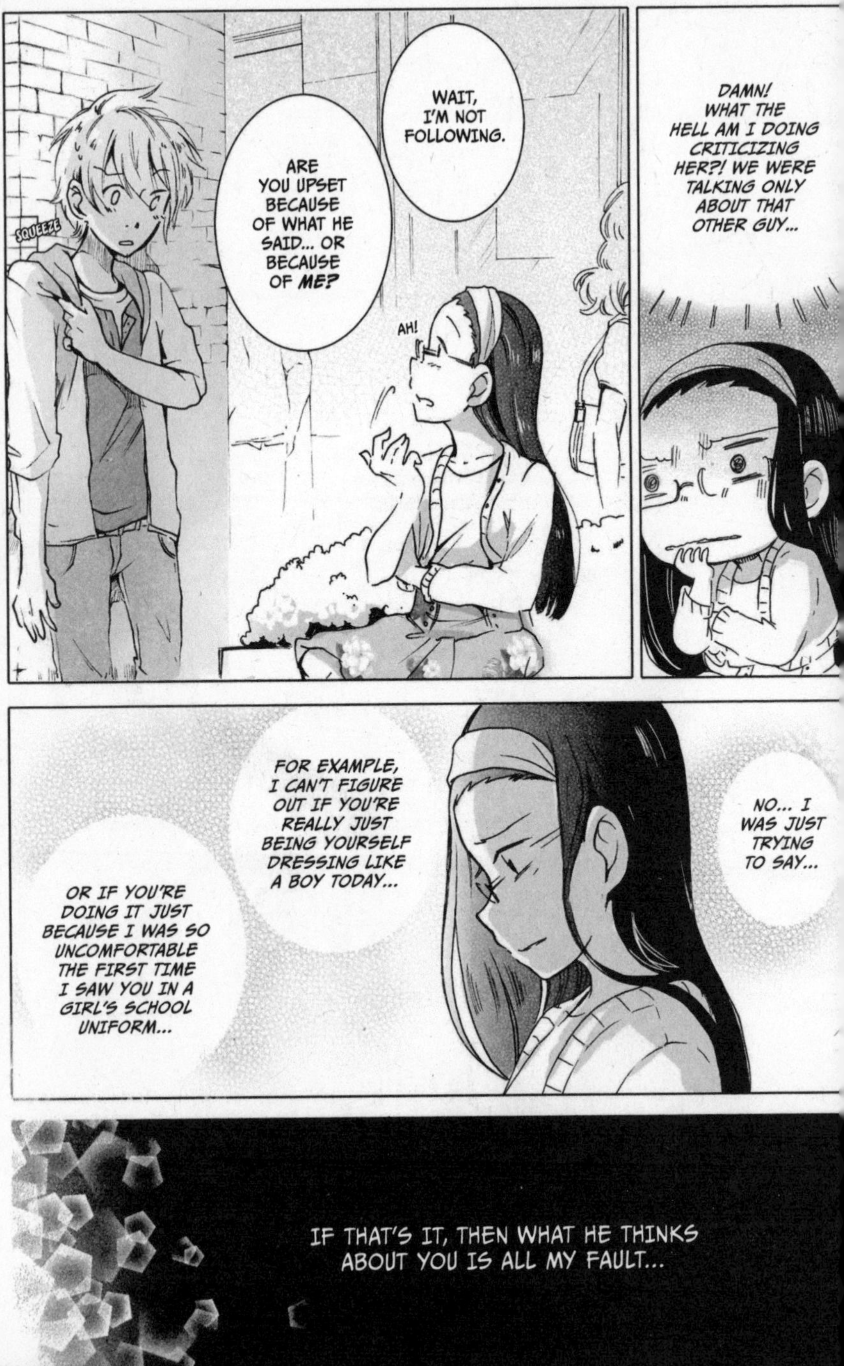
DAMN! WHAT THE HELL AM I DOING CRITICIZING HER?! WE WERE TALKING ONLY ABOUT THAT OTHER GUY...
WAIT, I'M NOT FOLLOWING.
ARE YOU UPSET BECAUSE OF WHAT HE SAID... OR BECAUSE OF ME?
AH!
SQUEEZE
NO... I WAS JUST TRYING TO SAY...
FOR EXAMPLE, I CAN'T FIGURE OUT IF YOU'RE REALLY JUST BEING YOURSELF DRESSING LIKE A BOY TODAY...
OR IF YOU'RE DOING IT JUST BECAUSE I WAS SO UNCOMFORTABLE THE FIRST TIME I SAW YOU IN A GIRL'S SCHOOL UNIFORM...
IF THAT'S IT, THEN WHAT HE THINKS ABOUT YOU IS ALL MY FAULT...

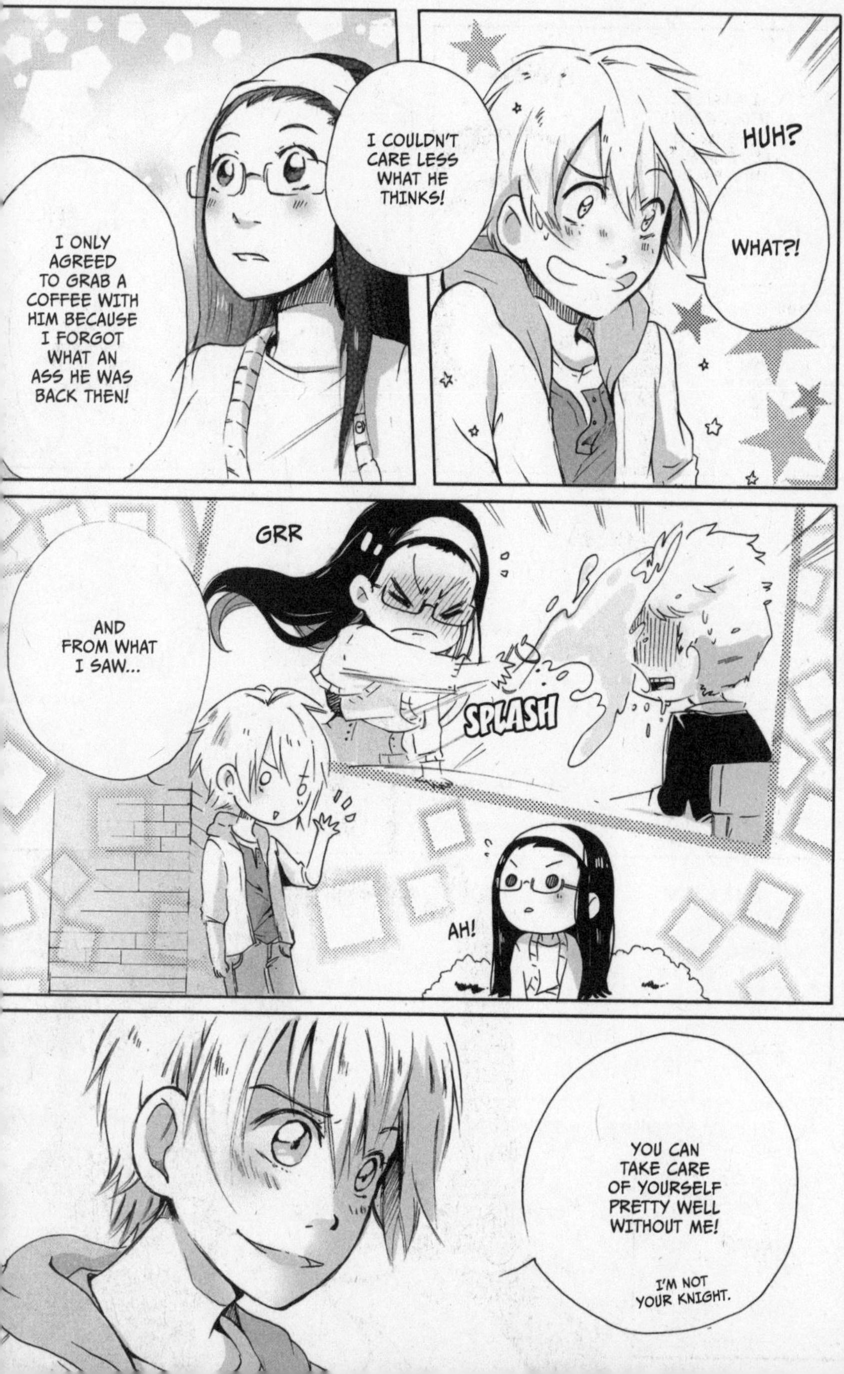
HUH?
WHAT?!
I COULDN'T CARE LESS WHAT HE THINKS!
I ONLY AGREED TO GRAB A COFFEE WITH HIM BECAUSE I FORGOT WHAT AN ASS HE WAS BACK THEN!
GRR
AND FROM WHAT I SAW...
SPLASH
AH!
YOU CAN TAKE CARE OF YOURSELF PRETTY WELL WITHOUT ME!
I'M NOT YOUR KNIGHT.

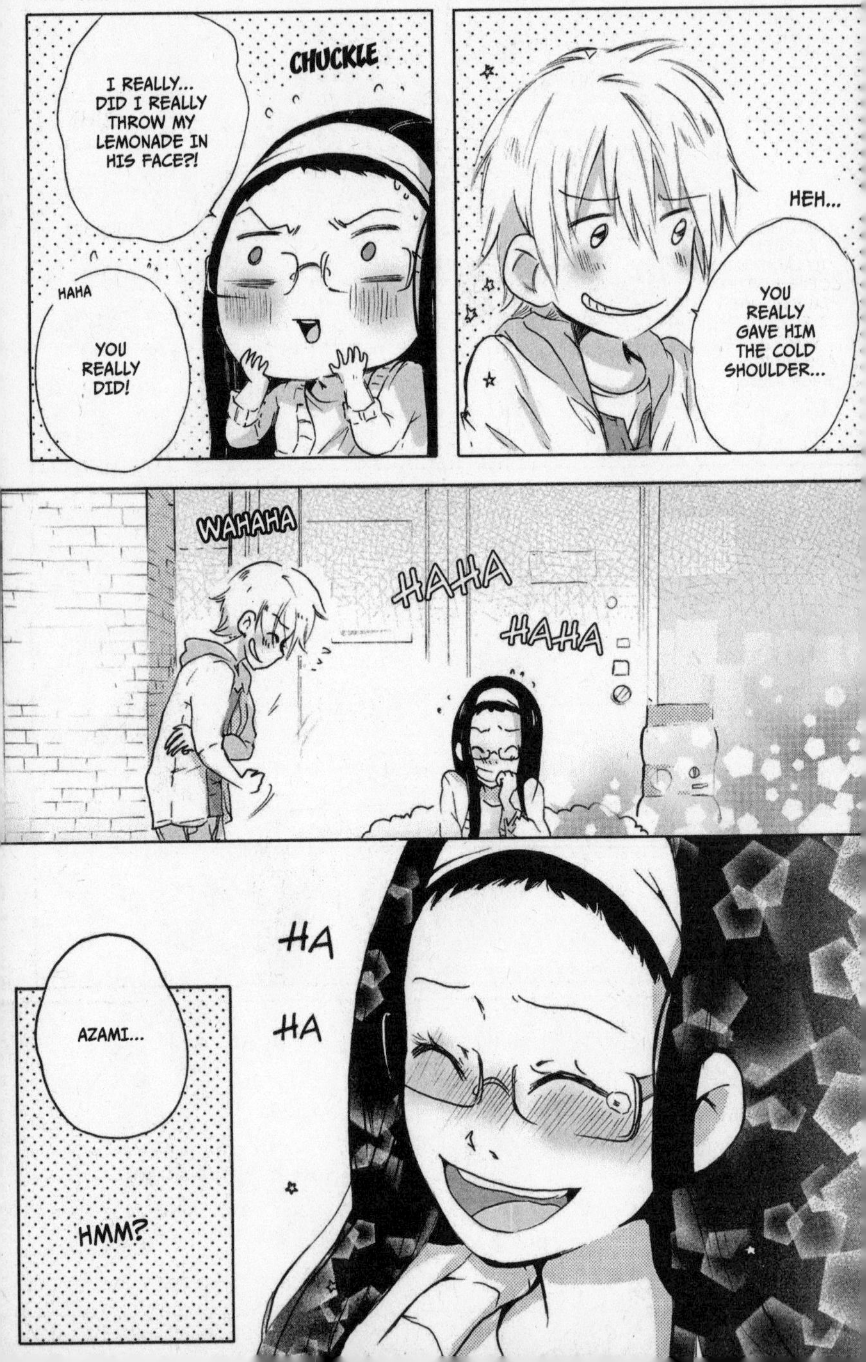
HEH...
YOU REALLY GAVE HIM THE COLD SHOULDER...
CHUCKLE
I REALLY... DID I REALLY THROW MY LEMONADE IN HIS FACE?!
HAHA
YOU REALLY DID!
HAHA
HAHA
WAHAHA
HA
HA
AZAMI...
HMM?

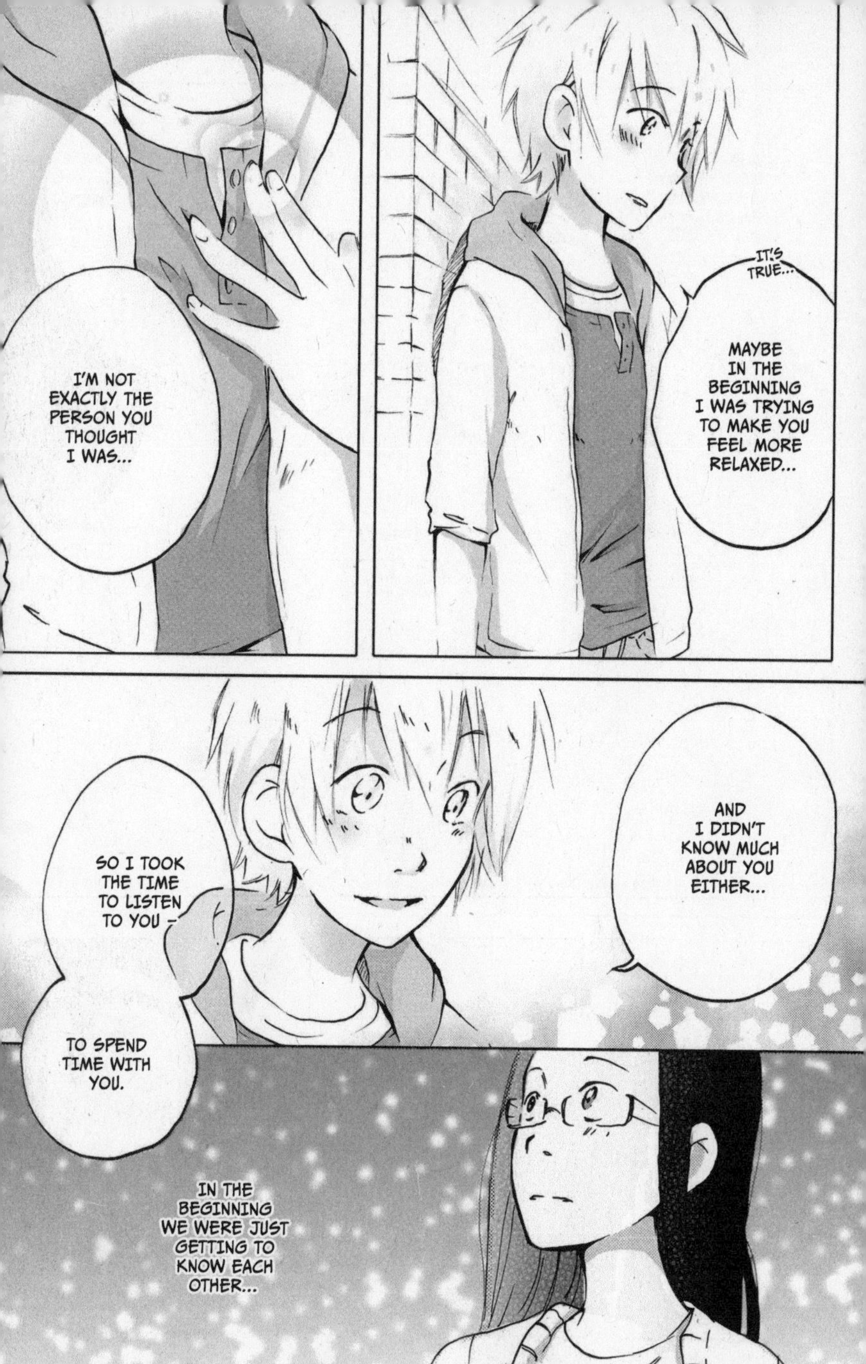
IT'S TRUE...
MAYBE IN THE BEGINNING I WAS TRYING TO MAKE YOU FEEL MORE RELAXED...
I'M NOT EXACTLY THE PERSON YOU THOUGHT I WAS...
AND I DIDN'T KNOW MUCH ABOUT YOU EITHER...
SO I TOOK THE TIME TO LISTEN TO YOU –
TO SPEND TIME WITH YOU.
IN THE BEGINNING WE WERE JUST GETTING TO KNOW EACH OTHER...

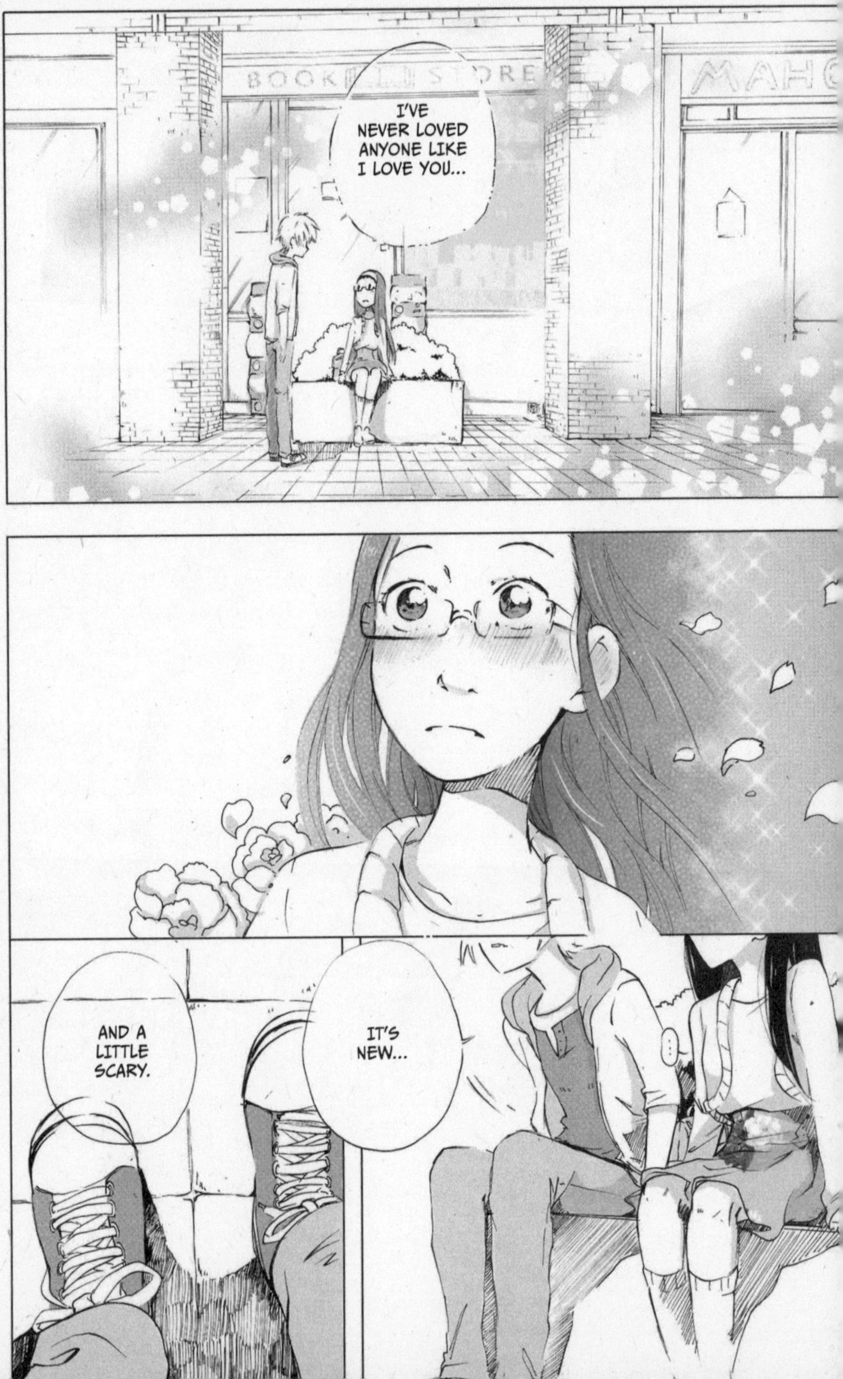
BOOK STORE
I'VE NEVER LOVED ANYONE LIKE I LOVE YOU...
...
IT'S NEW...
AND A LITTLE SCARY.

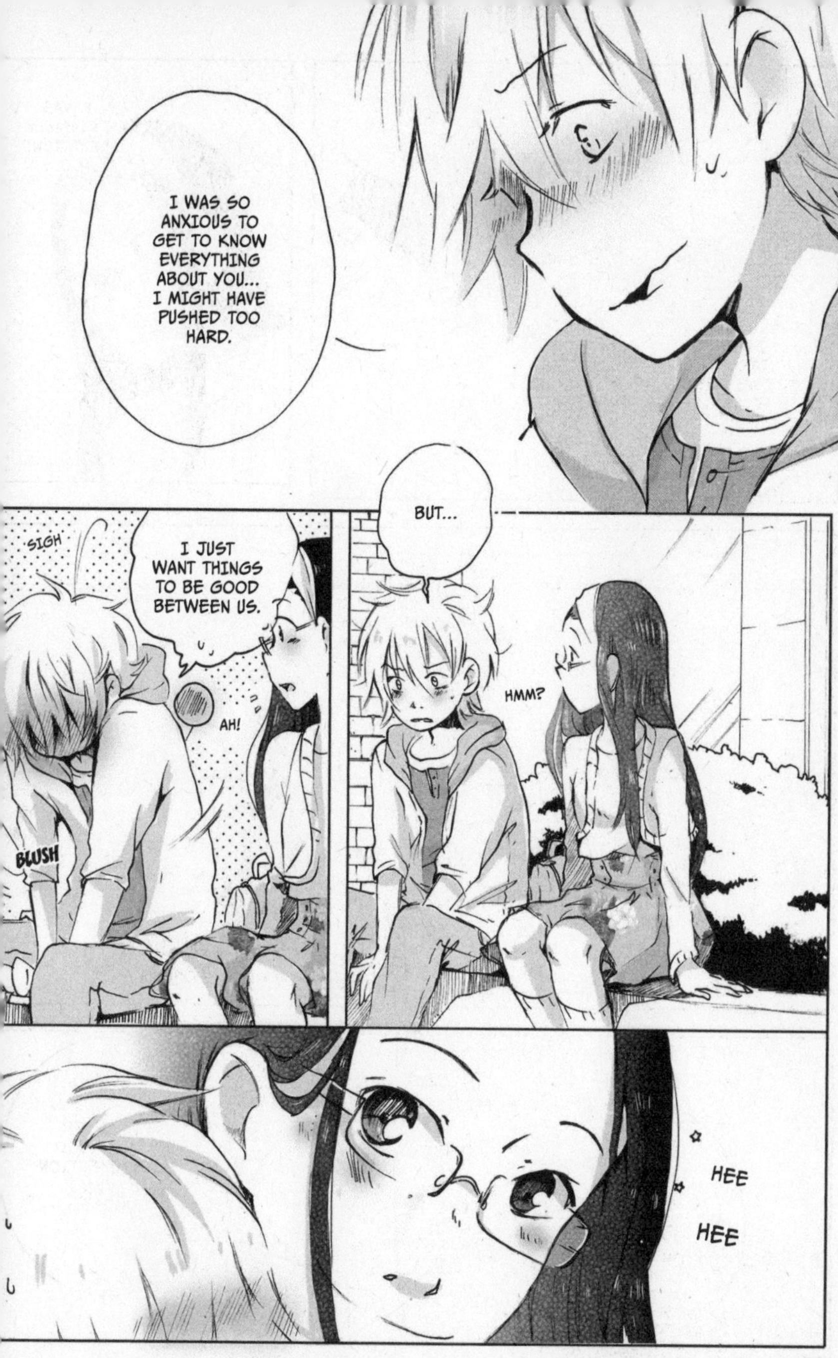
I WAS SO ANXIOUS TO GET TO KNOW EVERYTHING ABOUT YOU... I MIGHT HAVE PUSHED TOO HARD.
BUT...
HMM?
SIGH
I JUST WANT THINGS TO BE GOOD BETWEEN US.
AH!
BLUSH
HEE
HEE

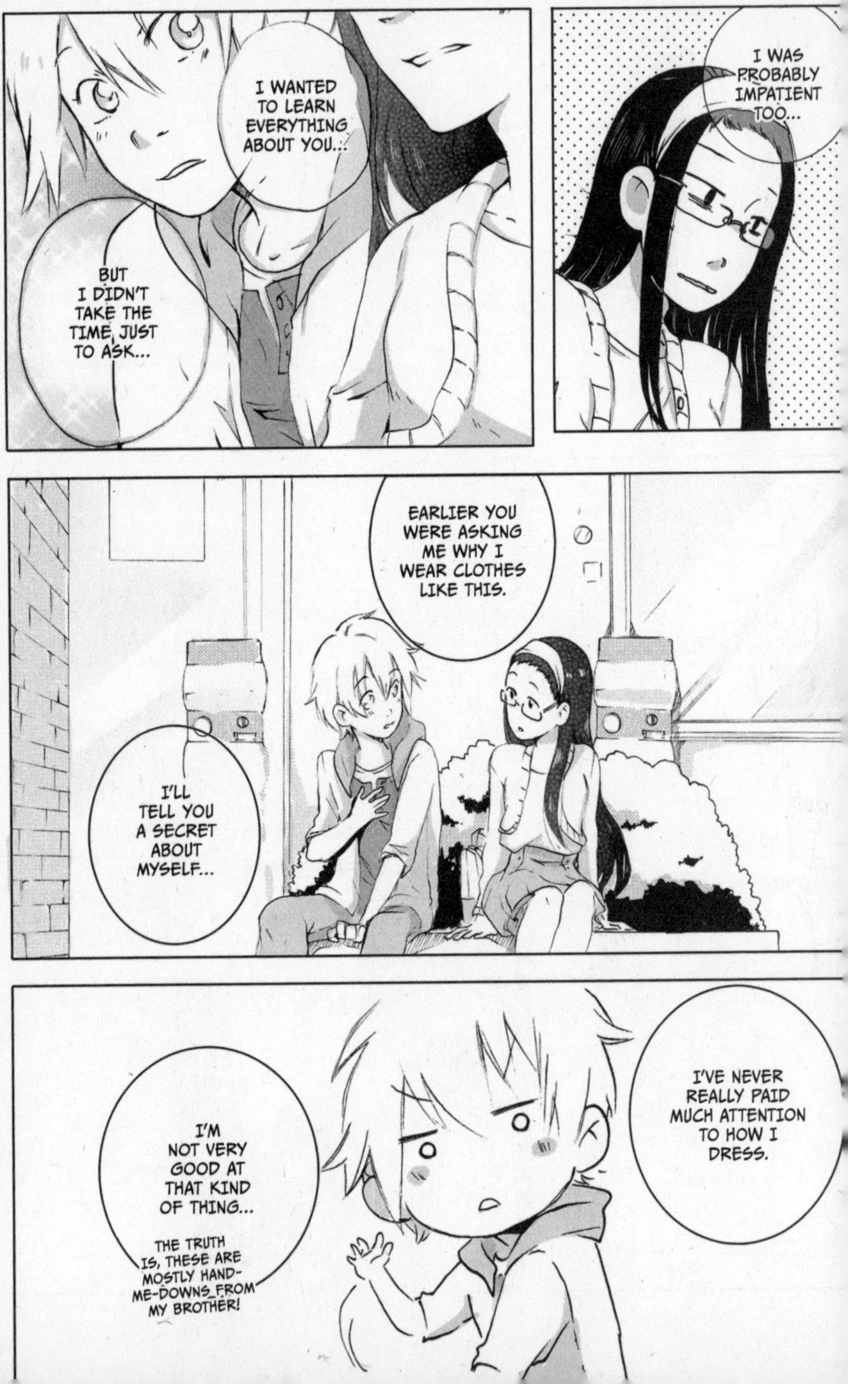
I WAS PROBABLY IMPATIENT TOO...
I WANTED TO LEARN EVERYTHING ABOUT YOU...
BUT I DIDN'T TAKE THE TIME, JUST TO ASK...
EARLIER YOU WERE ASKING ME WHY I WEAR CLOTHES LIKE THIS.
I'LL TELL YOU A SECRET ABOUT MYSELF...
I'VE NEVER REALLY PAID MUCH ATTENTION TO HOW I DRESS.
I'M NOT VERY GOOD AT THAT KIND OF THING...
THE TRUTH IS, THESE ARE MOSTLY HAND-ME-DOWNS FROM MY BROTHER!

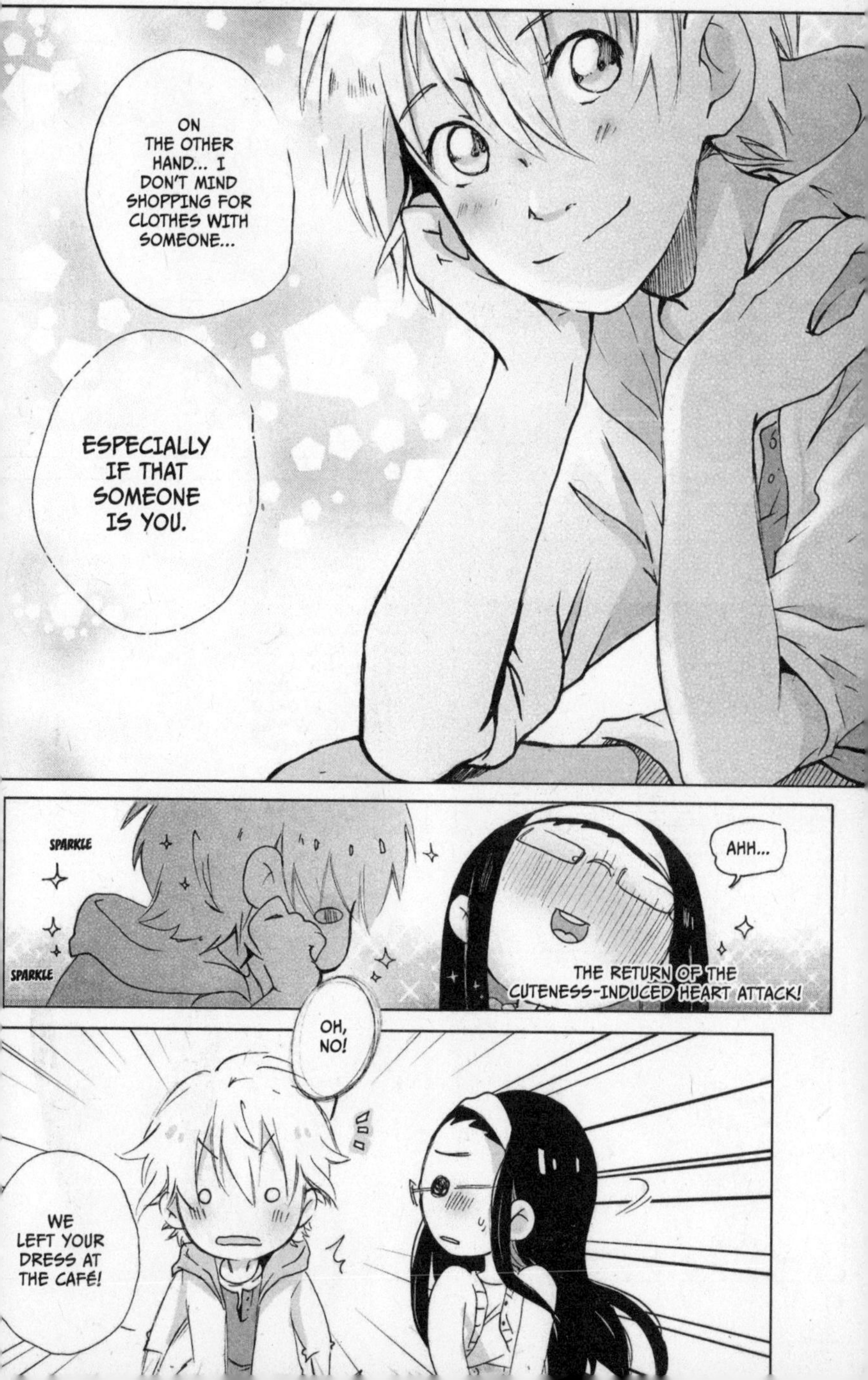
ON THE OTHER HAND... I DON'T MIND SHOPPING FOR CLOTHES WITH SOMEONE...
ESPECIALLY IF THAT SOMEONE IS YOU.
AHH...
THE RETURN OF THE CUTENESS-INDUCED HEART ATTACK!
SPARKLE
SPARKLE
OH, NO!
WE LEFT YOUR DRESS AT THE CAFÉ!

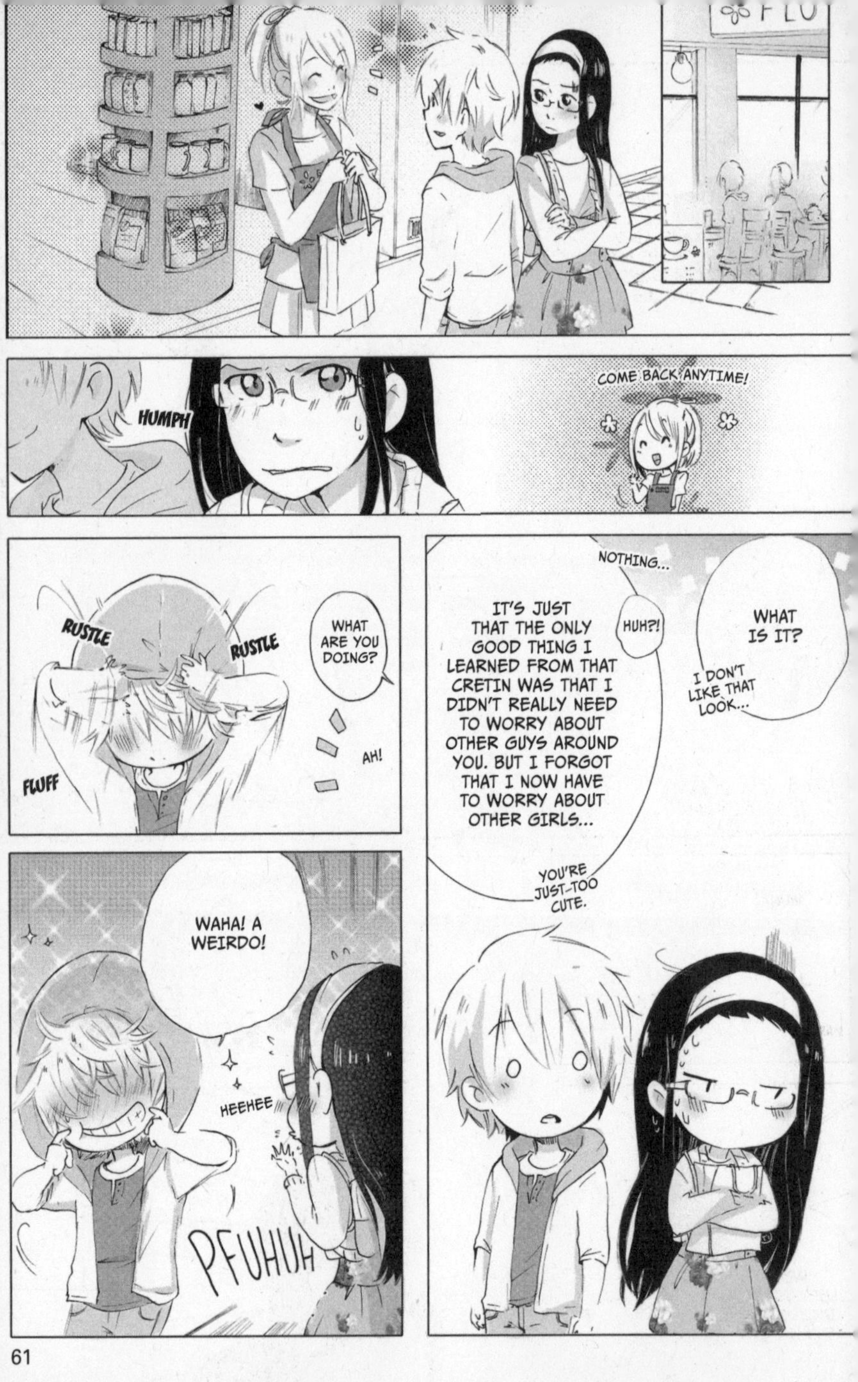
COME BACK ANYTIME!
HUMPH
WHAT IS IT?
I DON'T LIKE THAT LOOK...
HUH?!
NOTHING...
IT'S JUST THAT THE ONLY GOOD THING I LEARNED FROM THAT CRETIN WAS THAT I DIDN'T REALLY NEED TO WORRY ABOUT OTHER GUYS AROUND YOU. BUT I FORGOT THAT I NOW HAVE TO WORRY ABOUT OTHER GIRLS...
YOU'RE JUST-TOO CUTE.
WHAT ARE YOU DOING?
RUSTLE
RUSTLE
AH!
FLUFF
WAHA! A WEIRDO!
HEEHEE
PFUHUH

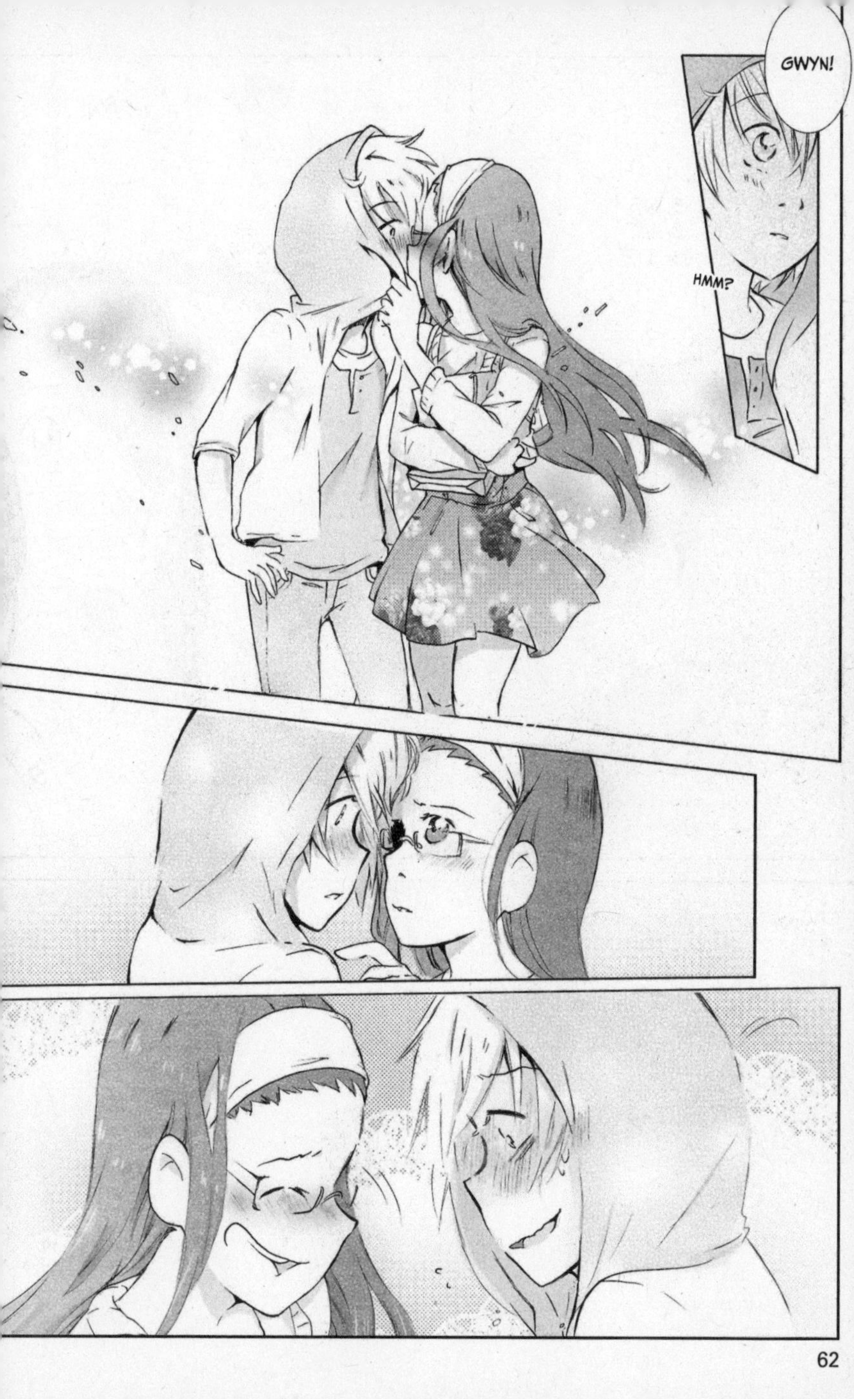
GWYN!
HMM?

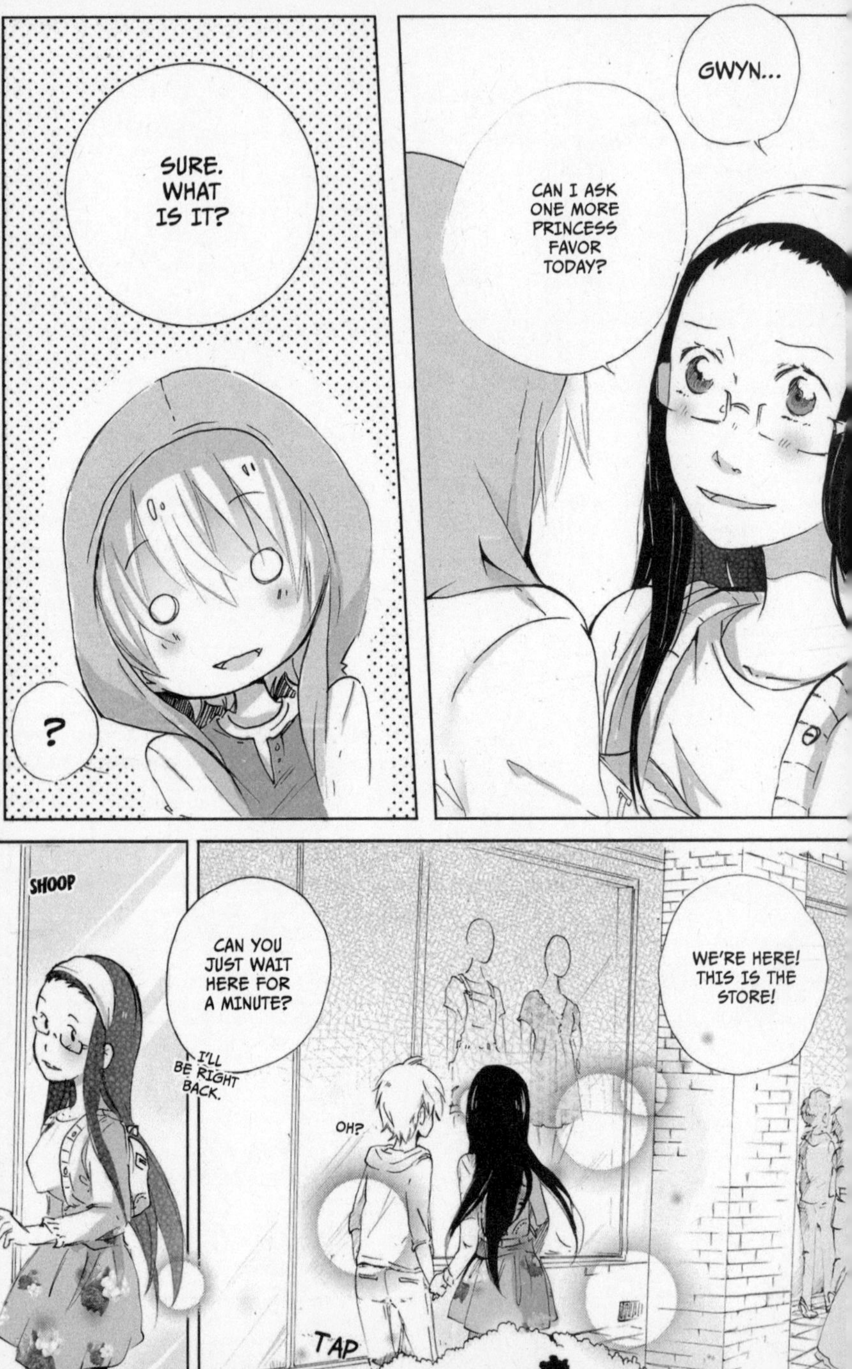
GWYN...
CAN I ASK ONE MORE PRINCESS FAVOR TODAY?
SURE. WHAT IS IT?
?
WE'RE HERE! THIS IS THE STORE!
CAN YOU JUST WAIT HERE FOR A MINUTE?
I'LL BE RIGHT BACK.
OH?
TAP
SHOOP

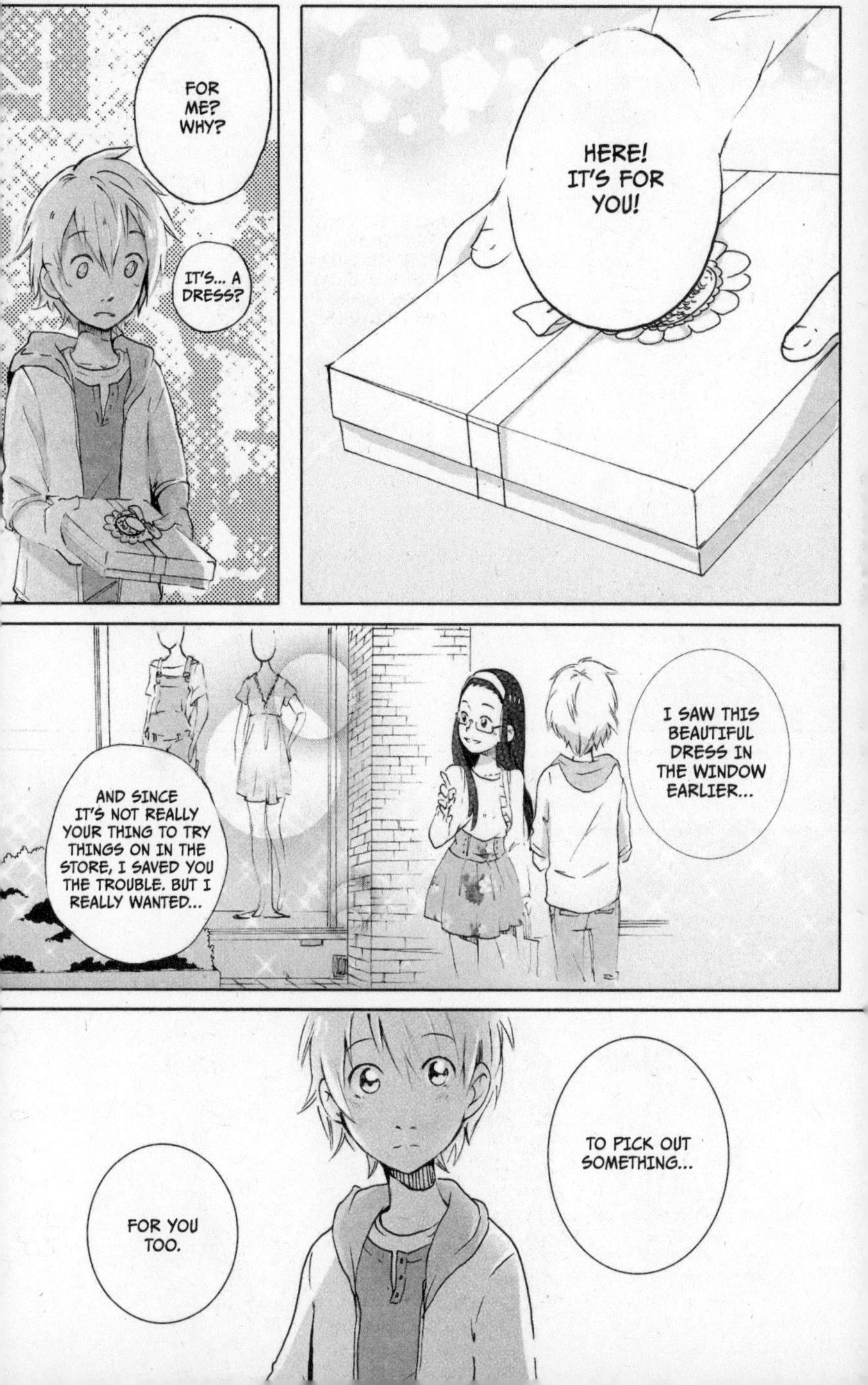
HERE! IT'S FOR YOU!
FOR ME? WHY?
IT'S... A DRESS?
I SAW THIS BEAUTIFUL DRESS IN THE WINDOW EARLIER...
AND SINCE IT'S NOT REALLY YOUR THING TO TRY THINGS ON IN THE STORE, I SAVED YOU THE TROUBLE. BUT I REALLY WANTED...
TO PICK OUT SOMETHING...
FOR YOU TOO.

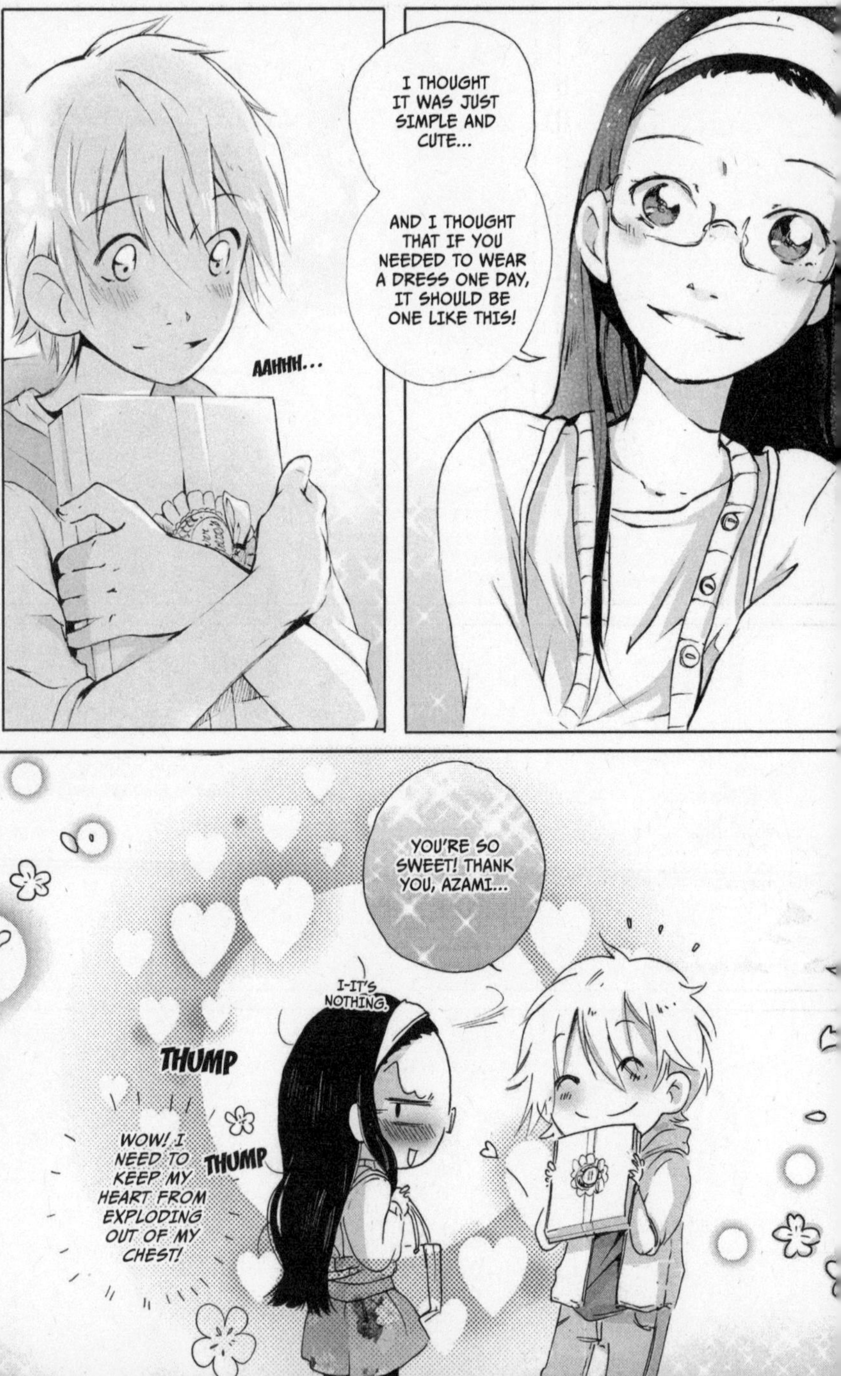
I THOUGHT IT WAS JUST SIMPLE AND CUTE...
AND I THOUGHT THAT IF YOU NEEDED TO WEAR A DRESS ONE DAY, IT SHOULD BE ONE LIKE THIS!
AAHHH...
YOU'RE SO SWEET! THANK YOU, AZAMI...
I-IT'S NOTHING.
THUMP
WOW! I NEED TO KEEP MY HEART FROM EXPLODING OUT OF MY CHEST!
THUMP

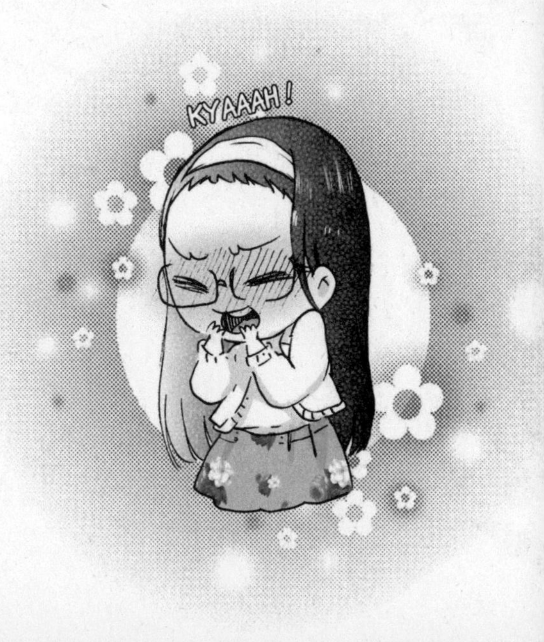
KYAAAH!

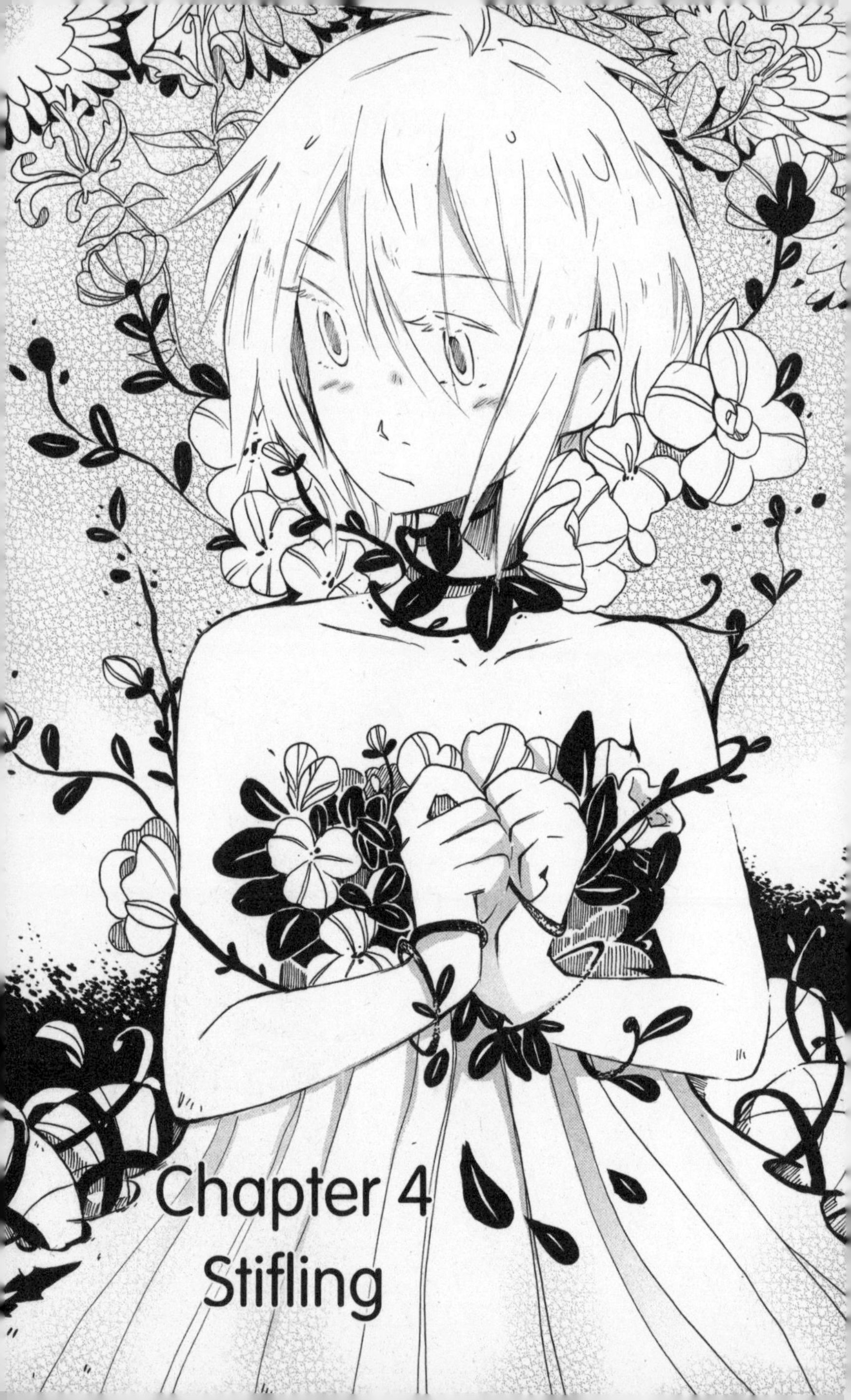
Chapter 4
Stifling

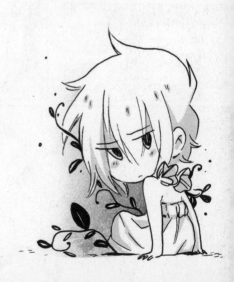

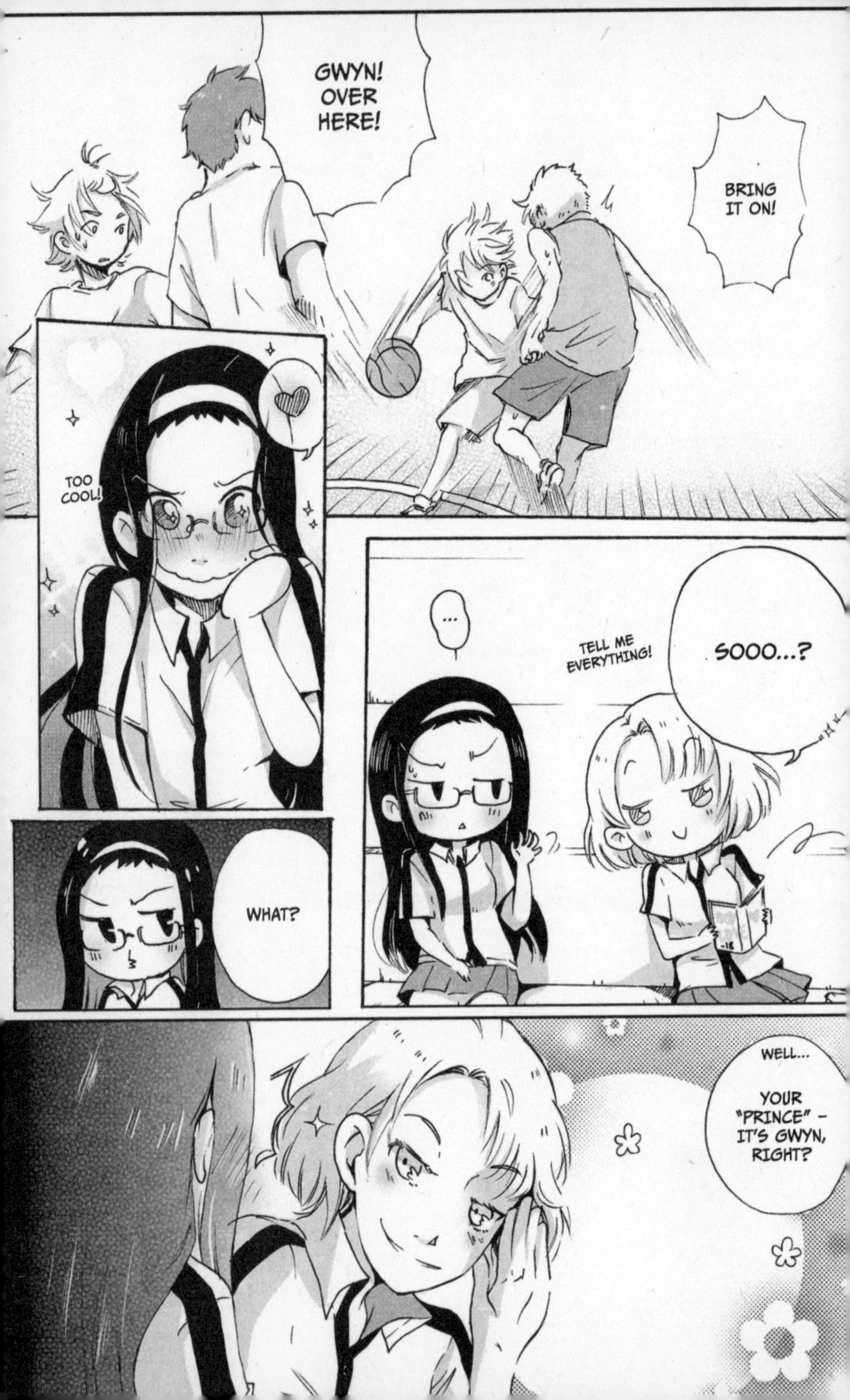
GWYN! OVER HERE!
BRING IT ON!
SOOO...?
TELL ME EVERYTHING!
...
TOO COOL!
WHAT?
WELL...
YOUR "PRINCE" – IT'S GWYN, RIGHT?

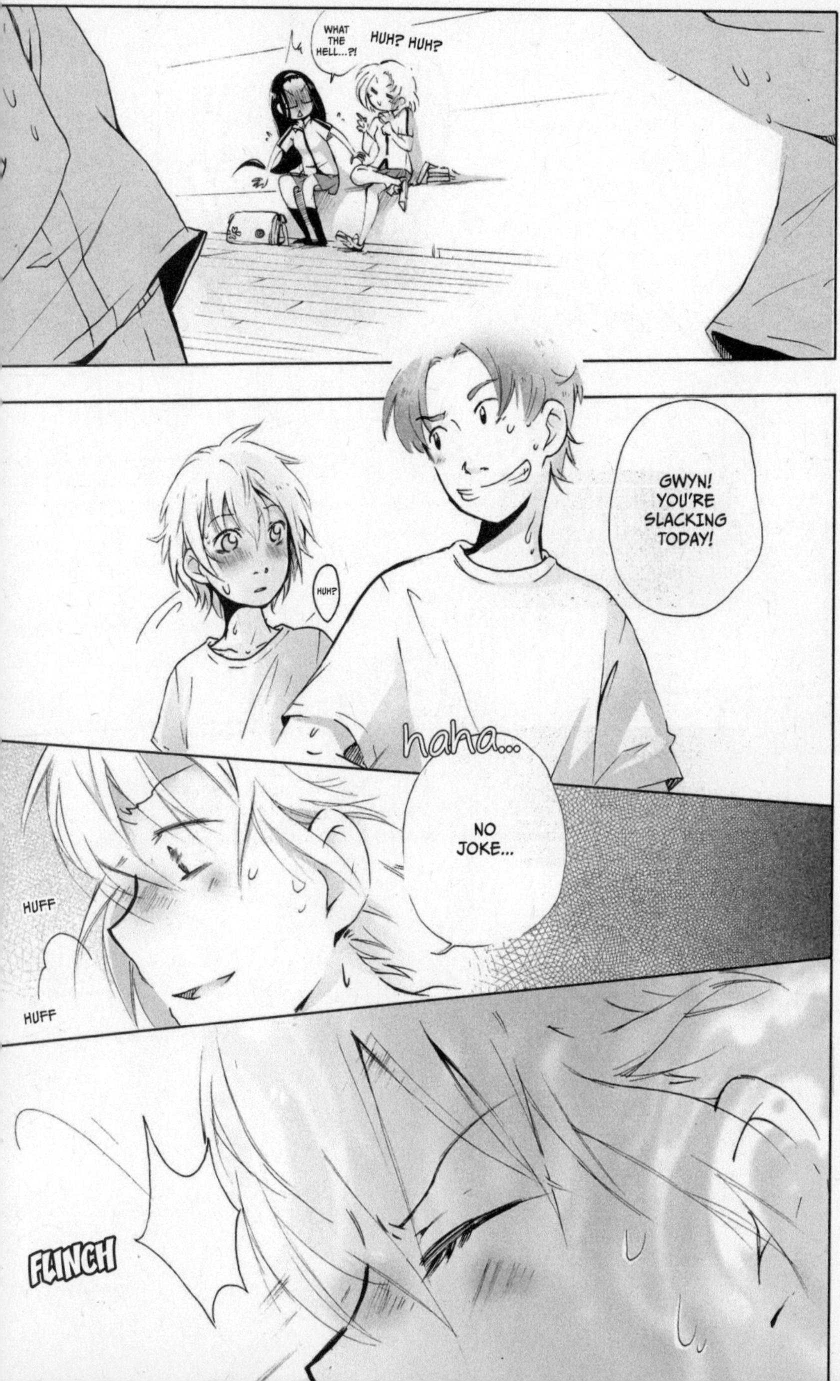
HUH? HUH?
WHAT THE HELL...?!
GWYN! YOU'RE SLACKING TODAY!
HUH?
haha...
NO JOKE...
HUFF
HUFF
FLINCH

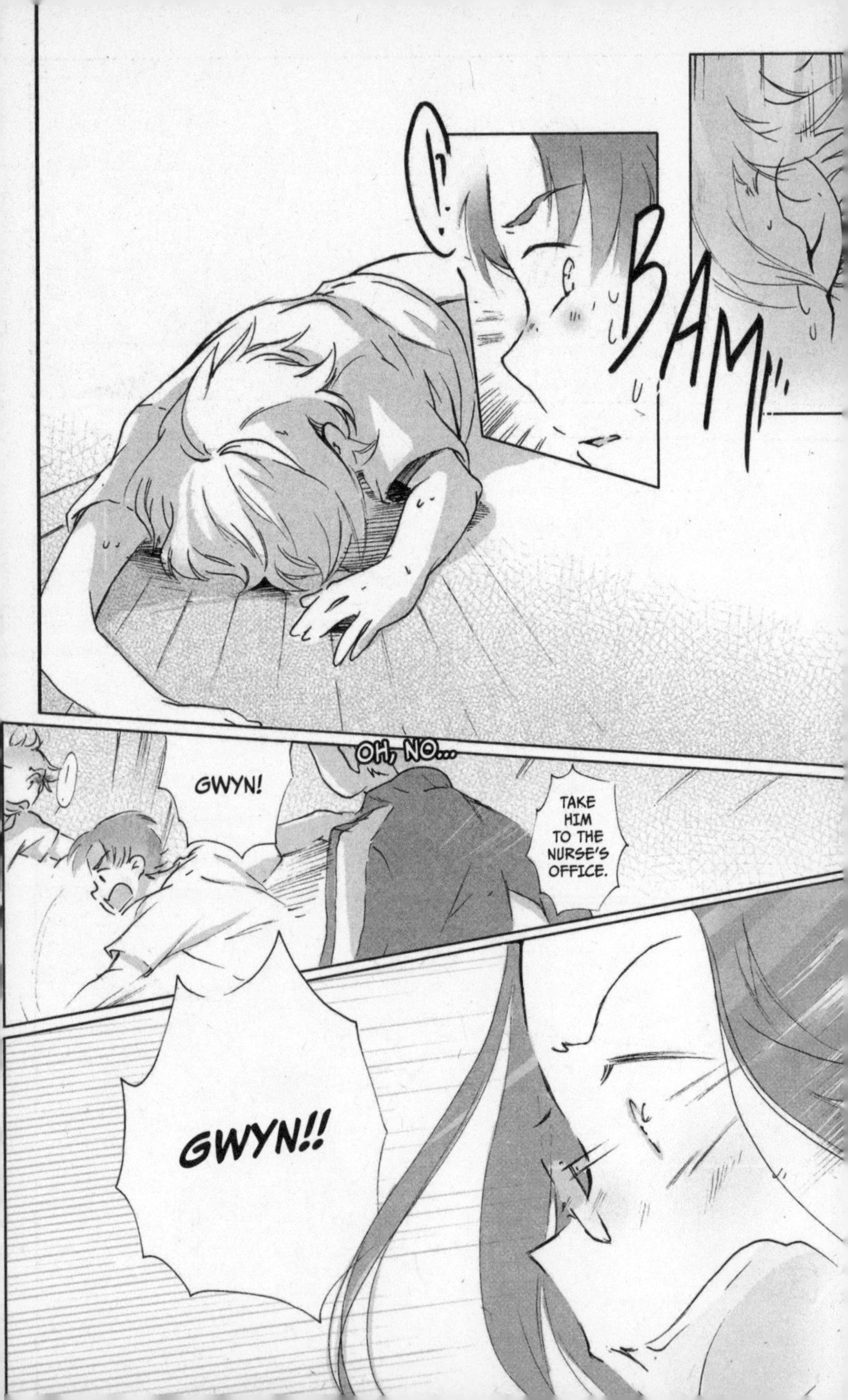
!?
BAM
OH, NO...
TAKE HIM TO THE NURSE'S OFFICE.
!
GWYN!
GWYN!!

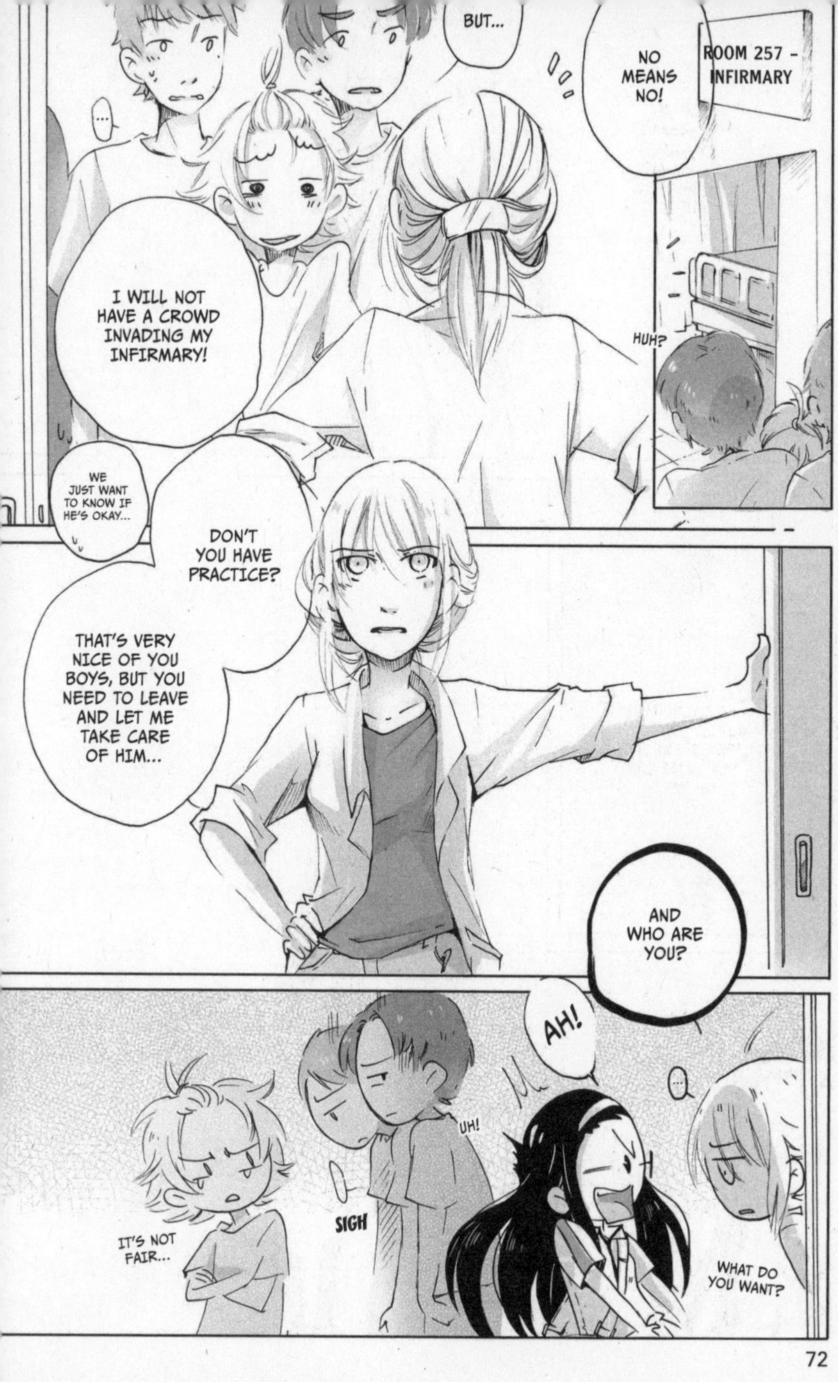

ROOM 257 - INFIRMARY
NO MEANS NO!
BUT...
...
HUH?
I WILL NOT HAVE A CROWD INVADING MY INFIRMARY!
WE JUST WANT TO KNOW IF HE'S OKAY...
DON'T YOU HAVE PRACTICE?
THAT'S VERY NICE OF YOU BOYS, BUT YOU NEED TO LEAVE AND LET ME TAKE CARE OF HIM...
AND WHO ARE YOU?
...
AH!
WHAT DO YOU WANT?
UH!
SIGH
IT'S NOT FAIR...

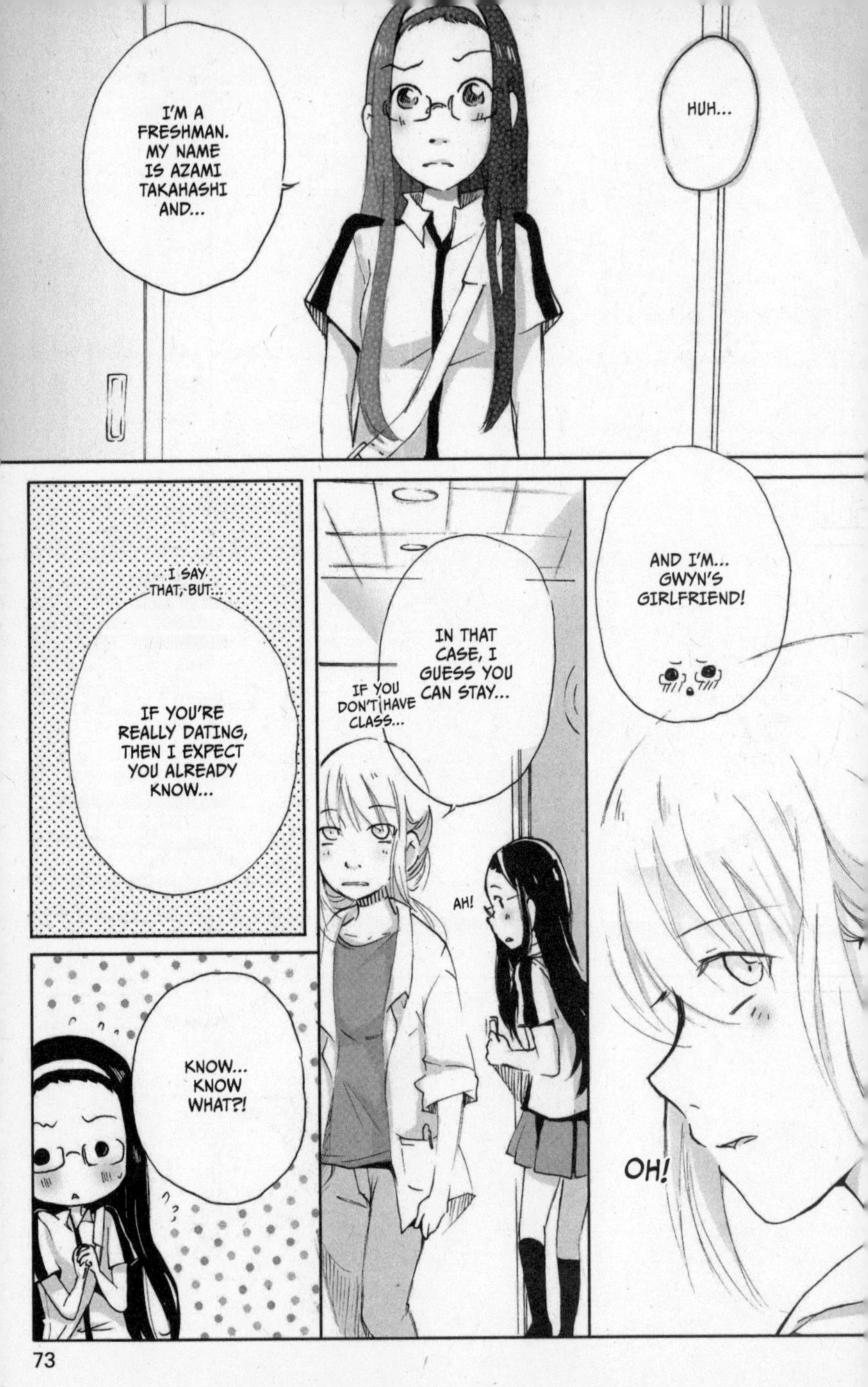
HUH...
I'M A FRESHMAN. MY NAME IS AZAMI TAKAHASHI AND...
AND I'M... GWYN'S GIRLFRIEND!
OH!
IN THAT CASE, I GUESS YOU CAN STAY...
IF YOU DON'T HAVE CLASS...
AH!
I SAY THAT, BUT...
IF YOU'RE REALLY DATING, THEN I EXPECT YOU ALREADY KNOW...
KNOW... KNOW WHAT?!

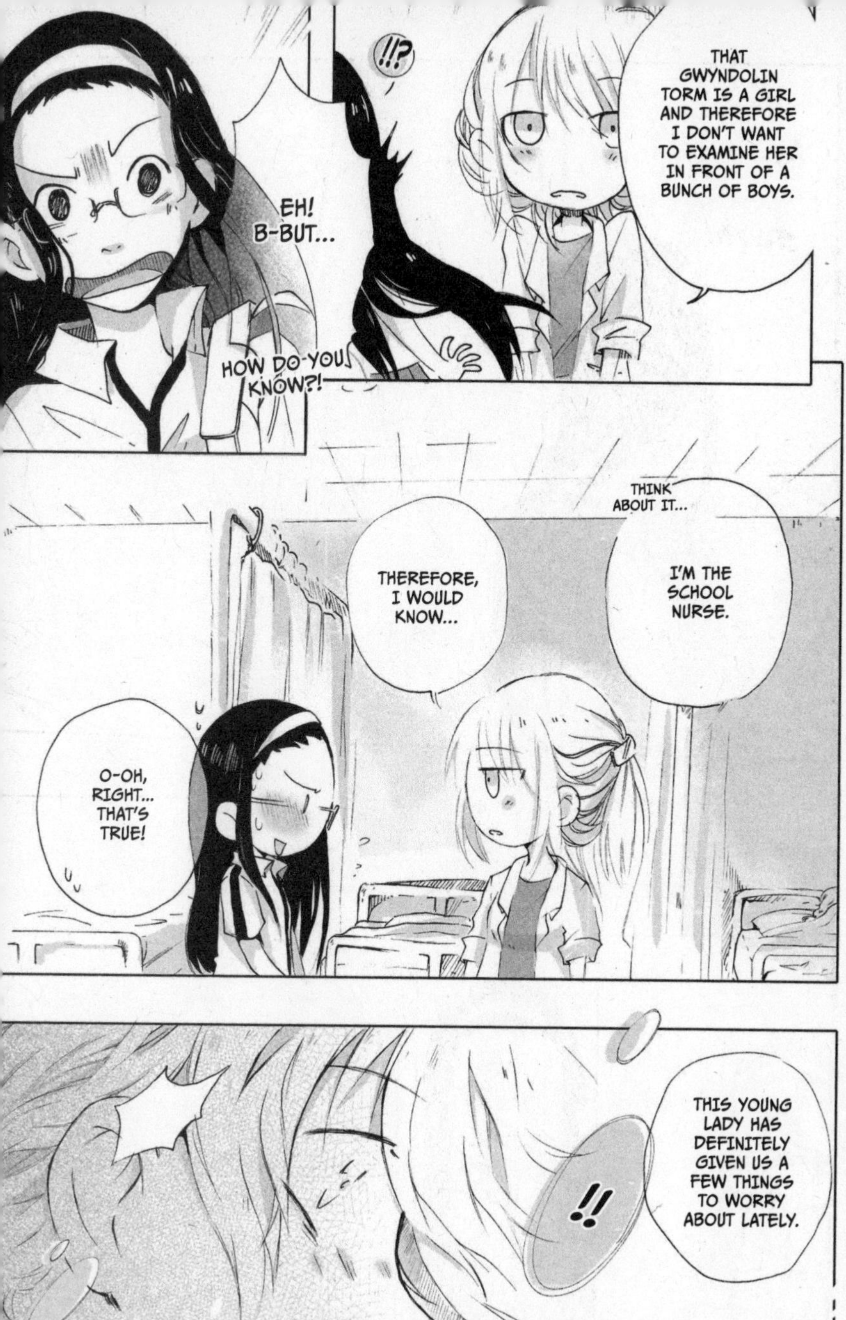
THAT GWYNDOLIN TORM IS A GIRL AND THEREFORE I DON'T WANT TO EXAMINE HER IN FRONT OF A BUNCH OF BOYS.
!!?
EH! B-BUT...
HOW DO-YOU KNOW?!
THINK ABOUT IT...
I'M THE SCHOOL NURSE.
THEREFORE, I WOULD KNOW...
O-OH, RIGHT... THAT'S TRUE!
THIS YOUNG LADY HAS DEFINITELY GIVEN US A FEW THINGS TO WORRY ABOUT LATELY.
!!

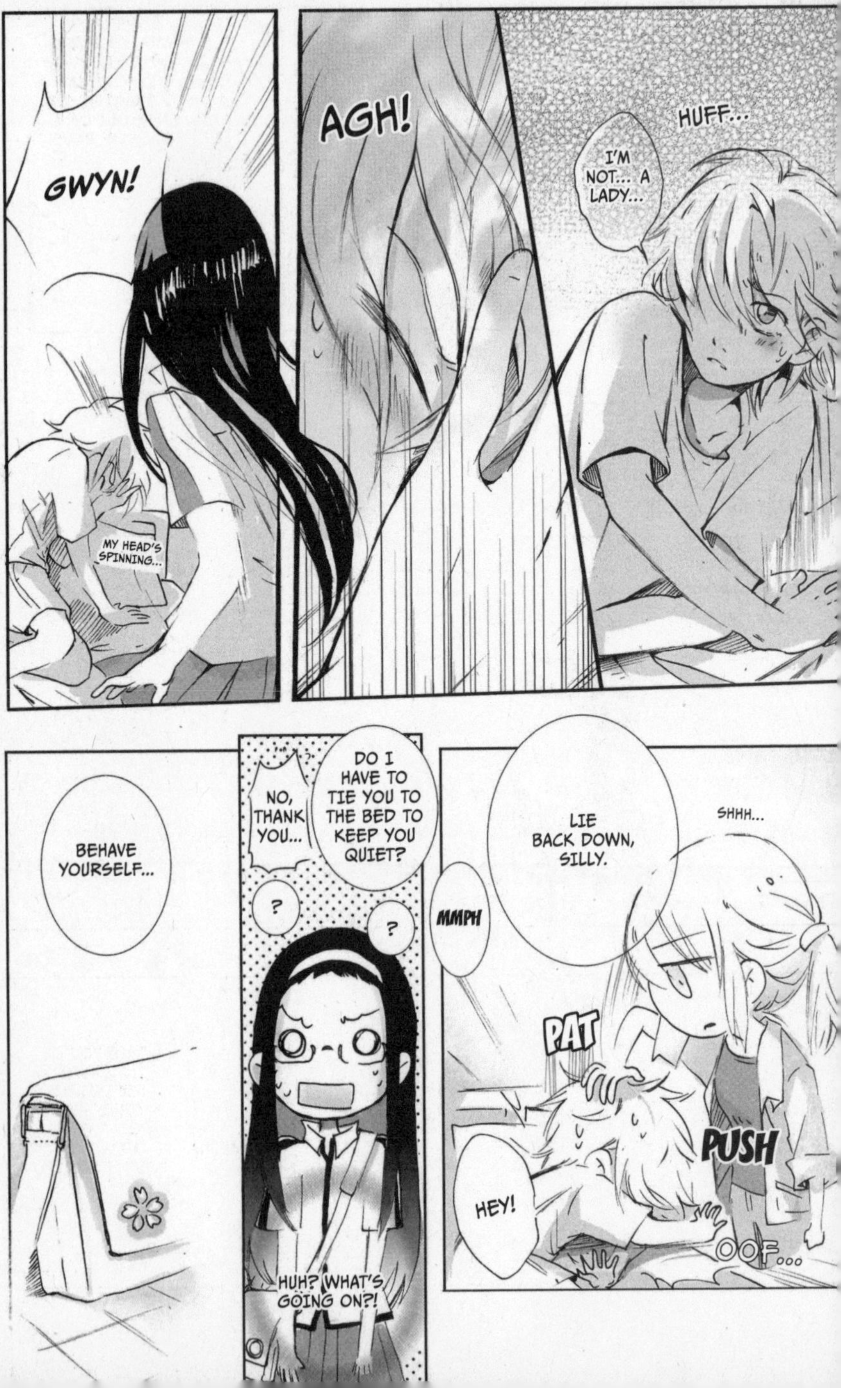
HUFF...
I'M NOT... A LADY...
AGH!
GWYN!
MY HEAD'S SPINNING...
SHHH...
LIE BACK DOWN, SILLY.
MMPH
PAT
PUSH
HEY!
OOF...
DO I HAVE TO TIE YOU TO THE BED TO KEEP YOU QUIET?
NO, THANK YOU...
?
?
HUH? WHAT'S GOING ON?!
BEHAVE YOURSELF...

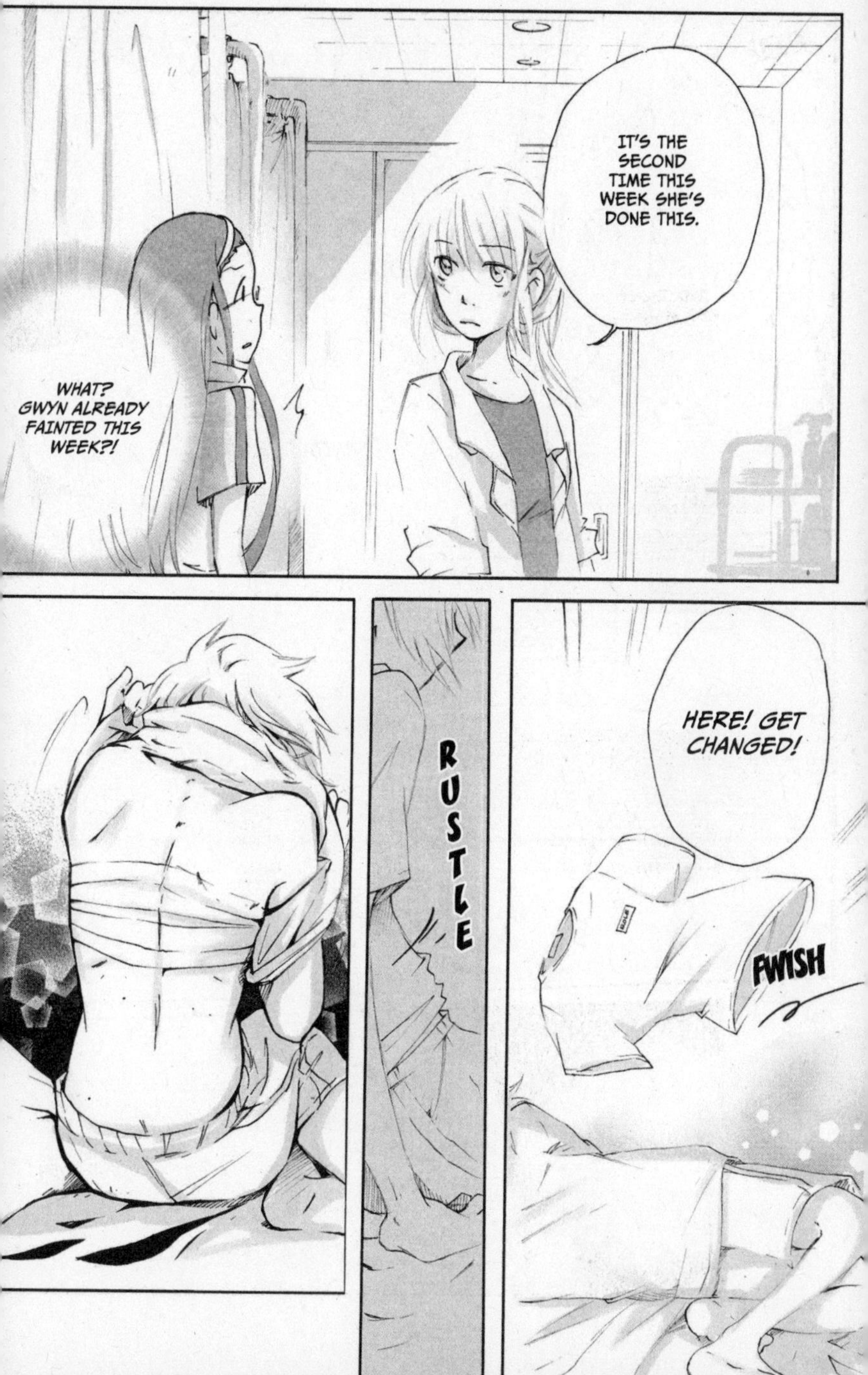
IT'S THE SECOND TIME THIS WEEK SHE'S DONE THIS.
WHAT? GWYN ALREADY FAINTED THIS WEEK?!
HERE! GET CHANGED!
FWISH
RUSTLE

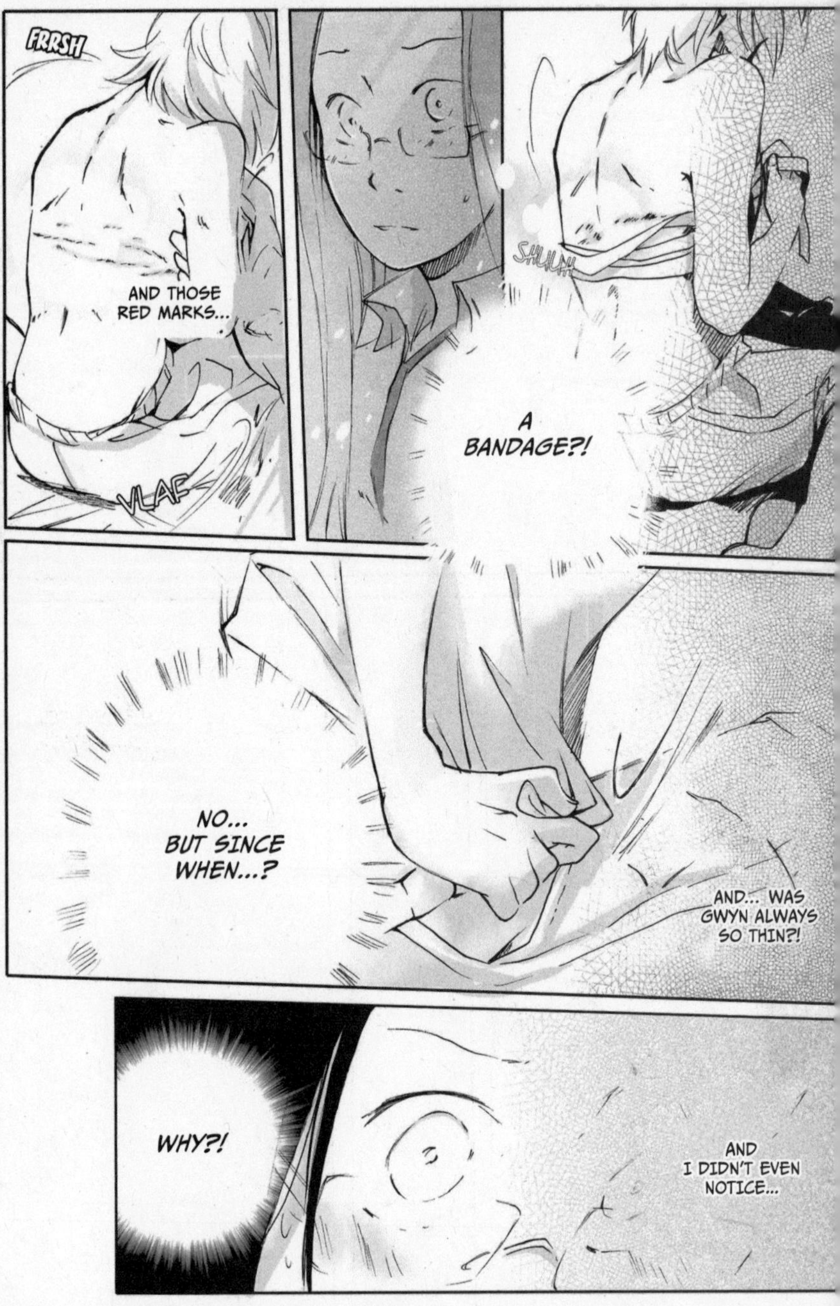
SHUUH
A BANDAGE?!
FRRSH
AND THOSE RED MARKS...
VLAF
AND... WAS GWYN ALWAYS SO THIN?!
NO... BUT SINCE WHEN...?
AND I DIDN'T EVEN NOTICE...
WHY?!

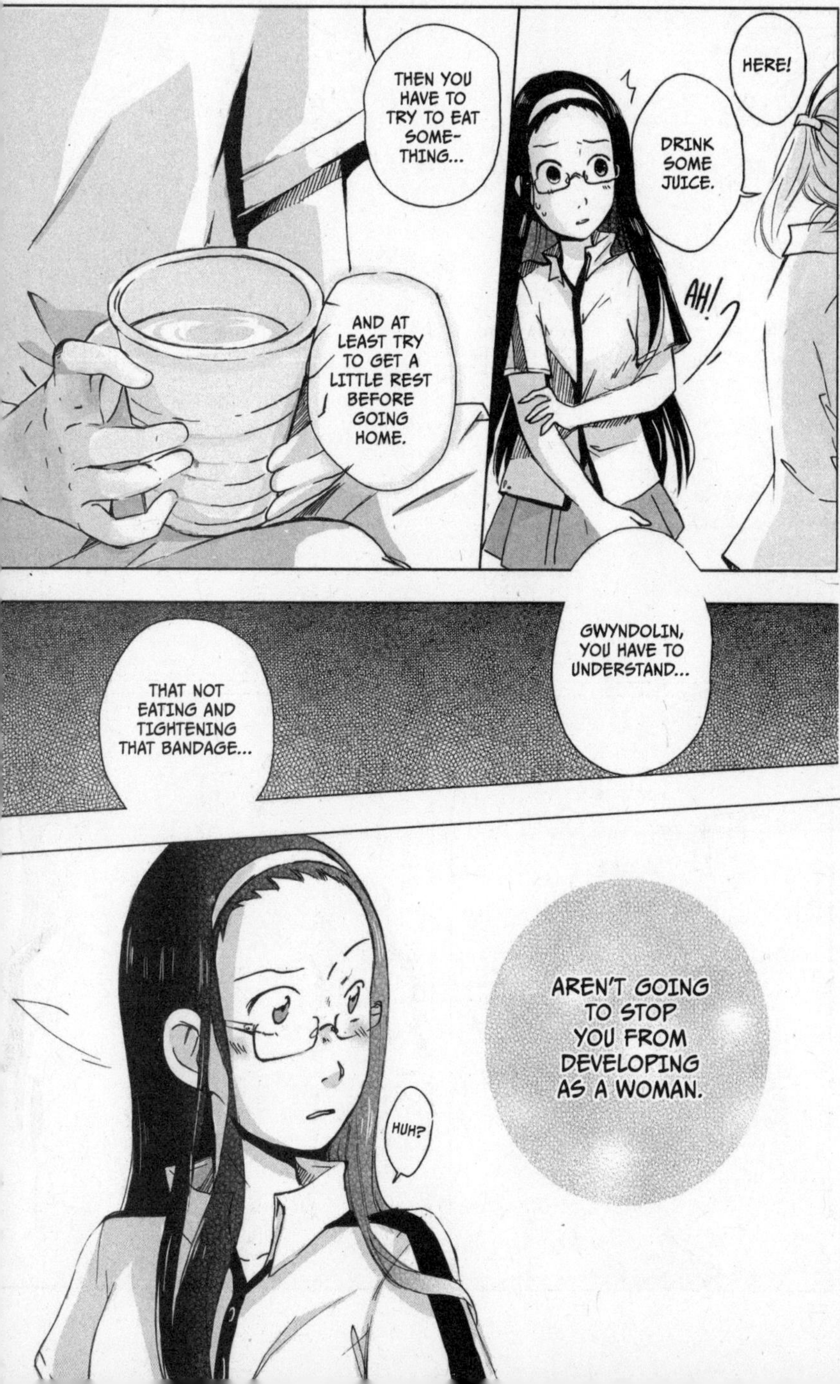
HERE!
DRINK SOME JUICE.
AH!
THEN YOU HAVE TO TRY TO EAT SOME-THING...
AND AT LEAST TRY TO GET A LITTLE REST BEFORE GOING HOME.
GWYNDOLIN, YOU HAVE TO UNDERSTAND...
THAT NOT EATING AND TIGHTENING THAT BANDAGE...
AREN'T GOING TO STOP YOU FROM DEVELOPING AS A WOMAN.
HUH?

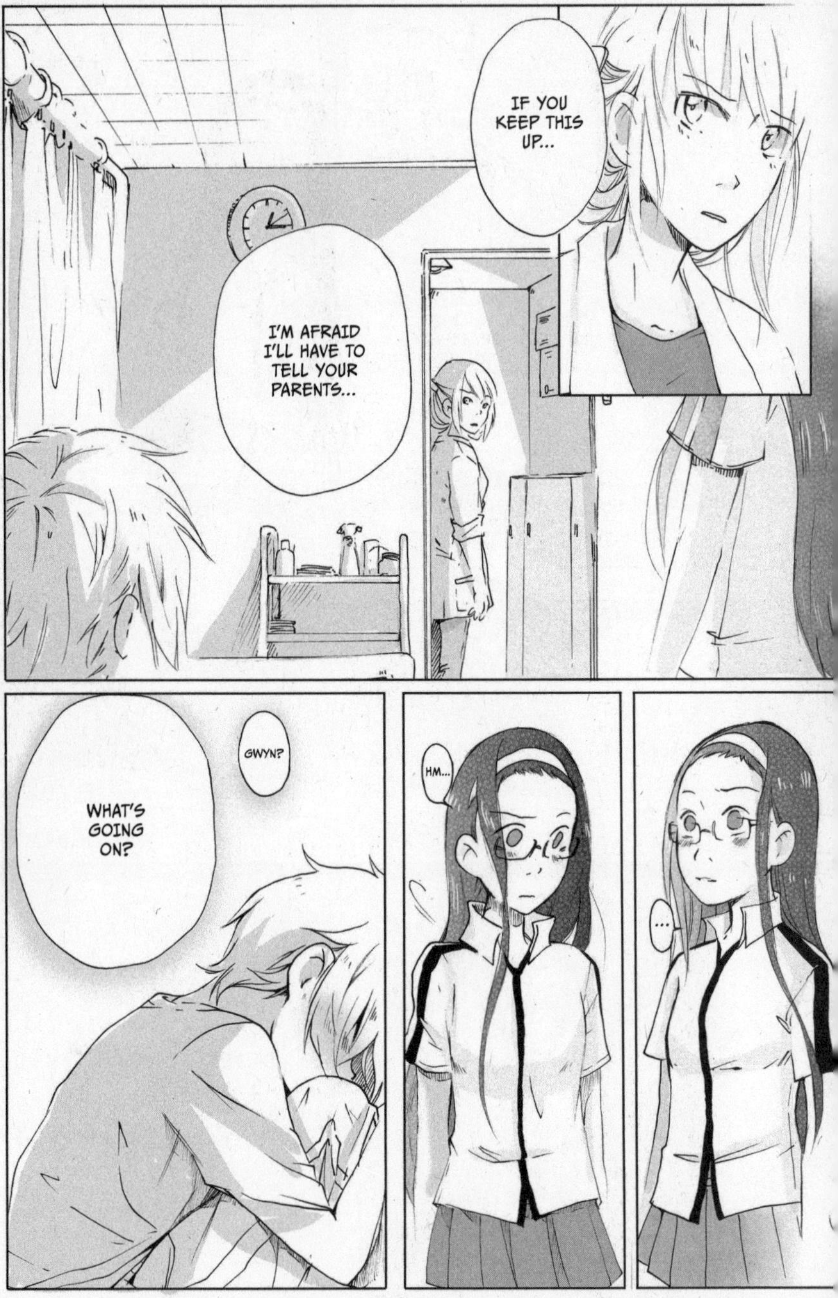

IF YOU KEEP THIS UP...
I'M AFRAID I'LL HAVE TO TELL YOUR PARENTS...
...
HM...
GWYN?
WHAT'S GOING ON?

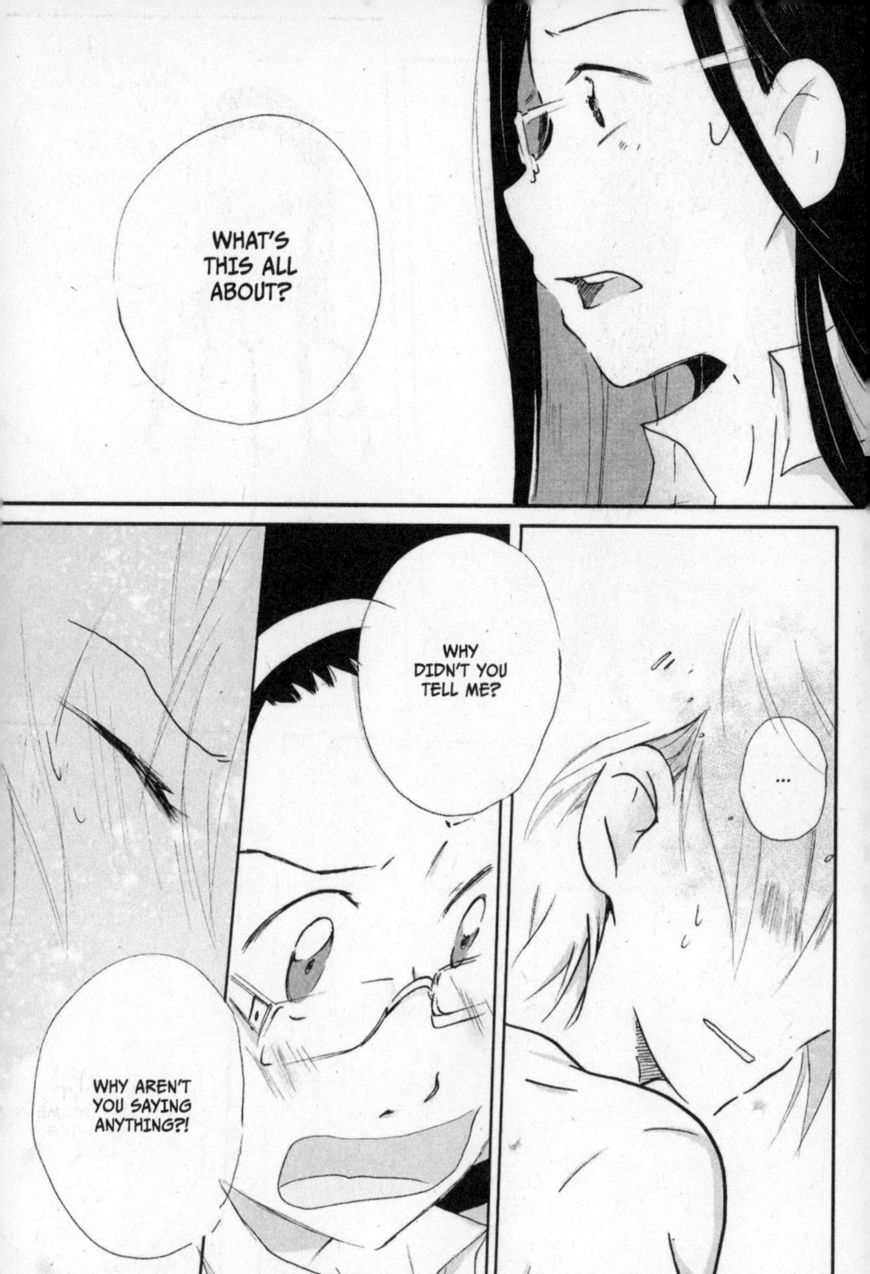
WHAT'S THIS ALL ABOUT?
...
WHY DIDN'T YOU TELL ME?
WHY AREN'T YOU SAYING ANYTHING?!

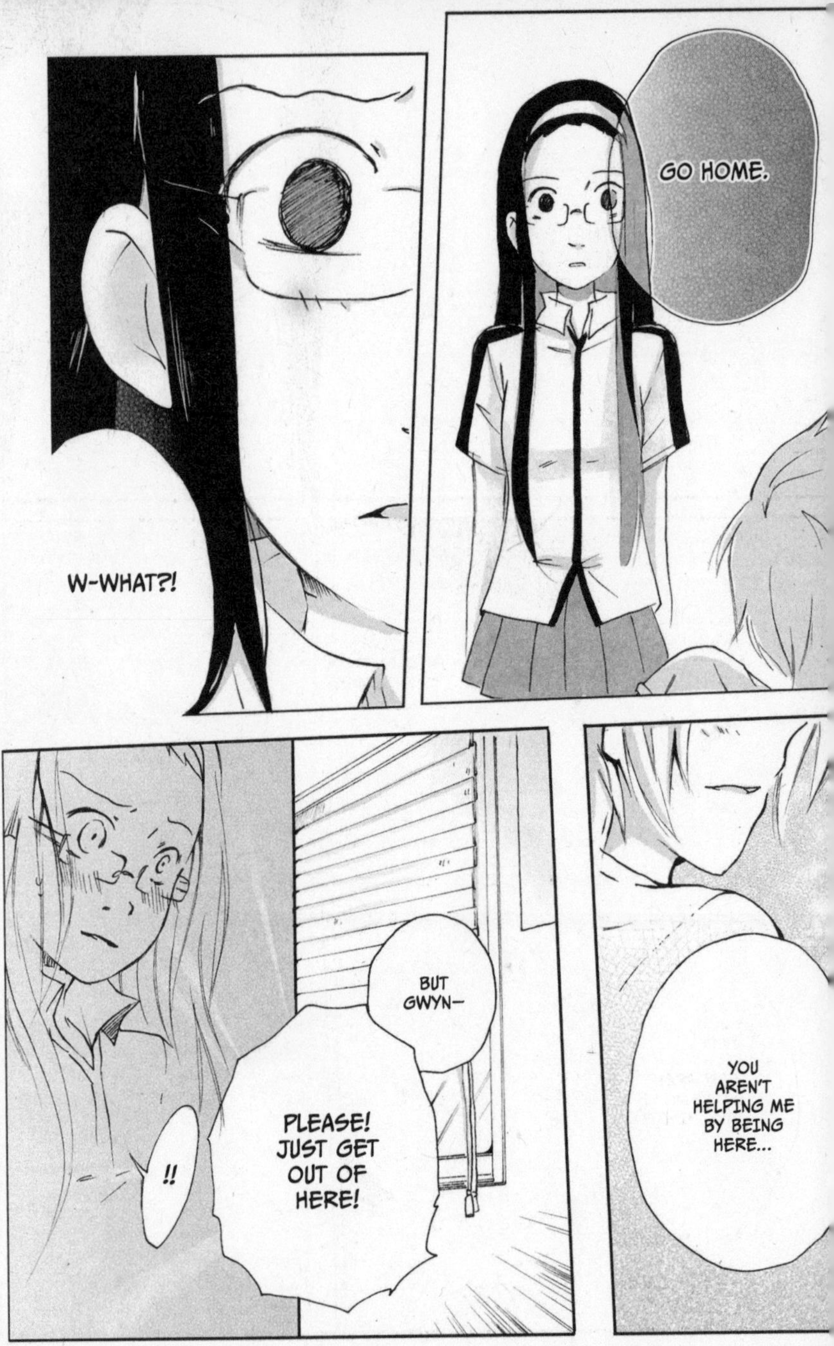
GO HOME.
W-WHAT?!
YOU AREN'T HELPING ME BY BEING HERE...
BUT GWYN—
PLEASE! JUST GET OUT OF HERE!
!!

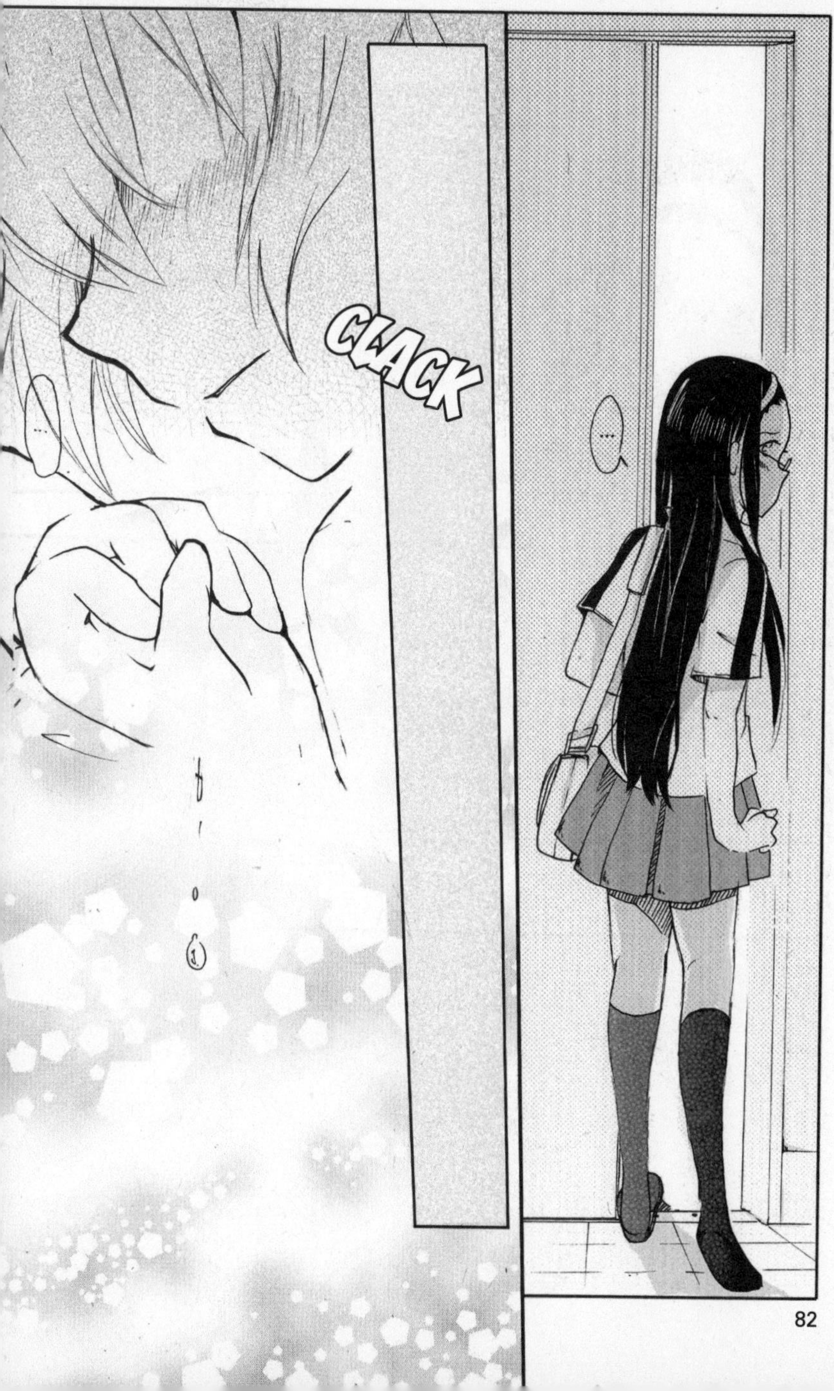
...
CLACK
...

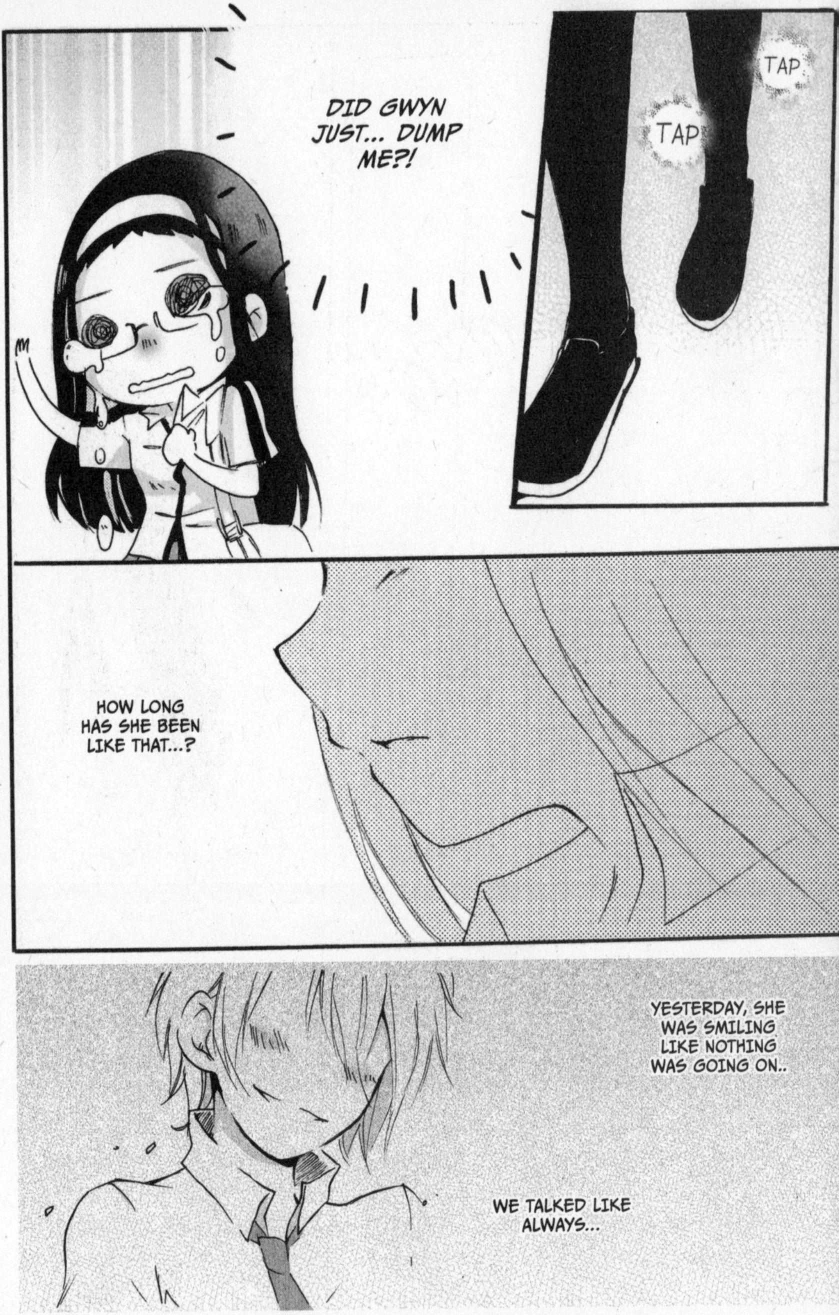
TAP
TAP
DID GWYN JUST... DUMP ME?!
HOW LONG HAS SHE BEEN LIKE THAT...?
YESTERDAY, SHE WAS SMILING LIKE NOTHING WAS GOING ON..
WE TALKED LIKE ALWAYS...

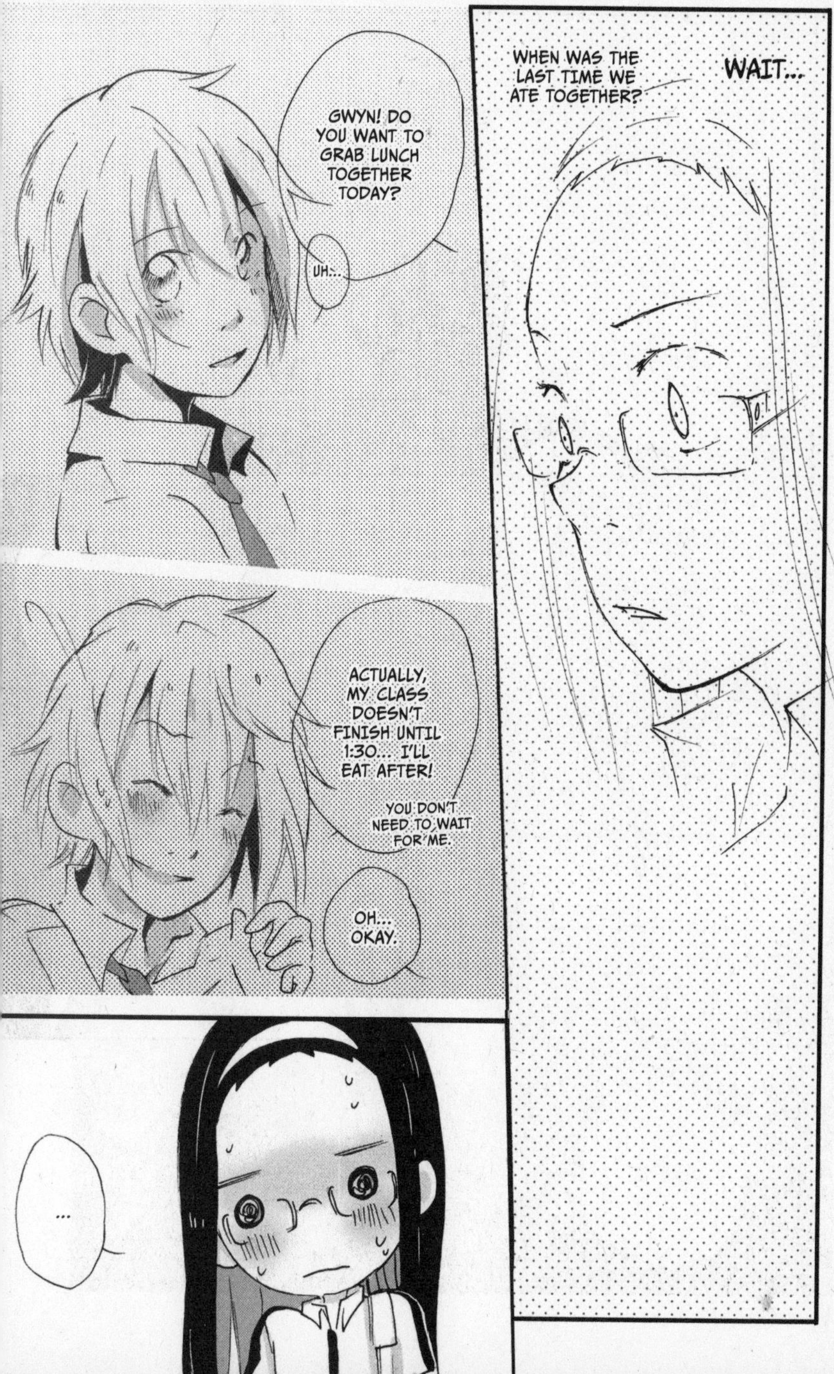
WAIT...
WHEN WAS THE LAST TIME WE ATE TOGETHER?
GWYN! DO YOU WANT TO GRAB LUNCH TOGETHER TODAY?
UH...
ACTUALLY, MY CLASS DOESN'T FINISH UNTIL 1:30... I'LL EAT AFTER!
YOU DON'T NEED TO WAIT FOR ME.
OH... OKAY.
...

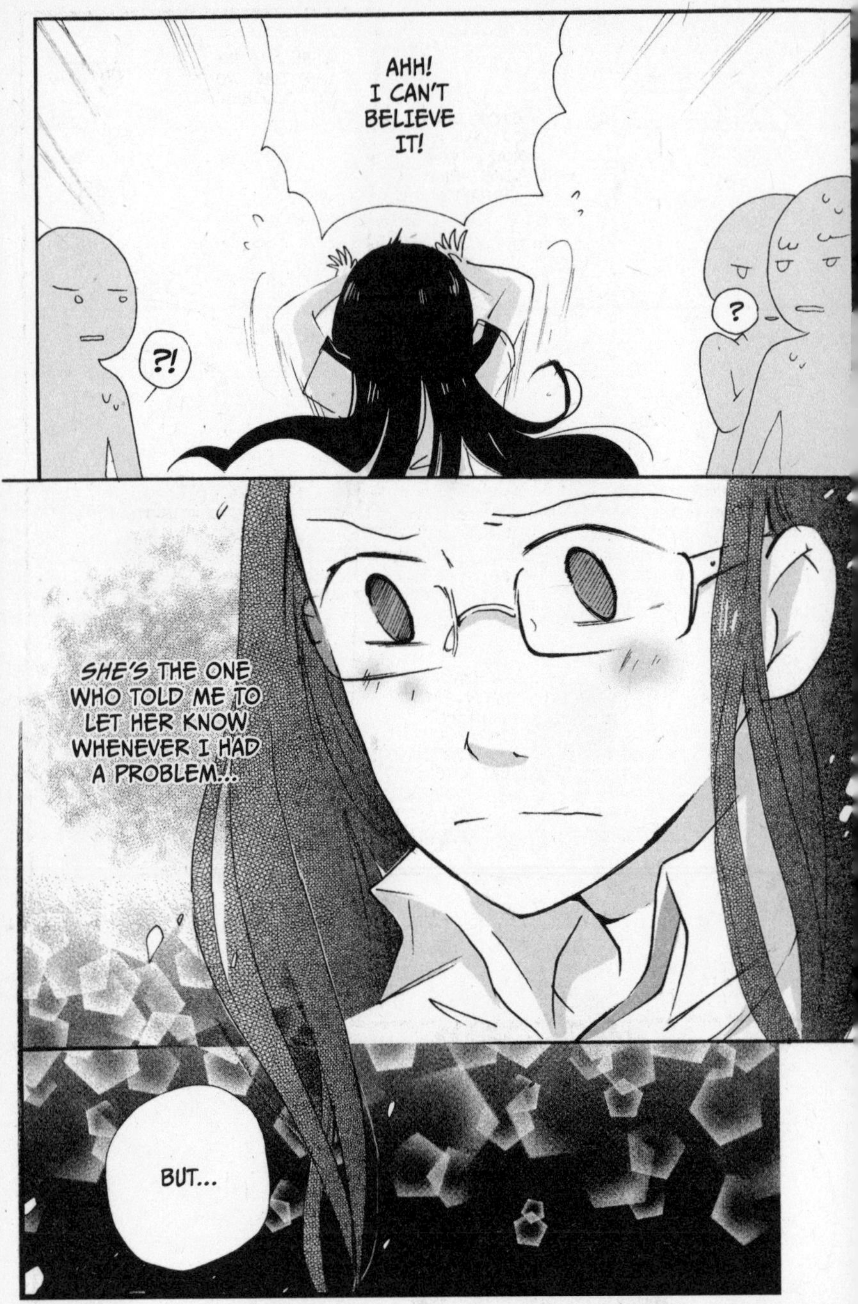
AHH! I CAN'T BELIEVE IT!
?
?!
SHE'S THE ONE WHO TOLD ME TO LET HER KNOW WHENEVER I HAD A PROBLEM...
BUT...

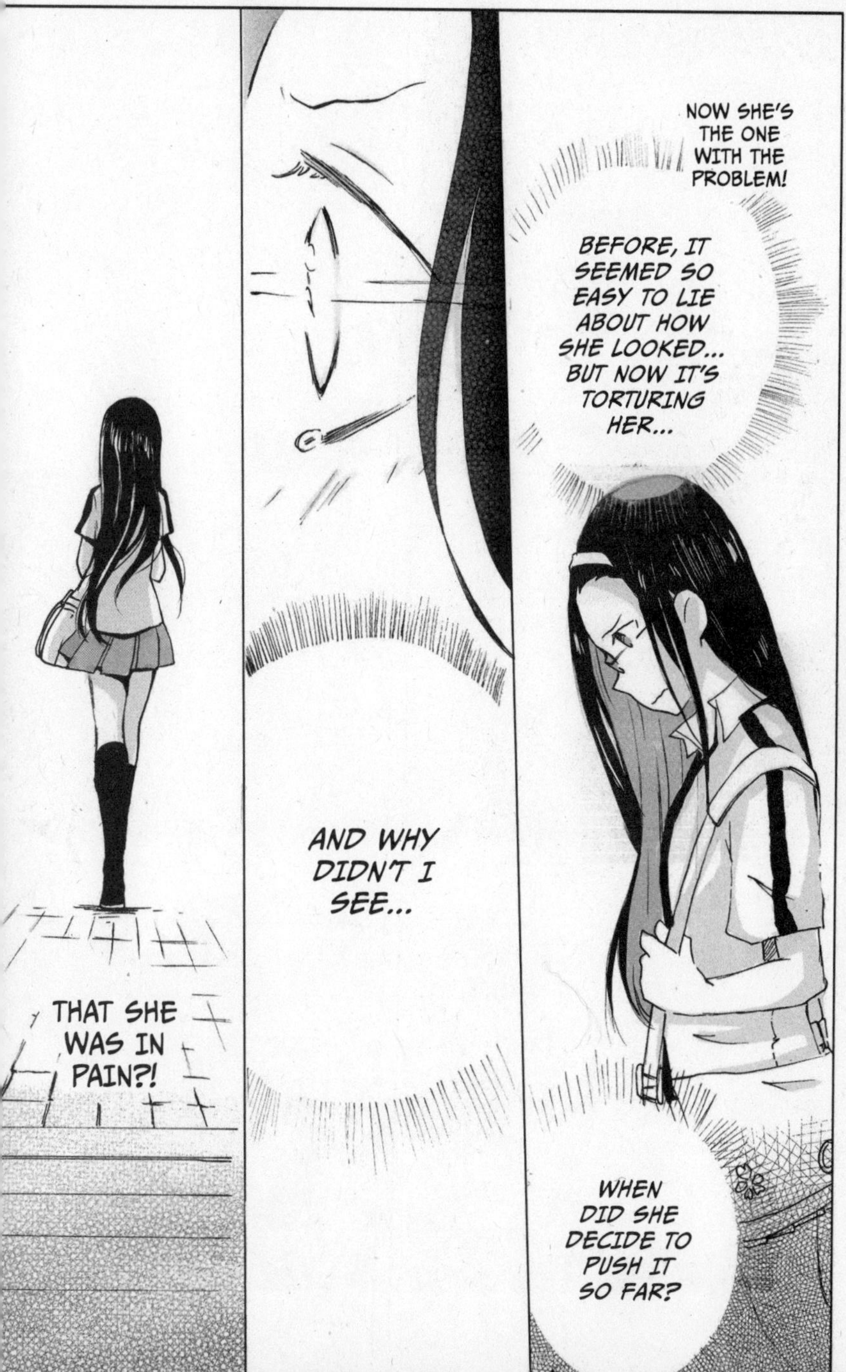
NOW SHE'S THE ONE WITH THE PROBLEM!
BEFORE, IT SEEMED SO EASY TO LIE ABOUT HOW SHE LOOKED... BUT NOW IT'S TORTURING HER...
WHEN DID SHE DECIDE TO PUSH IT SO FAR?
AND WHY DIDN'T I SEE...
THAT SHE WAS IN PAIN?!

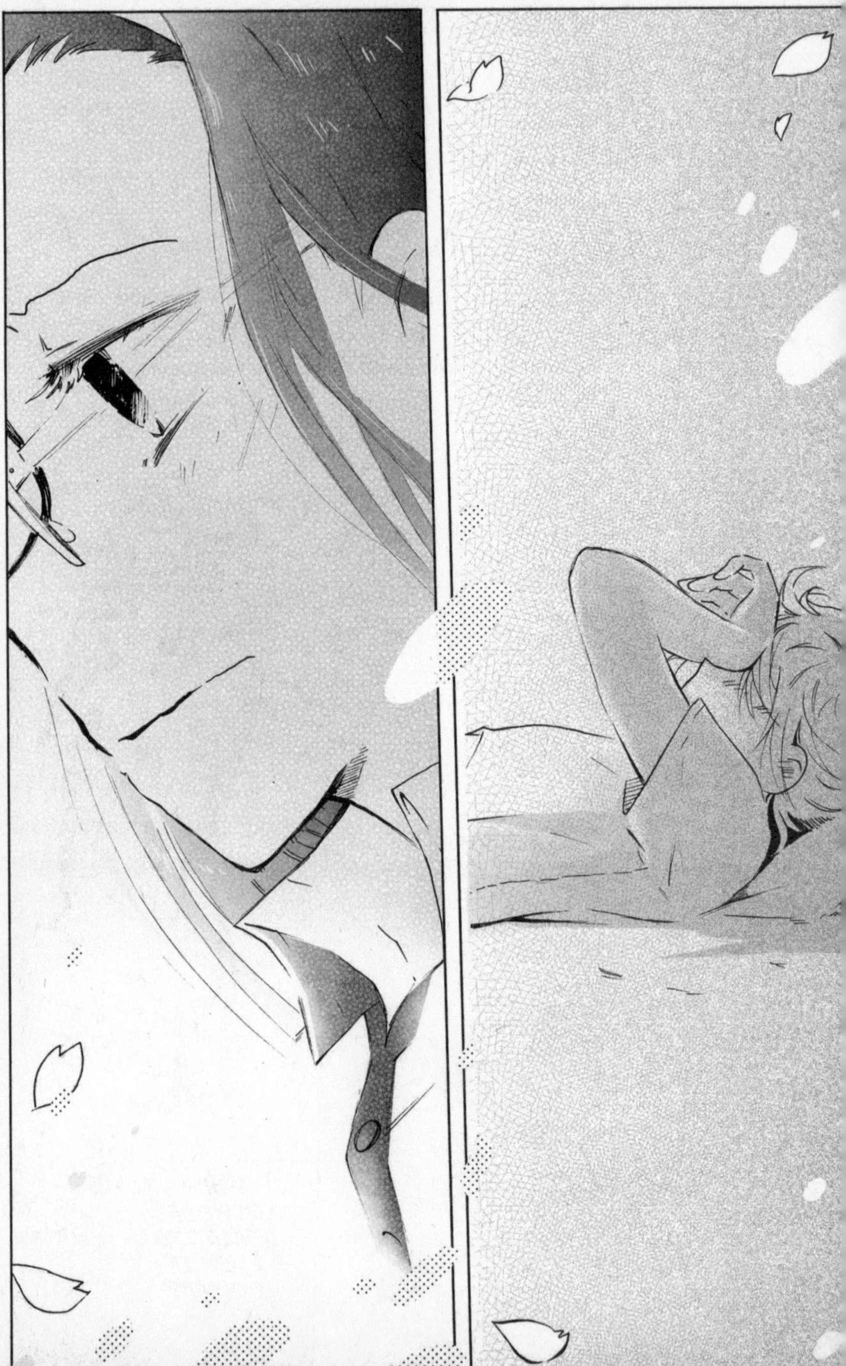

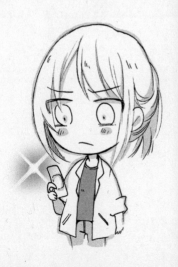

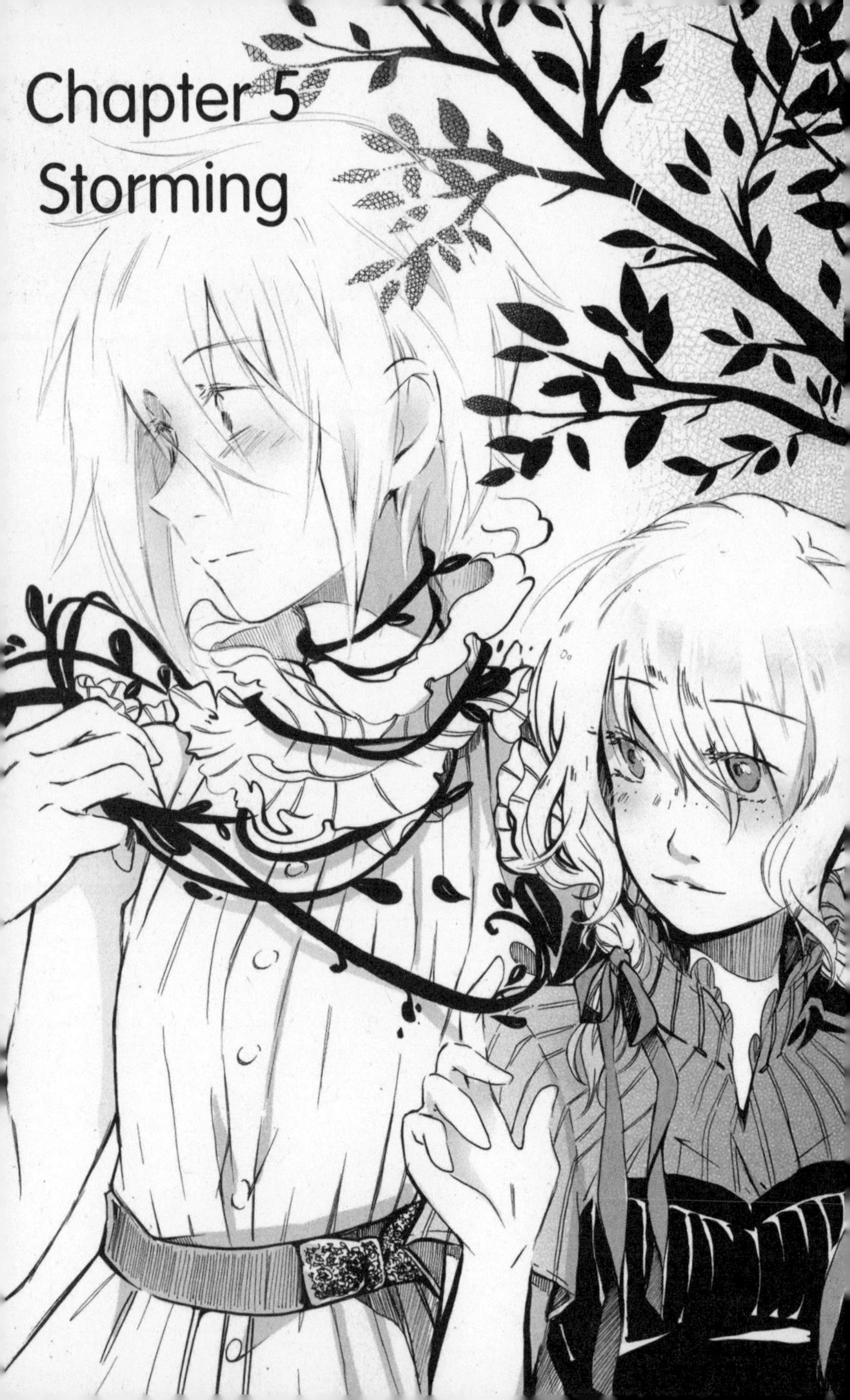
Chapter 5
Storming

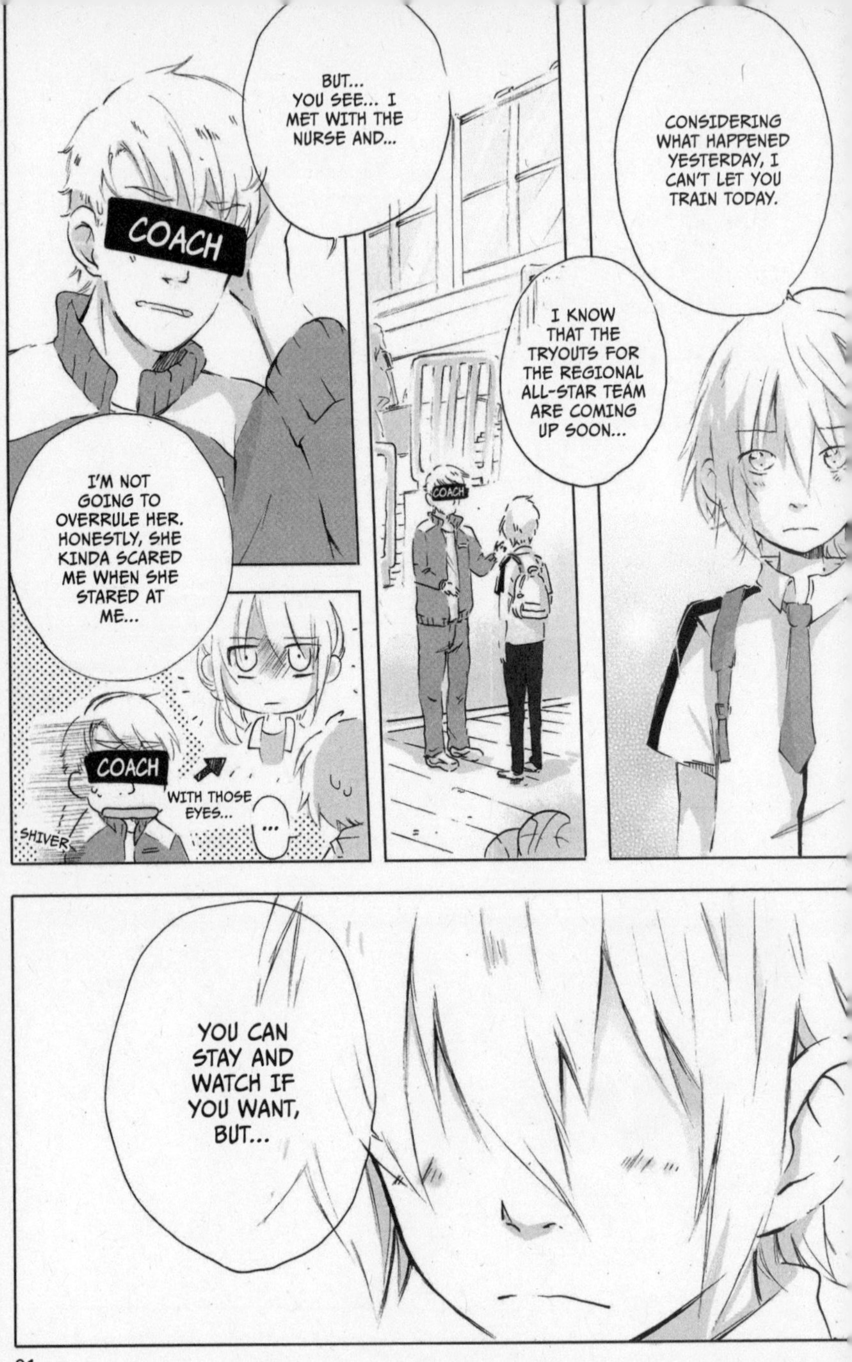
CONSIDERING WHAT HAPPENED YESTERDAY, I CAN'T LET YOU TRAIN TODAY.
I KNOW THAT THE TRYOUTS FOR THE REGIONAL ALL-STAR TEAM ARE COMING UP SOON...
COACH
BUT... YOU SEE... I MET WITH THE NURSE AND...
COACH
I'M NOT GOING TO OVERRULE HER. HONESTLY, SHE KINDA SCARED ME WHEN SHE STARED AT ME...
COACH
WITH THOSE EYES...
...
SHIVER
YOU CAN STAY AND WATCH IF YOU WANT, BUT...

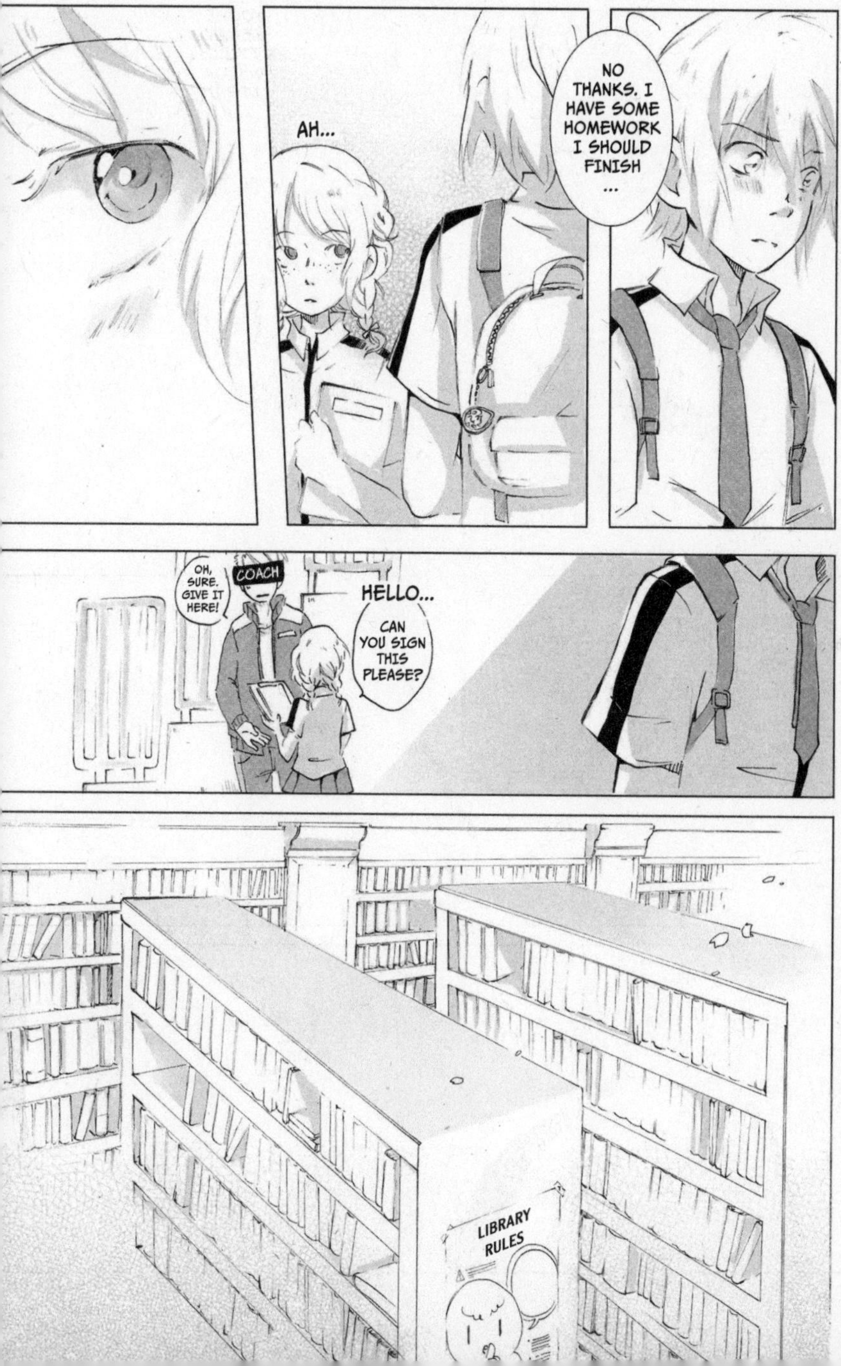
NO THANKS. I HAVE SOME HOMEWORK I SHOULD FINISH ...
AH...
HELLO...
CAN YOU SIGN THIS PLEASE?
COACH
OH, SURE. GIVE IT HERE!
LIBRARY RULES

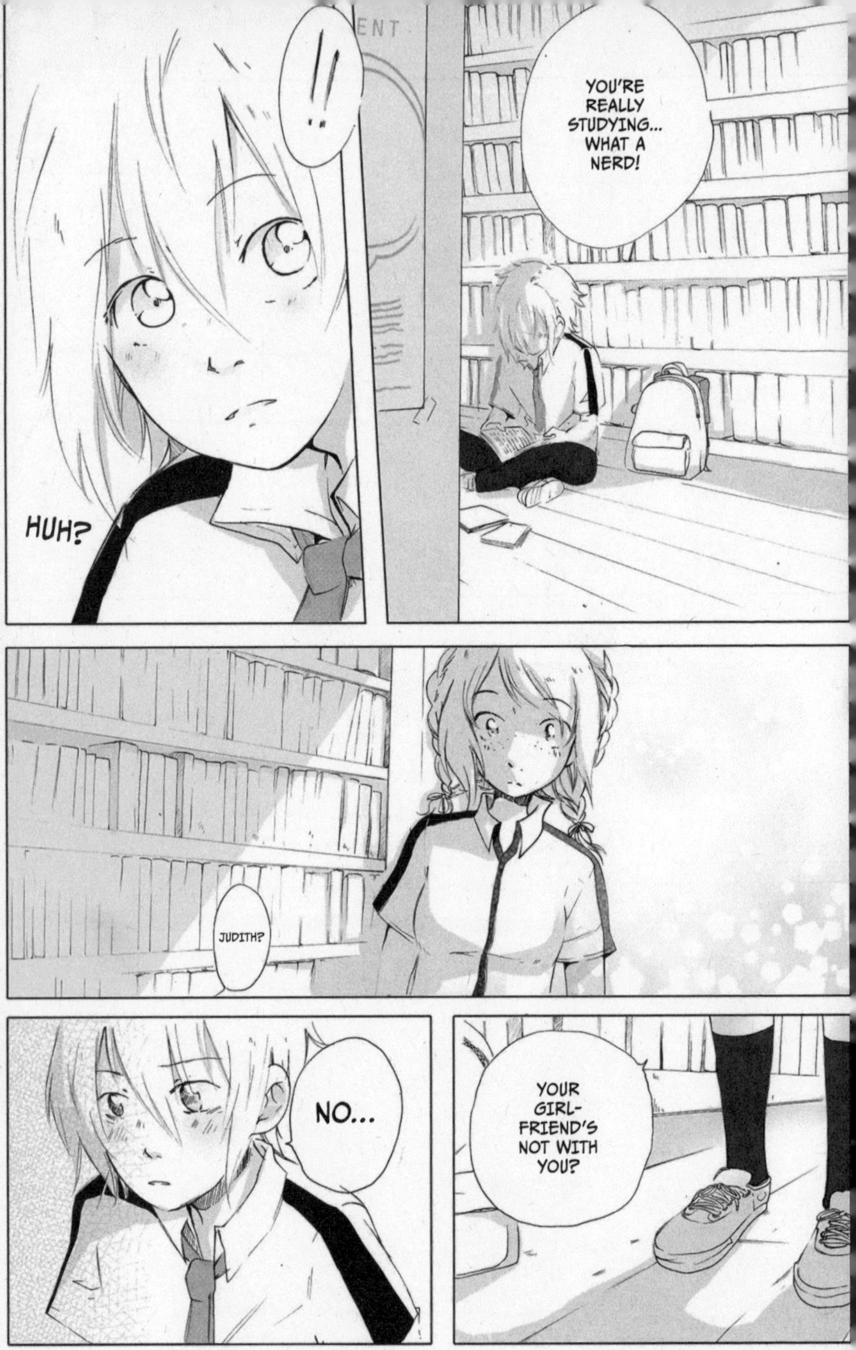
YOU'RE REALLY STUDYING... WHAT A NERD!
!!
HUH?
JUDITH?
YOUR GIRL-FRIEND'S NOT WITH YOU?
NO...

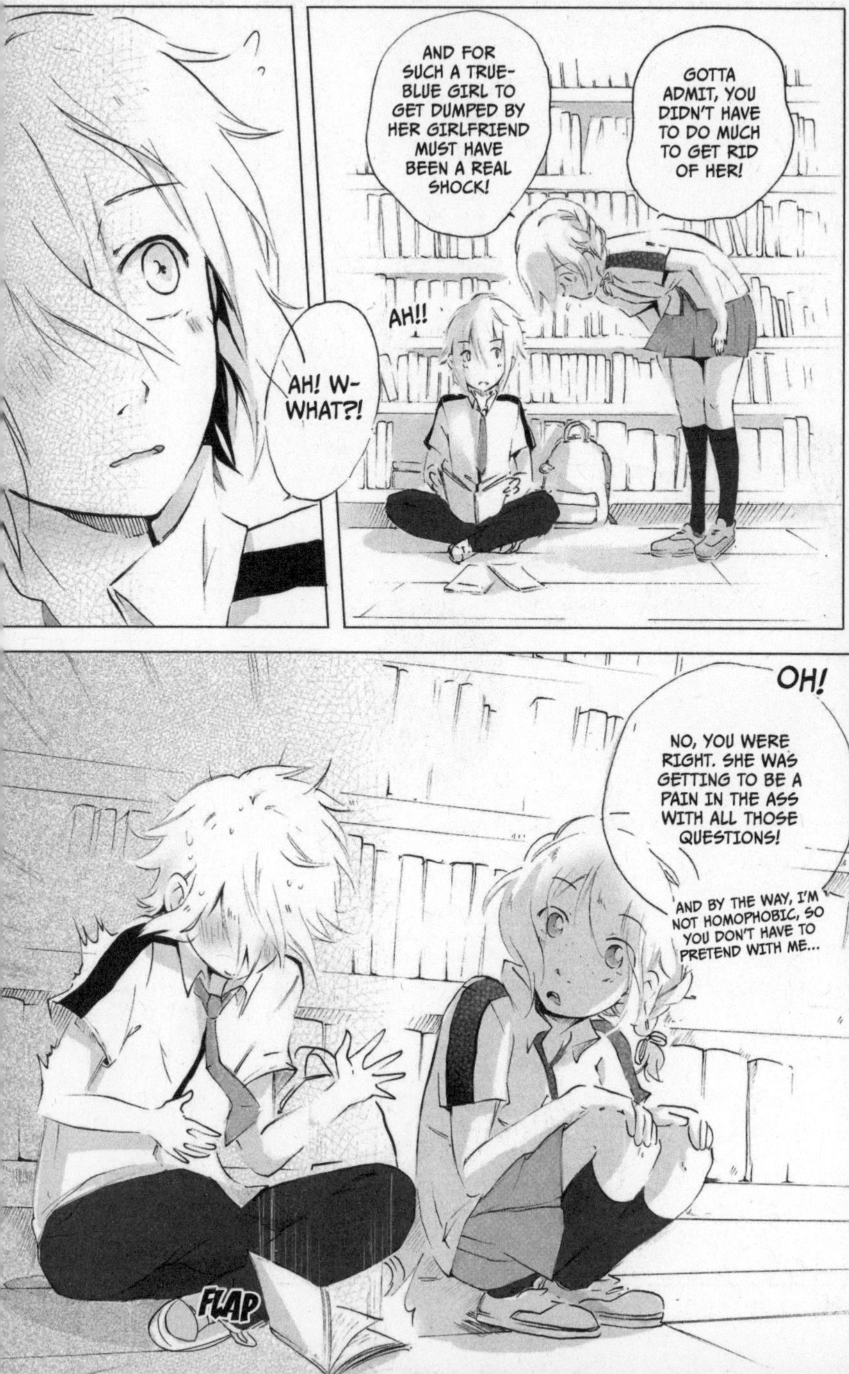
GOTTA ADMIT, YOU DIDN'T HAVE TO DO MUCH TO GET RID OF HER!
AND FOR SUCH A TRUE-BLUE GIRL TO GET DUMPED BY HER GIRLFRIEND MUST HAVE BEEN A REAL SHOCK!
AH!!
AH! W-WHAT?!
OH!
NO, YOU WERE RIGHT. SHE WAS GETTING TO BE A PAIN IN THE ASS WITH ALL THOSE QUESTIONS!
AND BY THE WAY, I'M NOT HOMOPHOBIC, SO YOU DON'T HAVE TO PRETEND WITH ME...
FLAP

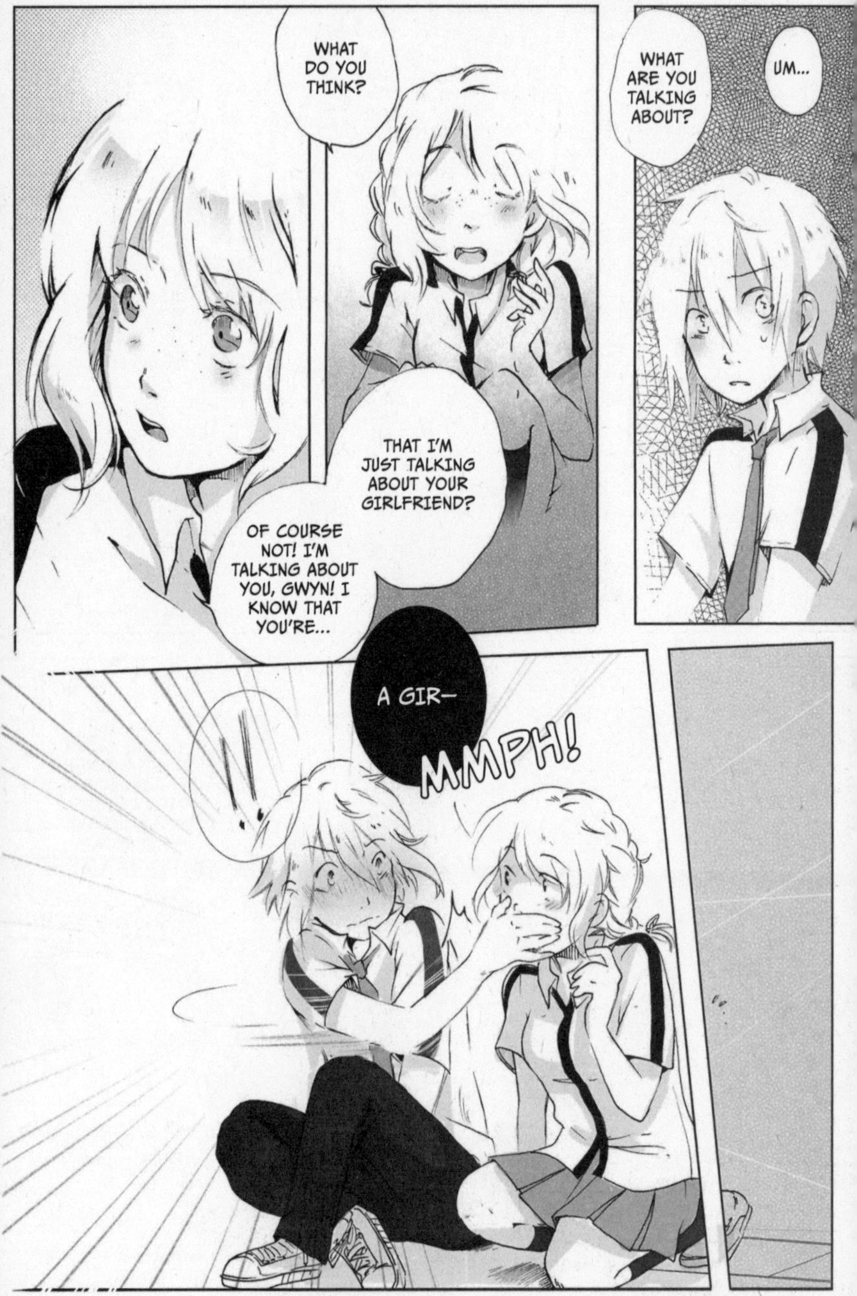
UM...
WHAT ARE YOU TALKING ABOUT?
WHAT DO YOU THINK?
THAT I'M JUST TALKING ABOUT YOUR GIRLFRIEND?
OF COURSE NOT! I'M TALKING ABOUT YOU, GWYN! I KNOW THAT YOU'RE...
A GIR—
MMPH!
!!

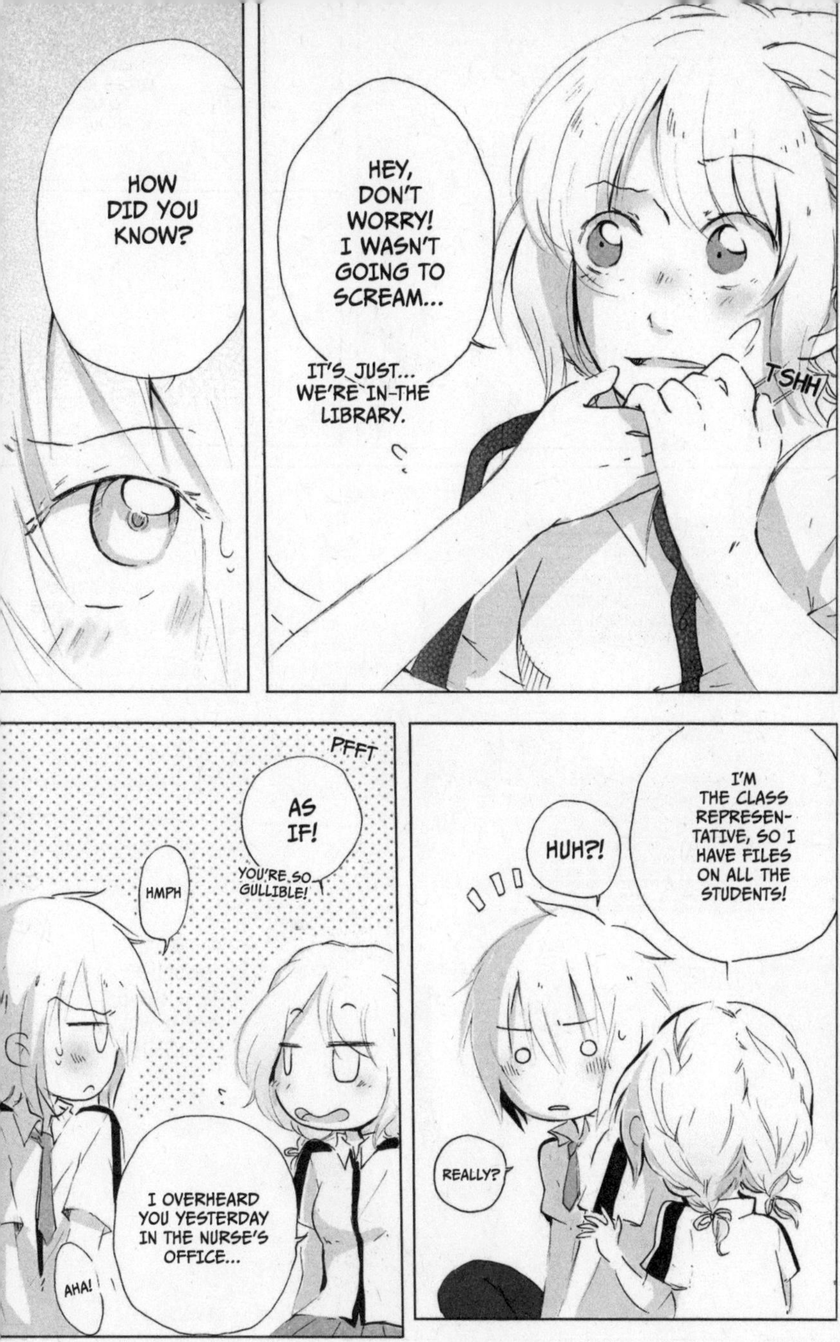
HEY, DON'T WORRY! I WASN'T GOING TO SCREAM...
IT'S JUST... WE'RE IN THE LIBRARY.
TSHH
HOW DID YOU KNOW?
I'M THE CLASS REPRESENTATIVE, SO I HAVE FILES ON ALL THE STUDENTS!
HUH?!
REALLY?
PFFT
AS IF!
YOU'RE SO GULLIBLE!
HMPH
I OVERHEARD YOU YESTERDAY IN THE NURSE'S OFFICE...
AHA!

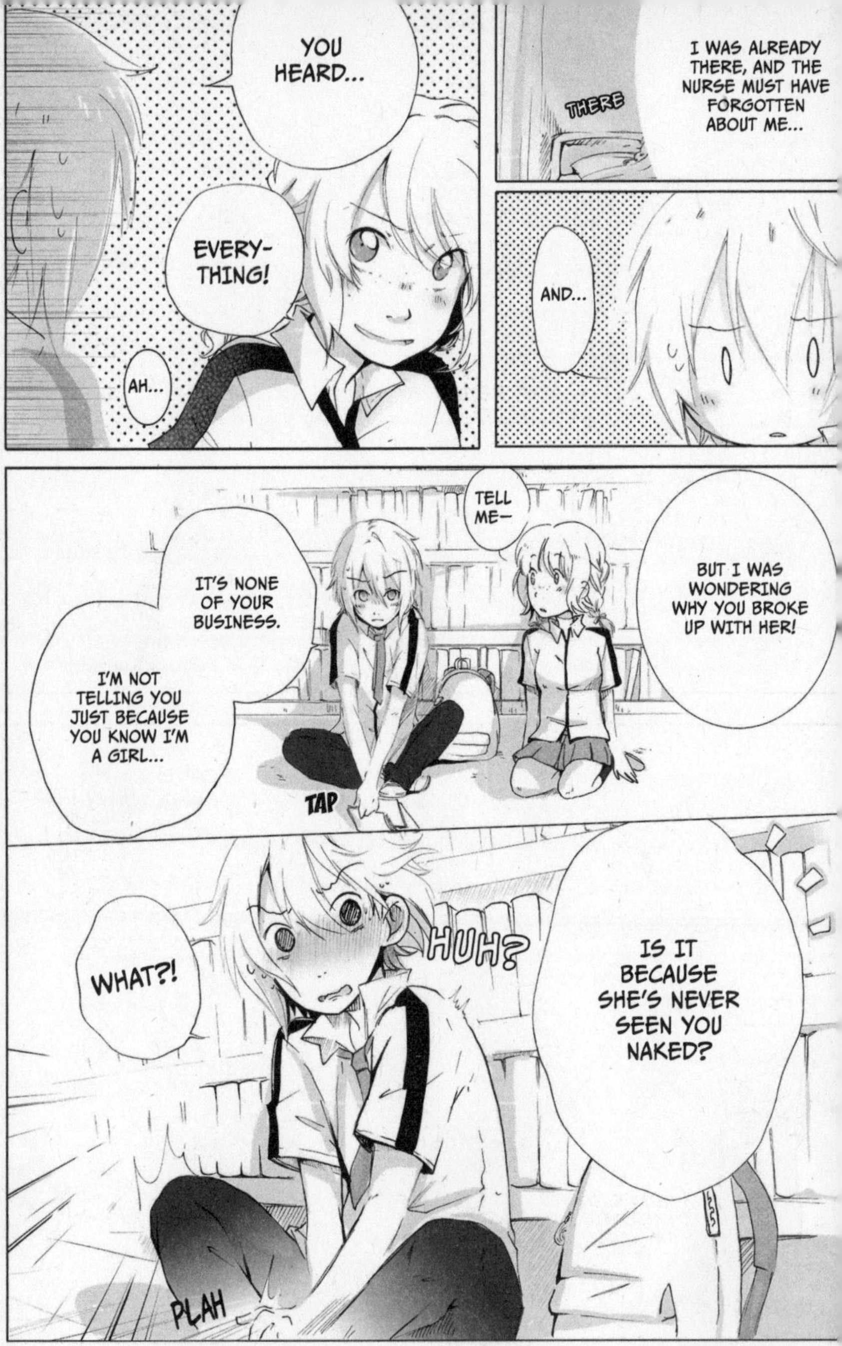
THERE
I WAS ALREADY THERE, AND THE NURSE MUST HAVE FORGOTTEN ABOUT ME...
AND...
YOU HEARD...
EVERY-THING!
AH...
TELL ME—
BUT I WAS WONDERING WHY YOU BROKE UP WITH HER!
IT'S NONE OF YOUR BUSINESS.
I'M NOT TELLING YOU JUST BECAUSE YOU KNOW I'M A GIRL...
TAP
IS IT BECAUSE SHE'S NEVER SEEN YOU NAKED?
HUH?
WHAT?!
PLAH

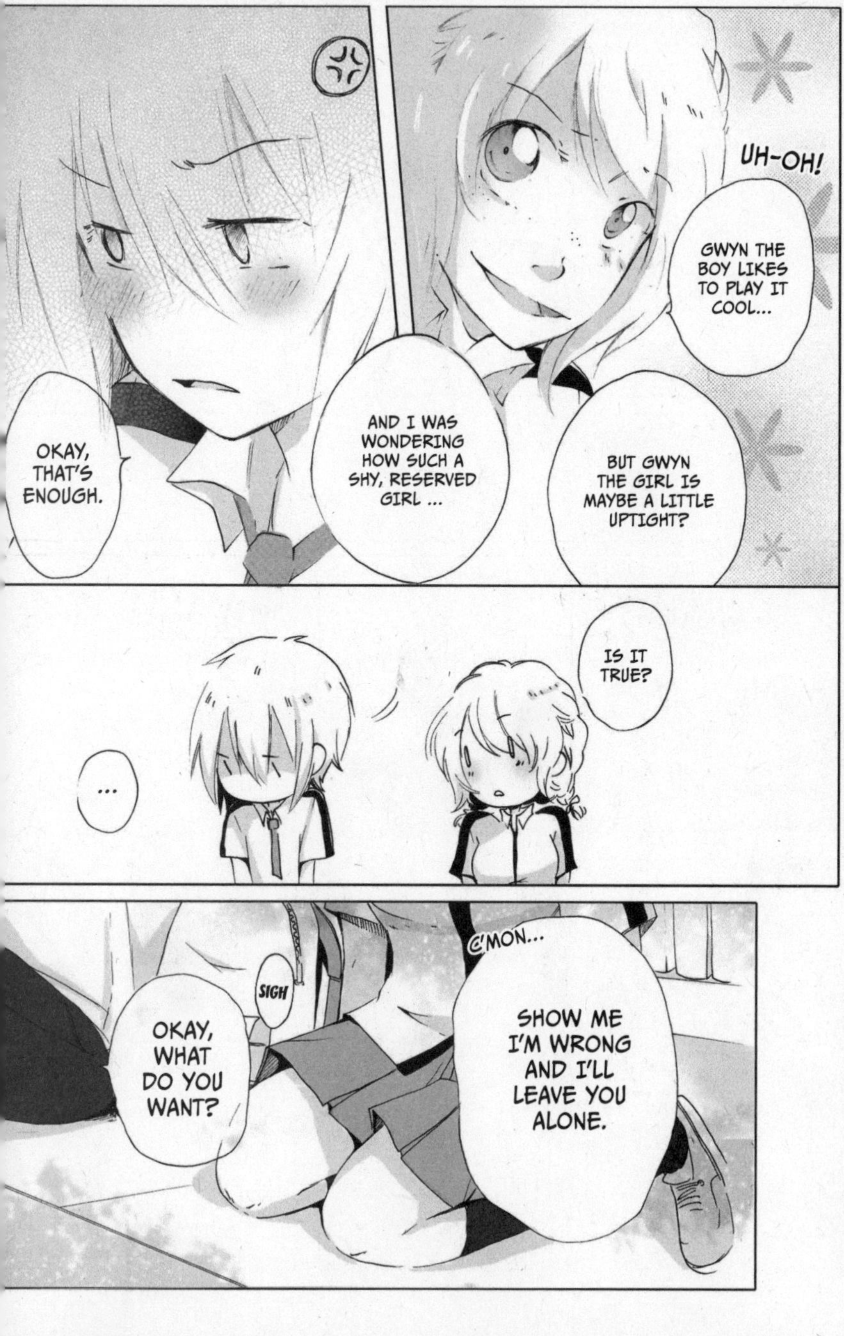
UH-OH!
GWYN THE BOY LIKES TO PLAY IT COOL...
BUT GWYN THE GIRL IS MAYBE A LITTLE UPTIGHT?
AND I WAS WONDERING HOW SUCH A SHY, RESERVED GIRL ...
OKAY, THAT'S ENOUGH.
IS IT TRUE?
...
C'MON...
SHOW ME I'M WRONG AND I'LL LEAVE YOU ALONE.
SIGH
OKAY, WHAT DO YOU WANT?

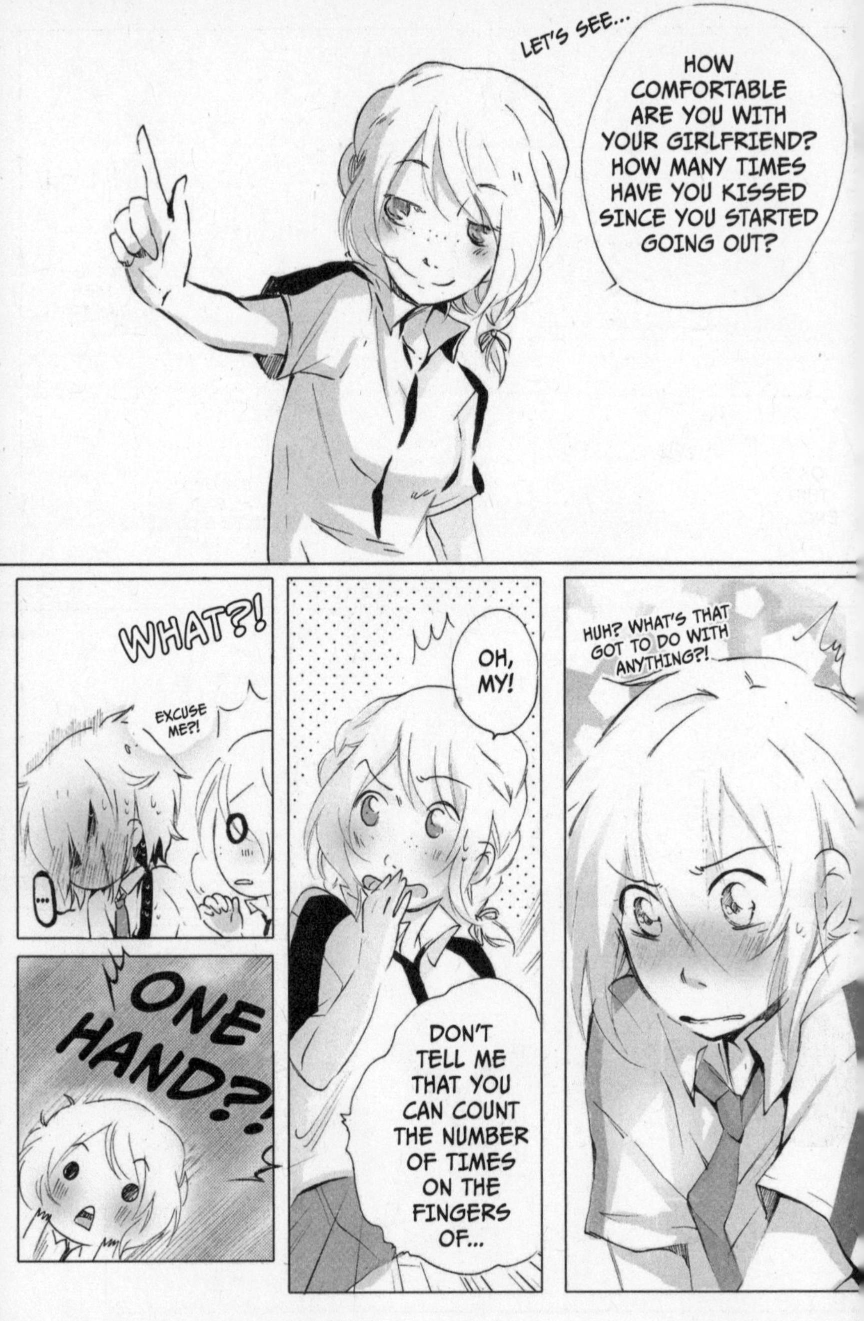
LET'S SEE...
HOW COMFORTABLE ARE YOU WITH YOUR GIRLFRIEND? HOW MANY TIMES HAVE YOU KISSED SINCE YOU STARTED GOING OUT?
HUH? WHAT'S THAT GOT TO DO WITH ANYTHING?!
OH, MY!
DON'T TELL ME THAT YOU CAN COUNT THE NUMBER OF TIMES ON THE FINGERS OF...
WHAT?!
EXCUSE ME?!
...
ONE HAND?!

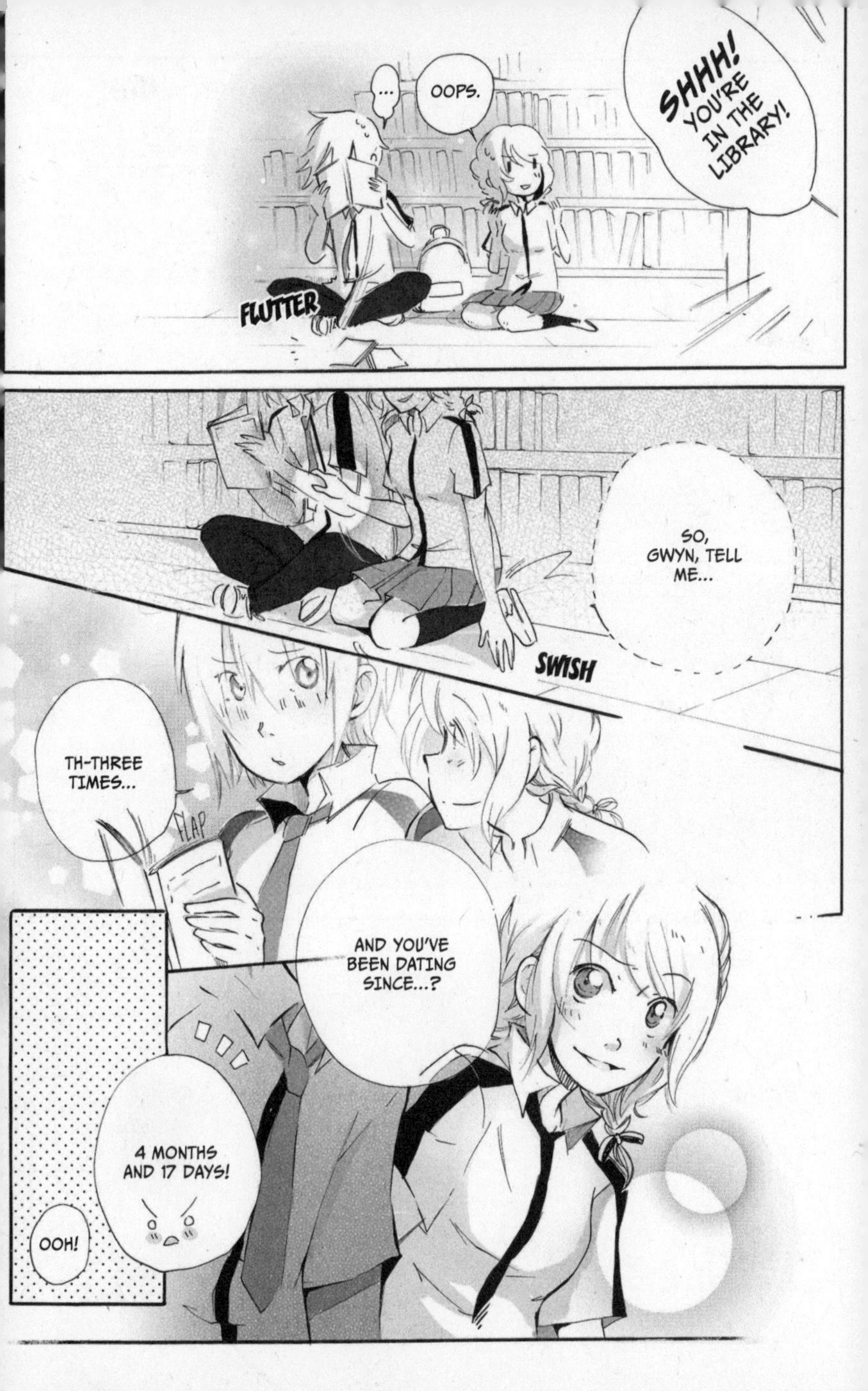
SHHH! YOU'RE IN THE LIBRARY!
OOPS.
...
FLUTTER
SO, GWYN, TELL ME...
SWISH
TH-THREE TIMES...
FLAP
AND YOU'VE BEEN DATING SINCE...?
4 MONTHS AND 17 DAYS!
OOH!

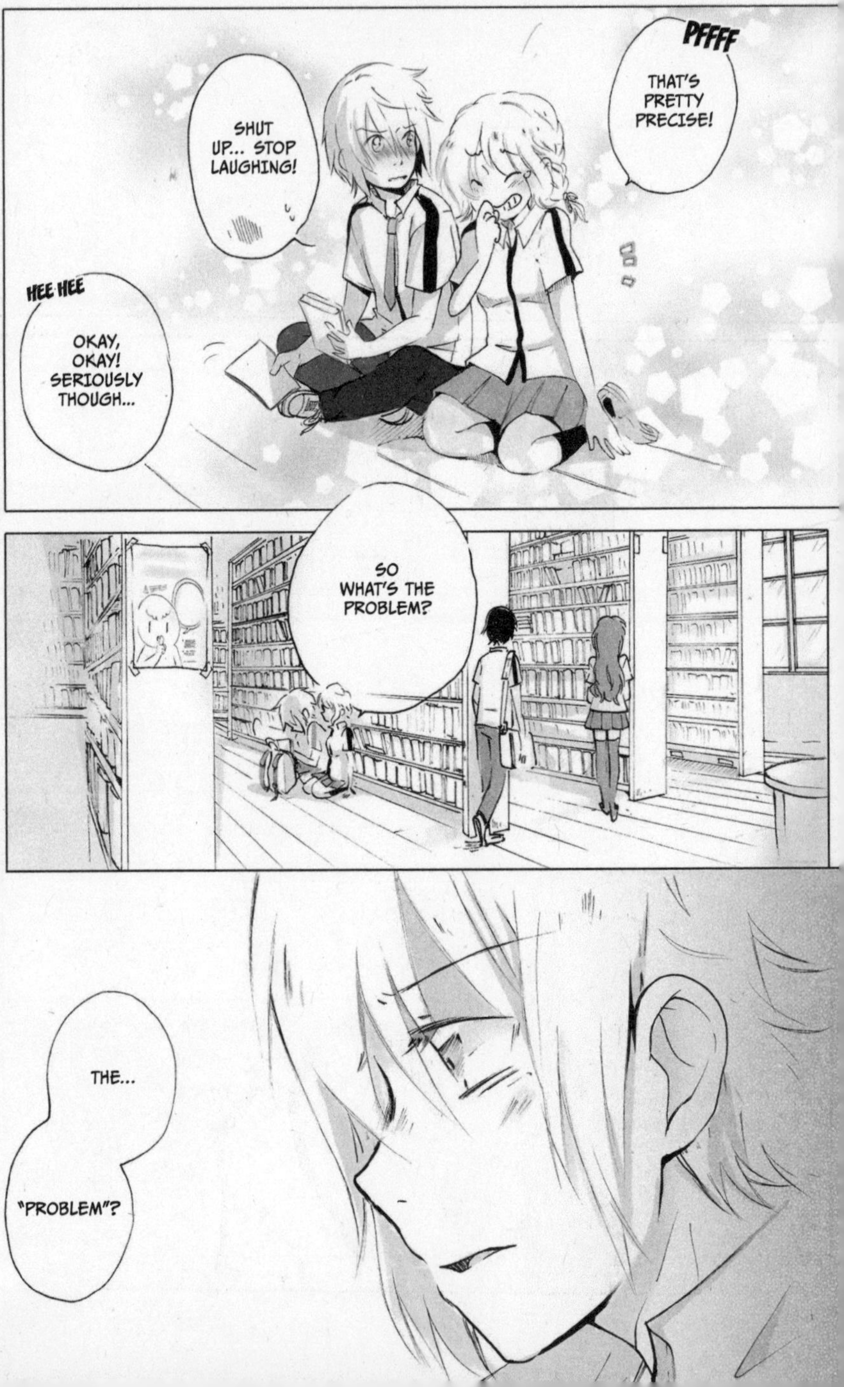
PFFFF
THAT'S PRETTY PRECISE!
SHUT UP... STOP LAUGHING!
HEE HEE
OKAY, OKAY! SERIOUSLY THOUGH...
SO WHAT'S THE PROBLEM?
THE... "PROBLEM"?

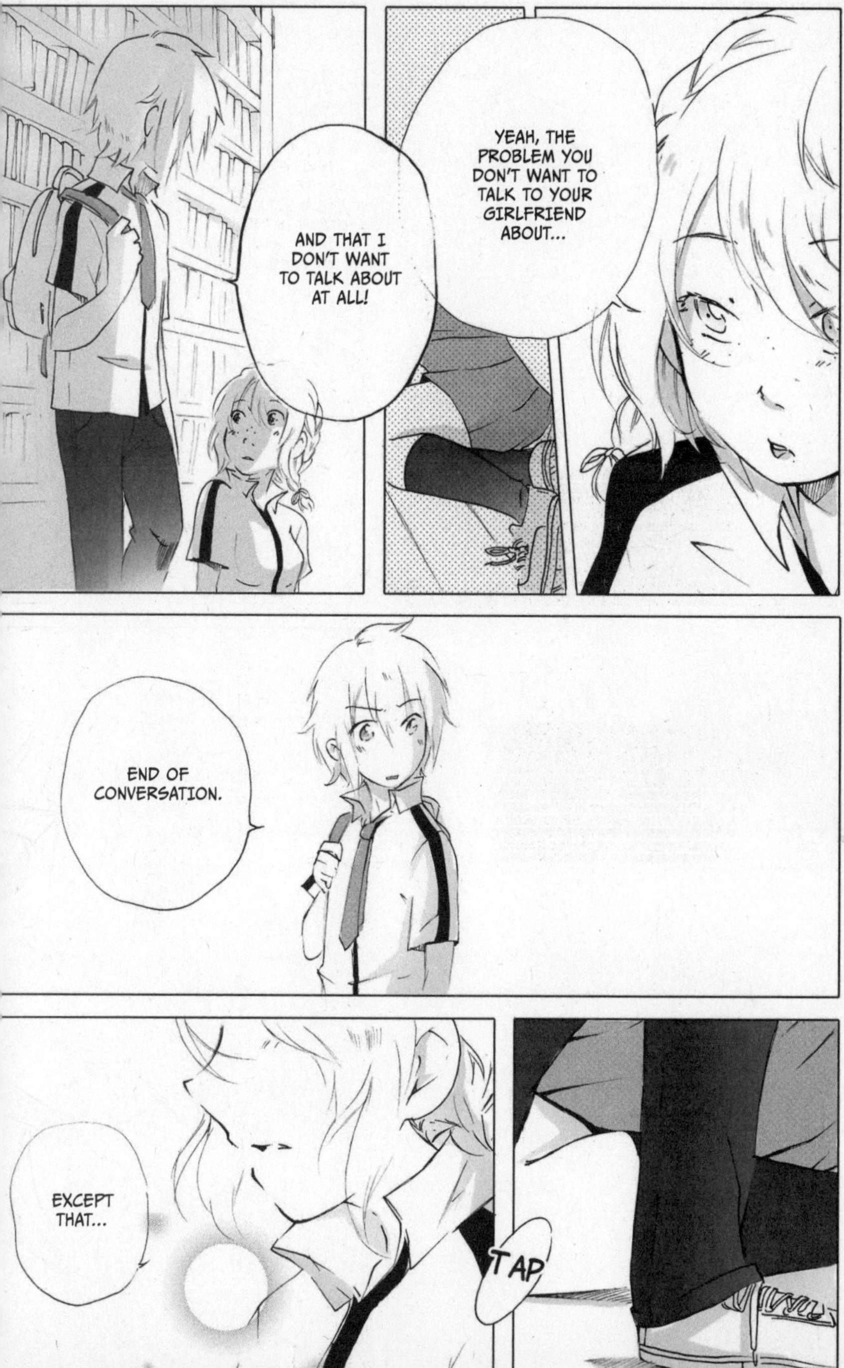
YEAH, THE PROBLEM YOU DON'T WANT TO TALK TO YOUR GIRLFRIEND ABOUT...
AND THAT I DON'T WANT TO TALK ABOUT AT ALL!
END OF CONVERSATION.
TAP
EXCEPT THAT...

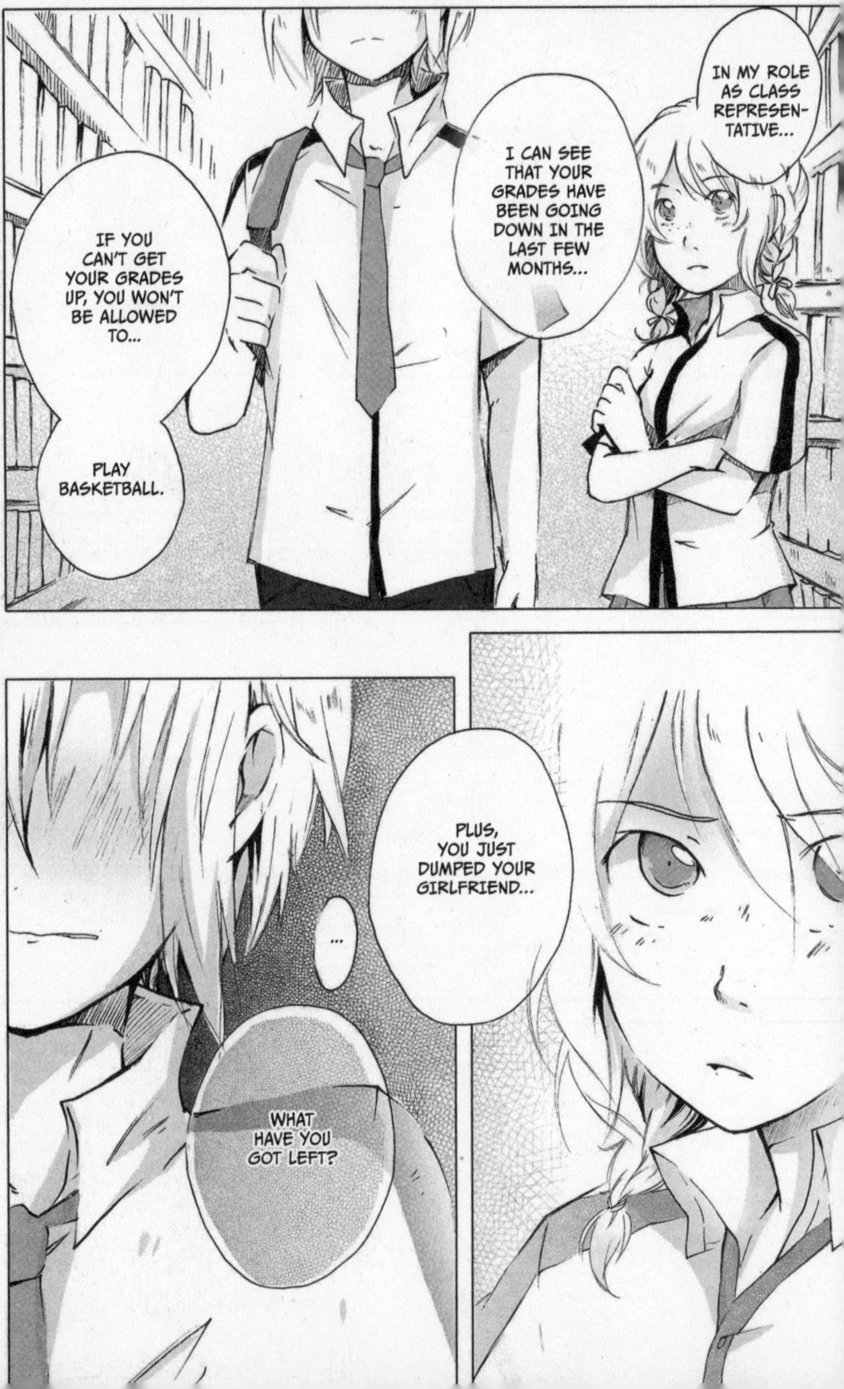
IN MY ROLE AS CLASS REPRESENTATIVE...
I CAN SEE THAT YOUR GRADES HAVE BEEN GOING DOWN IN THE LAST FEW MONTHS...
IF YOU CAN'T GET YOUR GRADES UP, YOU WON'T BE ALLOWED TO...
PLAY BASKETBALL.
PLUS, YOU JUST DUMPED YOUR GIRLFRIEND...
...
WHAT HAVE YOU GOT LEFT?

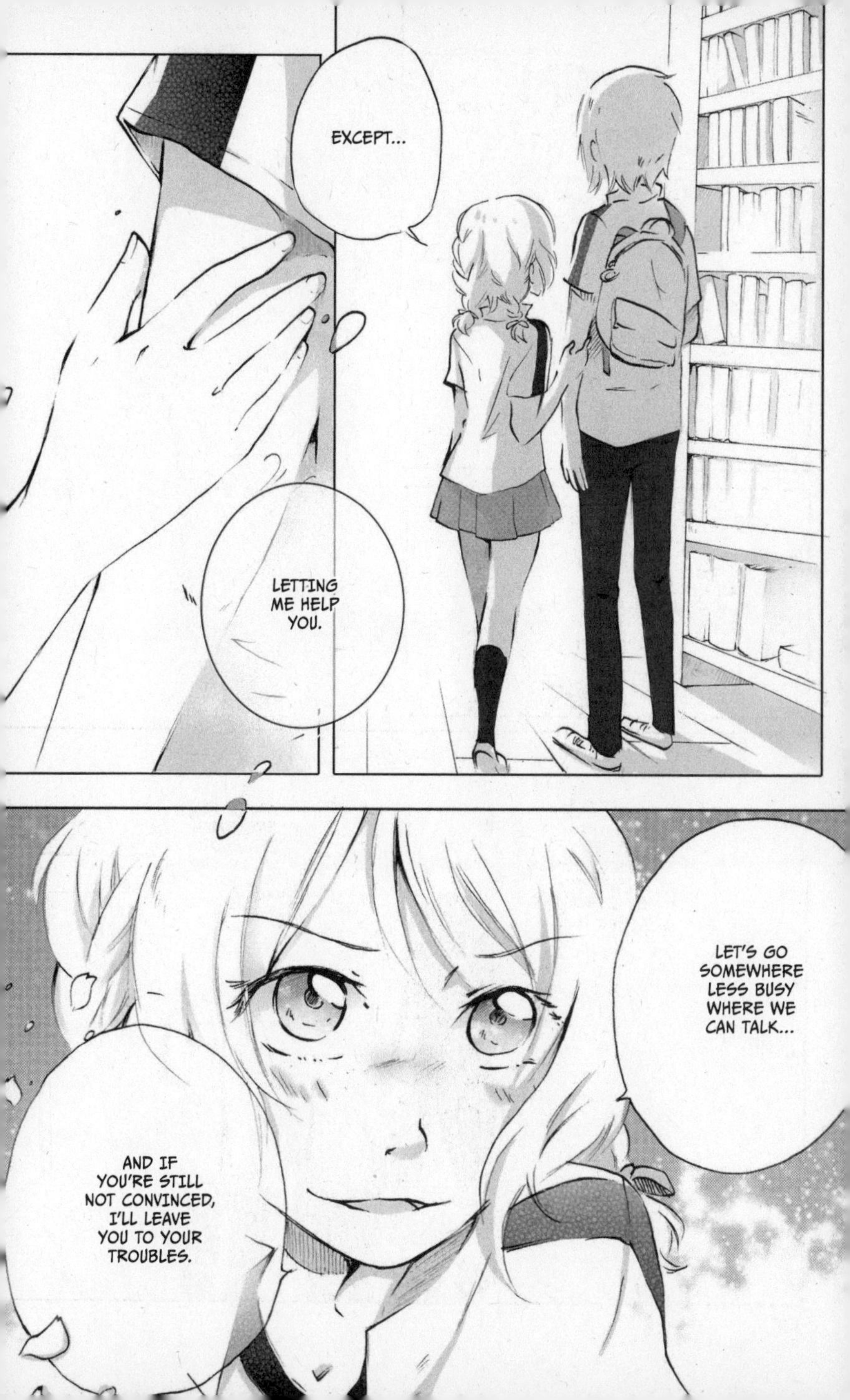
EXCEPT...
LETTING ME HELP YOU.
LET'S GO SOMEWHERE LESS BUSY WHERE WE CAN TALK...
AND IF YOU'RE STILL NOT CONVINCED, I'LL LEAVE YOU TO YOUR TROUBLES.

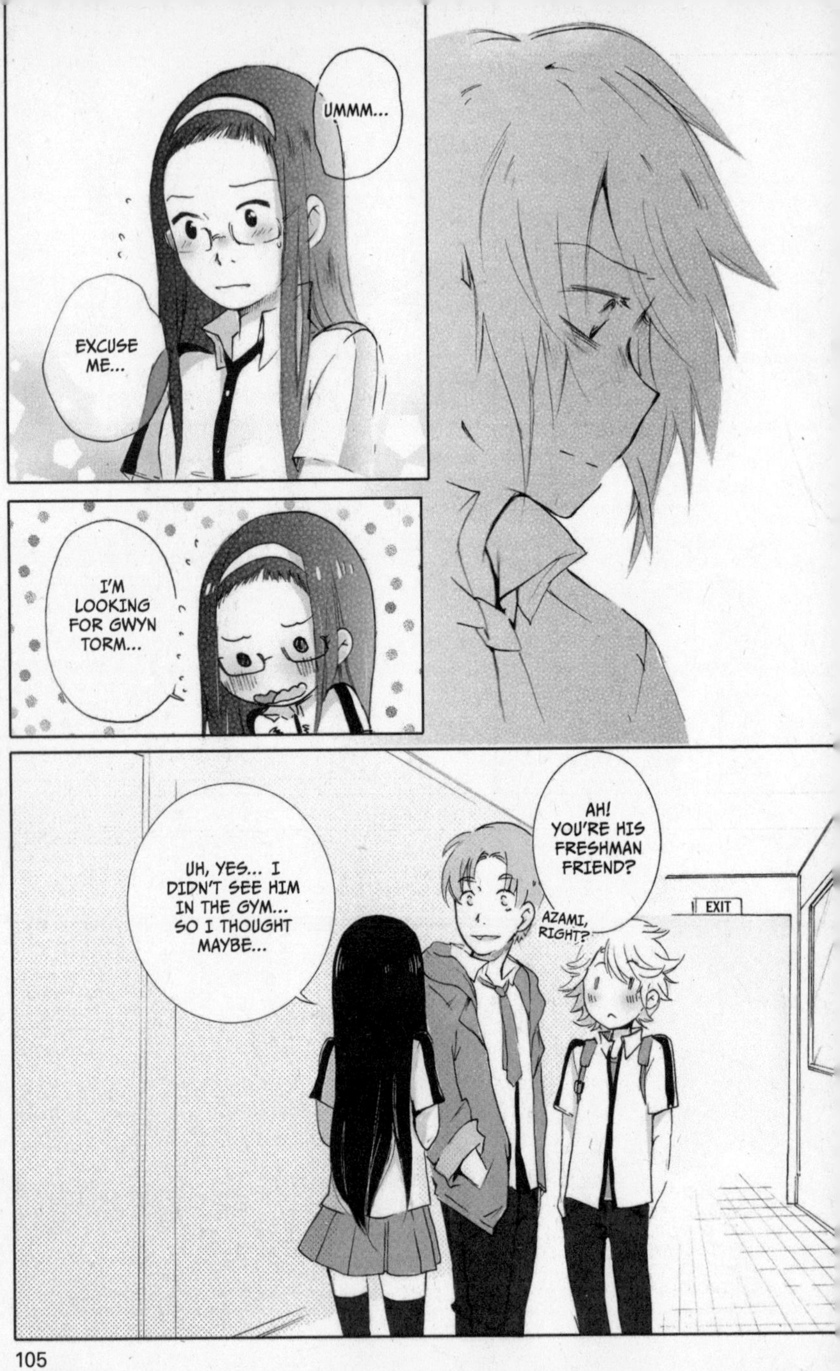
UMMM...
EXCUSE ME...
I'M LOOKING FOR GWYN TORM...
AH! YOU'RE HIS FRESHMAN FRIEND?
AZAMI, RIGHT?
UH, YES... I DIDN'T SEE HIM IN THE GYM... SO I THOUGHT MAYBE...
EXIT

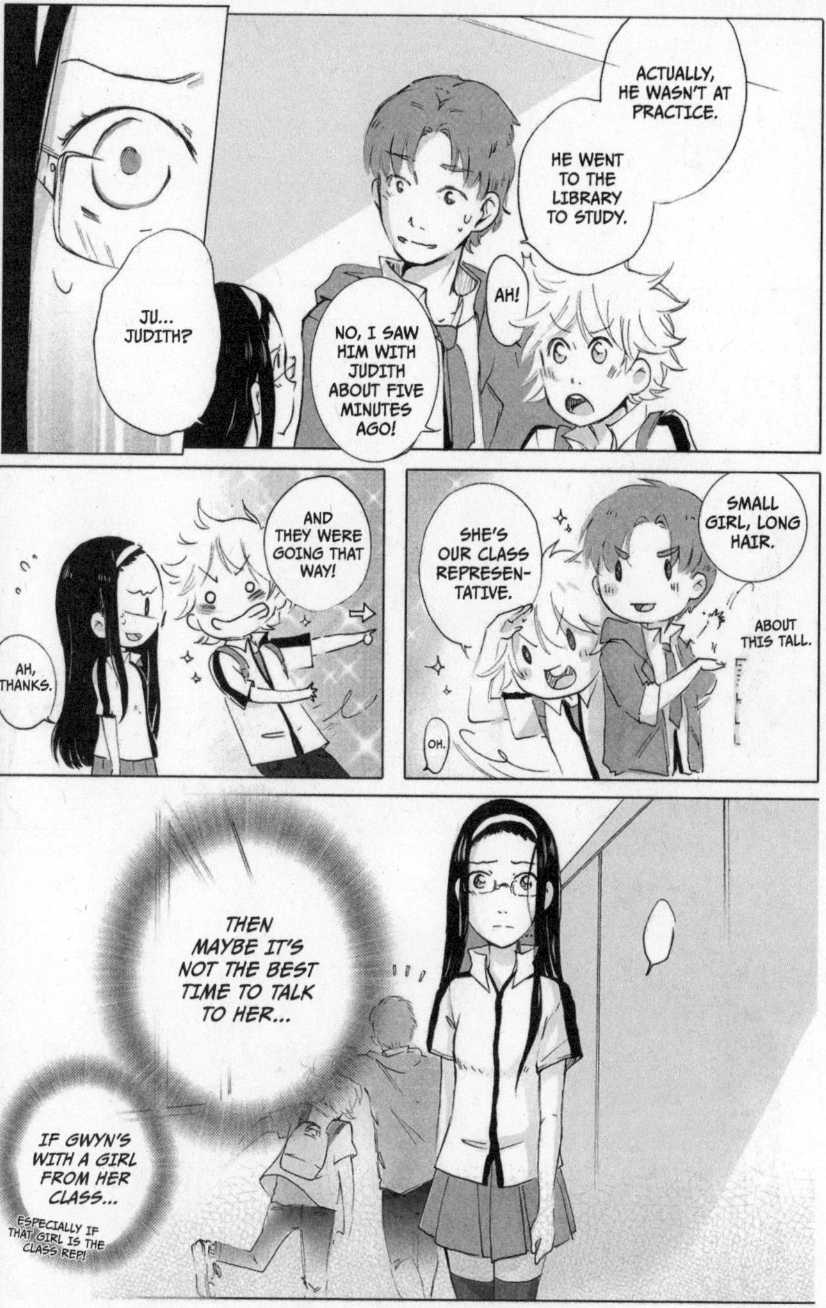
ACTUALLY, HE WASN'T AT PRACTICE.
HE WENT TO THE LIBRARY TO STUDY.
AH!
NO, I SAW HIM WITH JUDITH ABOUT FIVE MINUTES AGO!
JU... JUDITH?
SMALL GIRL, LONG HAIR.
SHE'S OUR CLASS REPRESEN-TATIVE.
ABOUT THIS TALL.
OH.
AND THEY WERE GOING THAT WAY!
AH, THANKS.
THEN MAYBE IT'S NOT THE BEST TIME TO TALK TO HER...
IF GWYN'S WITH A GIRL FROM HER CLASS...
ESPECIALLY IF THAT GIRL IS THE CLASS REP!

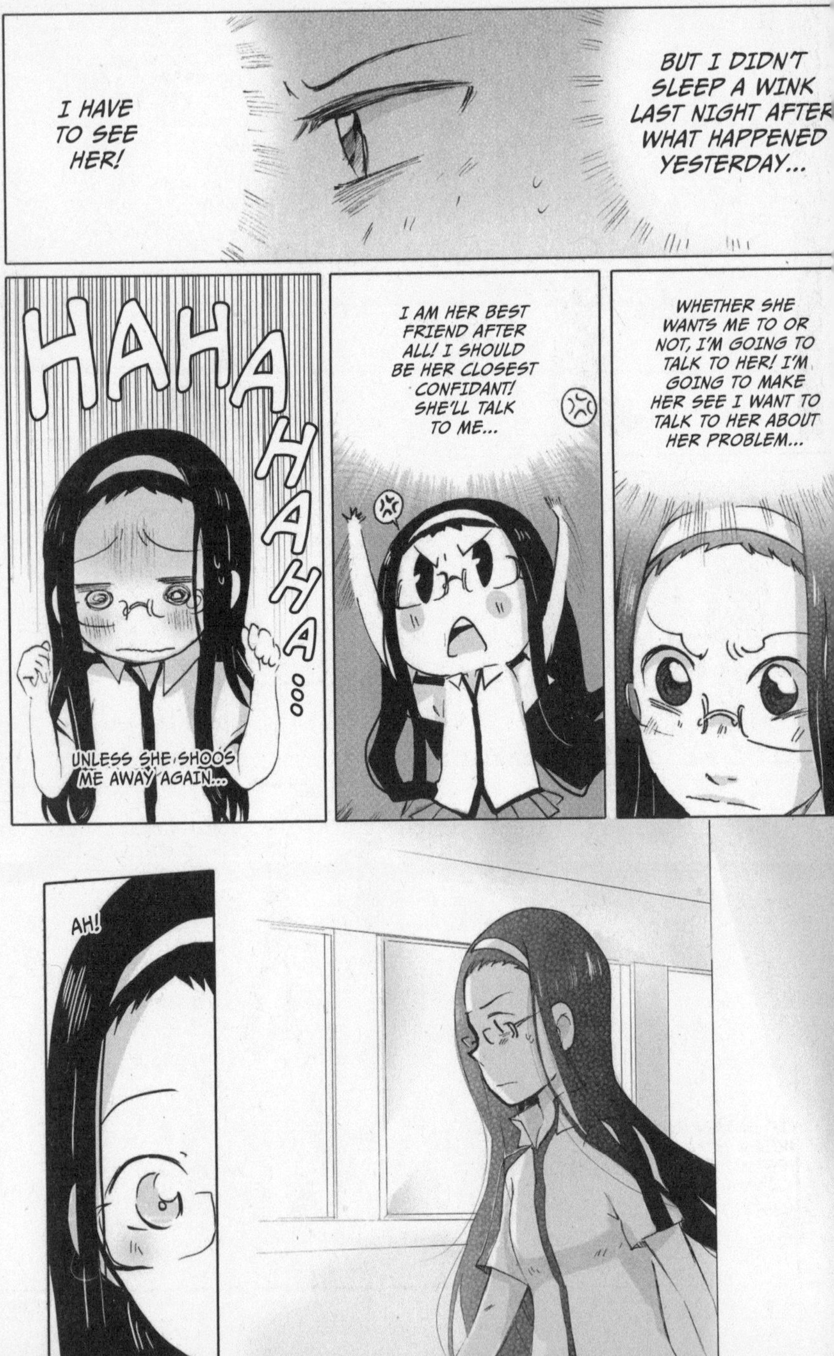
BUT I DIDN'T SLEEP A WINK LAST NIGHT AFTER WHAT HAPPENED YESTERDAY...
I HAVE TO SEE HER!
WHETHER SHE WANTS ME TO OR NOT, I'M GOING TO TALK TO HER! I'M GOING TO MAKE HER SEE I WANT TO TALK TO HER ABOUT HER PROBLEM...
I AM HER BEST FRIEND AFTER ALL! I SHOULD BE HER CLOSEST CONFIDANT! SHE'LL TALK TO ME...
HAHAHAHAHA...
UNLESS SHE SHOOS ME AWAY AGAIN...
AH!

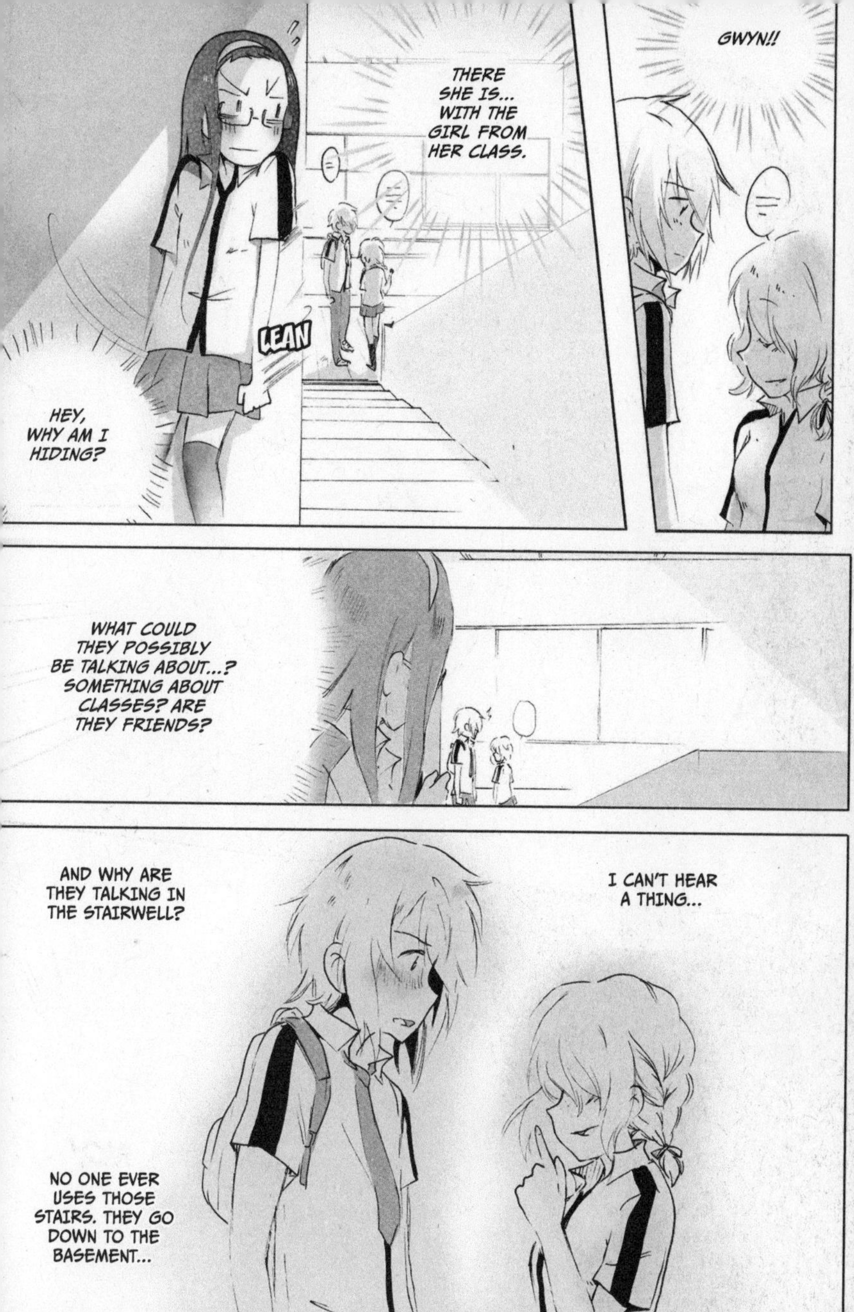
GWYN!!
THERE SHE IS... WITH THE GIRL FROM HER CLASS.
LEAN
HEY, WHY AM I HIDING?
WHAT COULD THEY POSSIBLY BE TALKING ABOUT...? SOMETHING ABOUT CLASSES? ARE THEY FRIENDS?
I CAN'T HEAR A THING...
AND WHY ARE THEY TALKING IN THE STAIRWELL?
NO ONE EVER USES THOSE STAIRS. THEY GO DOWN TO THE BASEMENT...

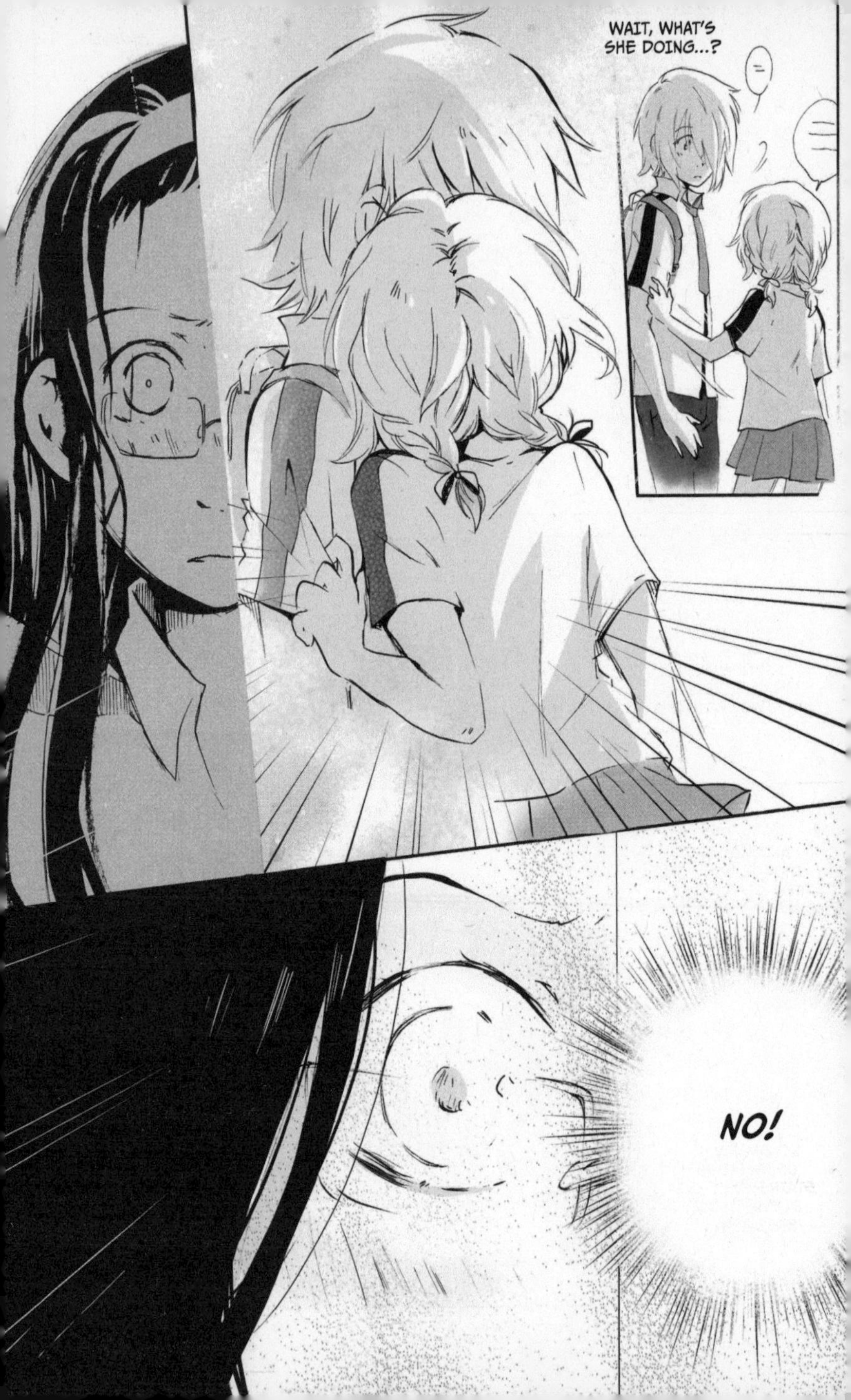
WAIT, WHAT'S SHE DOING...?
NO!

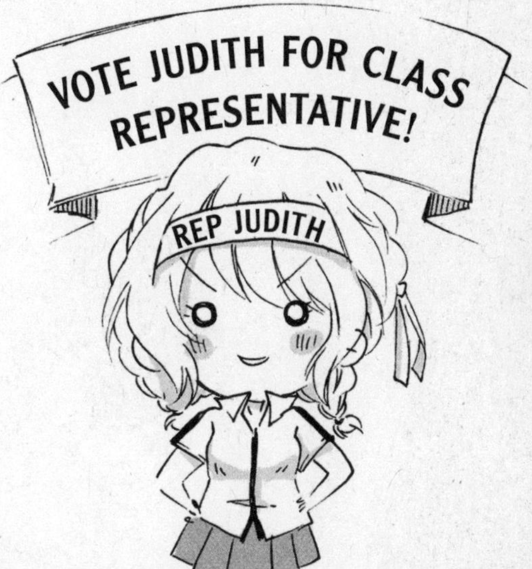
VOTE JUDITH FOR CLASS REPRESENTATIVE!
REP JUDITH

Chapter 6
Distrust

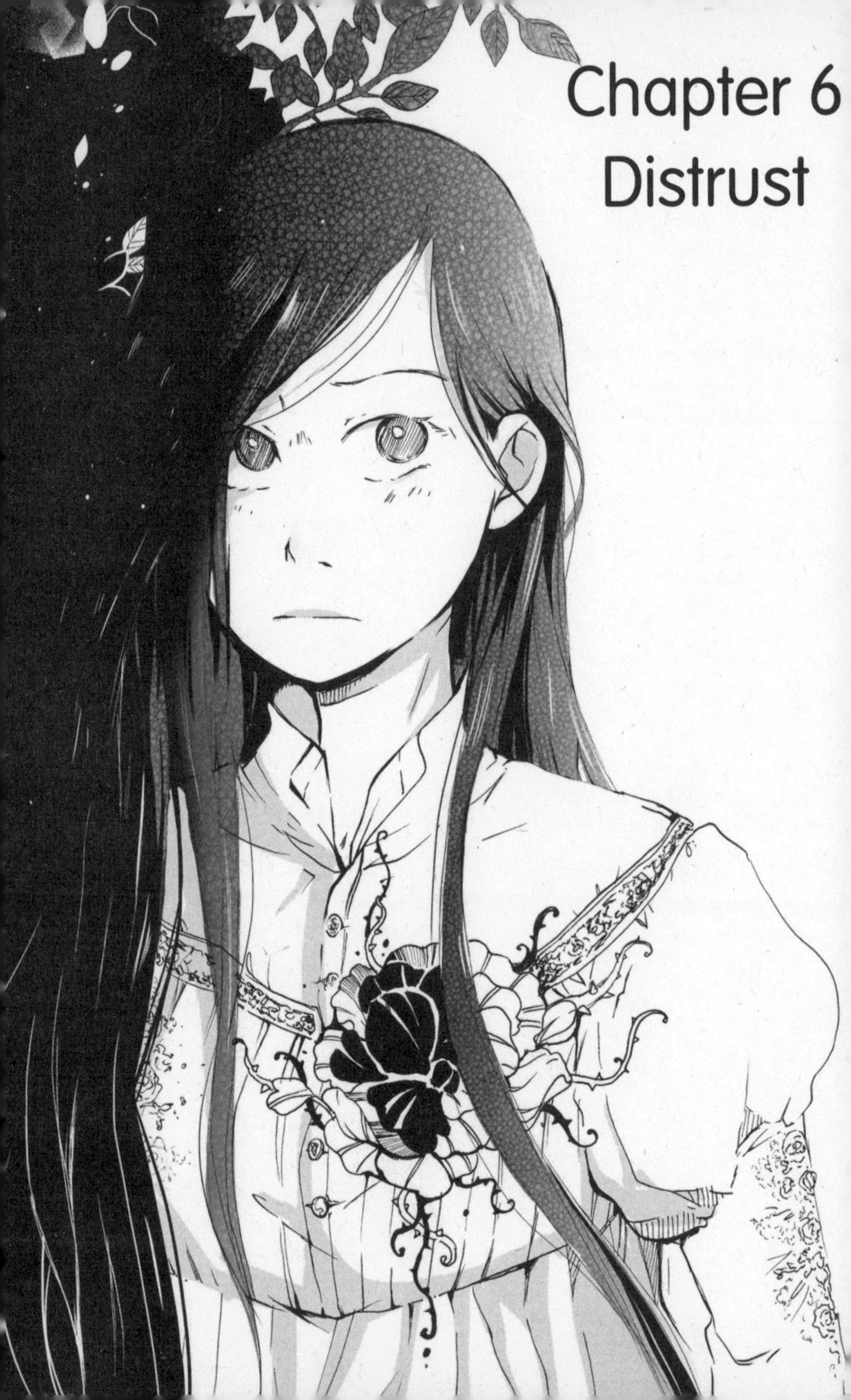

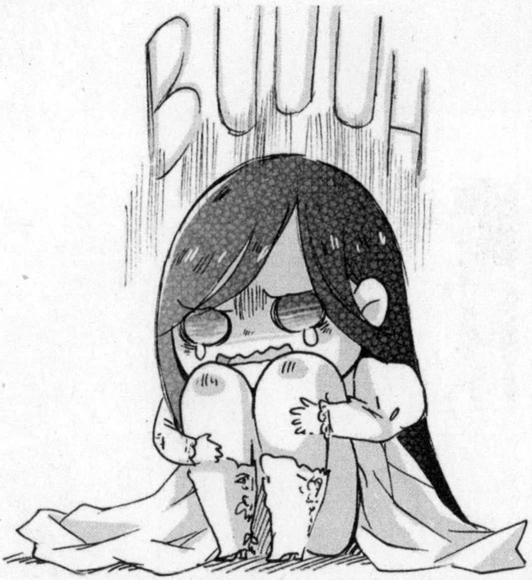
BUUUH

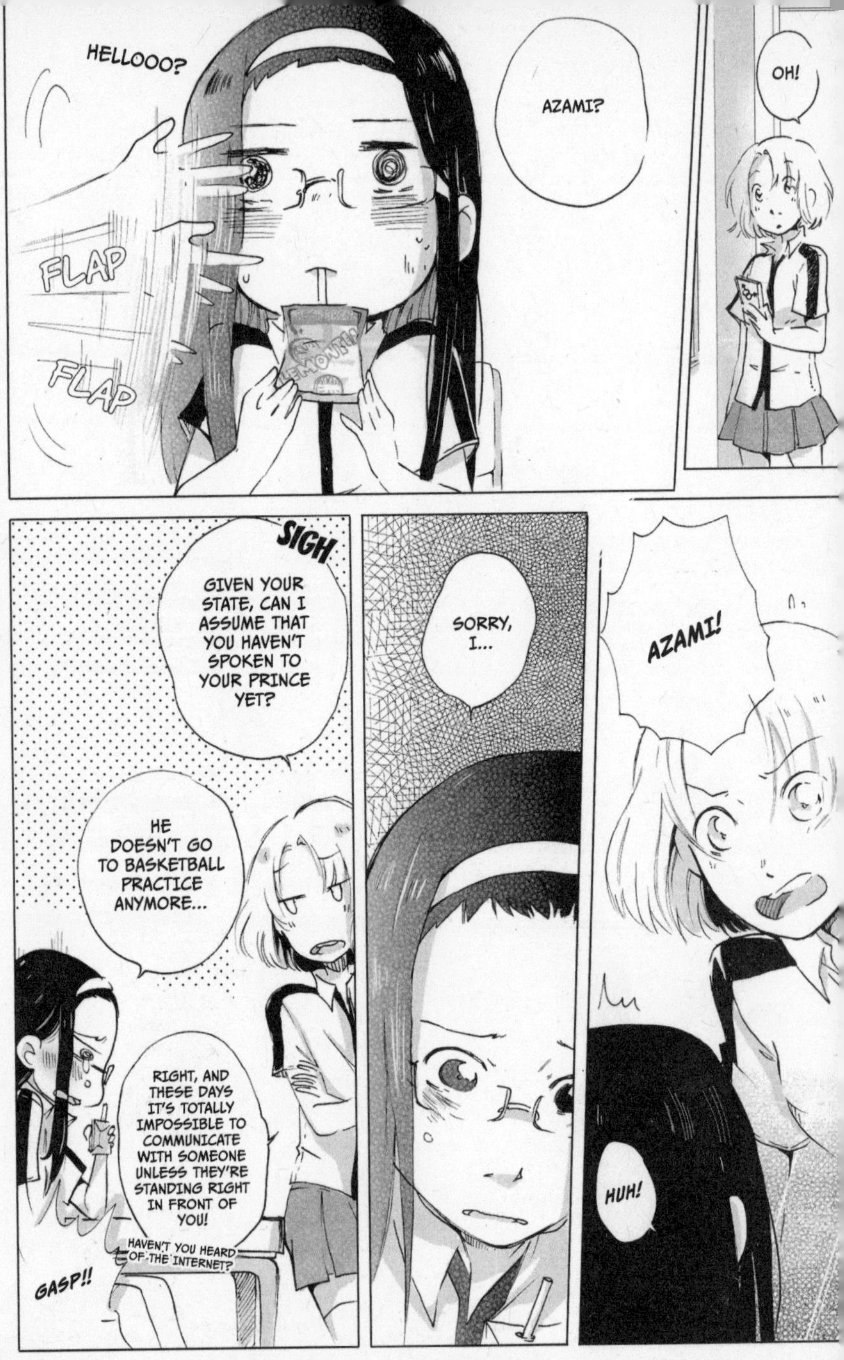
OH!
AZAMI?
HELLOOO?
FLAP
FLAP
AZAMI!
HUH!
SORRY, I...
SIGH
GIVEN YOUR STATE, CAN I ASSUME THAT YOU HAVEN'T SPOKEN TO YOUR PRINCE YET?
HE DOESN'T GO TO BASKETBALL PRACTICE ANYMORE...
RIGHT, AND THESE DAYS IT'S TOTALLY IMPOSSIBLE TO COMMUNICATE WITH SOMEONE UNLESS THEY'RE STANDING RIGHT IN FRONT OF YOU!
HAVEN'T YOU HEARD OF THE INTERNET?
GASP!!

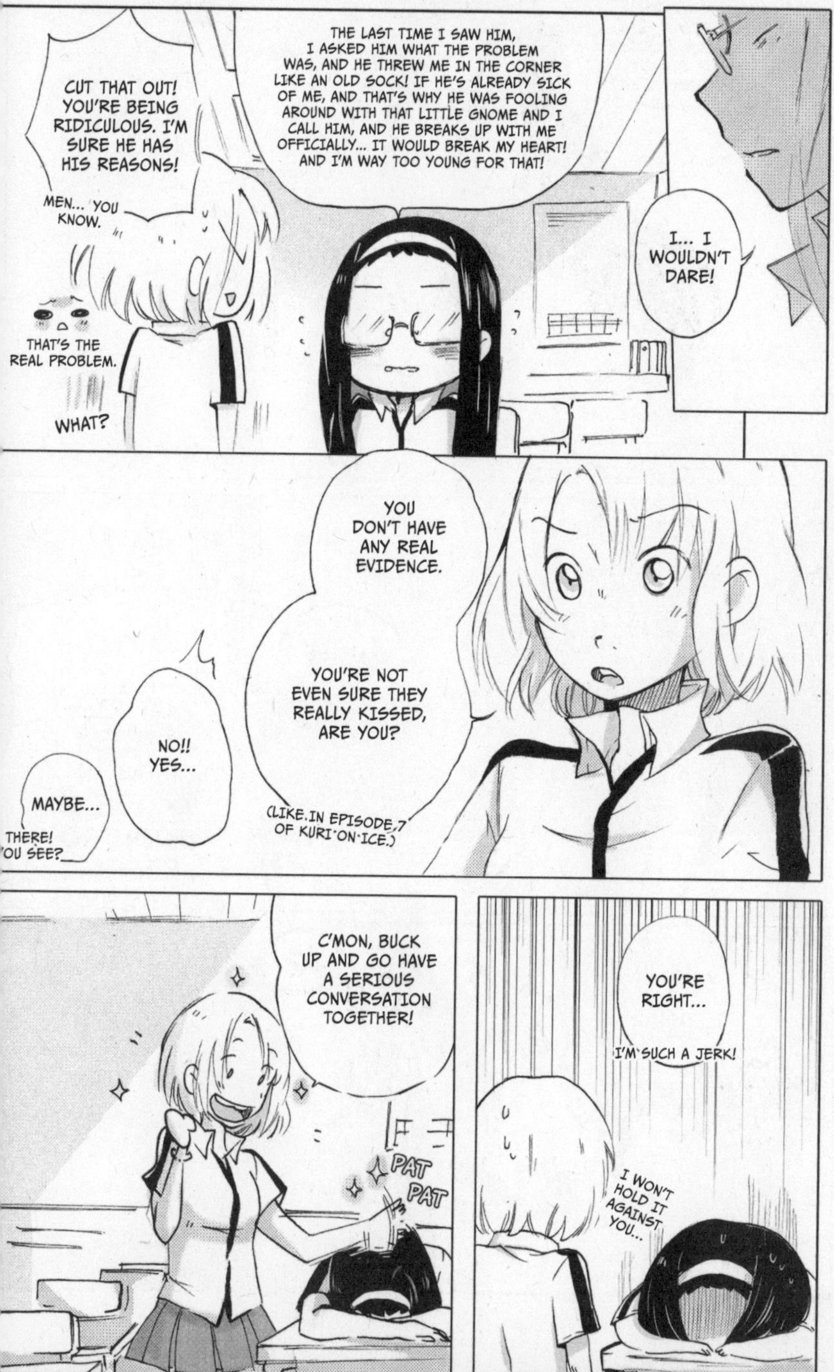
I... I WOULDN'T DARE!
THE LAST TIME I SAW HIM, I ASKED HIM WHAT THE PROBLEM WAS, AND HE THREW ME IN THE CORNER LIKE AN OLD SOCK! IF HE'S ALREADY SICK OF ME, AND THAT'S WHY HE WAS FOOLING AROUND WITH THAT LITTLE GNOME AND I CALL HIM, AND HE BREAKS UP WITH ME OFFICIALLY... IT WOULD BREAK MY HEART! AND I'M WAY TOO YOUNG FOR THAT!
CUT THAT OUT! YOU'RE BEING RIDICULOUS. I'M SURE HE HAS HIS REASONS!
MEN... YOU KNOW.
THAT'S THE REAL PROBLEM.
WHAT?
YOU DON'T HAVE ANY REAL EVIDENCE.
YOU'RE NOT EVEN SURE THEY REALLY KISSED, ARE YOU?
(LIKE IN EPISODE 7 OF KURI-ON-ICE.)
NO!! YES...
MAYBE...
THERE! OU SEE?
YOU'RE RIGHT...
I'M SUCH A JERK!
I WON'T HOLD IT AGAINST YOU...
C'MON, BUCK UP AND GO HAVE A SERIOUS CONVERSATION TOGETHER!
PAT PAT

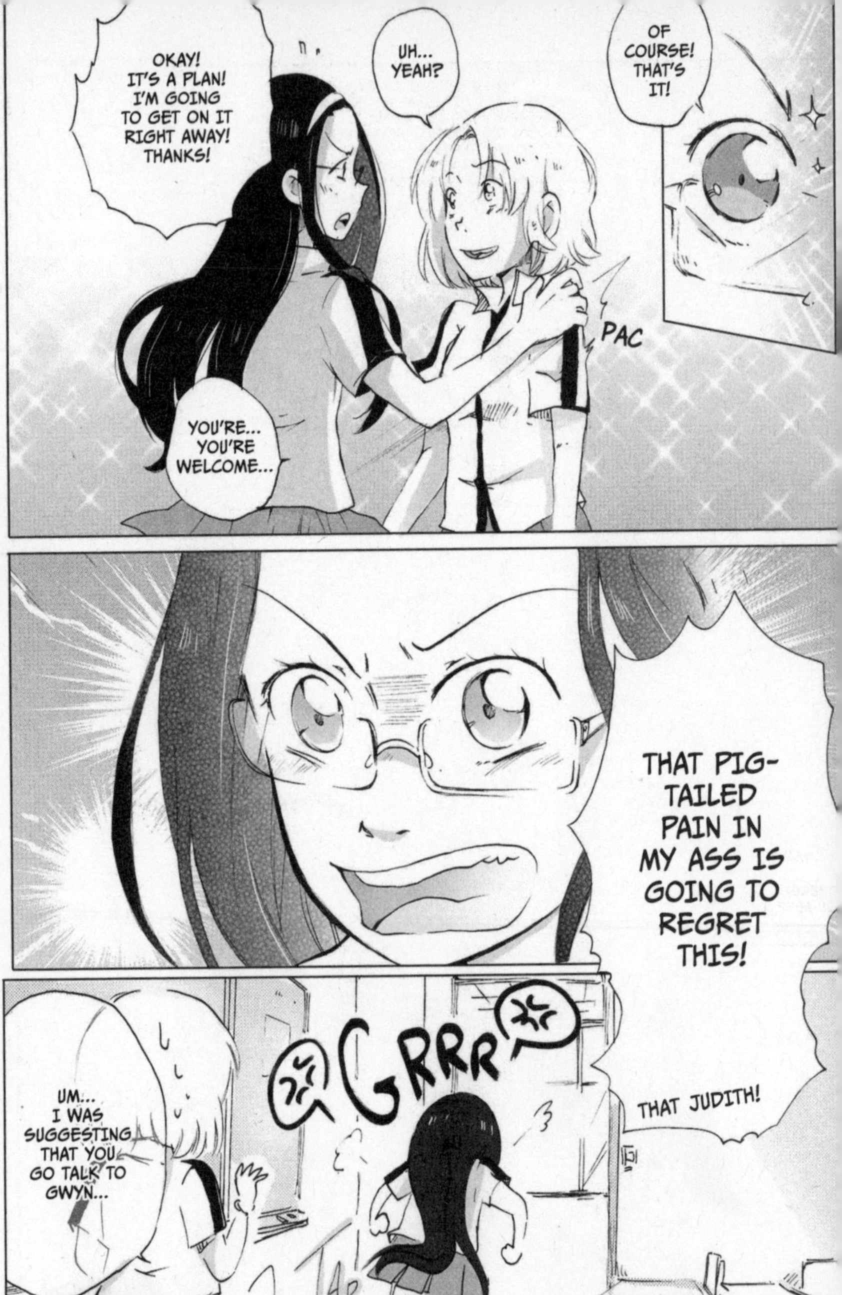
OF COURSE! THAT'S IT!
UH... YEAH?
OKAY! IT'S A PLAN! I'M GOING TO GET ON IT RIGHT AWAY! THANKS!
PAC
YOU'RE... YOU'RE WELCOME...
THAT PIG-TAILED PAIN IN MY ASS IS GOING TO REGRET THIS!
THAT JUDITH!
GRRR
UM... I WAS SUGGESTING THAT YOU GO TALK TO GWYN...
TAP
TAP

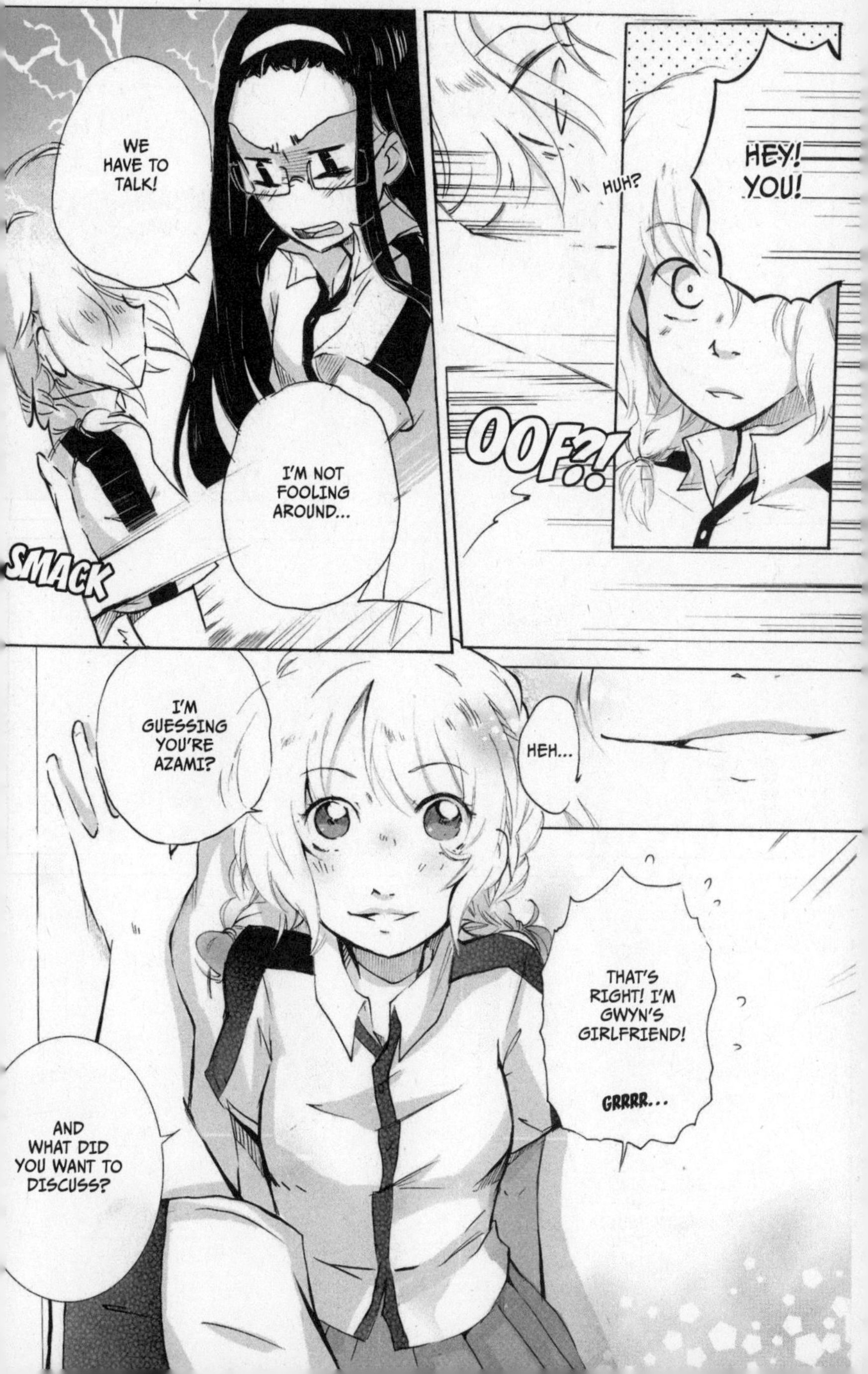
HEY! YOU!
HUH?
OOF?!
WE HAVE TO TALK!
I'M NOT FOOLING AROUND...
SMACK
HEH...
I'M GUESSING YOU'RE AZAMI?
THAT'S RIGHT! I'M GWYN'S GIRLFRIEND!
GRRRR...
AND WHAT DID YOU WANT TO DISCUSS?

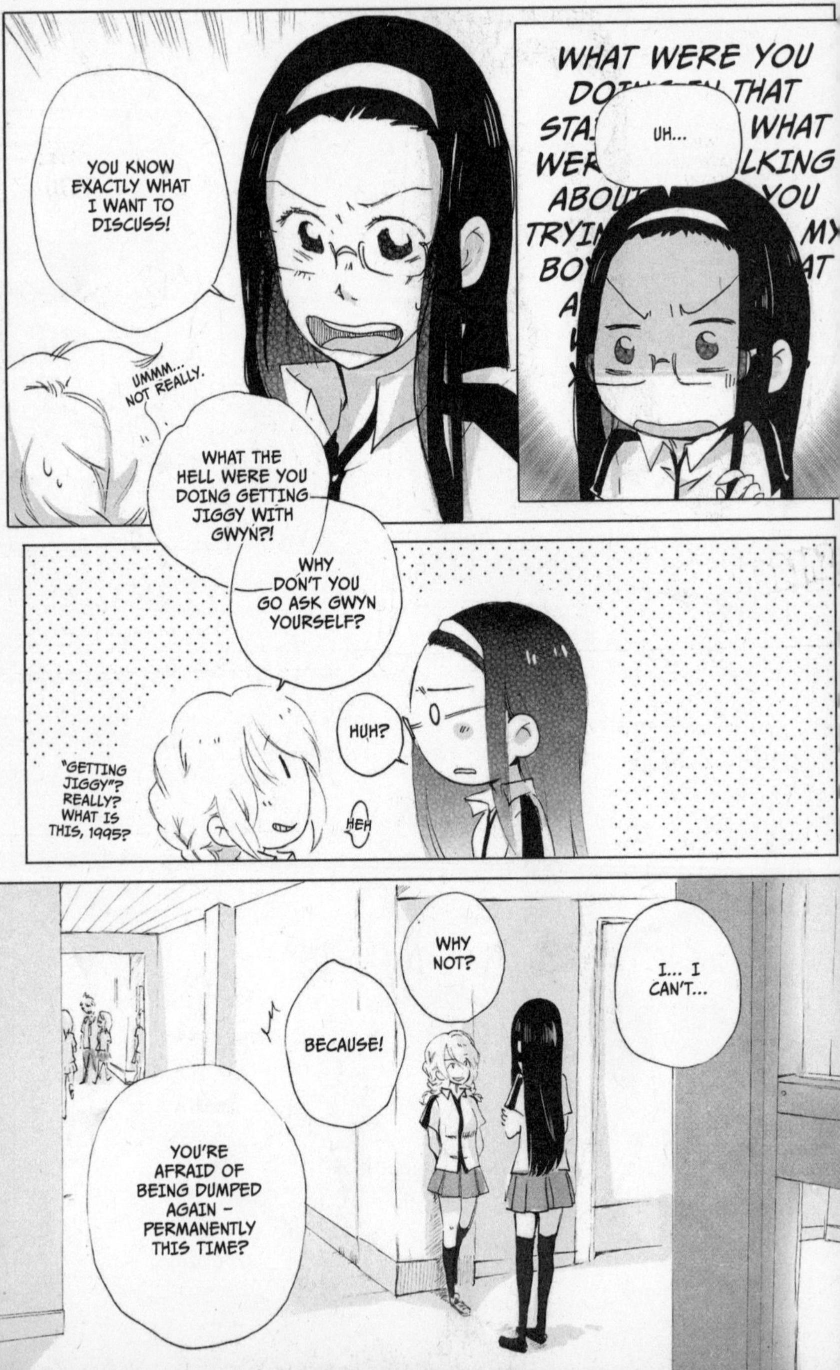
WHAT WERE YOU
THAT
WHAT
LKING
YOU
MY
AT
UH...
YOU KNOW EXACTLY WHAT I WANT TO DISCUSS!
UMMM... NOT REALLY.
WHAT THE HELL WERE YOU DOING GETTING JIGGY WITH GWYN?!
WHY DON'T YOU GO ASK GWYN YOURSELF?
HUH?
"GETTING JIGGY"? REALLY? WHAT IS THIS, 1995?
HEH
I... I CAN'T...
WHY NOT?
BECAUSE!
YOU'RE AFRAID OF BEING DUMPED AGAIN – PERMANENTLY THIS TIME?

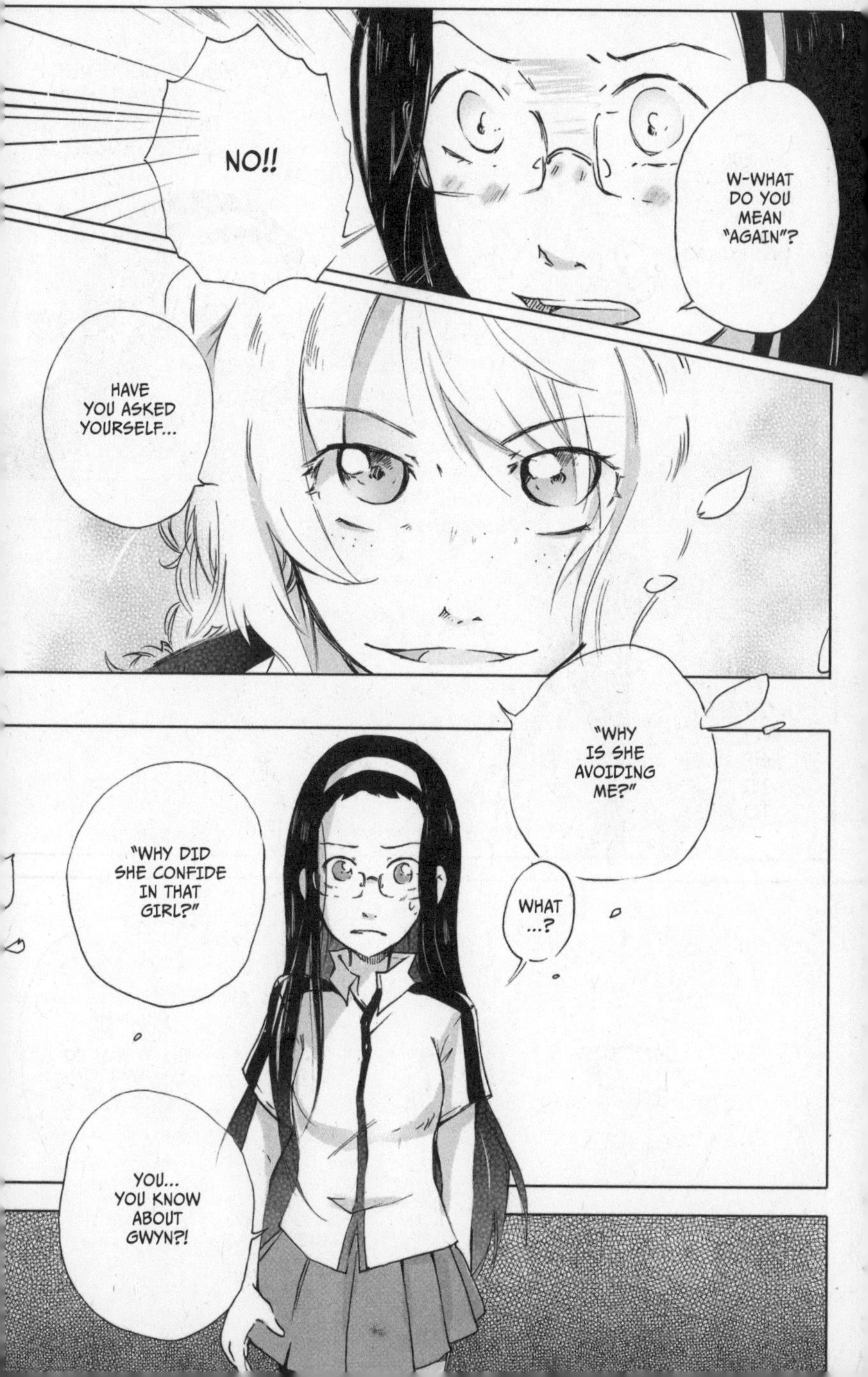
W-WHAT DO YOU MEAN "AGAIN"?
NO!!
HAVE YOU ASKED YOURSELF...
"WHY IS SHE AVOIDING ME?"
"WHY DID SHE CONFIDE IN THAT GIRL?"
WHAT ...?
YOU... YOU KNOW ABOUT GWYN?!

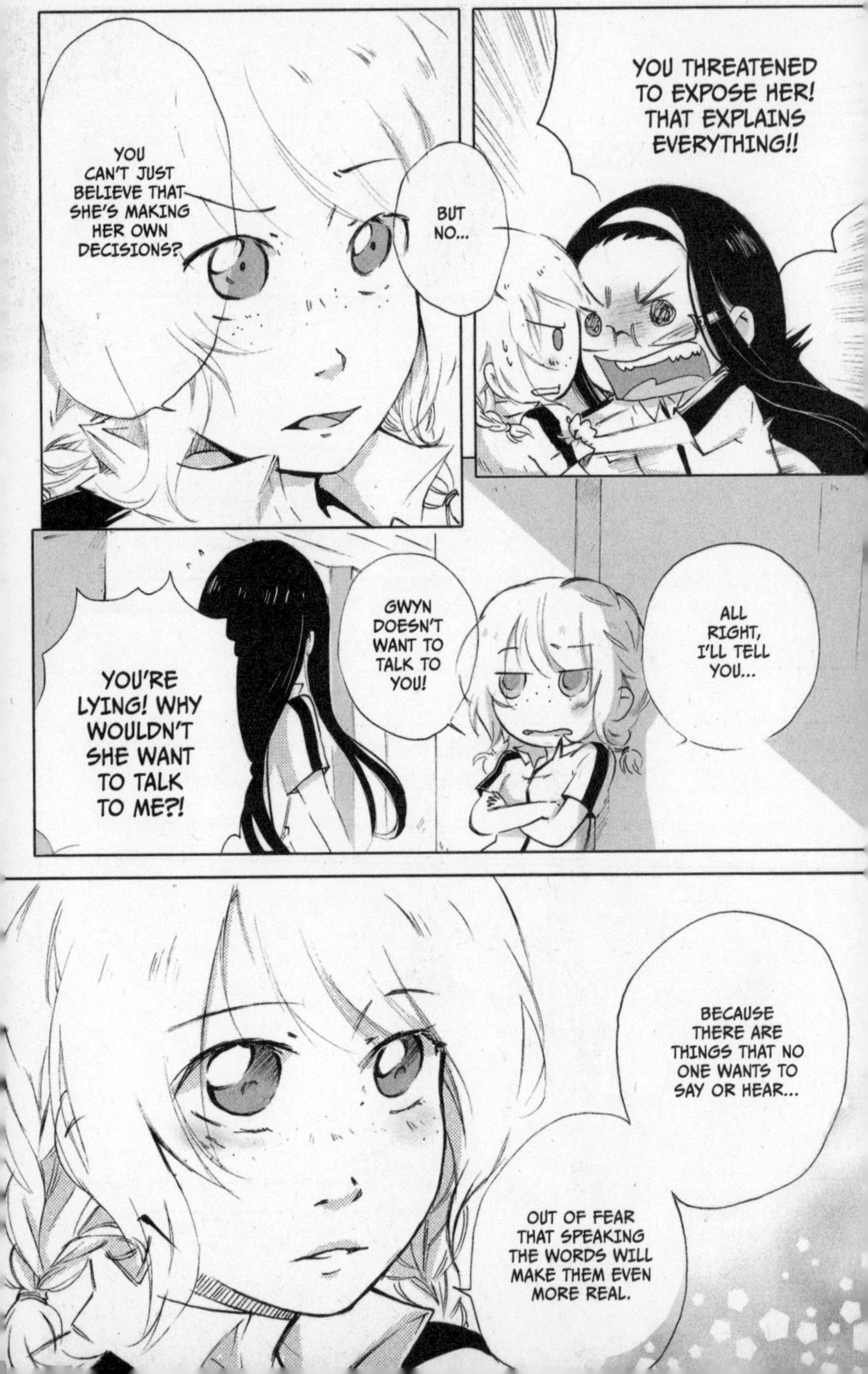

YOU THREATENED TO EXPOSE HER! THAT EXPLAINS EVERYTHING!!
BUT NO...
YOU CAN'T JUST BELIEVE THAT SHE'S MAKING HER OWN DECISIONS?
GWYN DOESN'T WANT TO TALK TO YOU!
YOU'RE LYING! WHY WOULDN'T SHE WANT TO TALK TO ME?!
ALL RIGHT, I'LL TELL YOU...
BECAUSE THERE ARE THINGS THAT NO ONE WANTS TO SAY OR HEAR...
OUT OF FEAR THAT SPEAKING THE WORDS WILL MAKE THEM EVEN MORE REAL.

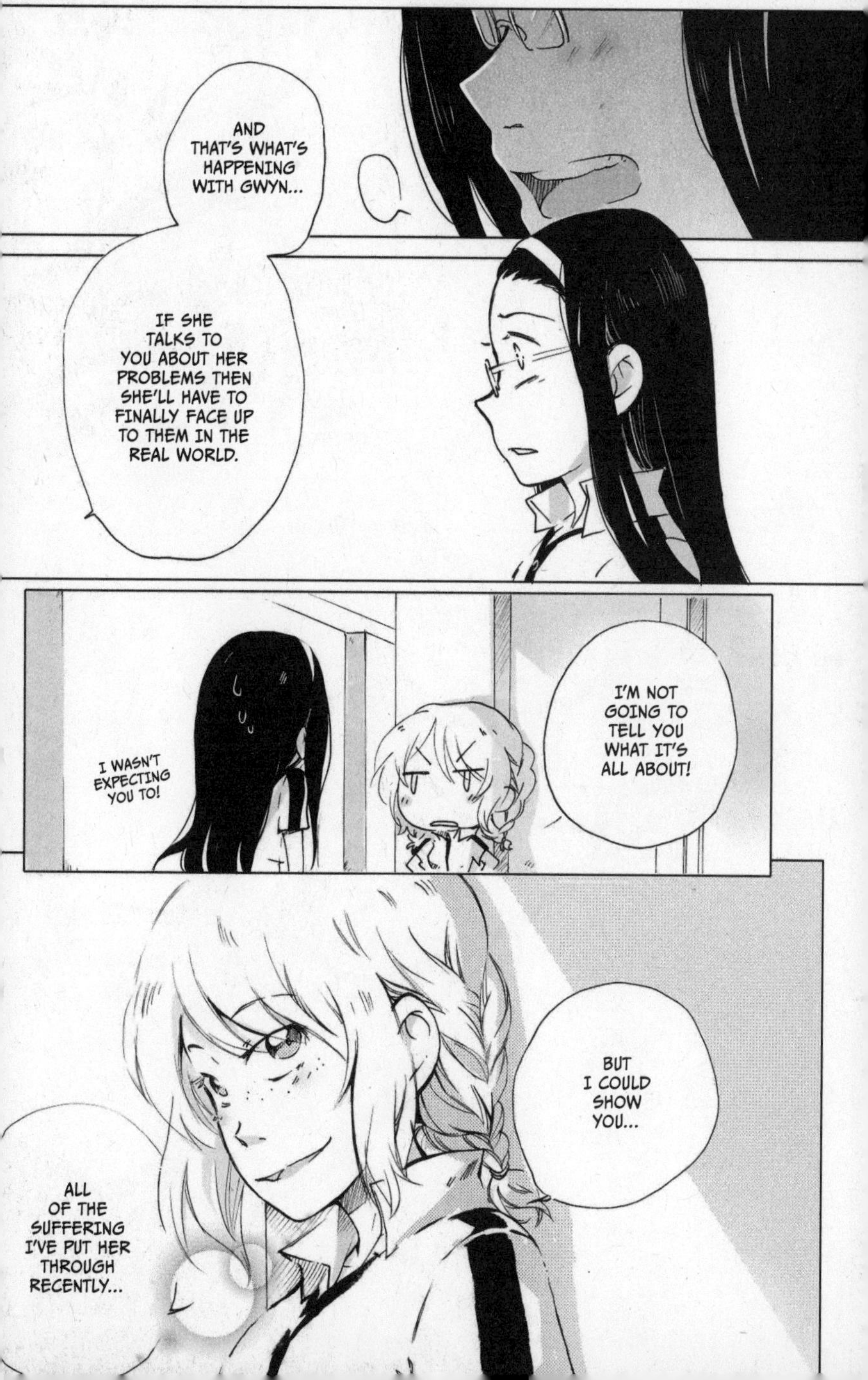
AND THAT'S WHAT'S HAPPENING WITH GWYN...
IF SHE TALKS TO YOU ABOUT HER PROBLEMS THEN SHE'LL HAVE TO FINALLY FACE UP TO THEM IN THE REAL WORLD.
I'M NOT GOING TO TELL YOU WHAT IT'S ALL ABOUT!
I WASN'T EXPECTING YOU TO!
BUT I COULD SHOW YOU...
ALL OF THE SUFFERING I'VE PUT HER THROUGH RECENTLY...

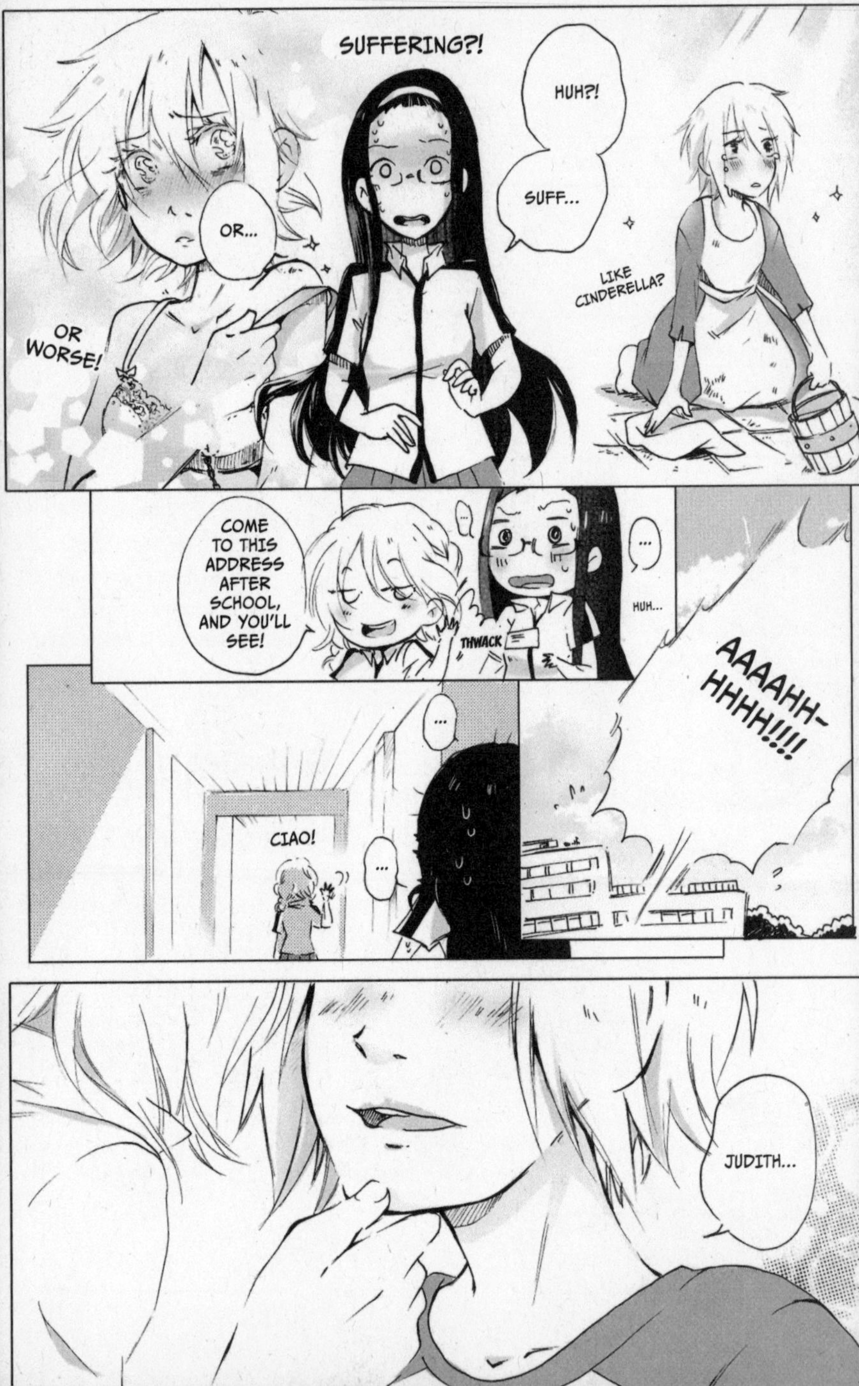
HUH?!
SUFF...
SUFFERING?!
LIKE CINDERELLA?
OR...
OR WORSE!
...
HUH...
...
COME TO THIS ADDRESS AFTER SCHOOL, AND YOU'LL SEE!
THWACK
AAAAHH-HHHH!!!!
...
CIAO!
...
JUDITH...

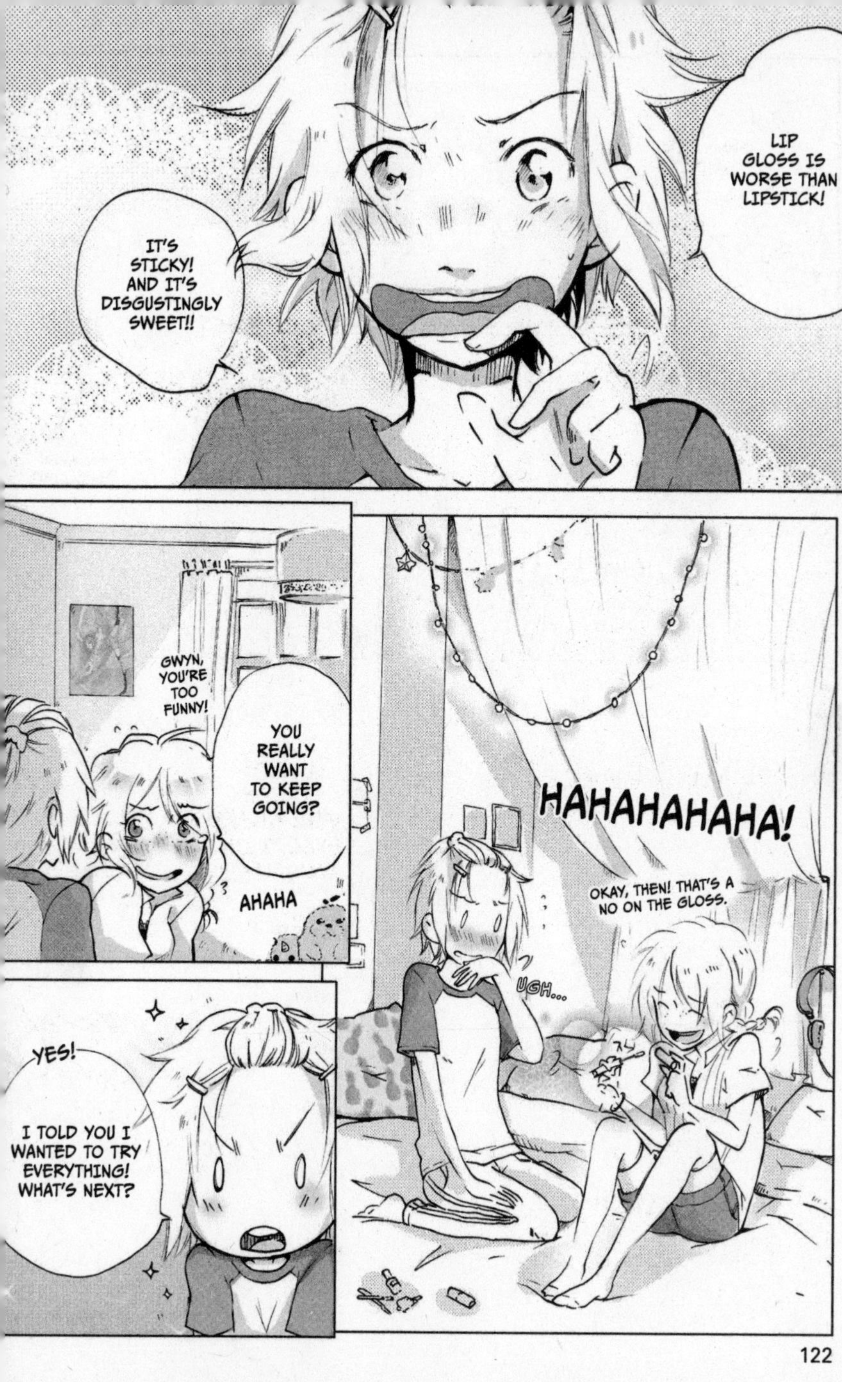

LIP GLOSS IS WORSE THAN LIPSTICK!
IT'S STICKY! AND IT'S DISGUSTINGLY SWEET!!
HAHAHAHAHA!
OKAY, THEN! THAT'S A NO ON THE GLOSS.
UGH...
GWYN, YOU'RE TOO FUNNY!
YOU REALLY WANT TO KEEP GOING?
AHAHA
YES!
I TOLD YOU I WANTED TO TRY EVERYTHING! WHAT'S NEXT?

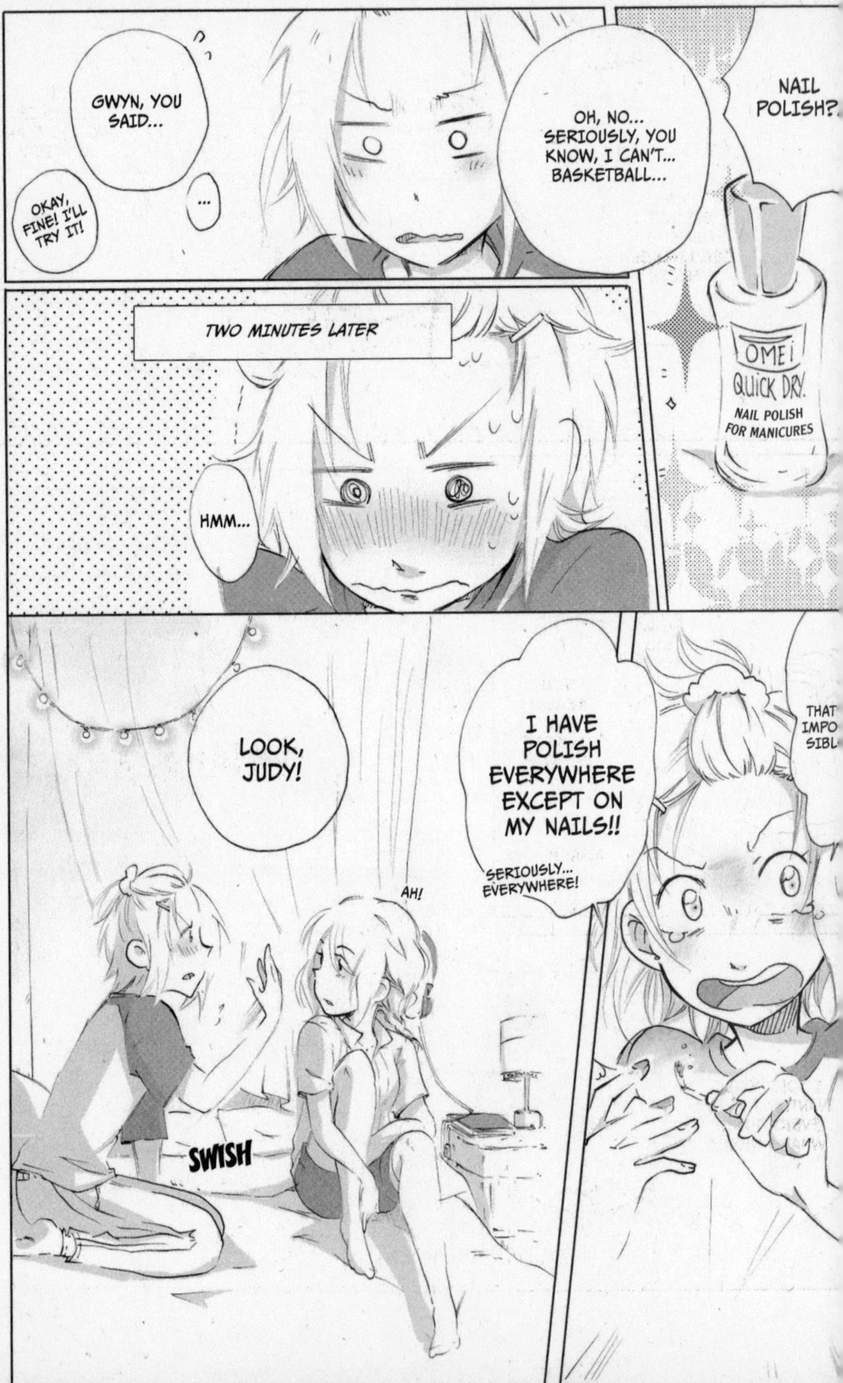
NAIL POLISH?
OMEI
QUICK DRY.
NAIL POLISH FOR MANICURES
OH, NO... SERIOUSLY, YOU KNOW, I CAN'T... BASKETBALL...
GWYN, YOU SAID...
...
OKAY, FINE! I'LL TRY IT!
TWO MINUTES LATER
HMM...
THAT IMPO SIBL
I HAVE POLISH EVERYWHERE EXCEPT ON MY NAILS!!
SERIOUSLY... EVERYWHERE!
LOOK, JUDY!
AH!
SWISH

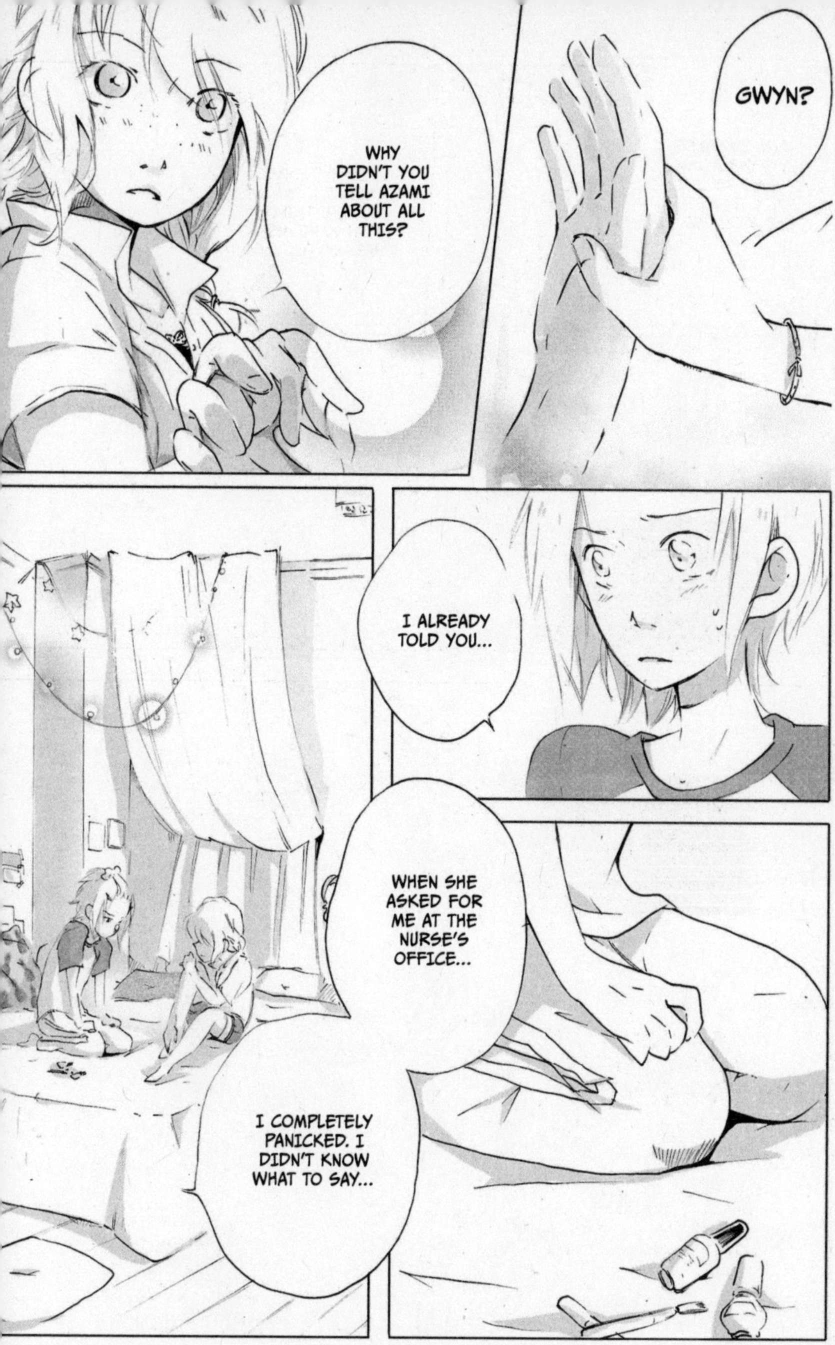
GWYN?
WHY DIDN'T YOU TELL AZAMI ABOUT ALL THIS?
I ALREADY TOLD YOU...
WHEN SHE ASKED FOR ME AT THE NURSE'S OFFICE...
I COMPLETELY PANICKED. I DIDN'T KNOW WHAT TO SAY...

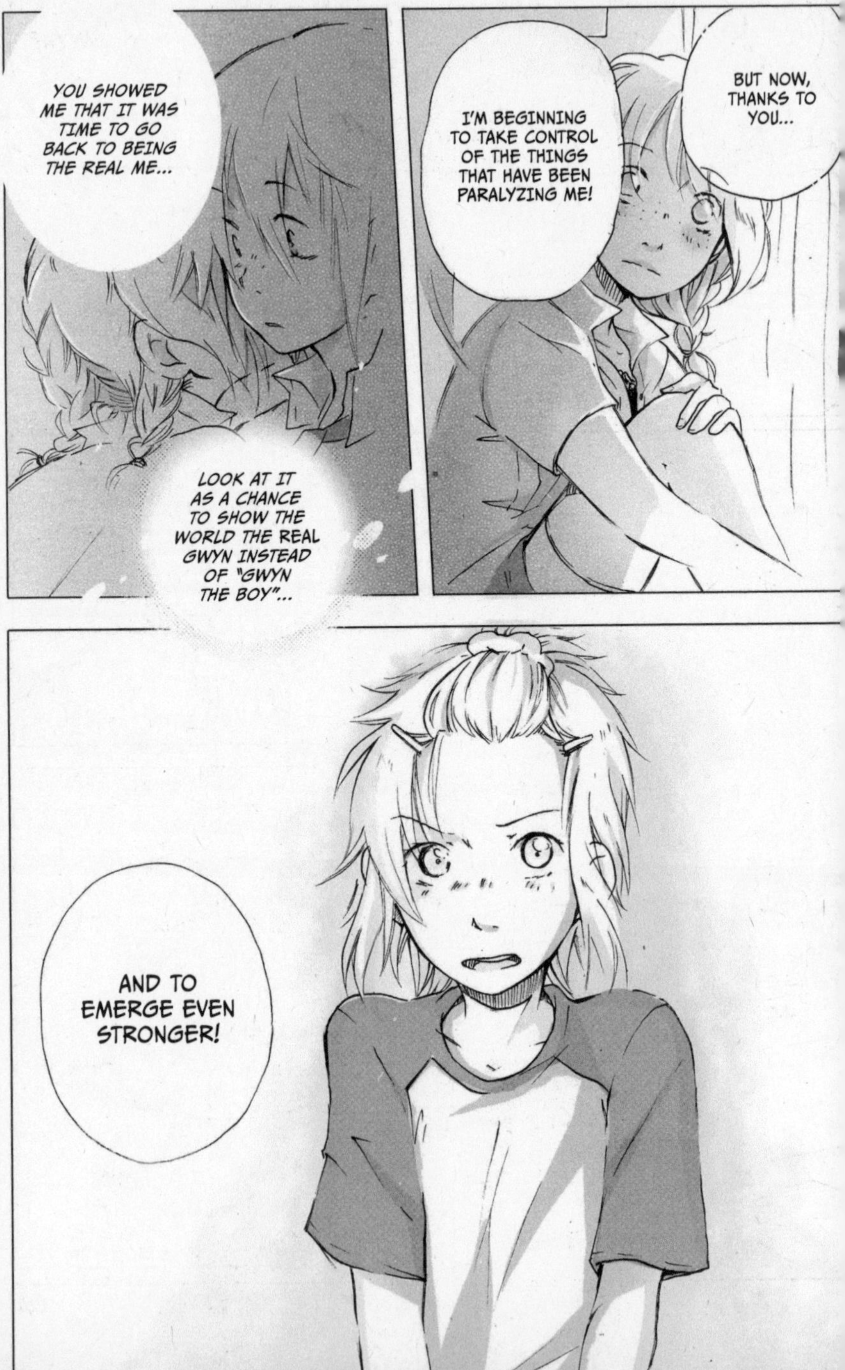
BUT NOW, THANKS TO YOU...
I'M BEGINNING TO TAKE CONTROL OF THE THINGS THAT HAVE BEEN PARALYZING ME!
YOU SHOWED ME THAT IT WAS TIME TO GO BACK TO BEING THE REAL ME...
LOOK AT IT AS A CHANCE TO SHOW THE WORLD THE REAL GWYN INSTEAD OF "GWYN THE BOY"...
AND TO EMERGE EVEN STRONGER!

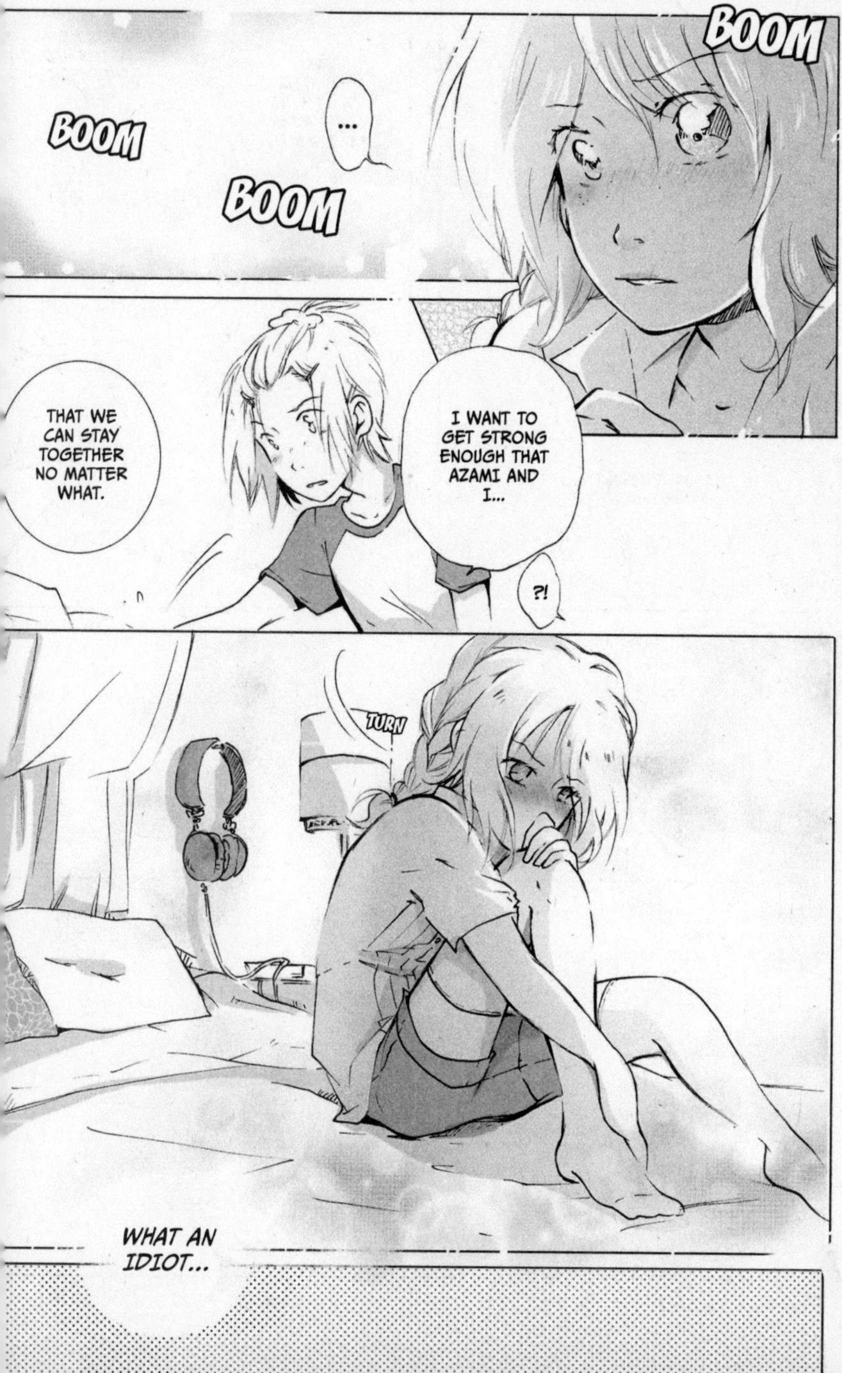
BOOM
...
BOOM
BOOM
I WANT TO GET STRONG ENOUGH THAT AZAMI AND I...
THAT WE CAN STAY TOGETHER NO MATTER WHAT.
?!
TURN
WHAT AN IDIOT...

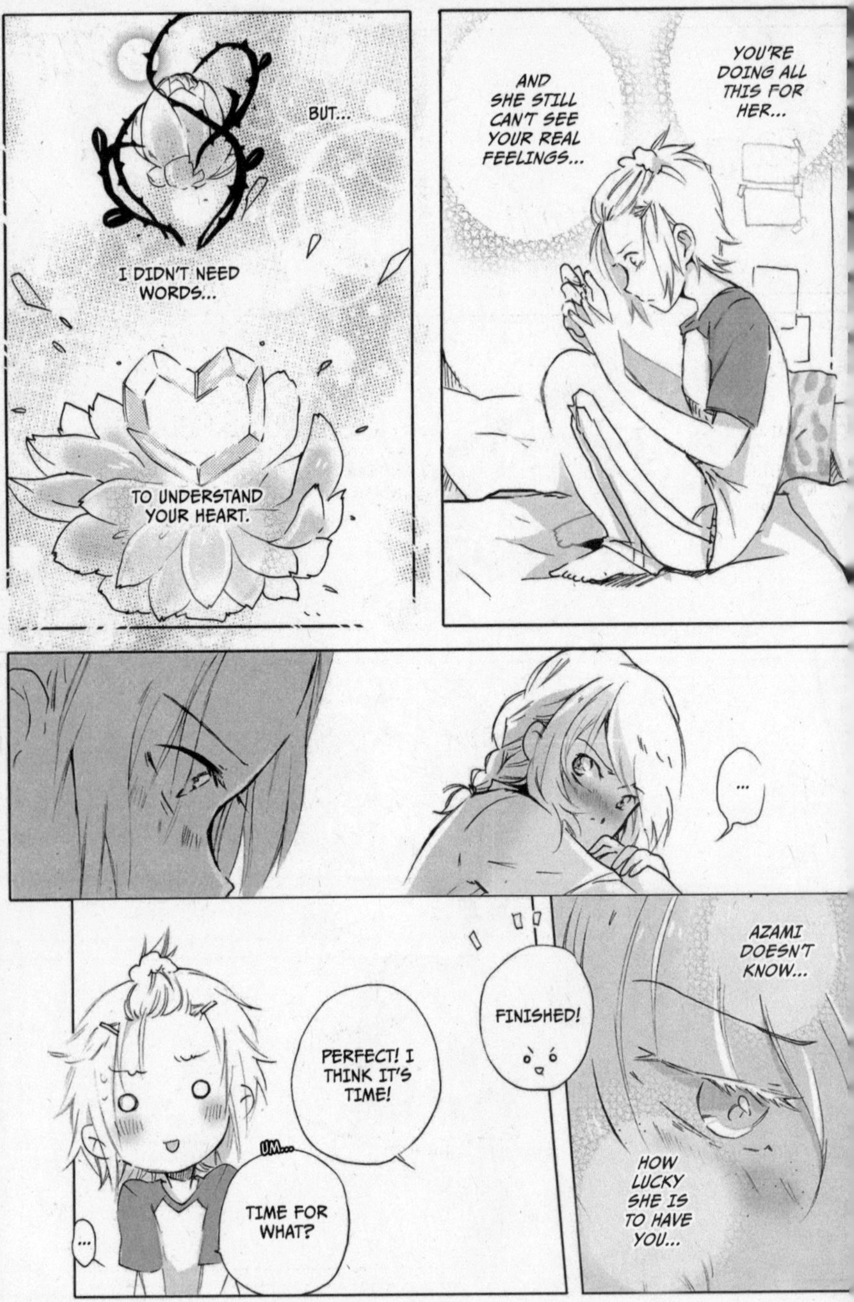
YOU'RE DOING ALL THIS FOR HER...
AND SHE STILL CAN'T SEE YOUR REAL FEELINGS...
BUT...
I DIDN'T NEED WORDS...
TO UNDERSTAND YOUR HEART.
...
AZAMI DOESN'T KNOW...
HOW LUCKY SHE IS TO HAVE YOU...
FINISHED!
PERFECT! I THINK IT'S TIME!
UM...
TIME FOR WHAT?
...

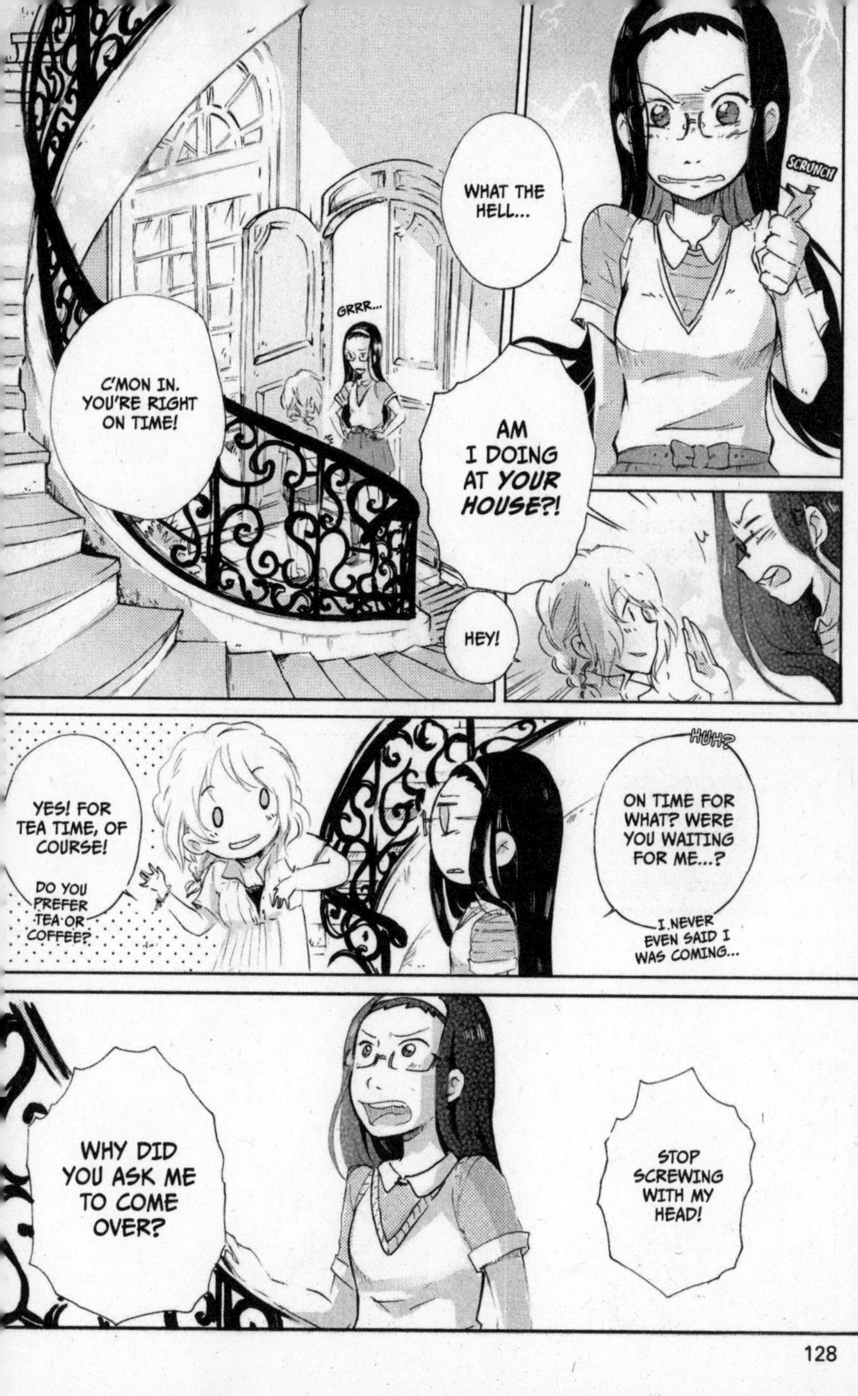
SCRUNCH
WHAT THE HELL...
AM I DOING AT YOUR HOUSE?!
HEY!
GRRR...
C'MON IN. YOU'RE RIGHT ON TIME!
HUH?
ON TIME FOR WHAT? WERE YOU WAITING FOR ME...?
I NEVER EVEN SAID I WAS COMING...
YES! FOR TEA TIME, OF COURSE!
DO YOU PREFER TEA OR COFFEE?
STOP SCREWING WITH MY HEAD!
WHY DID YOU ASK ME TO COME OVER?

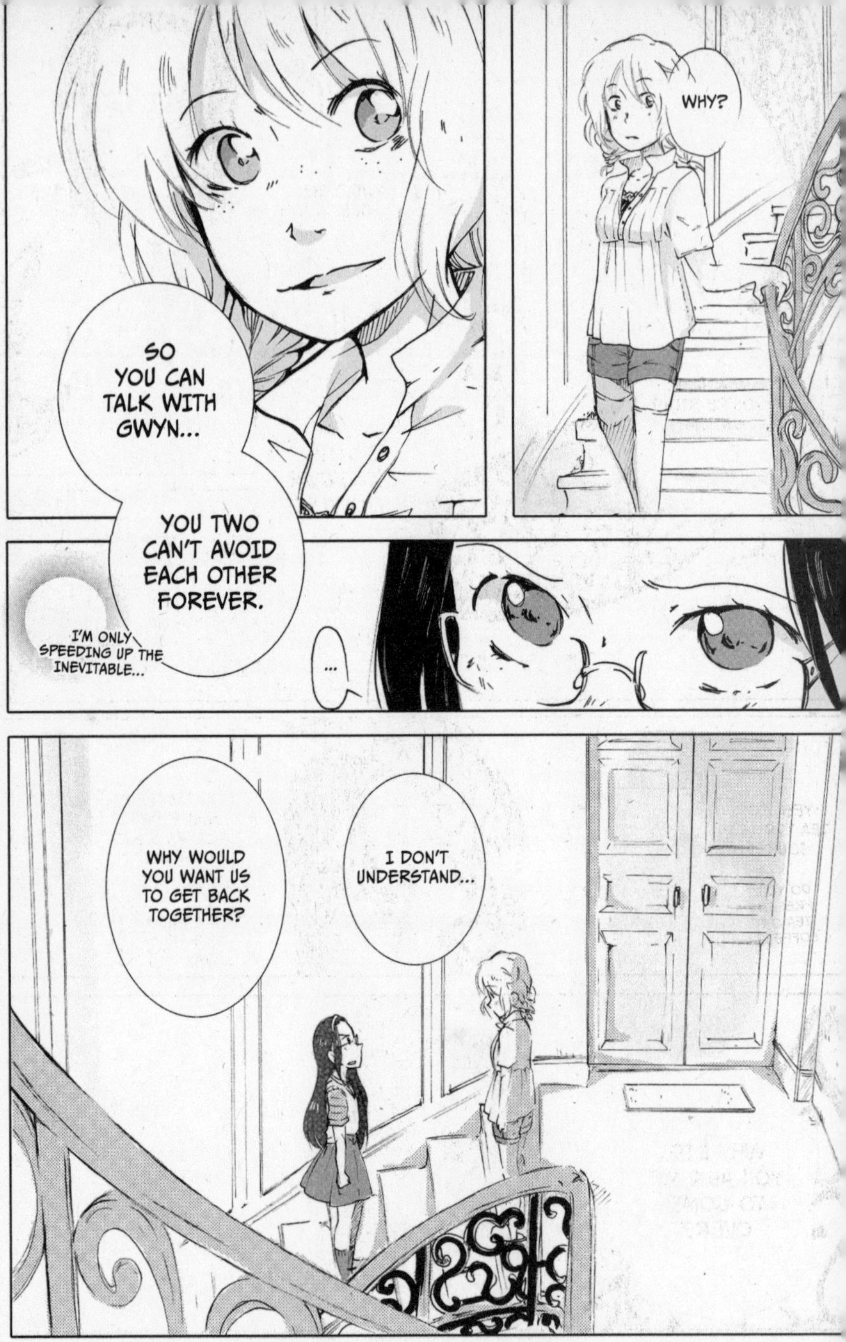

WHY?
SO YOU CAN TALK WITH GWYN...
YOU TWO CAN'T AVOID EACH OTHER FOREVER.
...
I'M ONLY SPEEDING UP THE INEVITABLE...
I DON'T UNDERSTAND...
WHY WOULD YOU WANT US TO GET BACK TOGETHER?

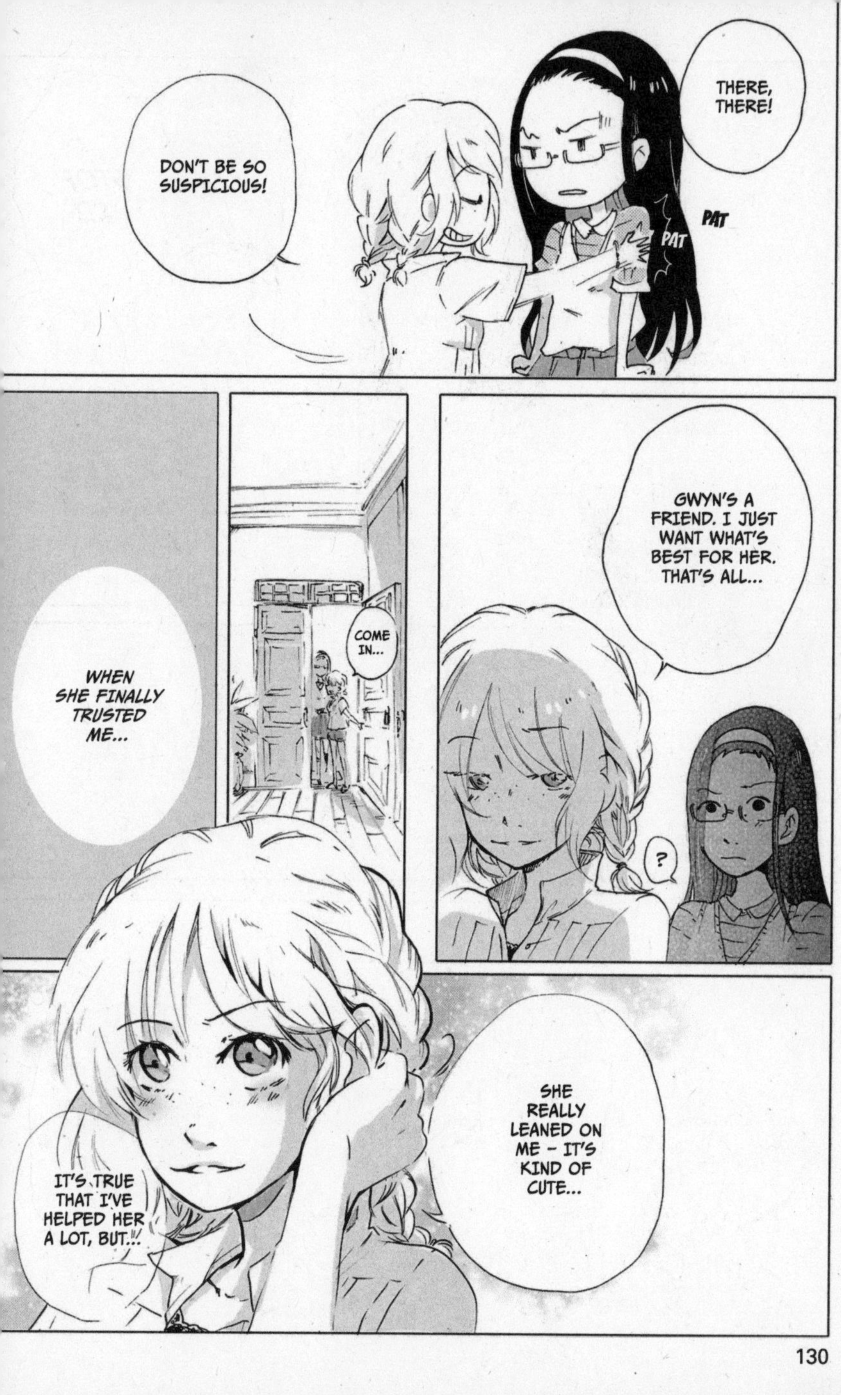
THERE, THERE!
PAT
PAT
DON'T BE SO SUSPICIOUS!
GWYN'S A FRIEND. I JUST WANT WHAT'S BEST FOR HER. THAT'S ALL...
?
COME IN...
WHEN SHE FINALLY TRUSTED ME...
SHE REALLY LEANED ON ME – IT'S KIND OF CUTE...
IT'S TRUE THAT I'VE HELPED HER A LOT, BUT...

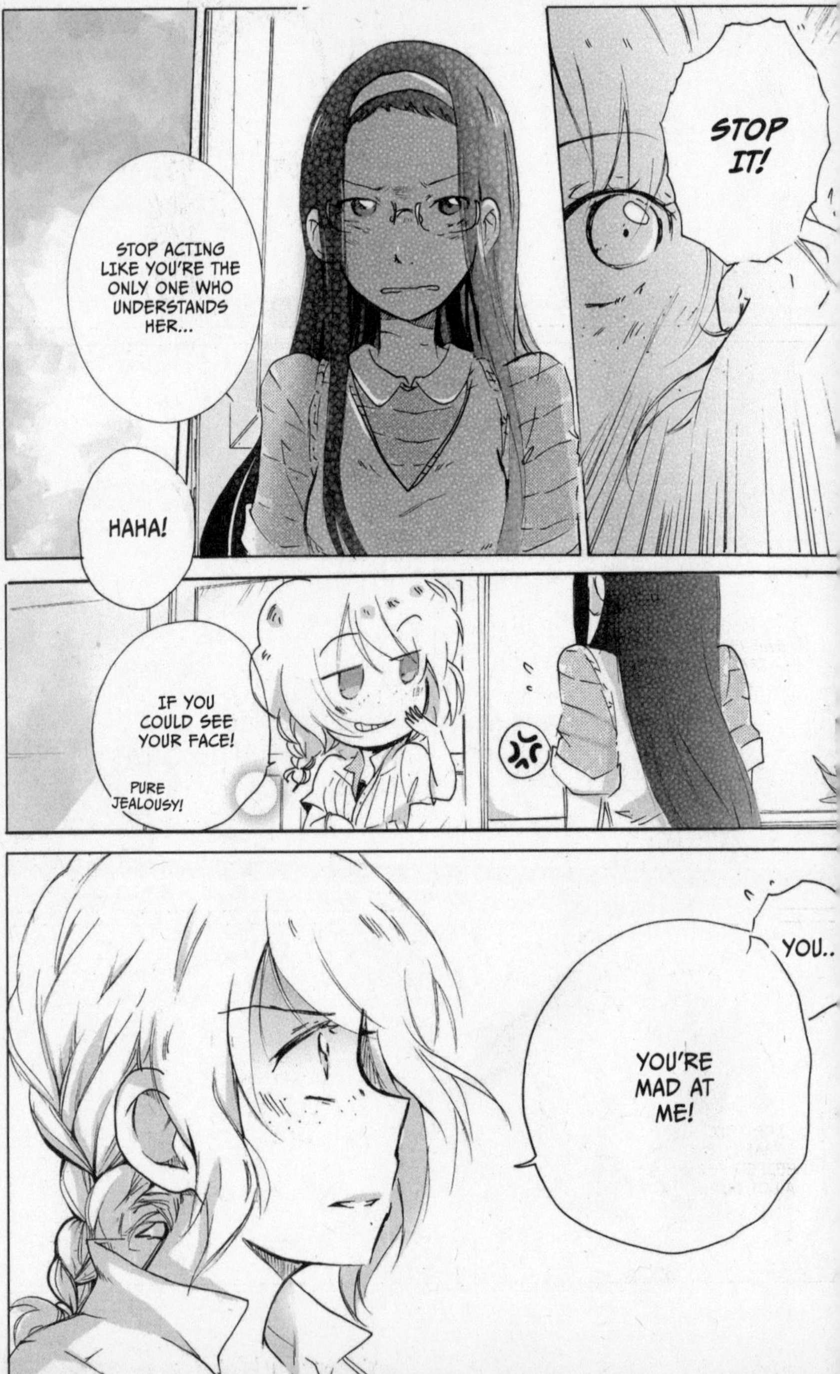
STOP IT!
STOP ACTING LIKE YOU'RE THE ONLY ONE WHO UNDERSTANDS HER...
HAHA!
IF YOU COULD SEE YOUR FACE!
PURE JEALOUSY!
YOU..
YOU'RE MAD AT ME!

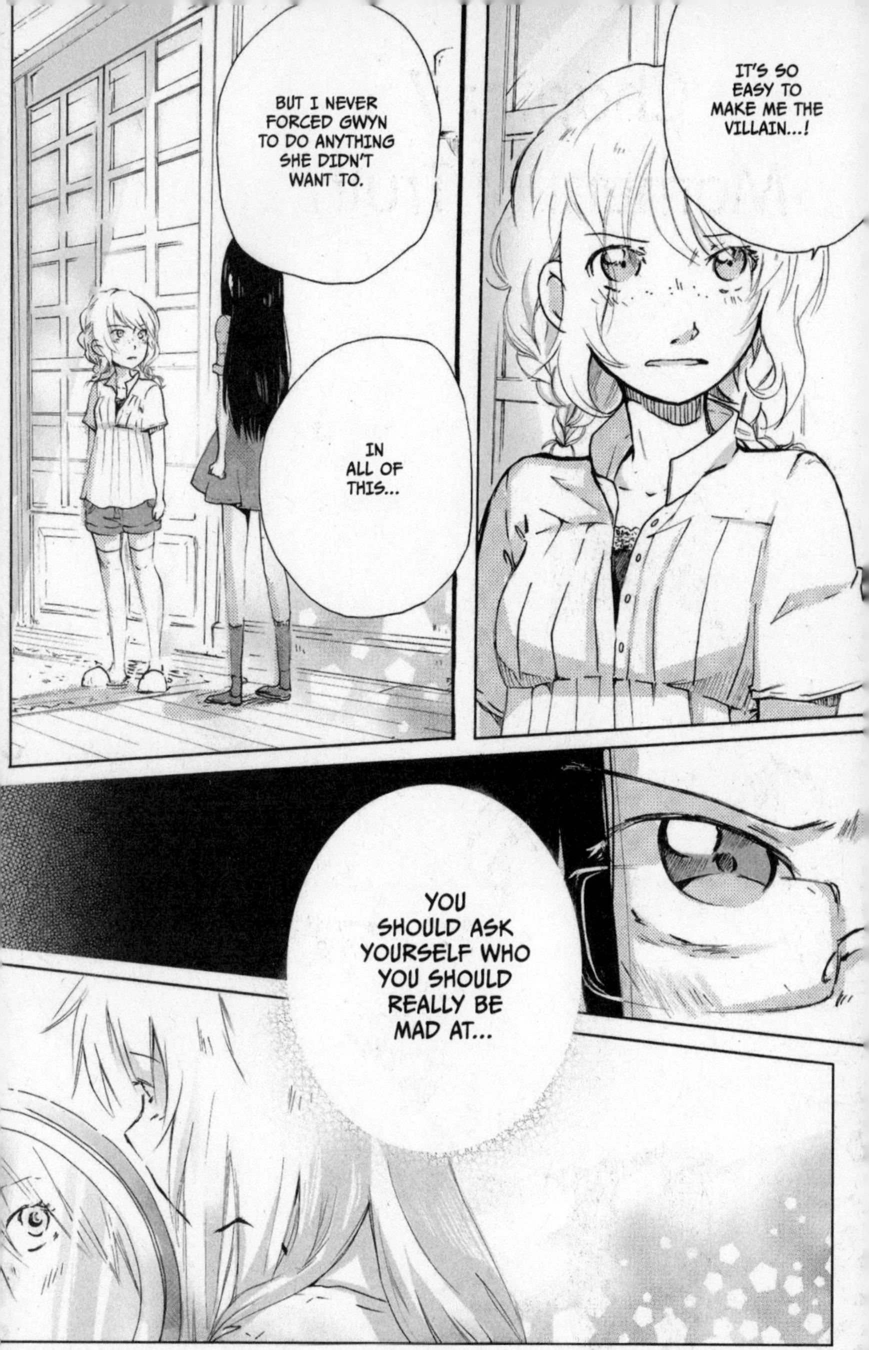
IT'S SO EASY TO MAKE ME THE VILLAIN...!
BUT I NEVER FORCED GWYN TO DO ANYTHING SHE DIDN'T WANT TO.
IN ALL OF THIS...
YOU SHOULD ASK YOURSELF WHO YOU SHOULD REALLY BE MAD AT...

Chapter 7
Moment of Truth

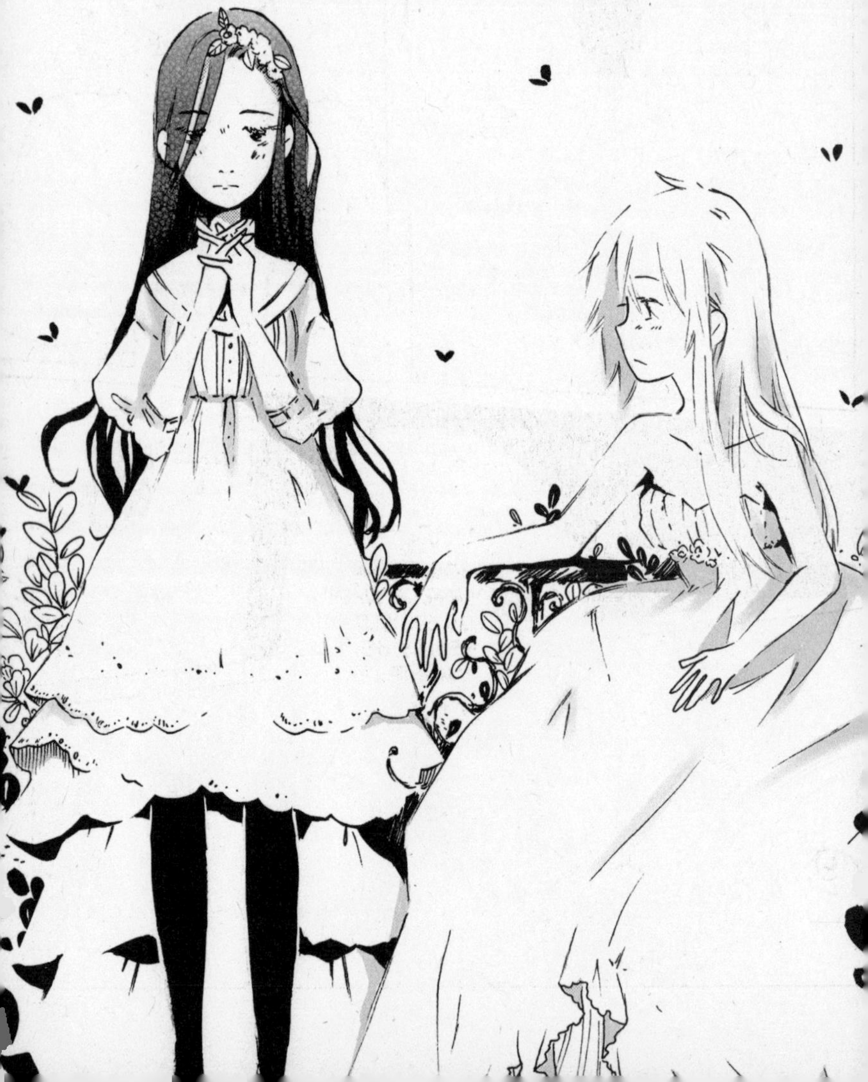

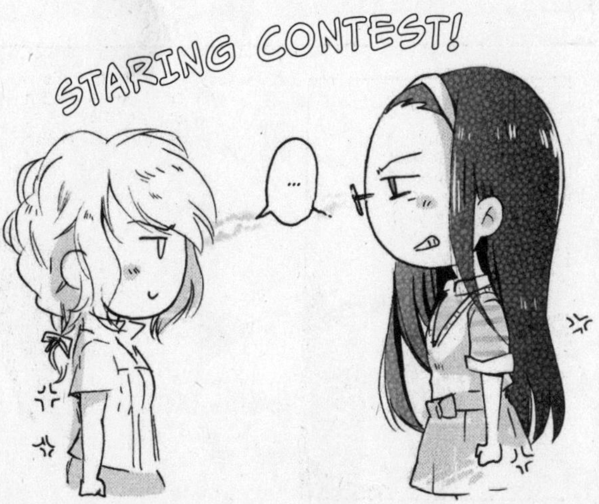
STARING CONTEST!
...

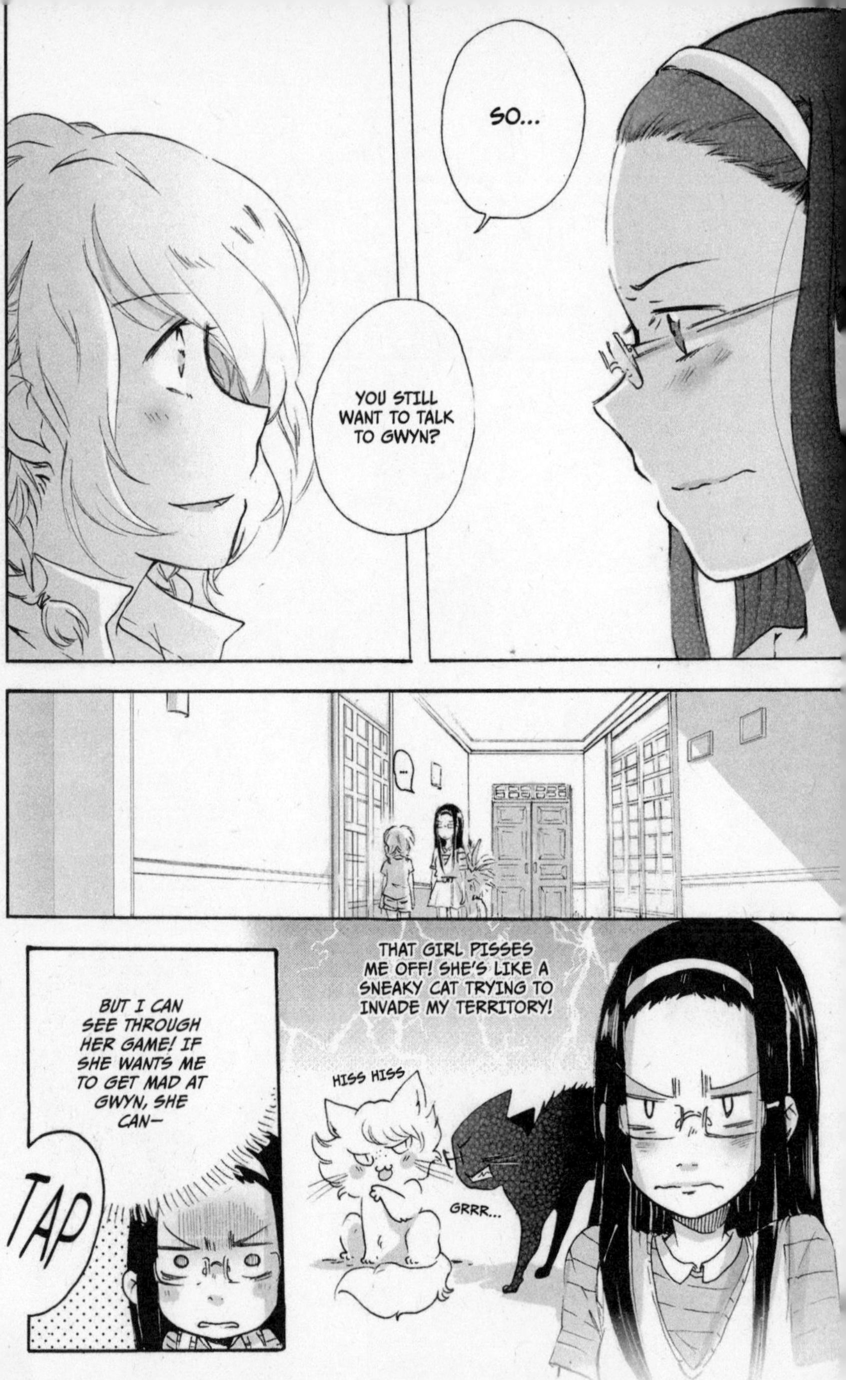
SO...
YOU STILL WANT TO TALK TO GWYN?
...
THAT GIRL PISSES ME OFF! SHE'S LIKE A SNEAKY CAT TRYING TO INVADE MY TERRITORY!
HISS HISS
GRRR...
BUT I CAN SEE THROUGH HER GAME! IF SHE WANTS ME TO GET MAD AT GWYN, SHE CAN–
TAP

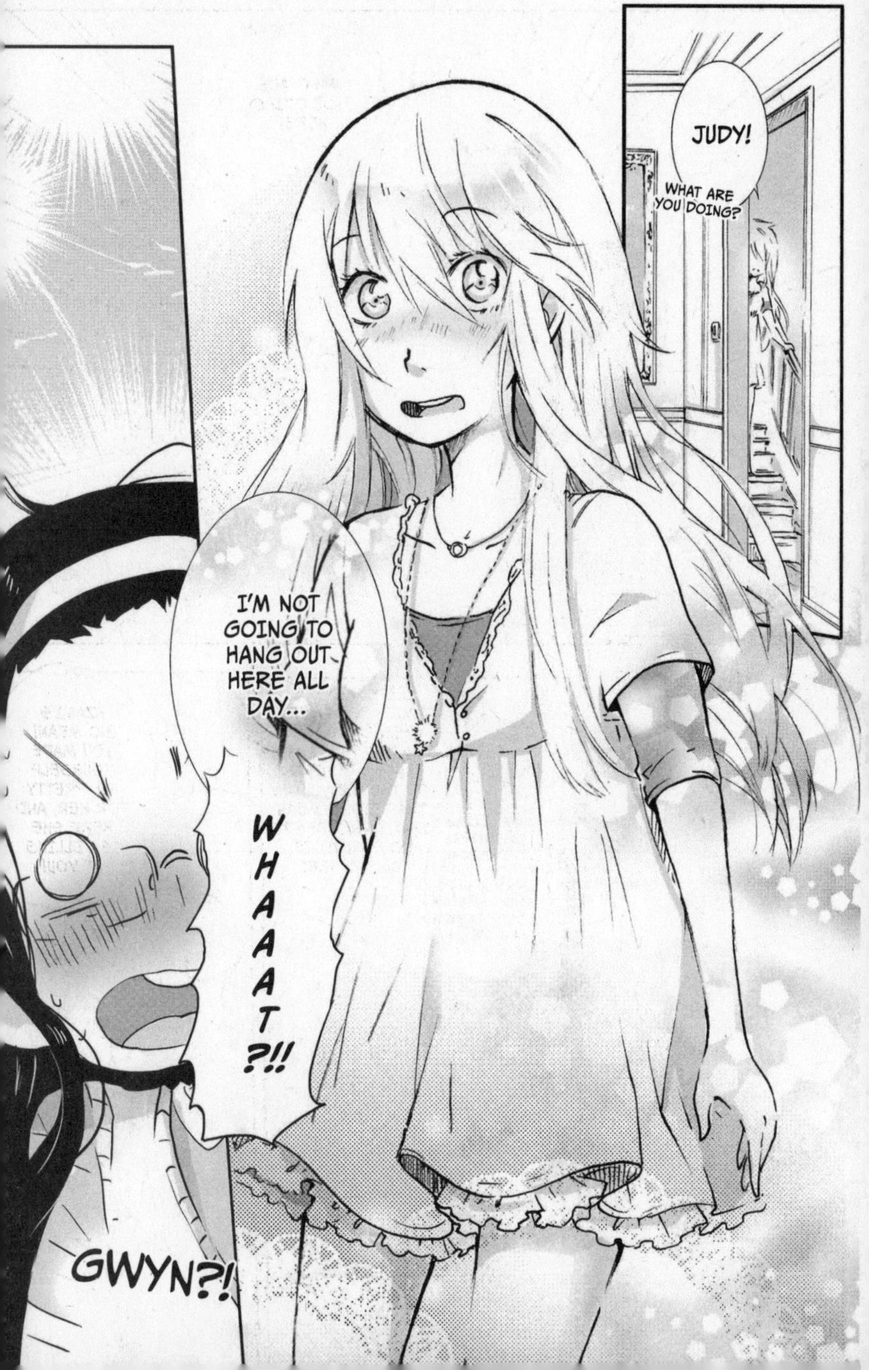
JUDY!
WHAT ARE YOU DOING?
I'M NOT GOING TO HANG OUT HERE ALL DAY...
WHAAAAT?!!
GWYN?!

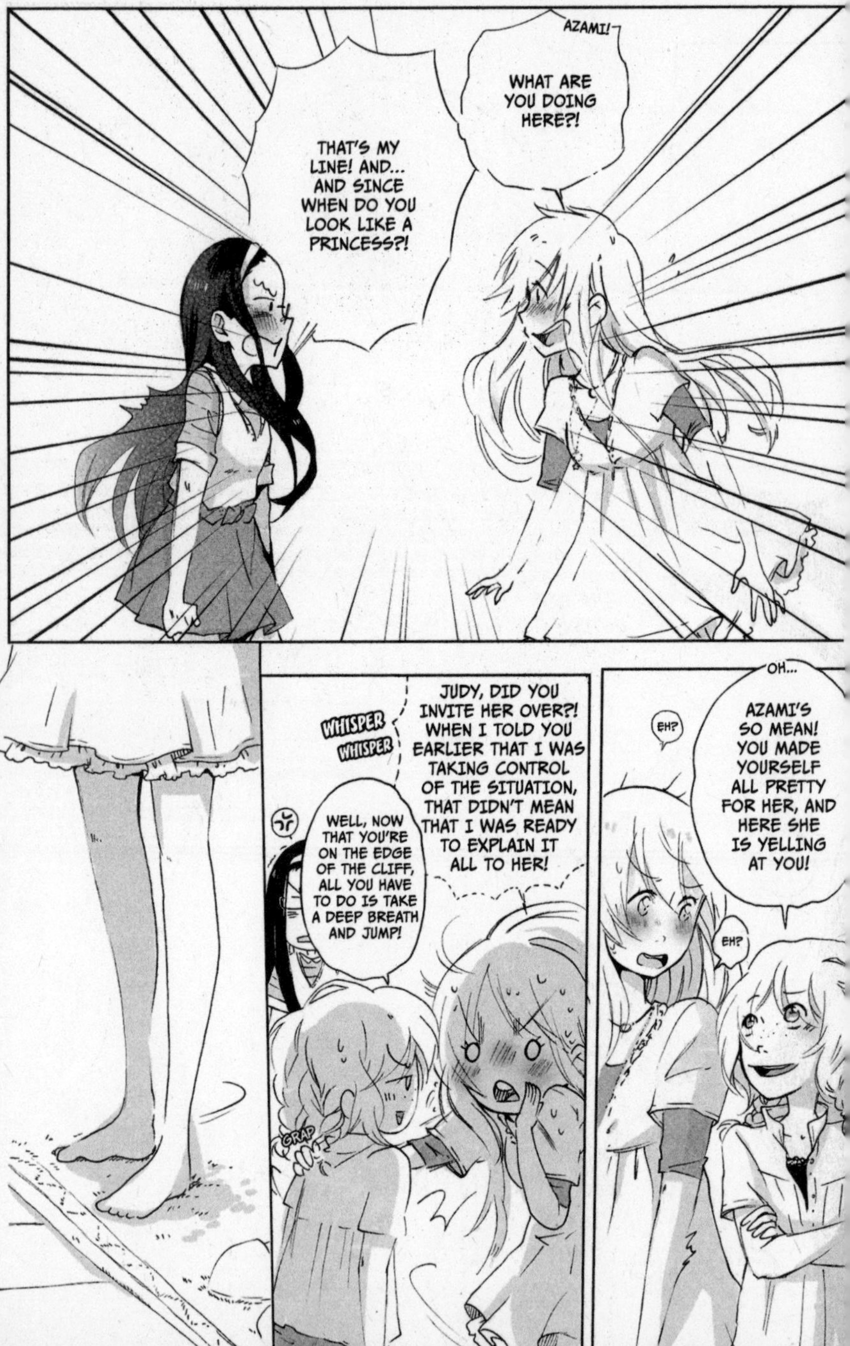
AZAMI!
WHAT ARE YOU DOING HERE?!
THAT'S MY LINE! AND... AND SINCE WHEN DO YOU LOOK LIKE A PRINCESS?!
OH...
AZAMI'S SO MEAN! YOU MADE YOURSELF ALL PRETTY FOR HER, AND HERE SHE IS YELLING AT YOU!
EH?
EH?
JUDY, DID YOU INVITE HER OVER?! WHEN I TOLD YOU EARLIER THAT I WAS TAKING CONTROL OF THE SITUATION, THAT DIDN'T MEAN THAT I WAS READY TO EXPLAIN IT ALL TO HER!
WHISPER
WHISPER
WELL, NOW THAT YOU'RE ON THE EDGE OF THE CLIFF, ALL YOU HAVE TO DO IS TAKE A DEEP BREATH AND JUMP!
GRAP

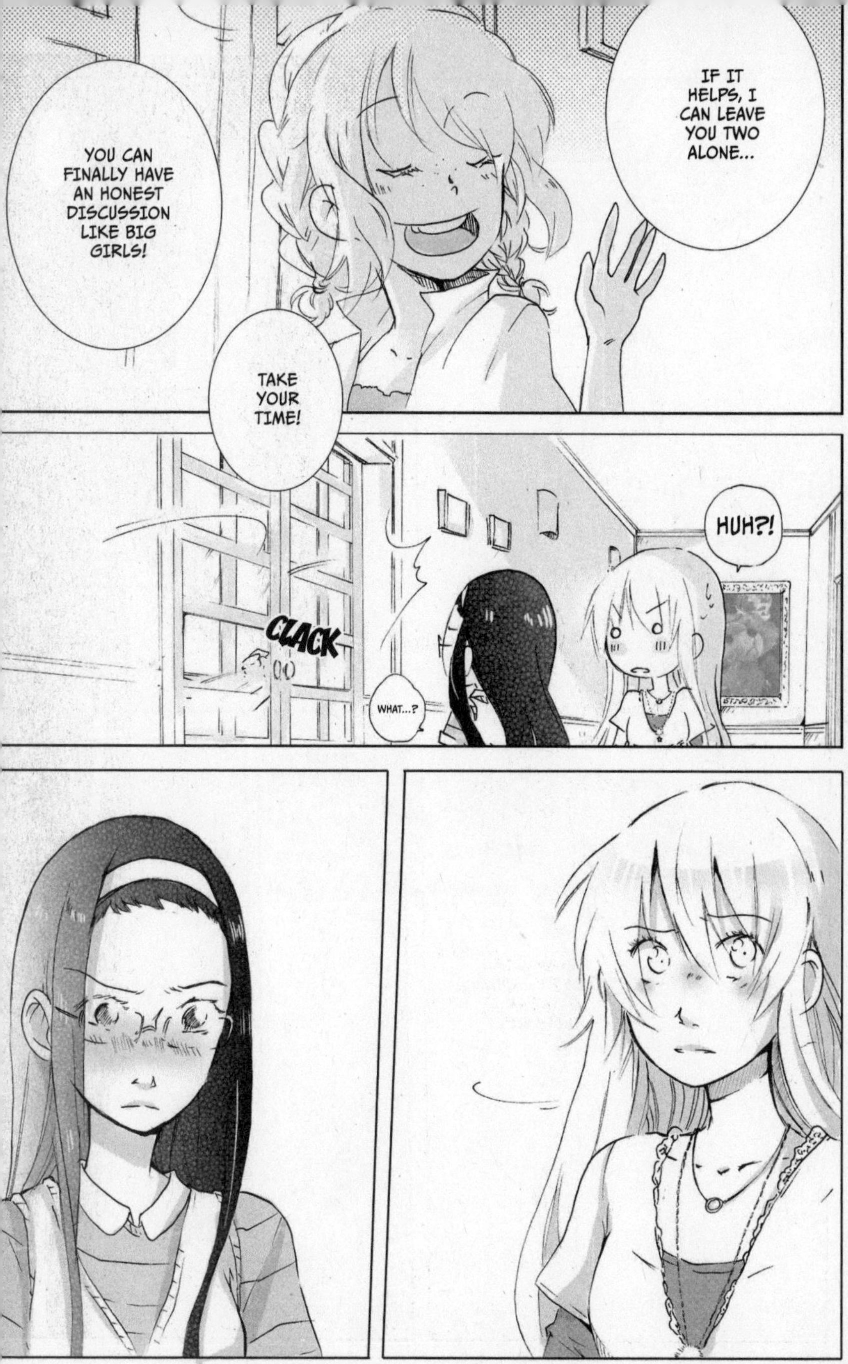
IF IT HELPS, I CAN LEAVE YOU TWO ALONE...
YOU CAN FINALLY HAVE AN HONEST DISCUSSION LIKE BIG GIRLS!
TAKE YOUR TIME!
HUH?!
CLACK
WHAT...?

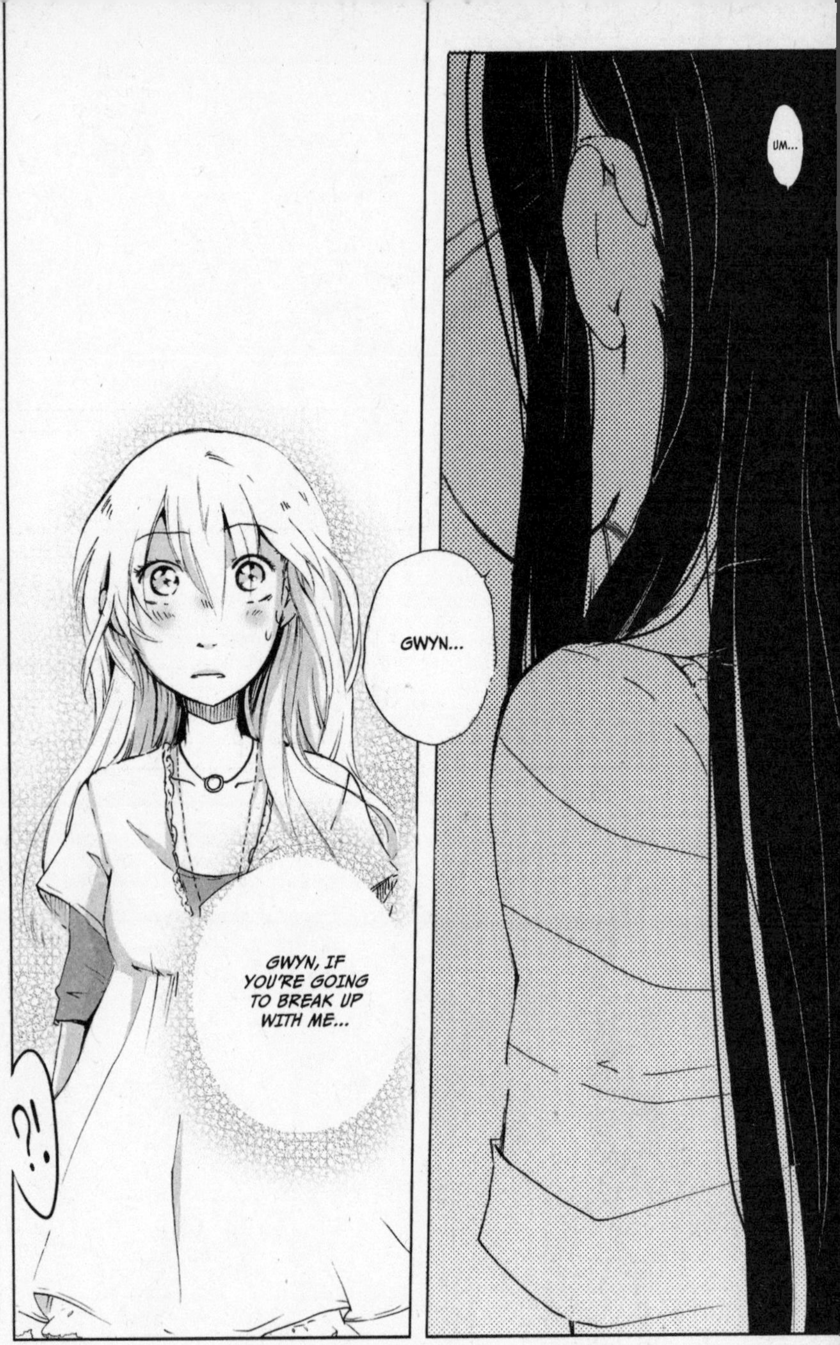
UM...
GWYN...
GWYN, IF YOU'RE GOING TO BREAK UP WITH ME...
?!

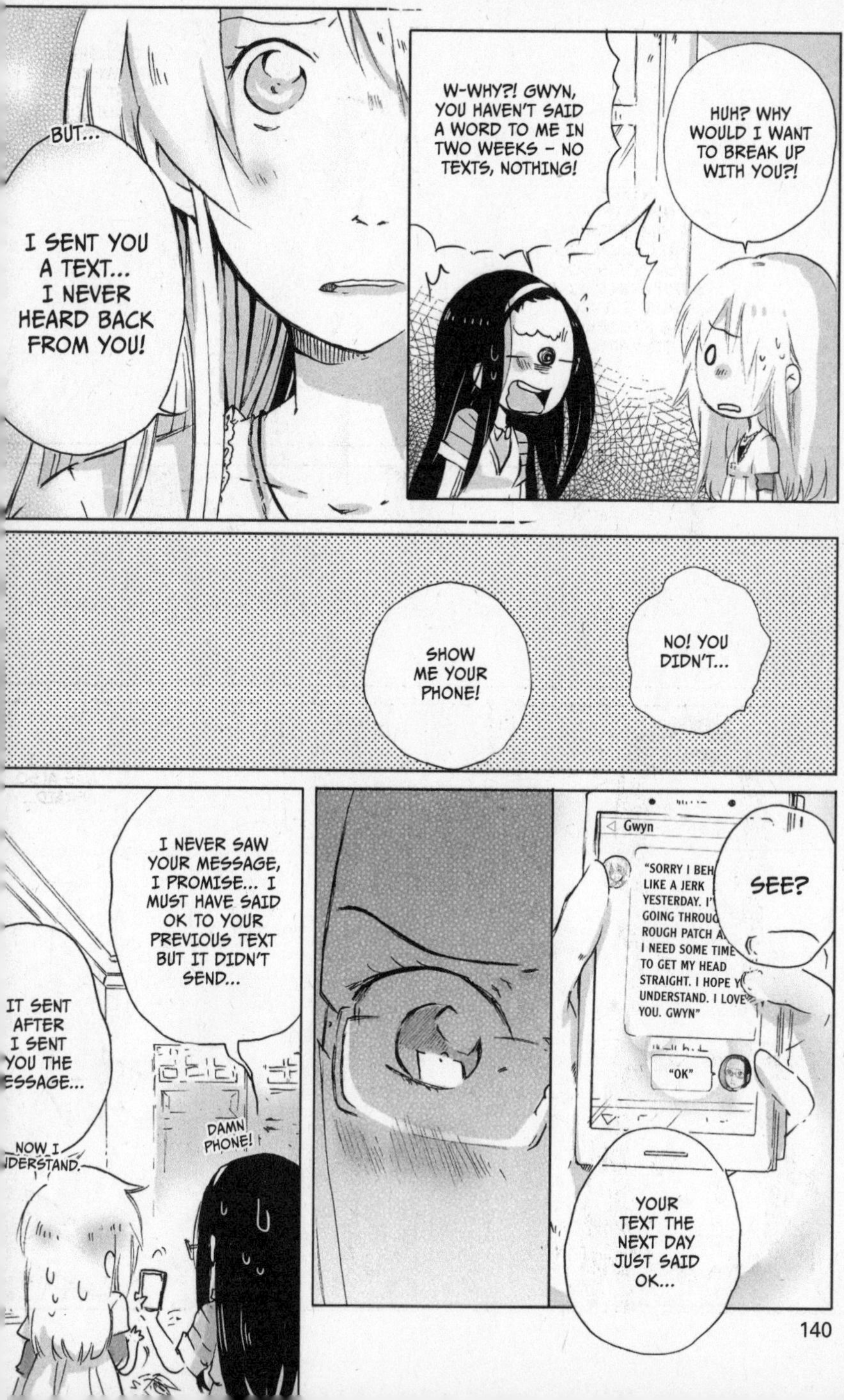
HUH? WHY WOULD I WANT TO BREAK UP WITH YOU?!
W-WHY?! GWYN, YOU HAVEN'T SAID A WORD TO ME IN TWO WEEKS - NO TEXTS, NOTHING!
BUT...
I SENT YOU A TEXT... I NEVER HEARD BACK FROM YOU!
NO! YOU DIDN'T...
SHOW ME YOUR PHONE!
SEE?
Gwyn
"SORRY I BEH
LIKE A JERK
YESTERDAY. I'
GOING THROUG
ROUGH PATCH A
I NEED SOME TIME
TO GET MY HEAD
STRAIGHT. I HOPE Y
UNDERSTAND. I LOVE
YOU. GWYN"
"OK"
YOUR TEXT THE NEXT DAY JUST SAID OK...
I NEVER SAW YOUR MESSAGE, I PROMISE... I MUST HAVE SAID OK TO YOUR PREVIOUS TEXT BUT IT DIDN'T SEND...
IT SENT AFTER I SENT YOU THE ESSAGE...
DAMN PHONE!
NOW I DERSTAND.

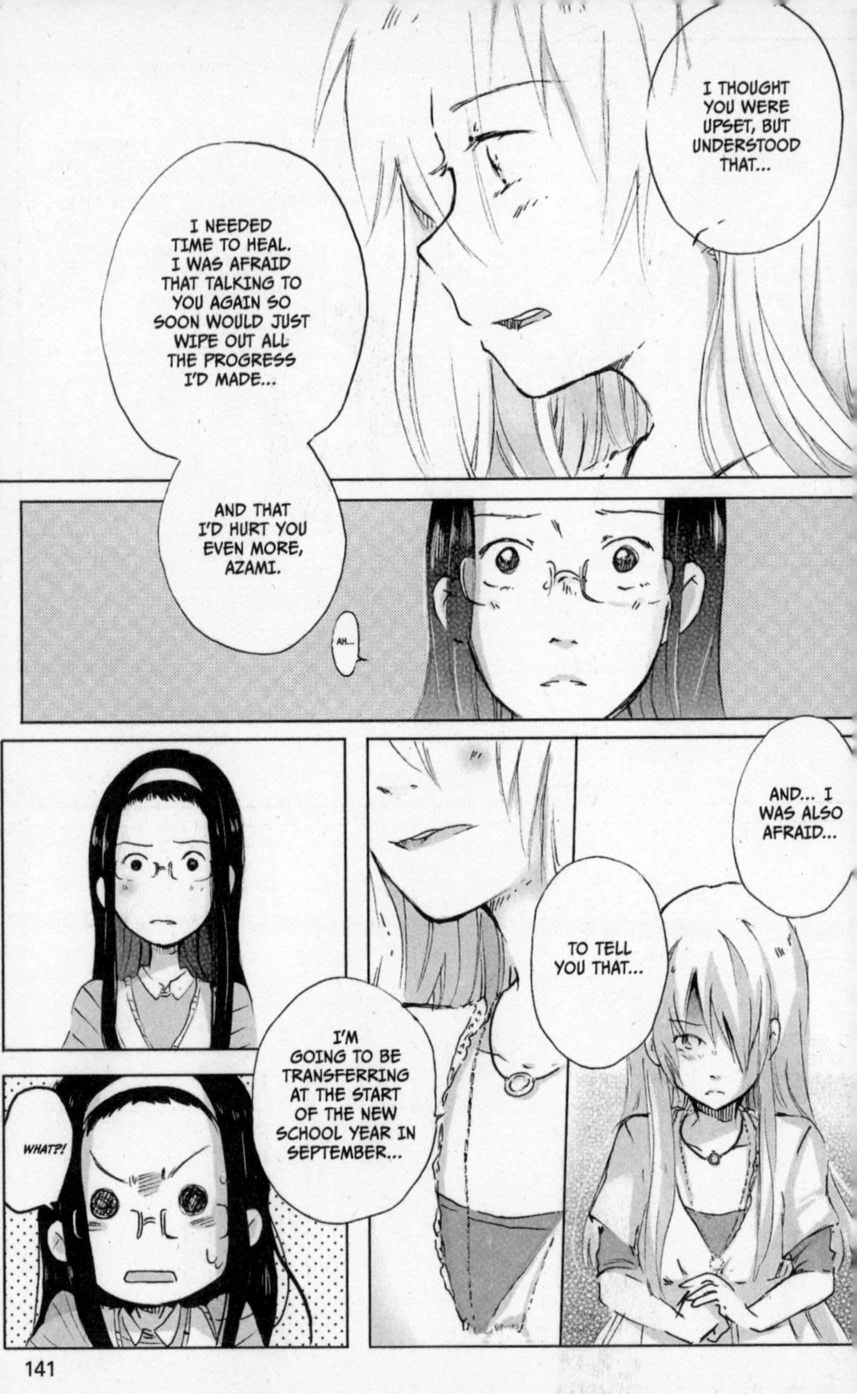
I THOUGHT YOU WERE UPSET, BUT UNDERSTOOD THAT...
I NEEDED TIME TO HEAL. I WAS AFRAID THAT TALKING TO YOU AGAIN SO SOON WOULD JUST WIPE OUT ALL THE PROGRESS I'D MADE...
AND THAT I'D HURT YOU EVEN MORE, AZAMI.
AH...
AND... I WAS ALSO AFRAID...
TO TELL YOU THAT...
I'M GOING TO BE TRANSFERRING AT THE START OF THE NEW SCHOOL YEAR IN SEPTEMBER...
WHAT?!

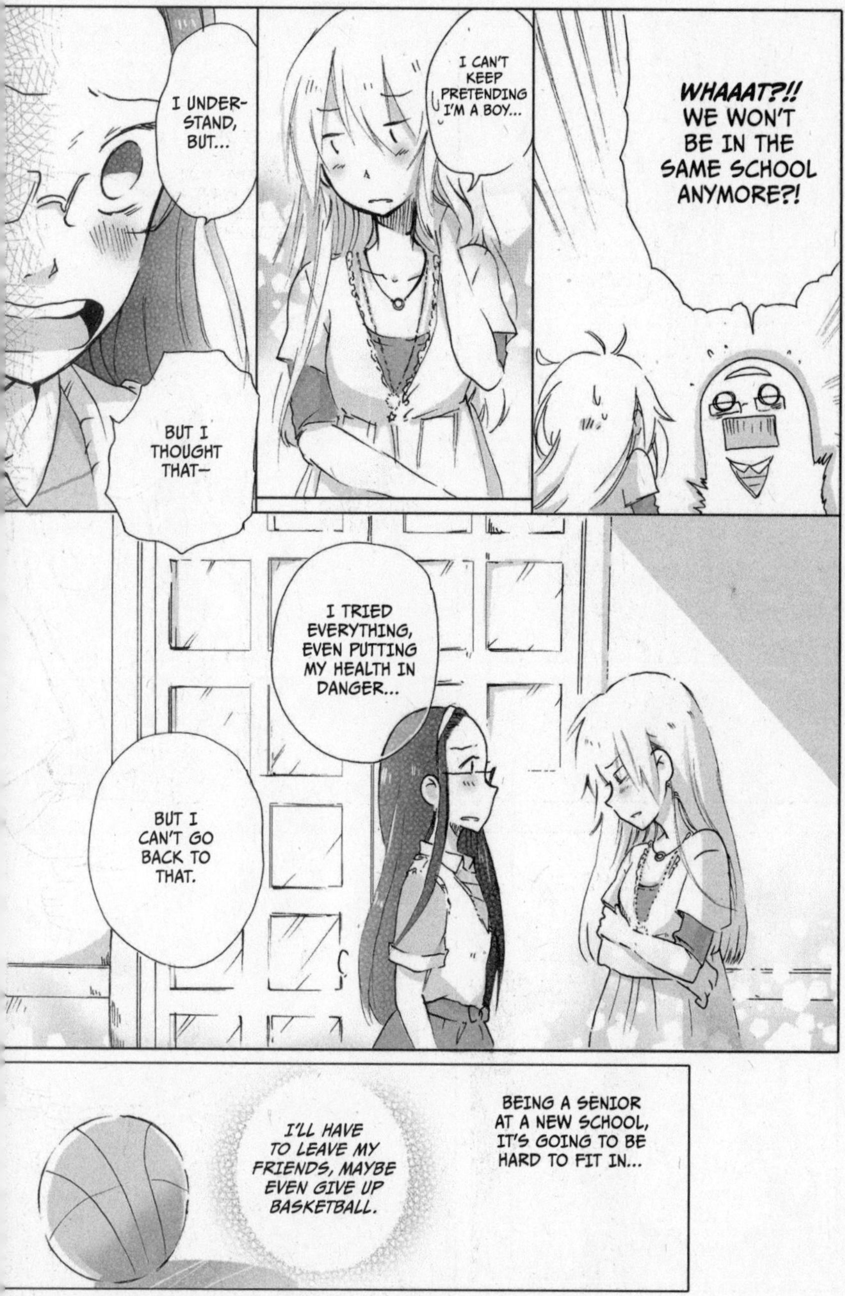
WHAAAT?!! WE WON'T BE IN THE SAME SCHOOL ANYMORE?!
I CAN'T KEEP PRETENDING I'M A BOY...
I UNDER-STAND, BUT...
BUT I THOUGHT THAT—
I TRIED EVERYTHING, EVEN PUTTING MY HEALTH IN DANGER...
BUT I CAN'T GO BACK TO THAT.
BEING A SENIOR AT A NEW SCHOOL, IT'S GOING TO BE HARD TO FIT IN...
I'LL HAVE TO LEAVE MY FRIENDS, MAYBE EVEN GIVE UP BASKETBALL.

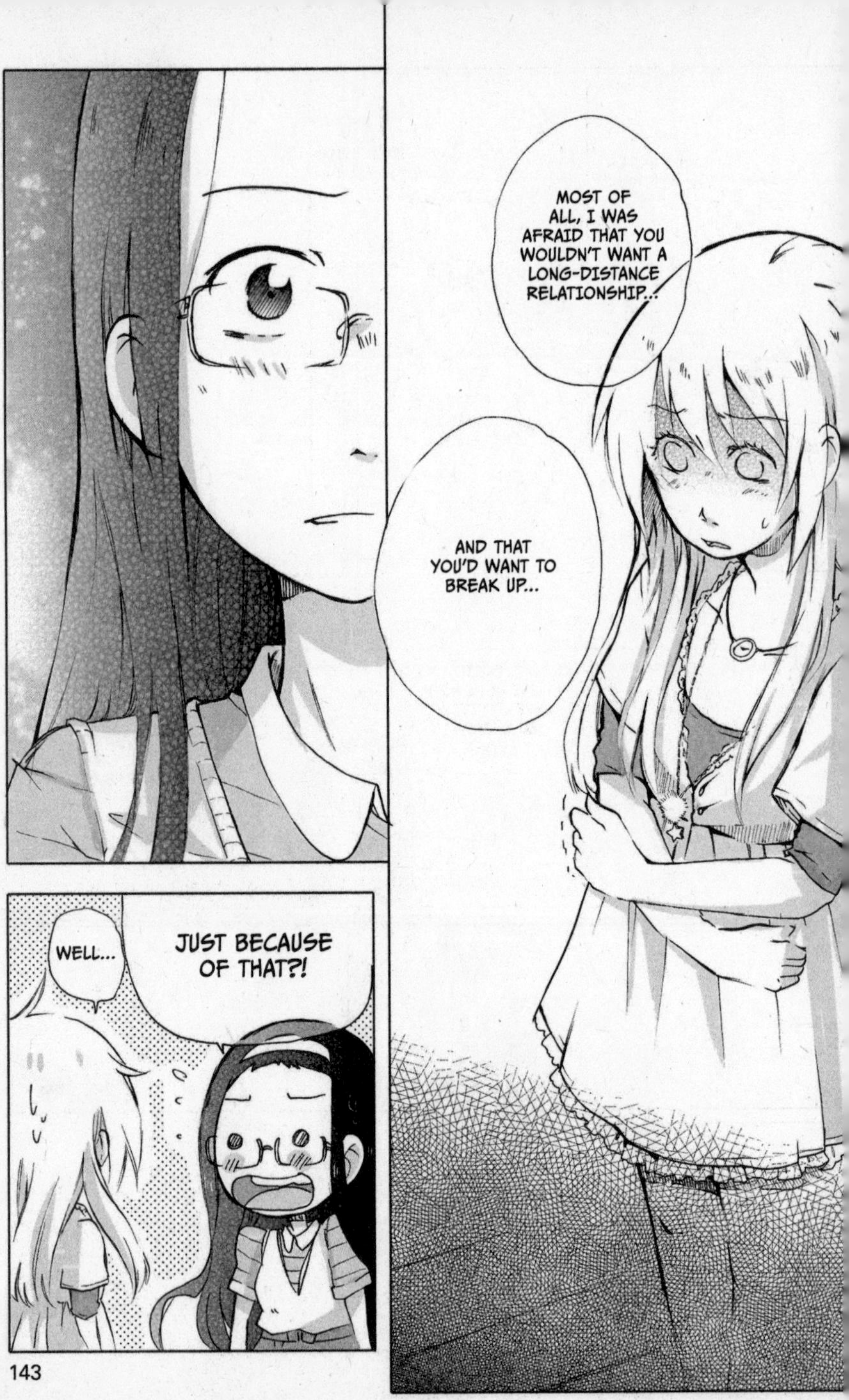
MOST OF ALL, I WAS AFRAID THAT YOU WOULDN'T WANT A LONG-DISTANCE RELATIONSHIP...
AND THAT YOU'D WANT TO BREAK UP...
JUST BECAUSE OF THAT?!
WELL...

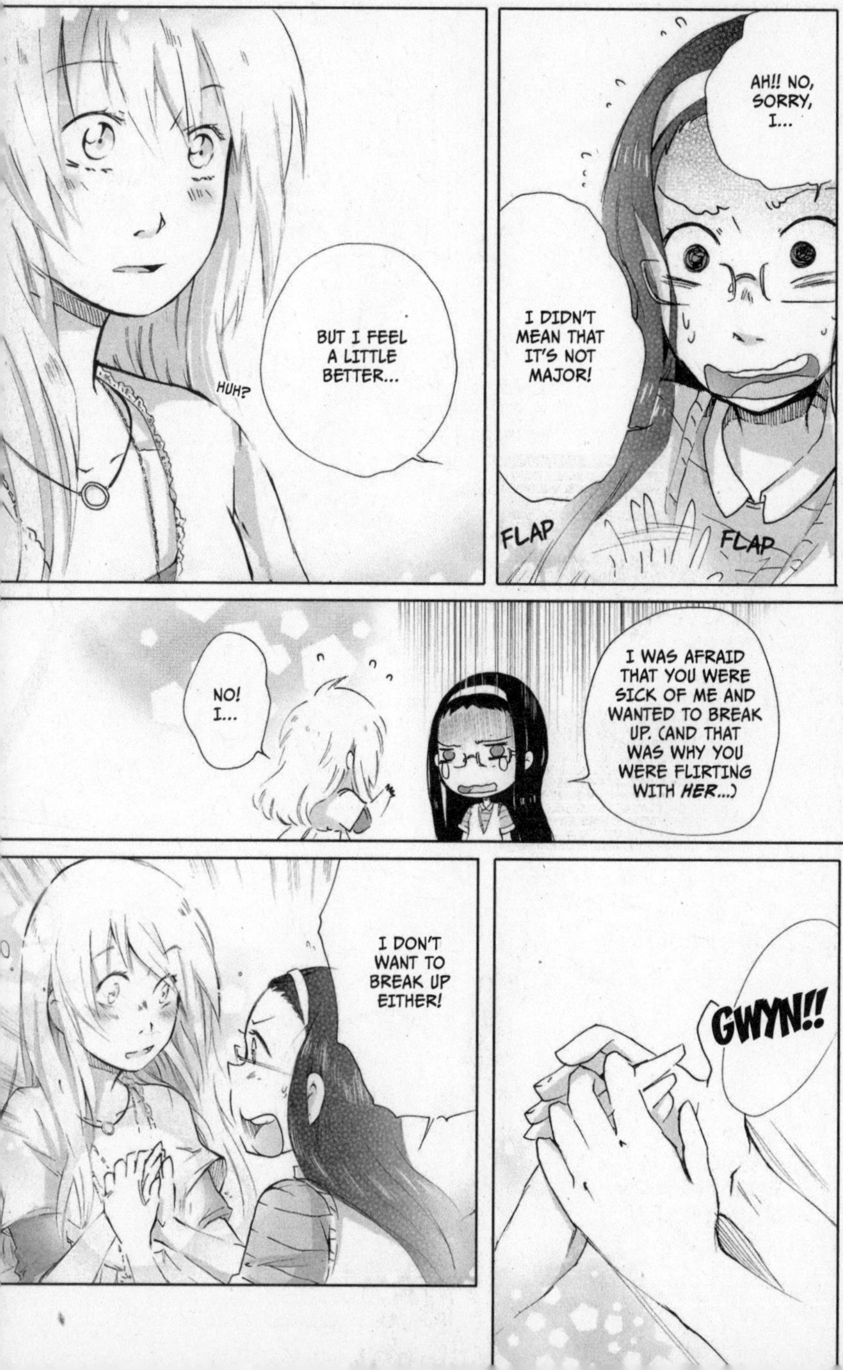
AH!! NO, SORRY, I...
I DIDN'T MEAN THAT IT'S NOT MAJOR!
FLAP
FLAP
HUH?
BUT I FEEL A LITTLE BETTER...
I WAS AFRAID THAT YOU WERE SICK OF ME AND WANTED TO BREAK UP. (AND THAT WAS WHY YOU WERE FLIRTING WITH HER...)
NO! I...
GWYN!!
I DON'T WANT TO BREAK UP EITHER!

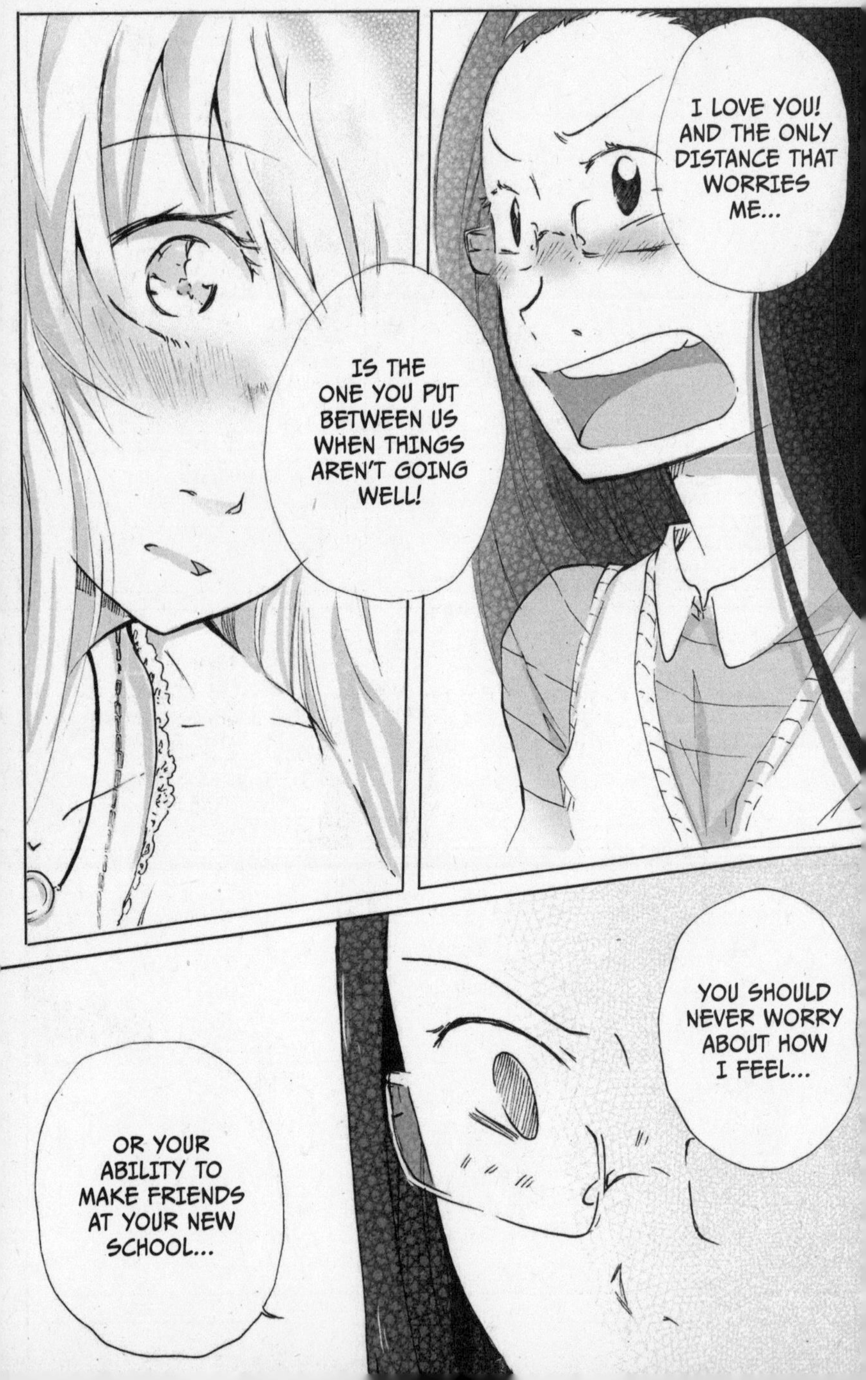
I LOVE YOU! AND THE ONLY DISTANCE THAT WORRIES ME...
IS THE ONE YOU PUT BETWEEN US WHEN THINGS AREN'T GOING WELL!
YOU SHOULD NEVER WORRY ABOUT HOW I FEEL...
OR YOUR ABILITY TO MAKE FRIENDS AT YOUR NEW SCHOOL...

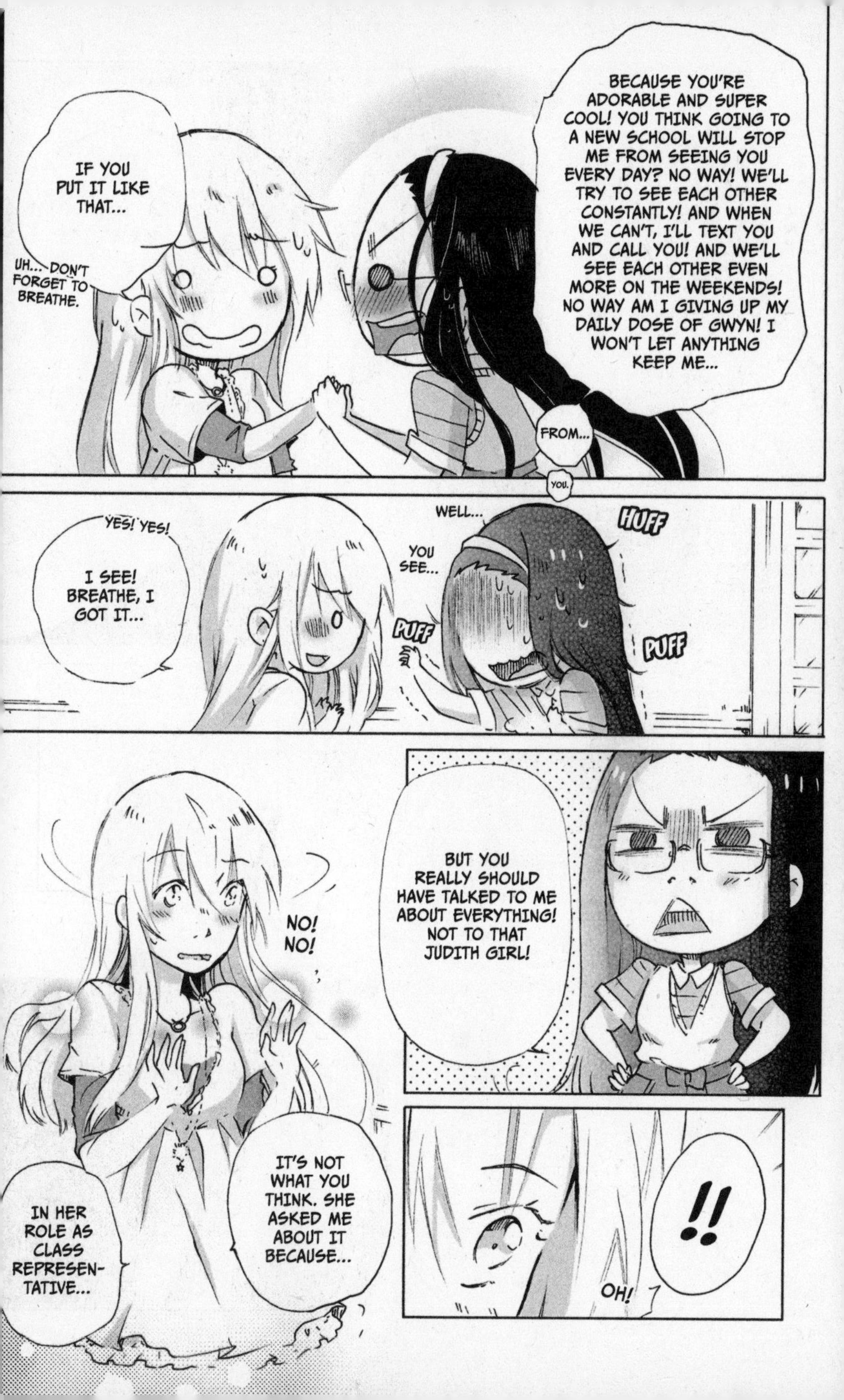
BECAUSE YOU'RE ADORABLE AND SUPER COOL! YOU THINK GOING TO A NEW SCHOOL WILL STOP ME FROM SEEING YOU EVERY DAY? NO WAY! WE'LL TRY TO SEE EACH OTHER CONSTANTLY! AND WHEN WE CAN'T, I'LL TEXT YOU AND CALL YOU! AND WE'LL SEE EACH OTHER EVEN MORE ON THE WEEKENDS! NO WAY AM I GIVING UP MY DAILY DOSE OF GWYN! I WON'T LET ANYTHING KEEP ME...
FROM...
YOU.
IF YOU PUT IT LIKE THAT...
UH... DON'T FORGET TO BREATHE.
HUFF
WELL...
YOU SEE...
PUFF
PUFF
YES! YES!
I SEE! BREATHE, I GOT IT...
BUT YOU REALLY SHOULD HAVE TALKED TO ME ABOUT EVERYTHING! NOT TO THAT JUDITH GIRL!
!!
OH!
NO! NO!
IT'S NOT WHAT YOU THINK. SHE ASKED ME ABOUT IT BECAUSE...
IN HER ROLE AS CLASS REPRESEN-TATIVE...

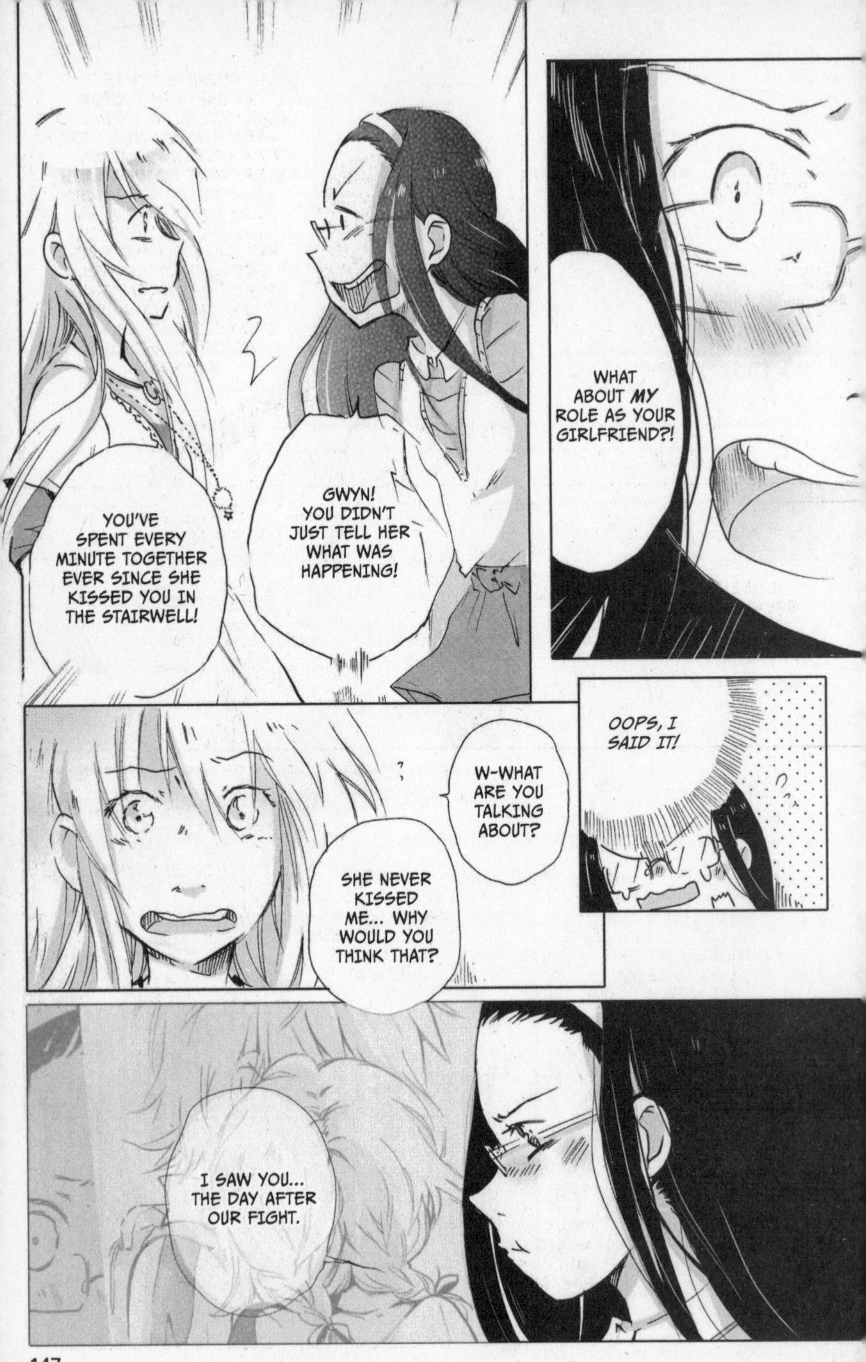
WHAT ABOUT *MY* ROLE AS YOUR GIRLFRIEND?!
GWYN! YOU DIDN'T JUST TELL HER WHAT WAS HAPPENING!
YOU'VE SPENT EVERY MINUTE TOGETHER EVER SINCE SHE KISSED YOU IN THE STAIRWELL!
OOPS, I SAID IT!
W-WHAT ARE YOU TALKING ABOUT?
SHE NEVER KISSED ME... WHY WOULD YOU THINK THAT?
I SAW YOU... THE DAY AFTER OUR FIGHT.

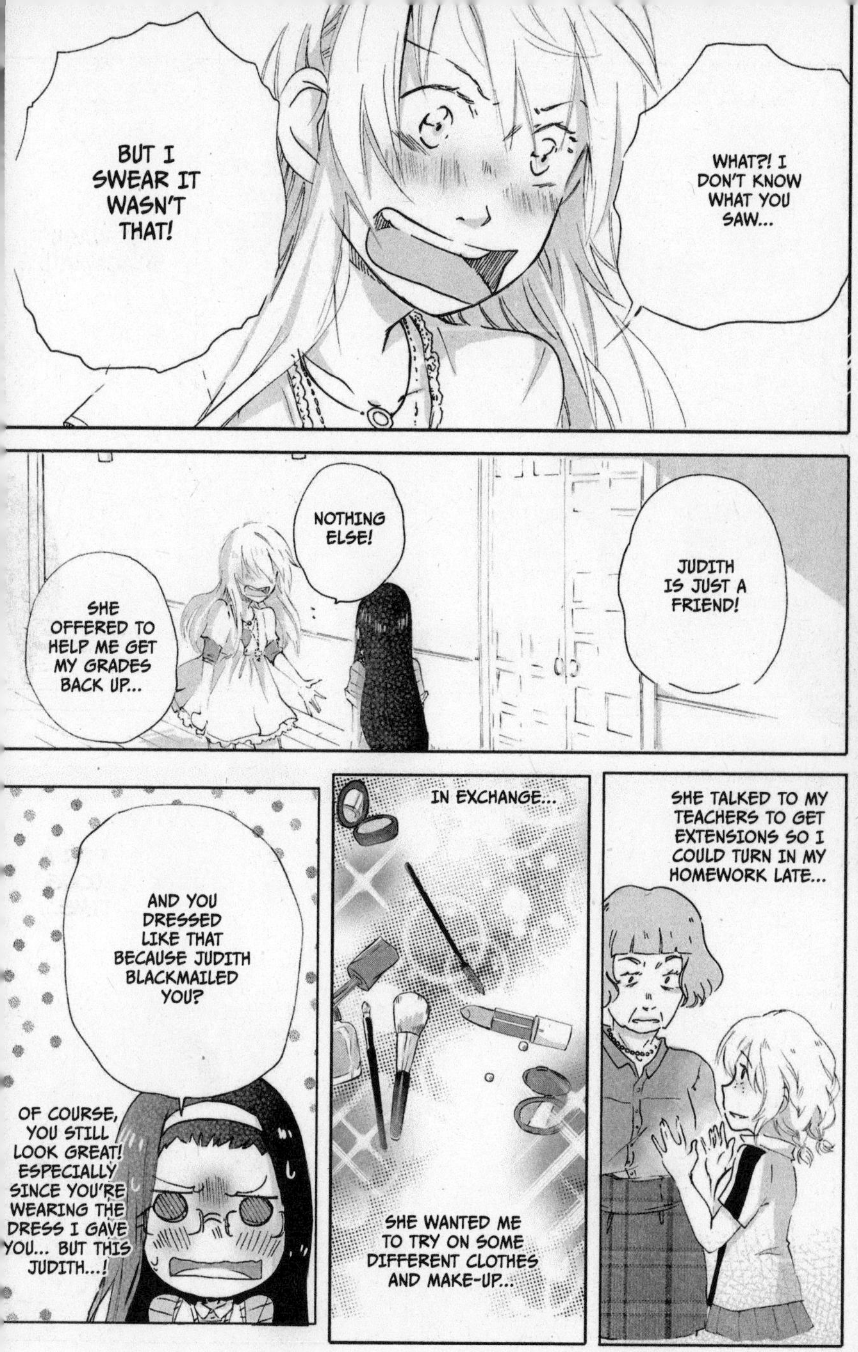
WHAT?! I DON'T KNOW WHAT YOU SAW...
BUT I SWEAR IT WASN'T THAT!
JUDITH IS JUST A FRIEND!
NOTHING ELSE!
SHE OFFERED TO HELP ME GET MY GRADES BACK UP...
SHE TALKED TO MY TEACHERS TO GET EXTENSIONS SO I COULD TURN IN MY HOMEWORK LATE...
IN EXCHANGE...
SHE WANTED ME TO TRY ON SOME DIFFERENT CLOTHES AND MAKE-UP...
AND YOU DRESSED LIKE THAT BECAUSE JUDITH BLACKMAILED YOU?
OF COURSE, YOU STILL LOOK GREAT! ESPECIALLY SINCE YOU'RE WEARING THE DRESS I GAVE YOU... BUT THIS JUDITH...!

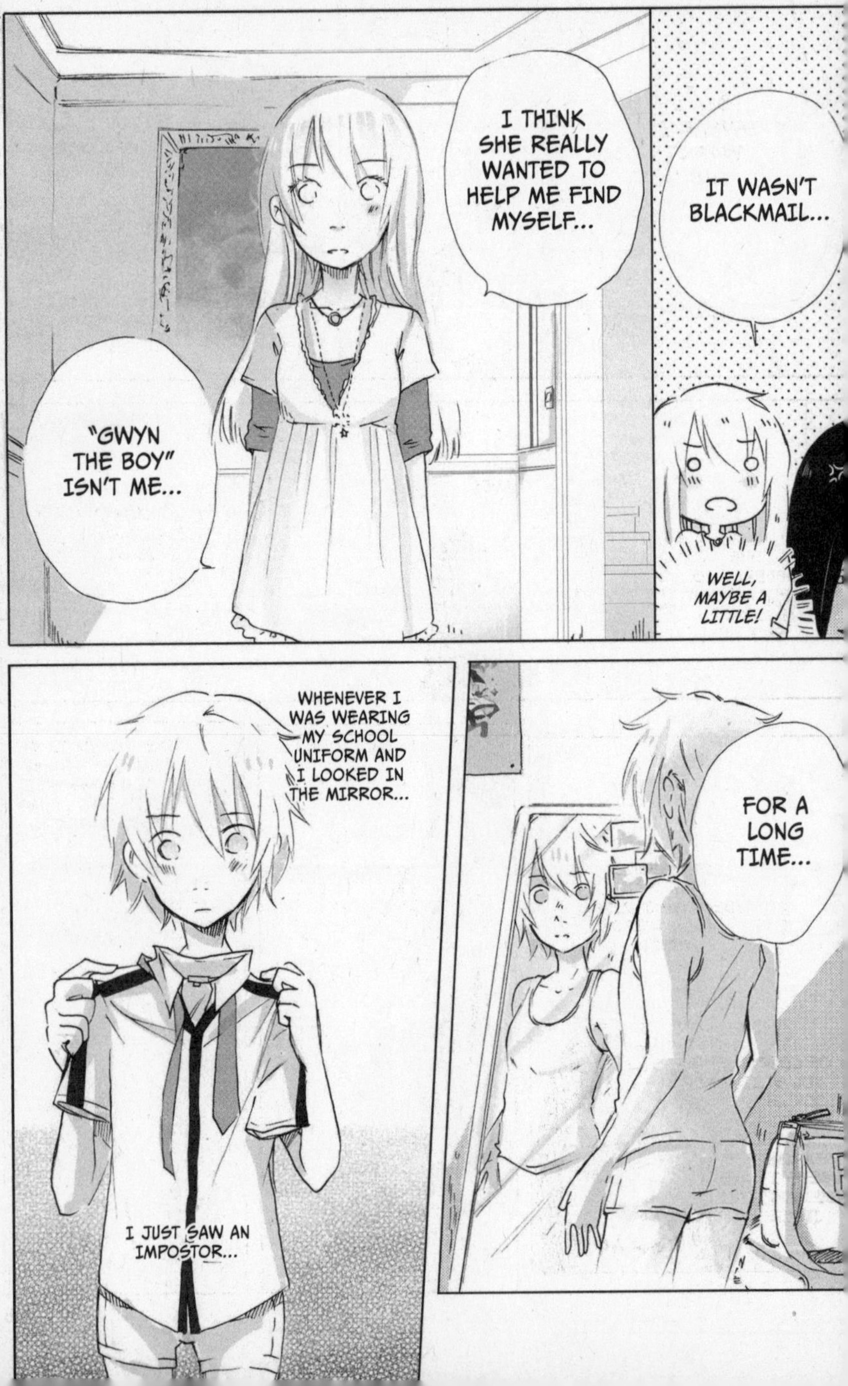
IT WASN'T BLACKMAIL...
WELL, MAYBE A LITTLE!
I THINK SHE REALLY WANTED TO HELP ME FIND MYSELF...
"GWYN THE BOY" ISN'T ME...
FOR A LONG TIME...
WHENEVER I WAS WEARING MY SCHOOL UNIFORM AND I LOOKED IN THE MIRROR...
I JUST SAW AN IMPOSTOR...

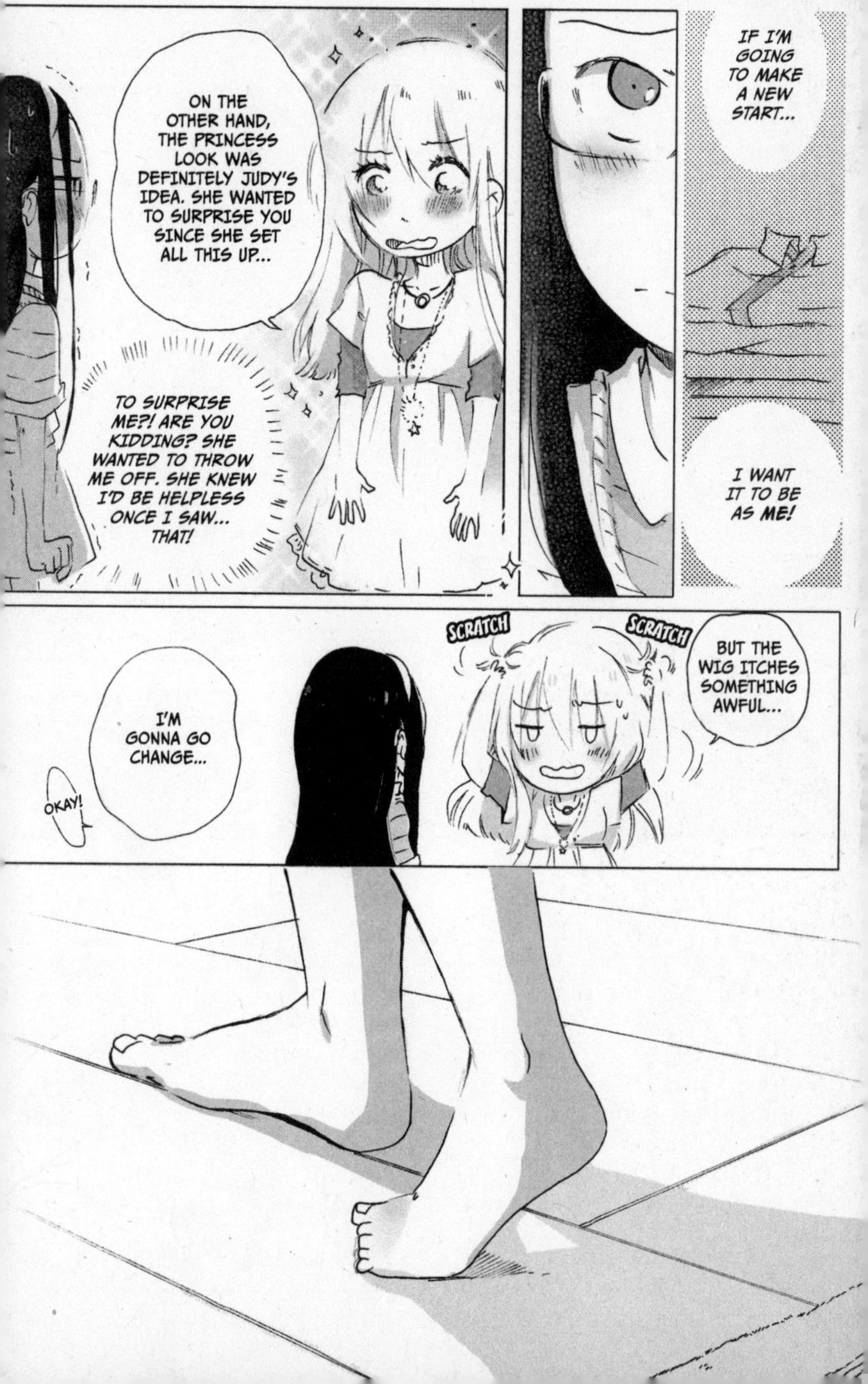
IF I'M GOING TO MAKE A NEW START...
I WANT IT TO BE AS ME!
ON THE OTHER HAND, THE PRINCESS LOOK WAS DEFINITELY JUDY'S IDEA. SHE WANTED TO SURPRISE YOU SINCE SHE SET ALL THIS UP...
TO SURPRISE ME?! ARE YOU KIDDING? SHE WANTED TO THROW ME OFF. SHE KNEW I'D BE HELPLESS ONCE I SAW... THAT!
SCRATCH
SCRATCH
BUT THE WIG ITCHES SOMETHING AWFUL...
I'M GONNA GO CHANGE...
OKAY!

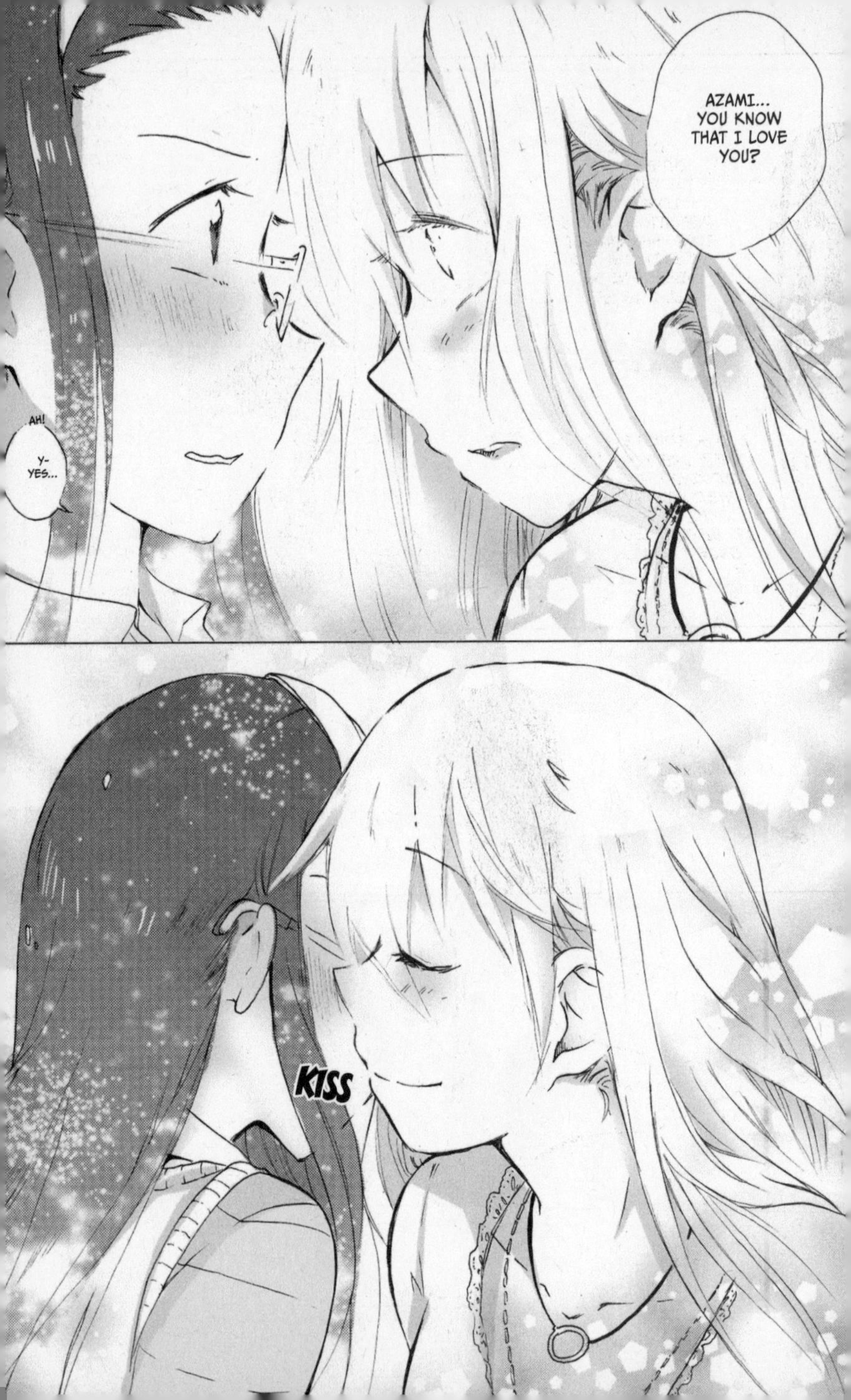
AZAMI... YOU KNOW THAT I LOVE YOU?
AH! Y- YES...
KISS

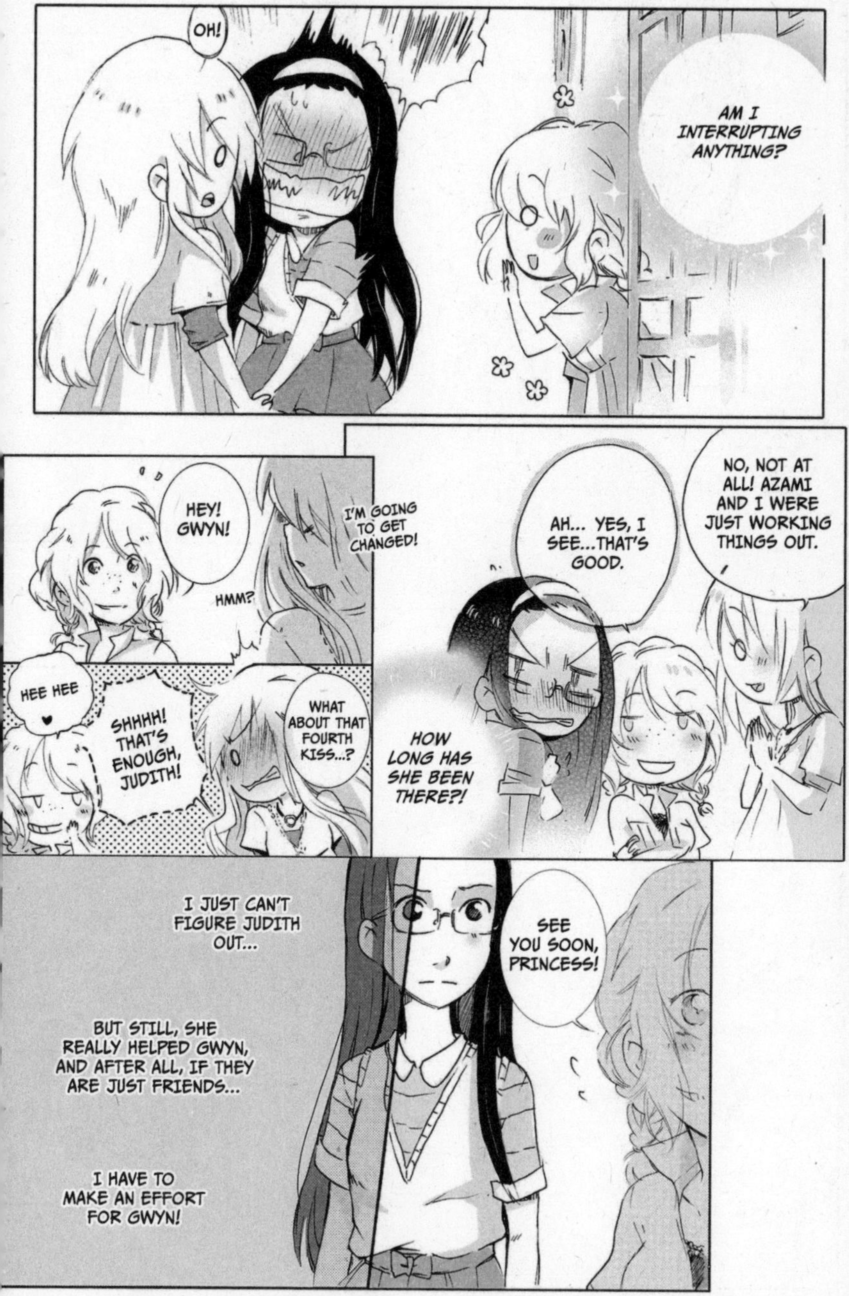
AM I INTERRUPTING ANYTHING?
OH!
NO, NOT AT ALL! AZAMI AND I WERE JUST WORKING THINGS OUT.
AH... YES, I SEE...THAT'S GOOD.
HOW LONG HAS SHE BEEN THERE?!
I'M GOING TO GET CHANGED!
HMM?
HEY! GWYN!
WHAT ABOUT THAT FOURTH KISS...?
SHHHH! THAT'S ENOUGH, JUDITH!
HEE HEE
SEE YOU SOON, PRINCESS!
I JUST CAN'T FIGURE JUDITH OUT...
BUT STILL, SHE REALLY HELPED GWYN, AND AFTER ALL, IF THEY ARE JUST FRIENDS...
I HAVE TO MAKE AN EFFORT FOR GWYN!

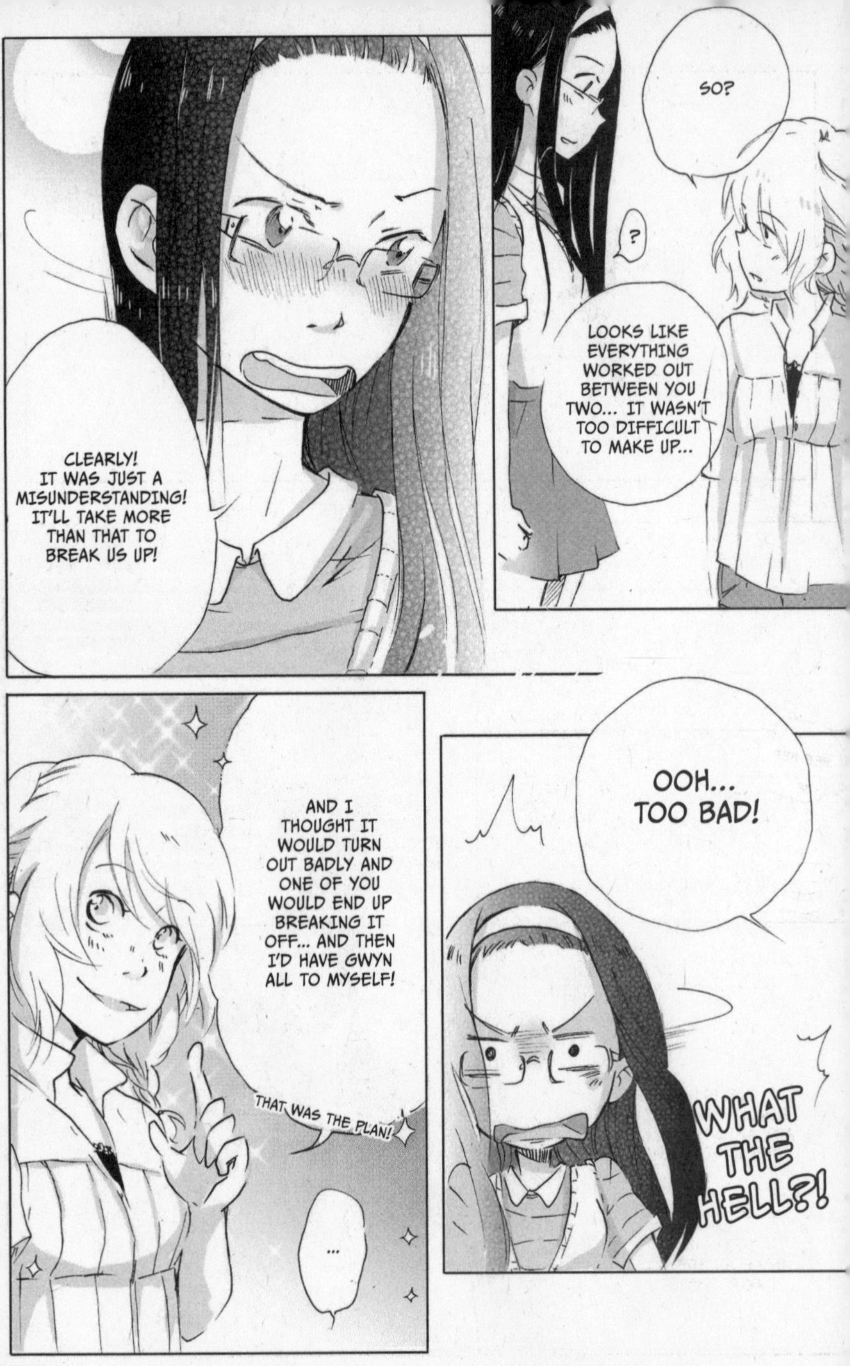
SO?
?
LOOKS LIKE EVERYTHING WORKED OUT BETWEEN YOU TWO... IT WASN'T TOO DIFFICULT TO MAKE UP...
CLEARLY! IT WAS JUST A MISUNDERSTANDING! IT'LL TAKE MORE THAN THAT TO BREAK US UP!
OOH... TOO BAD!
WHAT THE HELL?!
AND I THOUGHT IT WOULD TURN OUT BADLY AND ONE OF YOU WOULD END UP BREAKING IT OFF... AND THEN I'D HAVE GWYN ALL TO MYSELF!
THAT WAS THE PLAN!
...

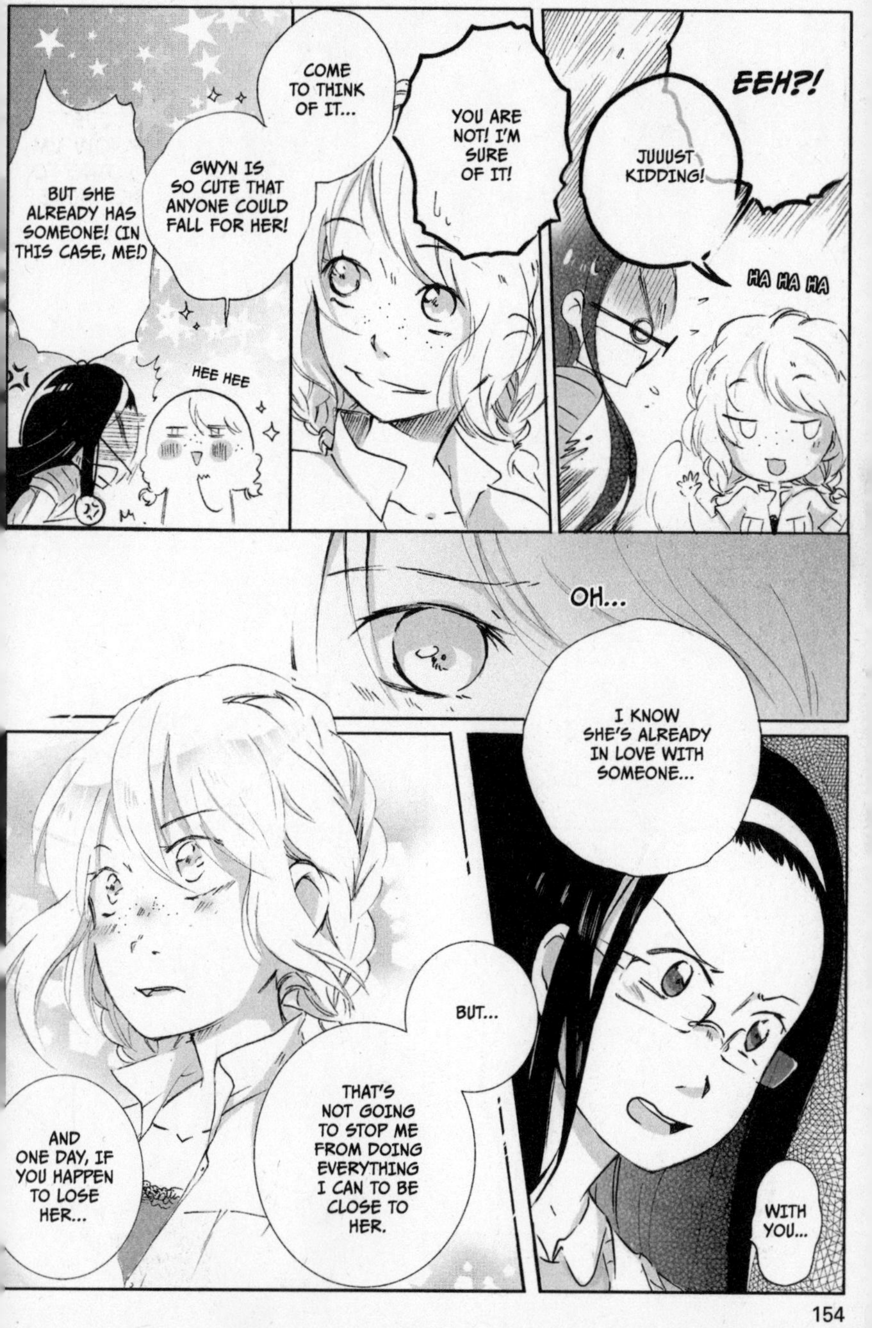
COME TO THINK OF IT...
GWYN IS SO CUTE THAT ANYONE COULD FALL FOR HER!
BUT SHE ALREADY HAS SOMEONE! (IN THIS CASE, ME!)
HEE HEE
YOU ARE NOT! I'M SURE OF IT!
EEH?!
JUUUST KIDDING!
HA HA HA
OH...
I KNOW SHE'S ALREADY IN LOVE WITH SOMEONE...
BUT...
THAT'S NOT GOING TO STOP ME FROM DOING EVERYTHING I CAN TO BE CLOSE TO HER.
AND ONE DAY, IF YOU HAPPEN TO LOSE HER...
WITH YOU...

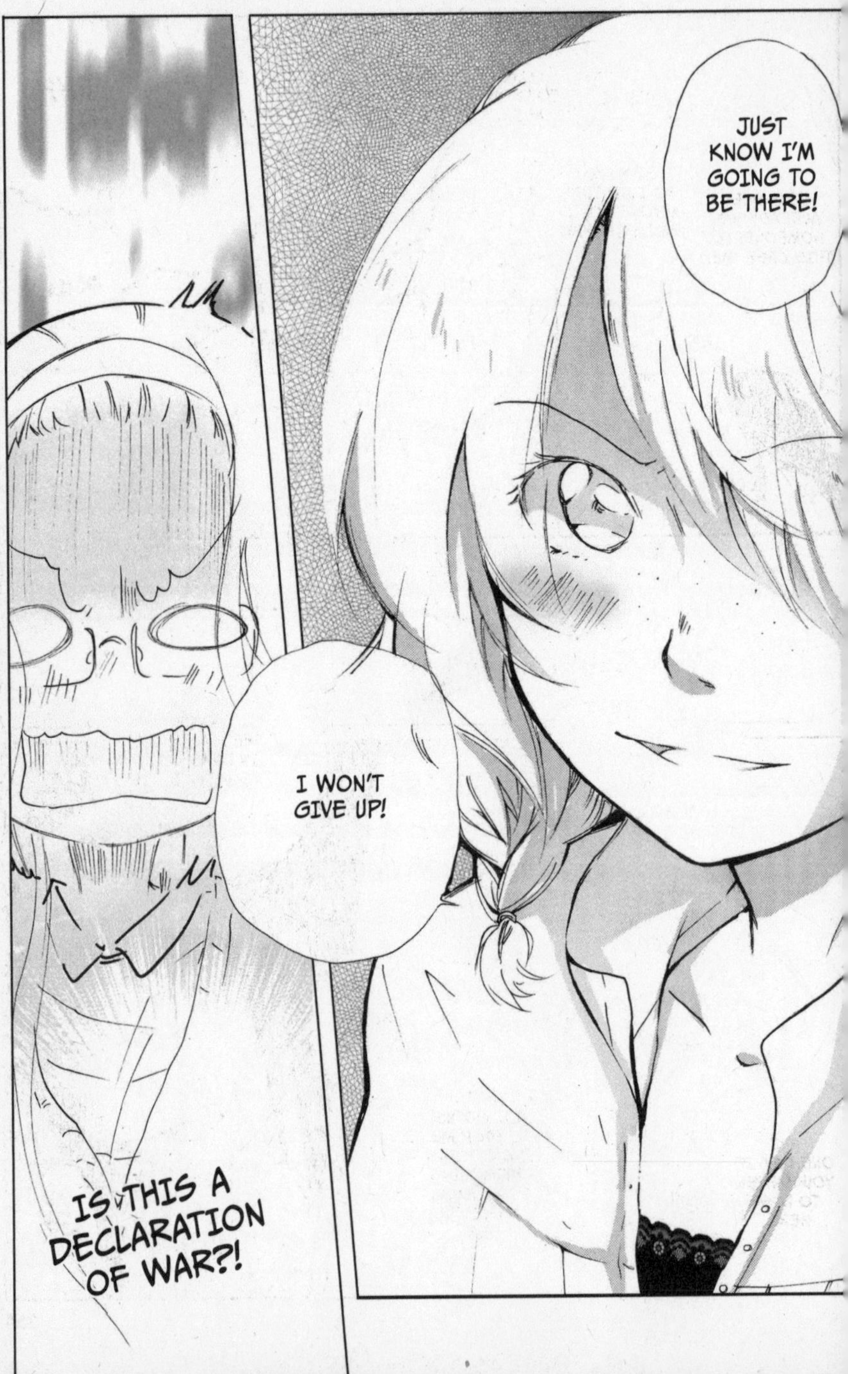
JUST KNOW I'M GOING TO BE THERE!
I WON'T GIVE UP!
IS THIS A DECLARATION OF WAR?!

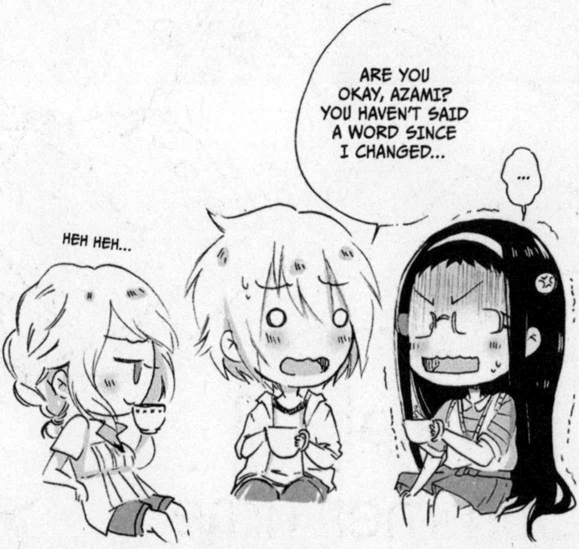
ARE YOU OKAY, AZAMI? YOU HAVEN'T SAID A WORD SINCE I CHANGED...
...
HEH HEH...

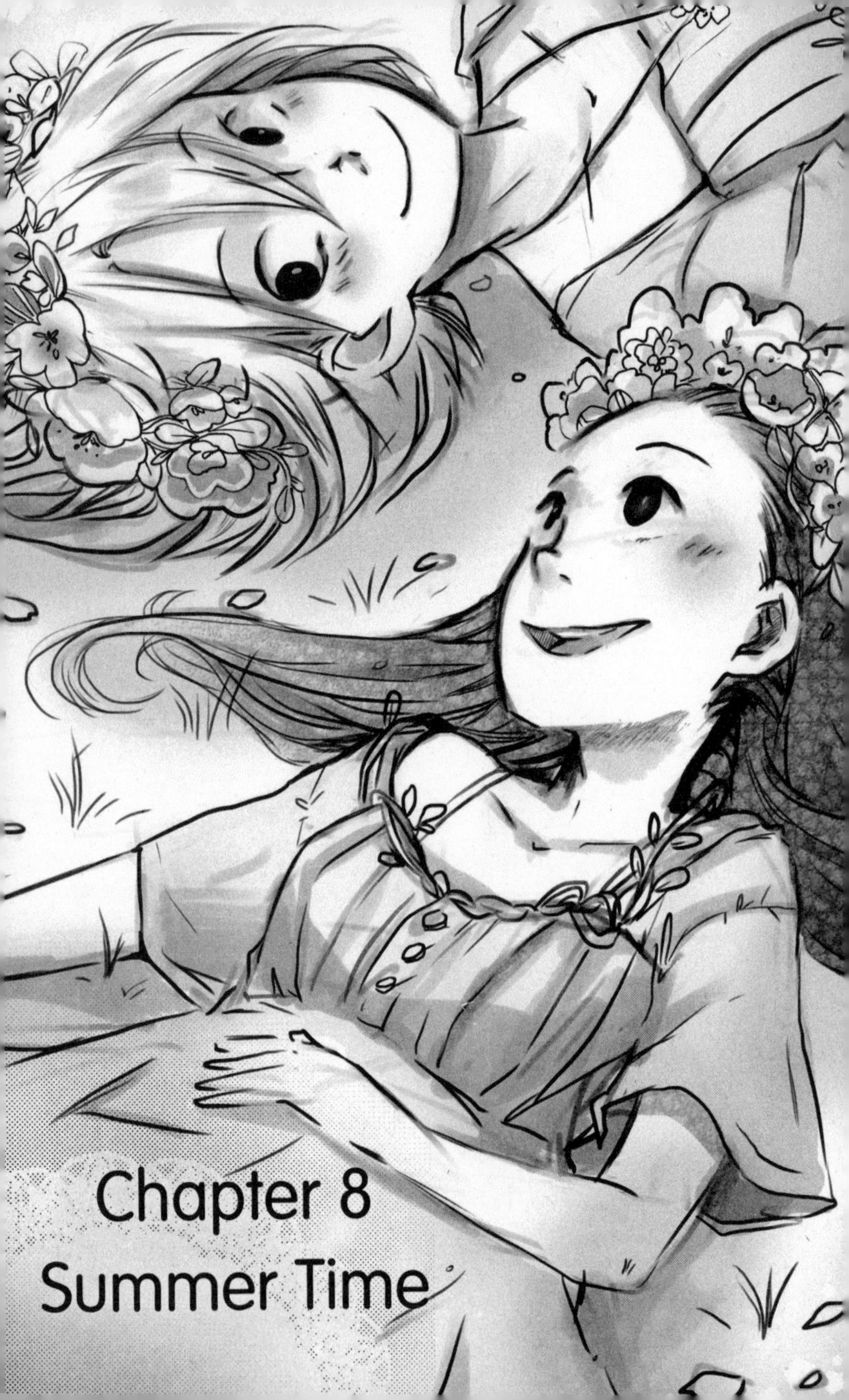
Chapter 8
Summer Time

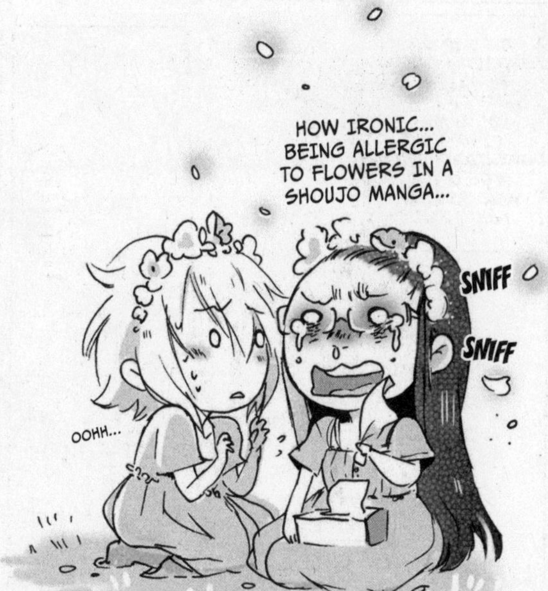
HOW IRONIC... BEING ALLERGIC TO FLOWERS IN A SHOUJO MANGA...
SNIFF
SNIFF
OOHH...

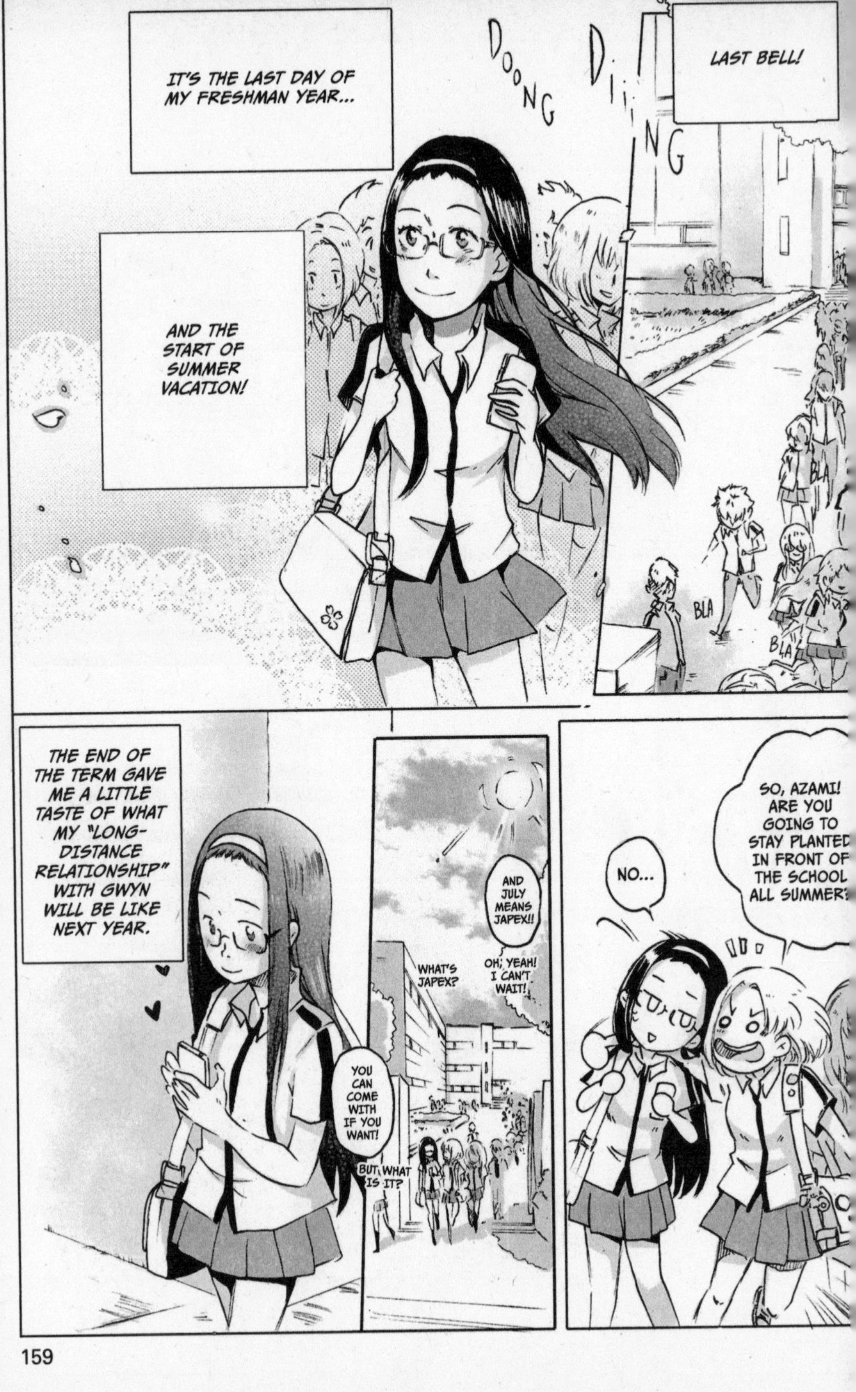
LAST BELL!
DIIING
DOONG
BLA
BLA
BLA
IT'S THE LAST DAY OF MY FRESHMAN YEAR...
AND THE START OF SUMMER VACATION!
SO, AZAMI! ARE YOU GOING TO STAY PLANTED IN FRONT OF THE SCHOOL ALL SUMMER?
NO...
AND JULY MEANS JAPEX!!
OH, YEAH! I CAN'T WAIT!
WHAT'S JAPEX?
YOU CAN COME WITH IF YOU WANT!
BUT, WHAT IS IT?
THE END OF THE TERM GAVE ME A LITTLE TASTE OF WHAT MY "LONG-DISTANCE RELATIONSHIP" WITH GWYN WILL BE LIKE NEXT YEAR.

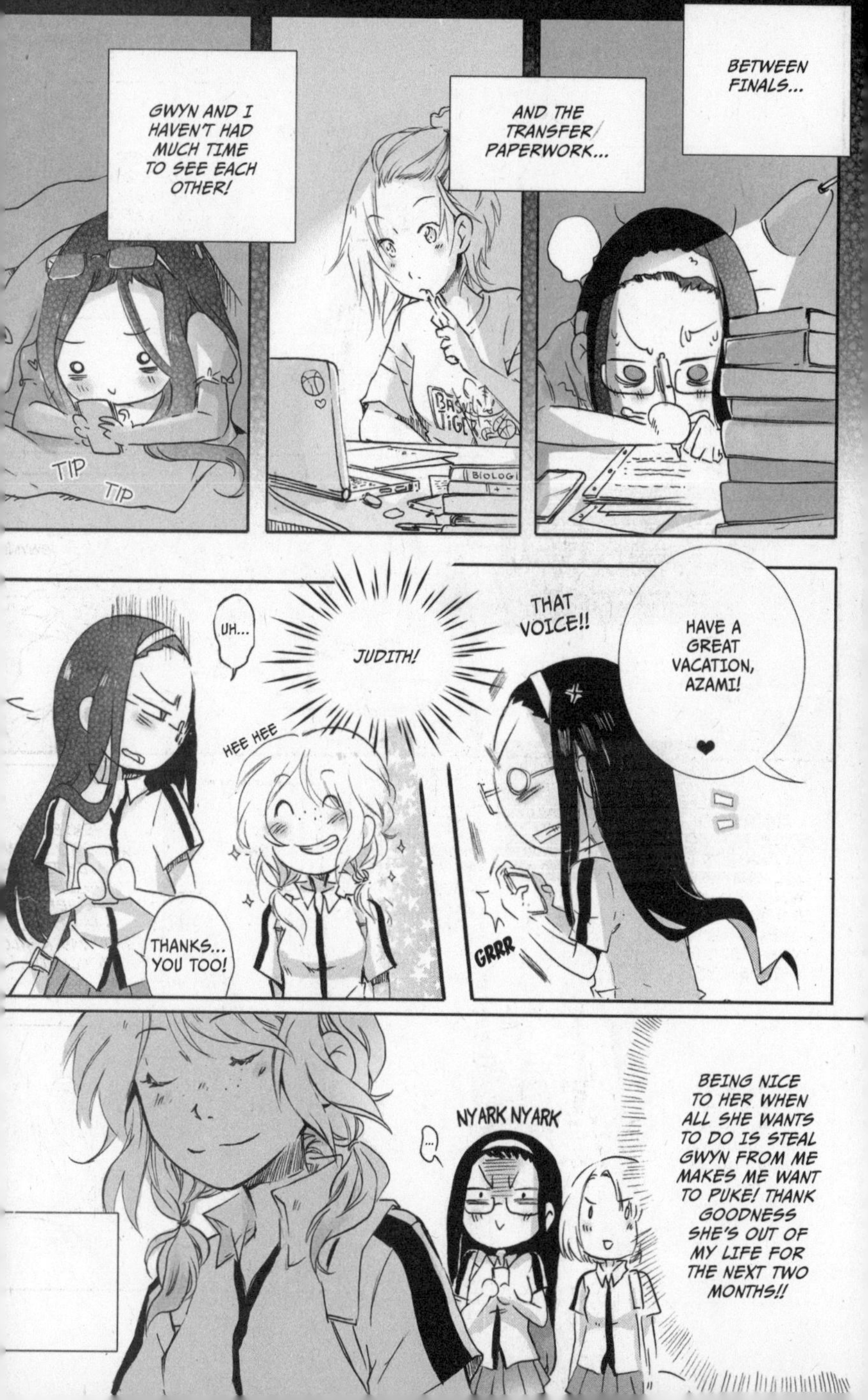
BETWEEN FINALS...
AND THE TRANSFER PAPERWORK...
GWYN AND I HAVEN'T HAD MUCH TIME TO SEE EACH OTHER!
TIP
TIP
HAVE A GREAT VACATION, AZAMI! ❤
THAT VOICE!!
GRRR
JUDITH!
UH...
HEE HEE
THANKS... YOU TOO!
BEING NICE TO HER WHEN ALL SHE WANTS TO DO IS STEAL GWYN FROM ME MAKES ME WANT TO PUKE! THANK GOODNESS SHE'S OUT OF MY LIFE FOR THE NEXT TWO MONTHS!!
NYARK NYARK
...

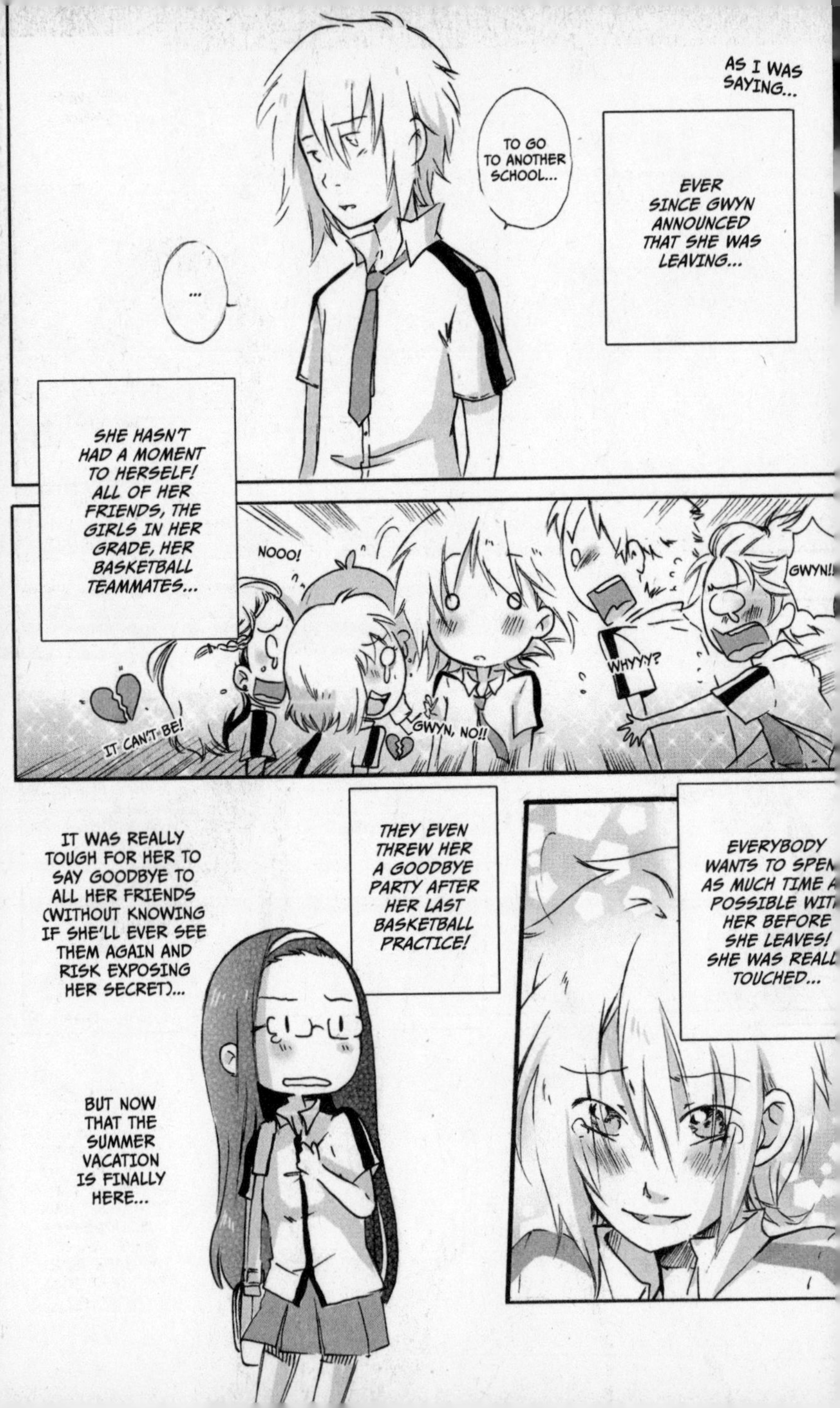
AS I WAS SAYING...
EVER SINCE GWYN ANNOUNCED THAT SHE WAS LEAVING...
TO GO TO ANOTHER SCHOOL...
...
SHE HASN'T HAD A MOMENT TO HERSELF! ALL OF HER FRIENDS, THE GIRLS IN HER GRADE, HER BASKETBALL TEAMMATES...
GWYN!!
WHYYY?
NOOO!
GWYN, NO!!
IT CAN'T BE!
EVERYBODY WANTS TO SPEN AS MUCH TIME A POSSIBLE WIT HER BEFORE SHE LEAVES! SHE WAS REALL TOUCHED...
THEY EVEN THREW HER A GOODBYE PARTY AFTER HER LAST BASKETBALL PRACTICE!
IT WAS REALLY TOUGH FOR HER TO SAY GOODBYE TO ALL HER FRIENDS (WITHOUT KNOWING IF SHE'LL EVER SEE THEM AGAIN AND RISK EXPOSING HER SECRET)...
BUT NOW THAT THE SUMMER VACATION IS FINALLY HERE...

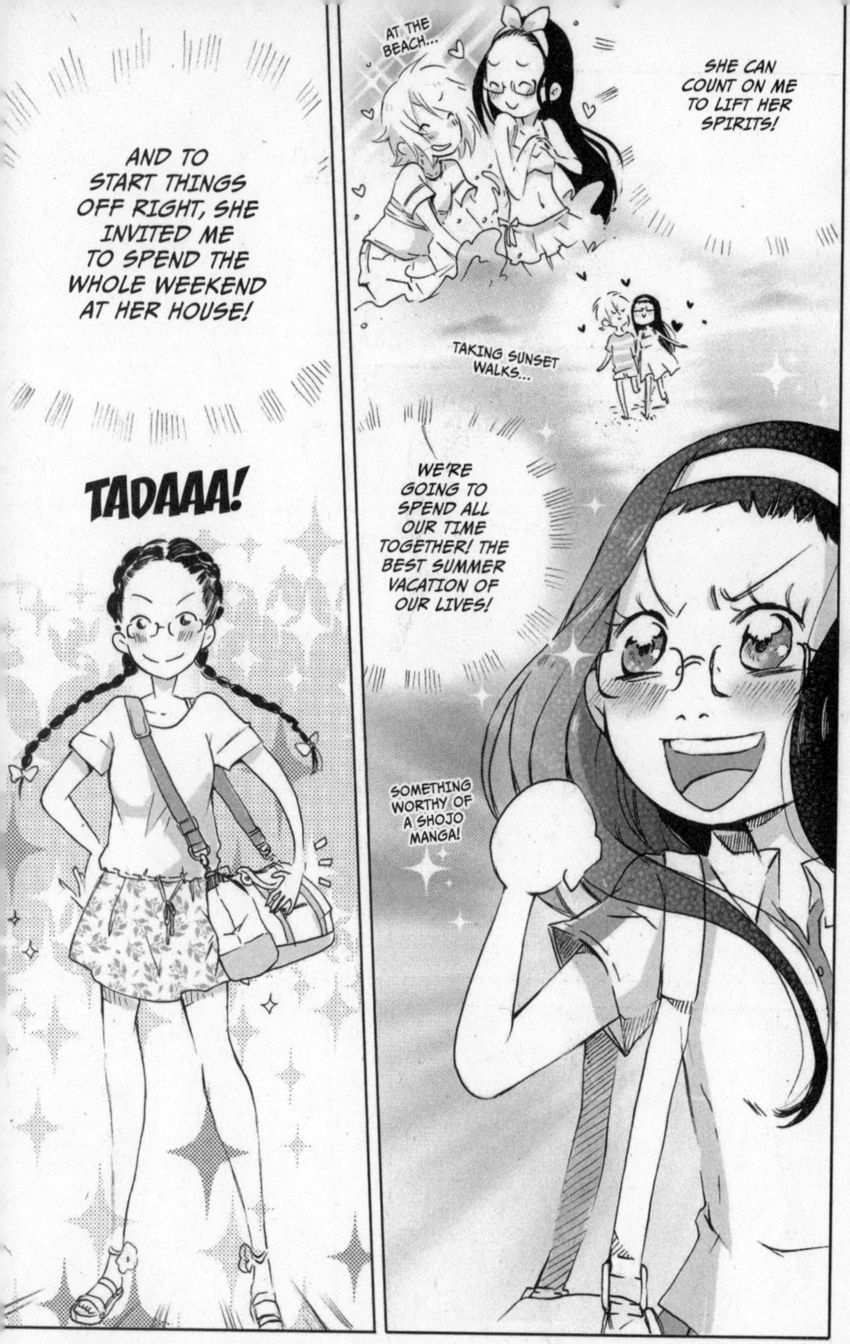
SHE CAN COUNT ON ME TO LIFT HER SPIRITS!
AT THE BEACH...
TAKING SUNSET WALKS...
WE'RE GOING TO SPEND ALL OUR TIME TOGETHER! THE BEST SUMMER VACATION OF OUR LIVES!
SOMETHING WORTHY OF A SHOJO MANGA!
AND TO START THINGS OFF RIGHT, SHE INVITED ME TO SPEND THE WHOLE WEEKEND AT HER HOUSE!
TADAAA!

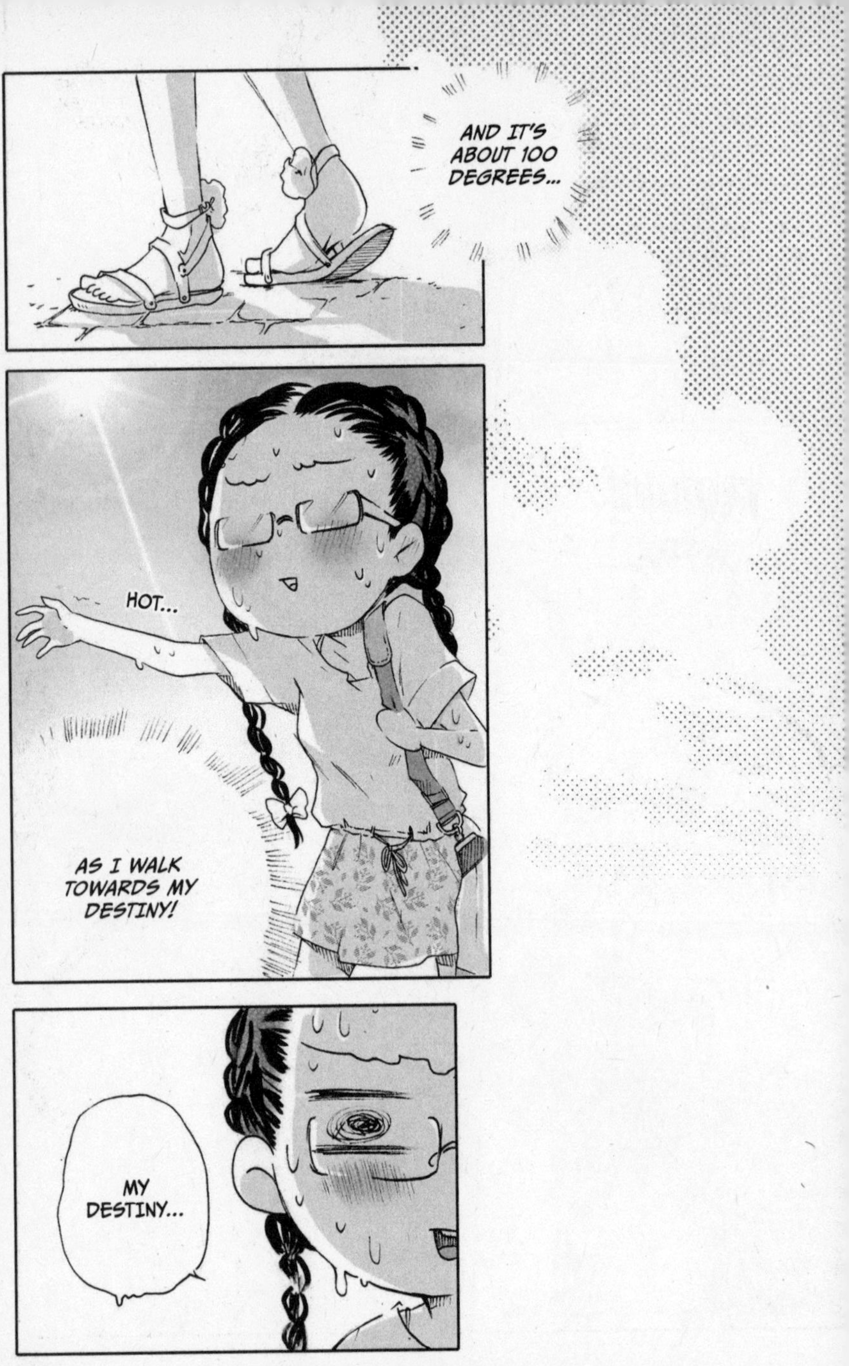
AND IT'S ABOUT 100 DEGREES...
HOT...
AS I WALK TOWARDS MY DESTINY!
MY DESTINY...

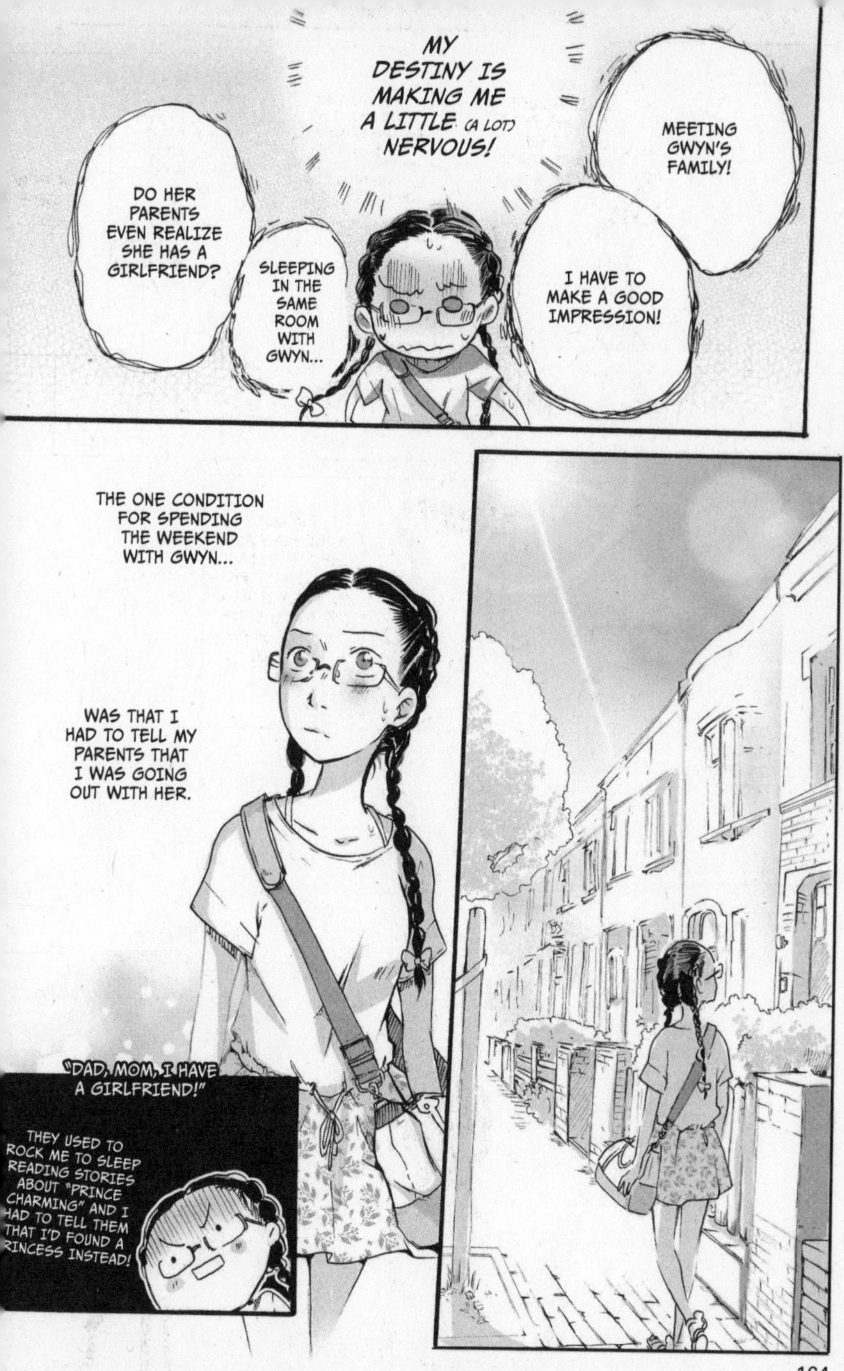
MY DESTINY IS MAKING ME A LITTLE (A LOT) NERVOUS!
MEETING GWYN'S FAMILY!
I HAVE TO MAKE A GOOD IMPRESSION!
SLEEPING IN THE SAME ROOM WITH GWYN...
DO HER PARENTS EVEN REALIZE SHE HAS A GIRLFRIEND?
THE ONE CONDITION FOR SPENDING THE WEEKEND WITH GWYN...
WAS THAT I HAD TO TELL MY PARENTS THAT I WAS GOING OUT WITH HER.
"DAD, MOM, I HAVE A GIRLFRIEND!"
THEY USED TO ROCK ME TO SLEEP READING STORIES ABOUT "PRINCE CHARMING" AND I HAD TO TELL THEM THAT I'D FOUND A PRINCESS INSTEAD!

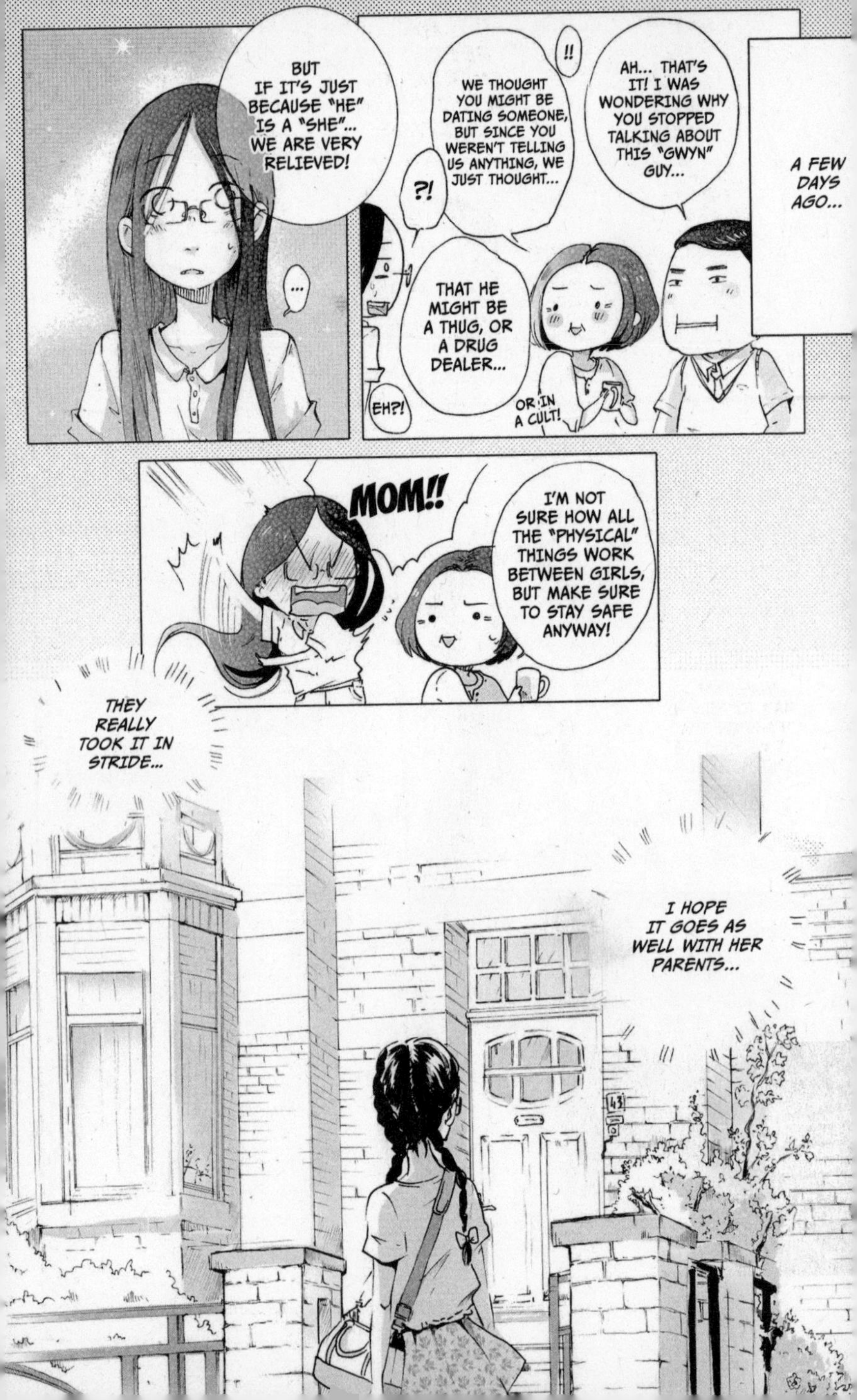
A FEW DAYS AGO...
AH... THAT'S IT! I WAS WONDERING WHY YOU STOPPED TALKING ABOUT THIS "GWYN" GUY...
!!
WE THOUGHT YOU MIGHT BE DATING SOMEONE, BUT SINCE YOU WEREN'T TELLING US ANYTHING, WE JUST THOUGHT...
?!
THAT HE MIGHT BE A THUG, OR A DRUG DEALER...
OR IN A CULT!
EH?!
BUT IF IT'S JUST BECAUSE "HE" IS A "SHE"... WE ARE VERY RELIEVED!
...
I'M NOT SURE HOW ALL THE "PHYSICAL" THINGS WORK BETWEEN GIRLS, BUT MAKE SURE TO STAY SAFE ANYWAY!
MOM!!
I HOPE IT GOES AS WELL WITH HER PARENTS...
43
THEY REALLY TOOK IT IN STRIDE...

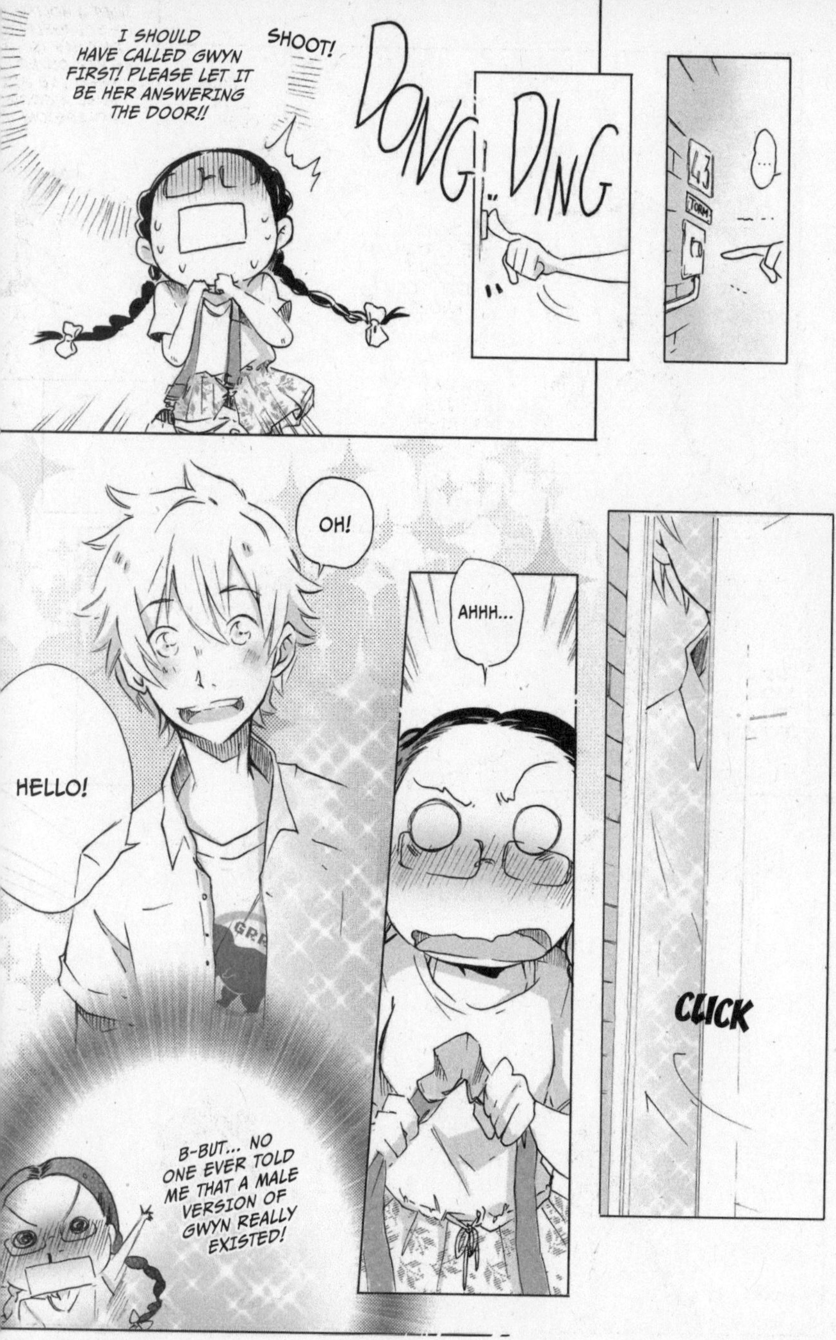

43
TORM
...
DING
DONG
SHOOT!
I SHOULD HAVE CALLED GWYN FIRST! PLEASE LET IT BE HER ANSWERING THE DOOR!!
CLICK
AHHH...
OH!
HELLO!
GRR
B-BUT... NO ONE EVER TOLD ME THAT A MALE VERSION OF GWYN REALLY EXISTED!

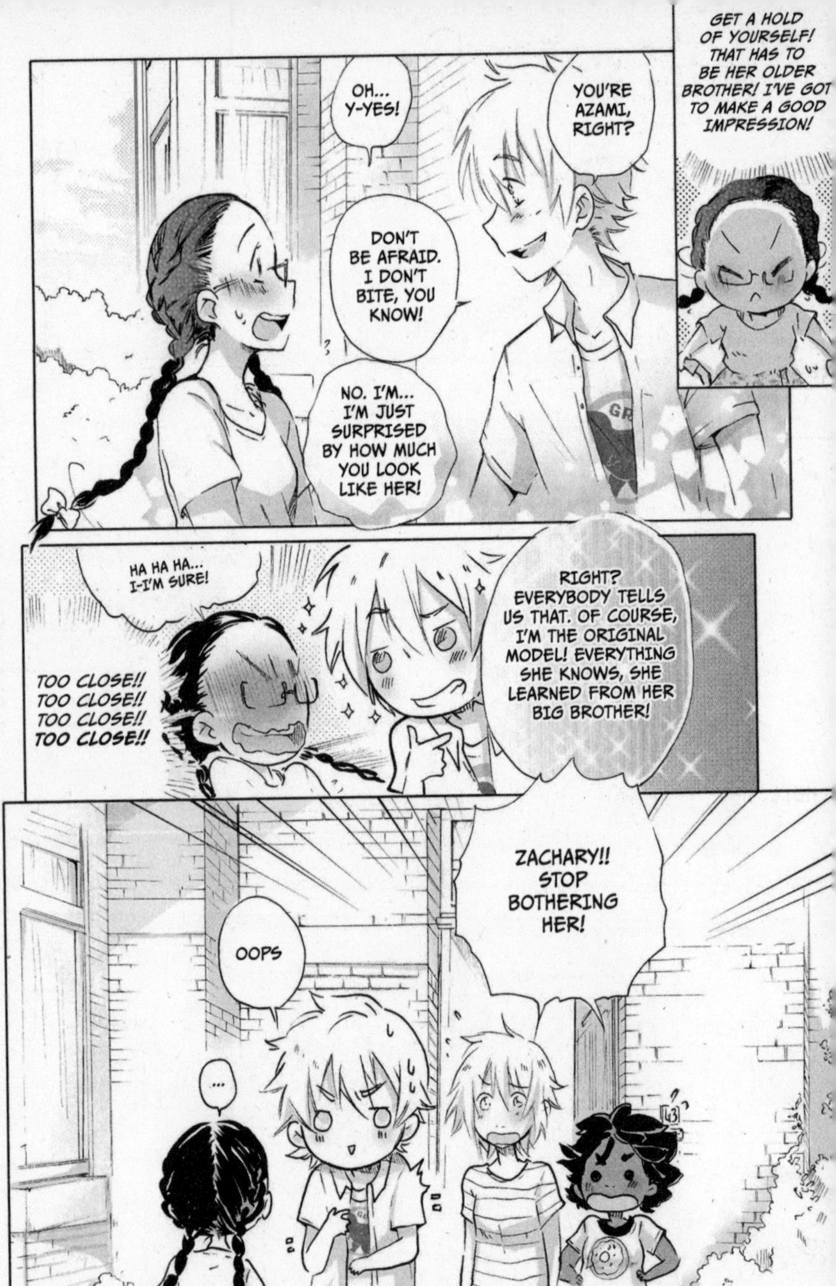
GET A HOLD OF YOURSELF! THAT HAS TO BE HER OLDER BROTHER! I'VE GOT TO MAKE A GOOD IMPRESSION!
YOU'RE AZAMI, RIGHT?
OH... Y-YES!
DON'T BE AFRAID. I DON'T BITE, YOU KNOW!
NO. I'M... I'M JUST SURPRISED BY HOW MUCH YOU LOOK LIKE HER!
RIGHT? EVERYBODY TELLS US THAT. OF COURSE, I'M THE ORIGINAL MODEL! EVERYTHING SHE KNOWS, SHE LEARNED FROM HER BIG BROTHER!
HA HA HA... I-I'M SURE!
TOO CLOSE!! TOO CLOSE!! TOO CLOSE!! TOO CLOSE!!
ZACHARY!! STOP BOTHERING HER!
OOPS
...

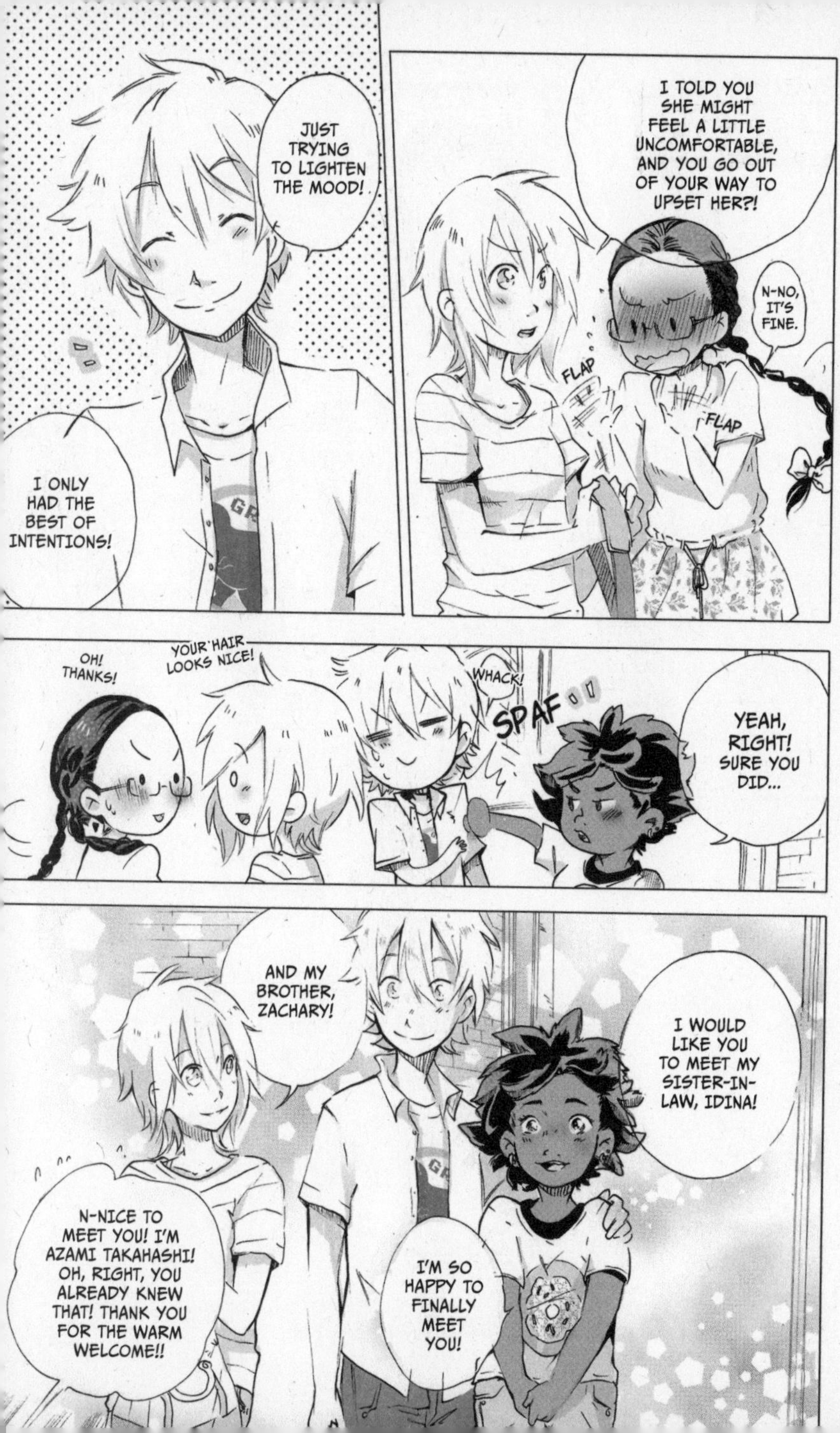
I TOLD YOU SHE MIGHT FEEL A LITTLE UNCOMFORTABLE, AND YOU GO OUT OF YOUR WAY TO UPSET HER?!
N-NO, IT'S FINE.
FLAP
FLAP
JUST TRYING TO LIGHTEN THE MOOD!
I ONLY HAD THE BEST OF INTENTIONS!
YEAH, RIGHT! SURE YOU DID...
SPAF
WHACK!
YOUR HAIR LOOKS NICE!
OH! THANKS!
I WOULD LIKE YOU TO MEET MY SISTER-IN-LAW, IDINA!
AND MY BROTHER, ZACHARY!
I'M SO HAPPY TO FINALLY MEET YOU!
N-NICE TO MEET YOU! I'M AZAMI TAKAHASHI! OH, RIGHT, YOU ALREADY KNEW THAT! THANK YOU FOR THE WARM WELCOME!!

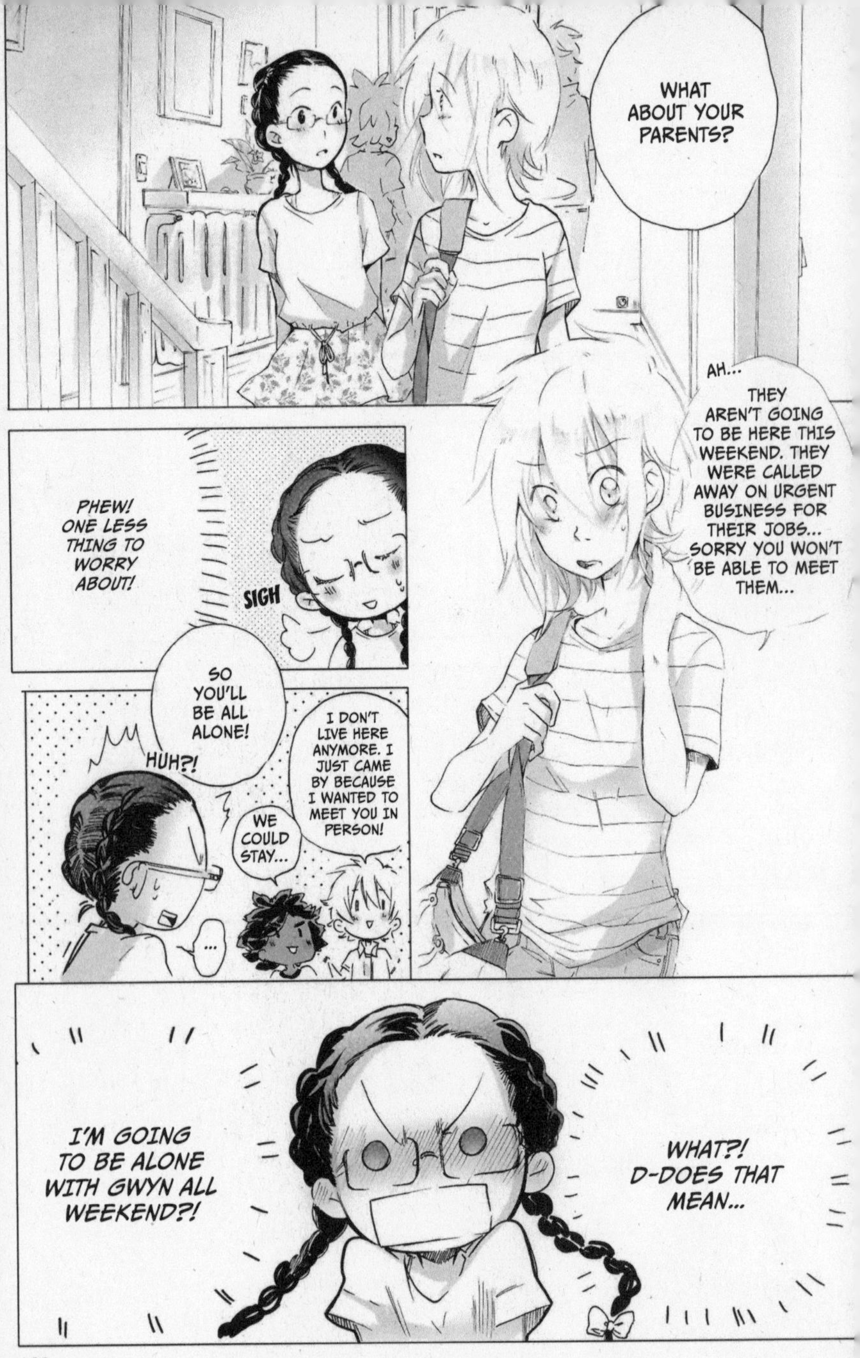
WHAT ABOUT YOUR PARENTS?
AH...
THEY AREN'T GOING TO BE HERE THIS WEEKEND. THEY WERE CALLED AWAY ON URGENT BUSINESS FOR THEIR JOBS... SORRY YOU WON'T BE ABLE TO MEET THEM...
PHEW! ONE LESS THING TO WORRY ABOUT!
SIGH
SO YOU'LL BE ALL ALONE!
HUH?!
I DON'T LIVE HERE ANYMORE. I JUST CAME BY BECAUSE I WANTED TO MEET YOU IN PERSON!
WE COULD STAY...
...
WHAT?! D-DOES THAT MEAN...
I'M GOING TO BE ALONE WITH GWYN ALL WEEKEND?!

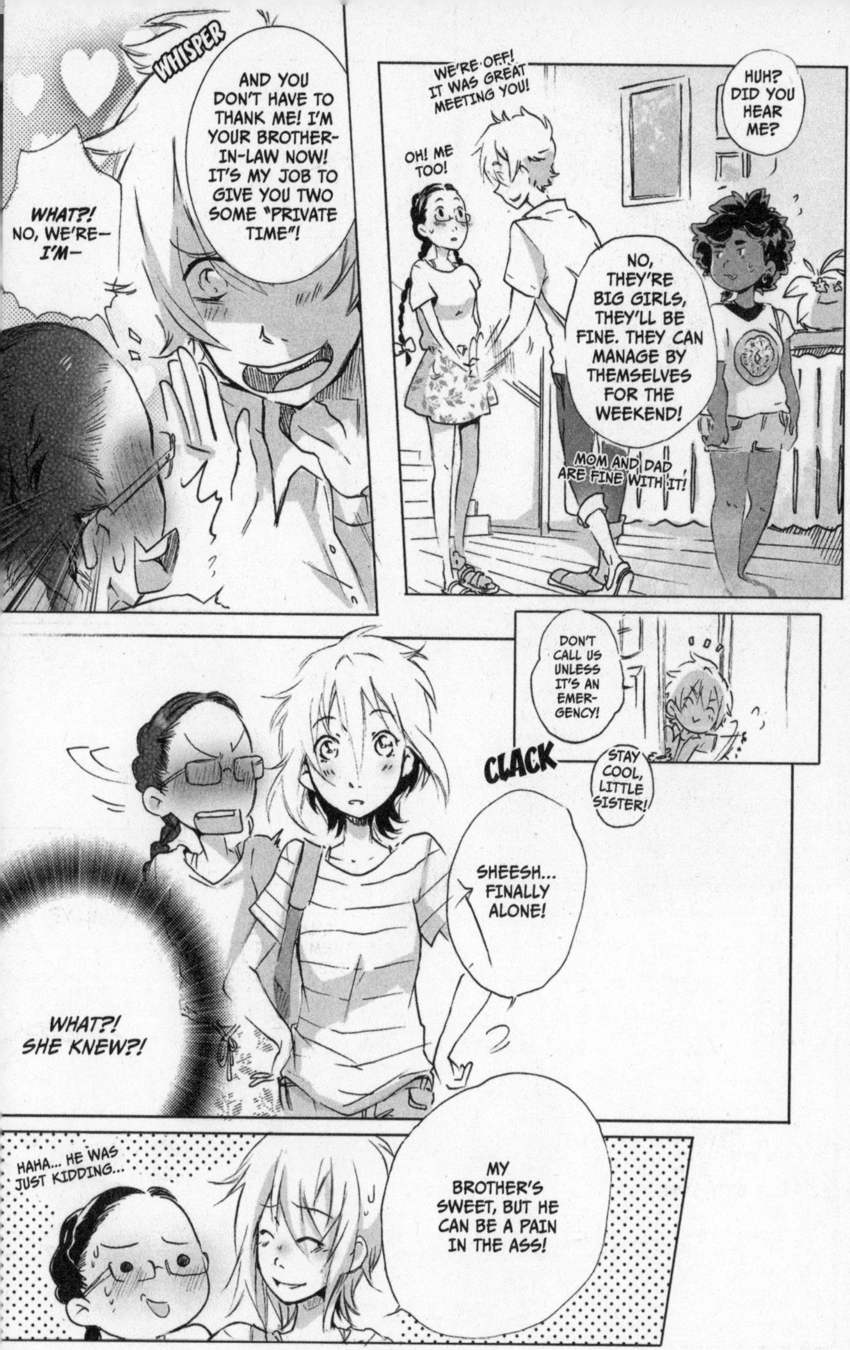
HUH? DID YOU HEAR ME?
WE'RE OFF! IT WAS GREAT MEETING YOU!
OH! ME TOO!
NO, THEY'RE BIG GIRLS, THEY'LL BE FINE. THEY CAN MANAGE BY THEMSELVES FOR THE WEEKEND!
MOM AND DAD ARE FINE WITH IT!
WHISPER
AND YOU DON'T HAVE TO THANK ME! I'M YOUR BROTHER-IN-LAW NOW! IT'S MY JOB TO GIVE YOU TWO SOME "PRIVATE TIME"!
WHAT?! NO, WE'RE— I'M—
DON'T CALL US UNLESS IT'S AN EMERGENCY!
STAY COOL, LITTLE SISTER!
CLACK
SHEESH... FINALLY ALONE!
WHAT?! SHE KNEW?!
MY BROTHER'S SWEET, BUT HE CAN BE A PAIN IN THE ASS!
HAHA... HE WAS JUST KIDDING...

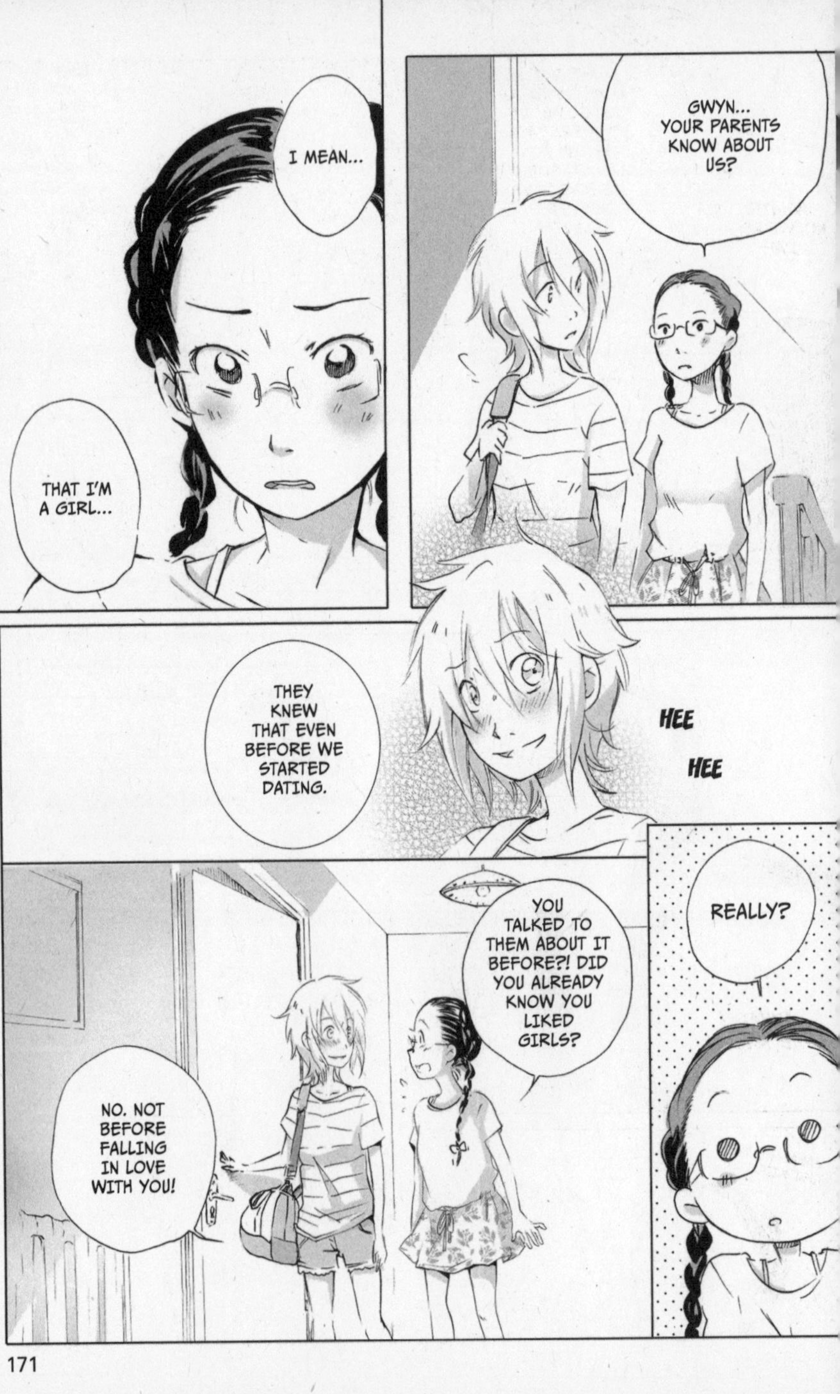
GWYN... YOUR PARENTS KNOW ABOUT US?
I MEAN...
THAT I'M A GIRL...
THEY KNEW THAT EVEN BEFORE WE STARTED DATING.
HEE
HEE
REALLY?
YOU TALKED TO THEM ABOUT IT BEFORE?! DID YOU ALREADY KNOW YOU LIKED GIRLS?
NO. NOT BEFORE FALLING IN LOVE WITH YOU!

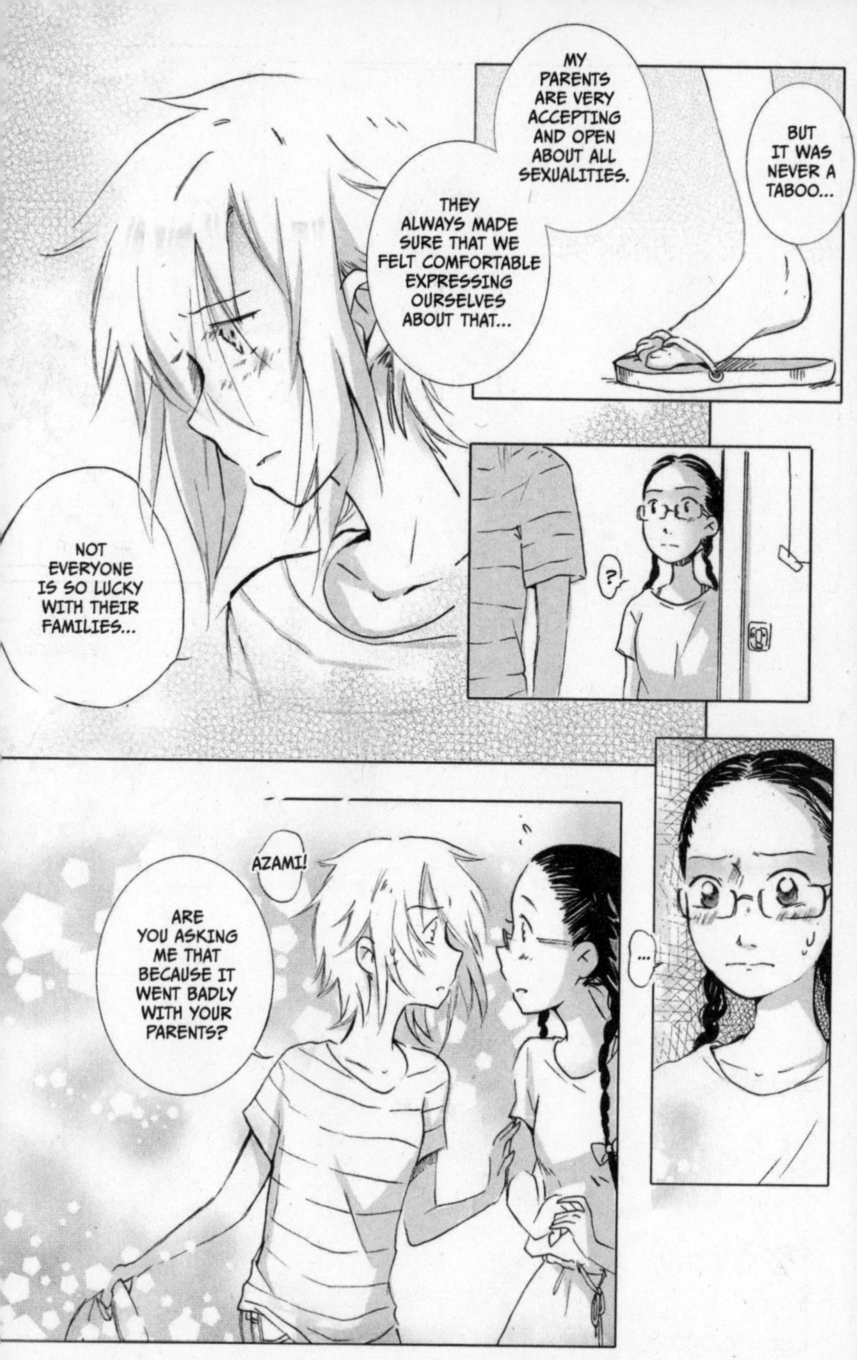
MY PARENTS ARE VERY ACCEPTING AND OPEN ABOUT ALL SEXUALITIES.
BUT IT WAS NEVER A TABOO...
THEY ALWAYS MADE SURE THAT WE FELT COMFORTABLE EXPRESSING OURSELVES ABOUT THAT...
?
NOT EVERYONE IS SO LUCKY WITH THEIR FAMILIES...
...
AZAMI!
ARE YOU ASKING ME THAT BECAUSE IT WENT BADLY WITH YOUR PARENTS?

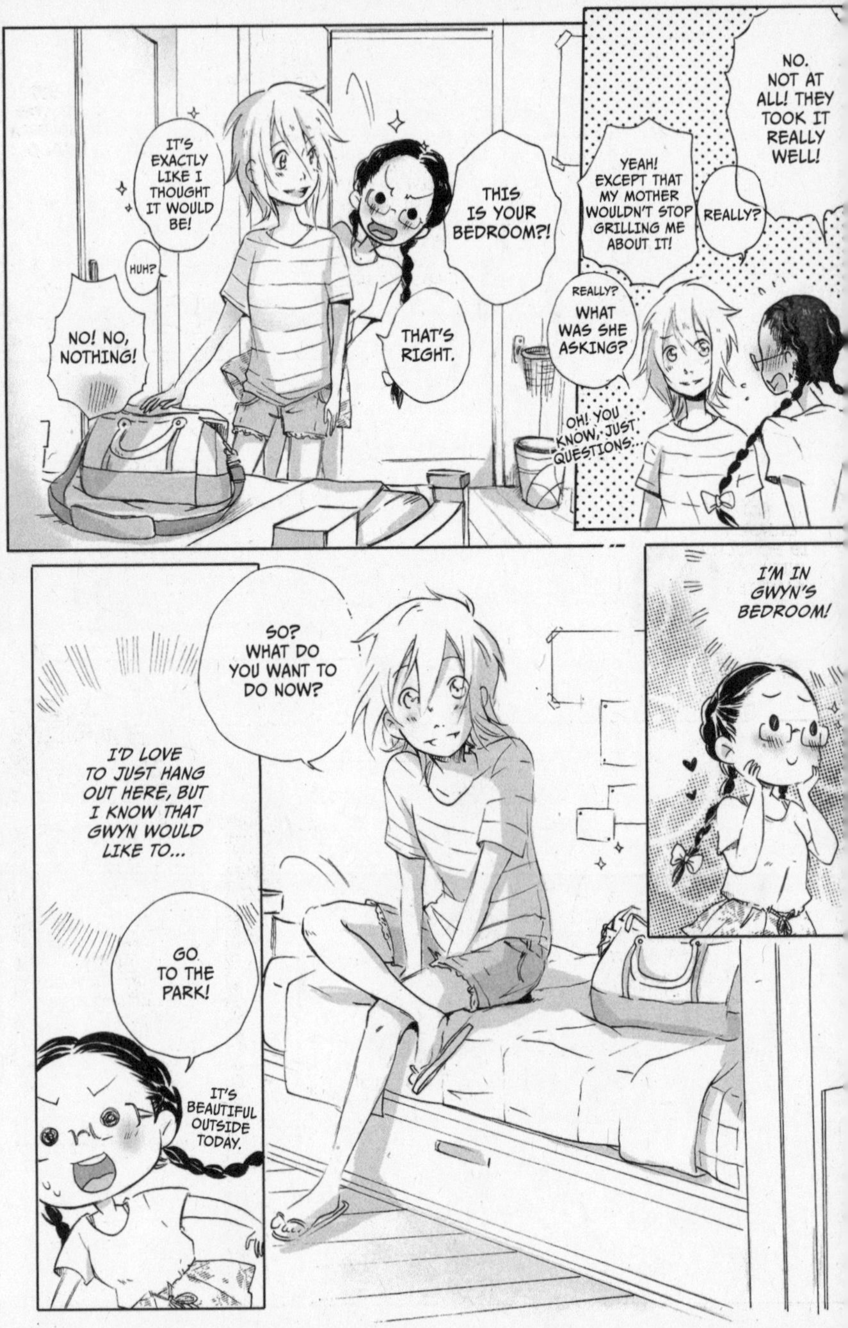
NO. NOT AT ALL! THEY TOOK IT REALLY WELL!
REALLY?
YEAH! EXCEPT THAT MY MOTHER WOULDN'T STOP GRILLING ME ABOUT IT!
REALLY? WHAT WAS SHE ASKING?
OH! YOU KNOW, JUST QUESTIONS...
THIS IS YOUR BEDROOM?!
THAT'S RIGHT.
IT'S EXACTLY LIKE I THOUGHT IT WOULD BE!
HUH?
NO! NO, NOTHING!
I'M IN GWYN'S BEDROOM!
SO? WHAT DO YOU WANT TO DO NOW?
I'D LOVE TO JUST HANG OUT HERE, BUT I KNOW THAT GWYN WOULD LIKE TO...
GO TO THE PARK!
IT'S BEAUTIFUL OUTSIDE TODAY.

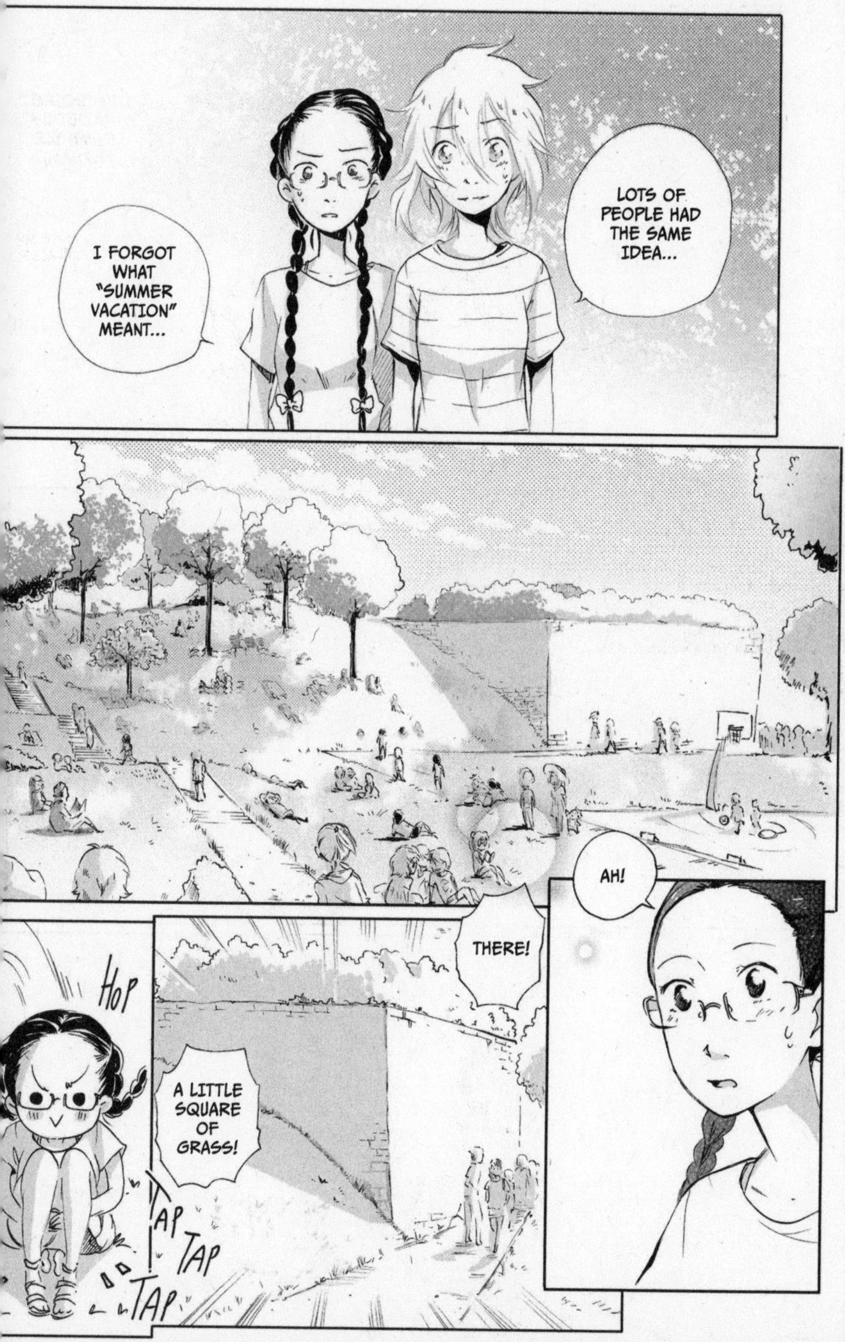
LOTS OF PEOPLE HAD THE SAME IDEA...
I FORGOT WHAT "SUMMER VACATION" MEANT...
AH!
THERE!
A LITTLE SQUARE OF GRASS!
HOP
TAP TAP TAP

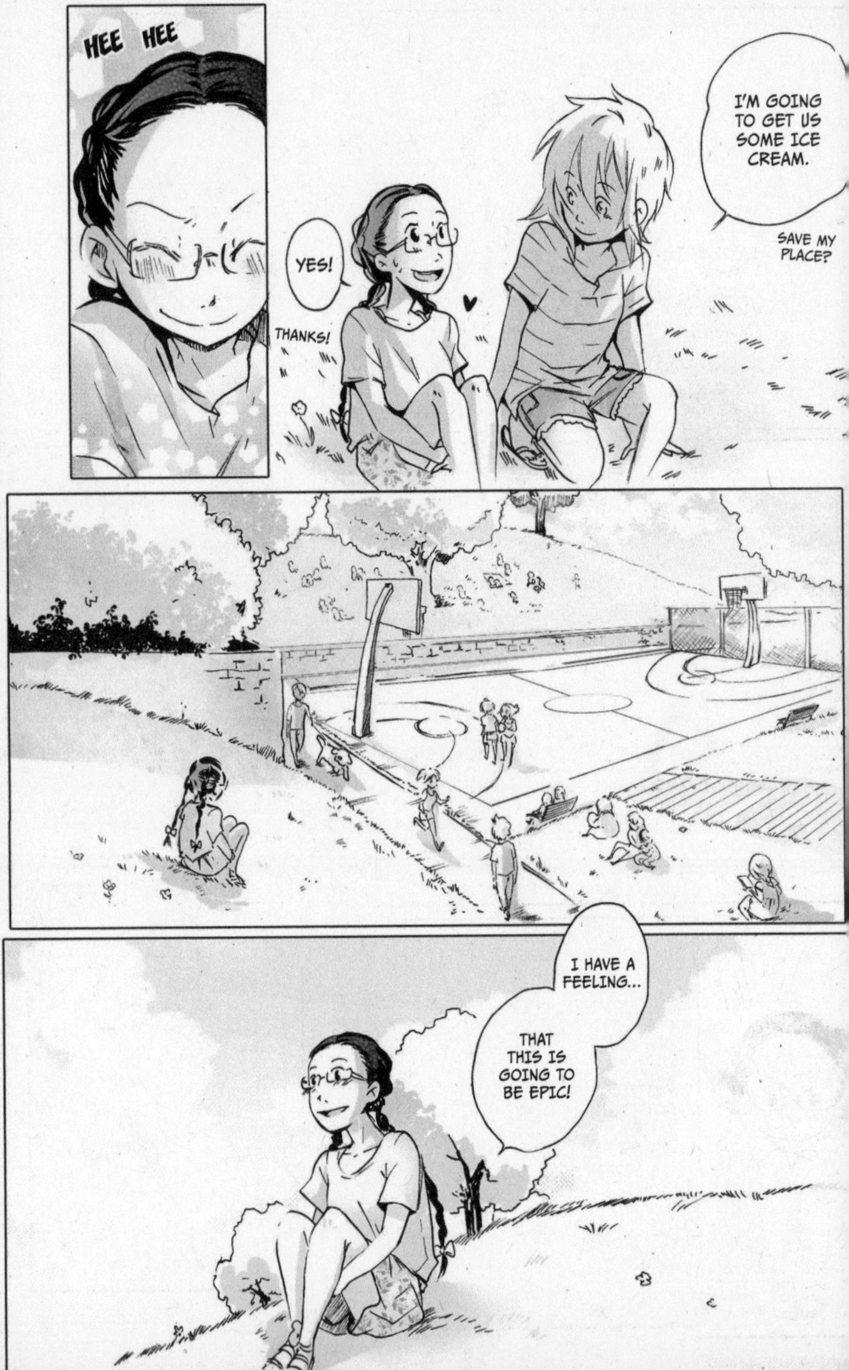
I'M GOING TO GET US SOME ICE CREAM.
SAVE MY PLACE?
YES!
THANKS!
HEE HEE
I HAVE A FEELING...
THAT THIS IS GOING TO BE EPIC!

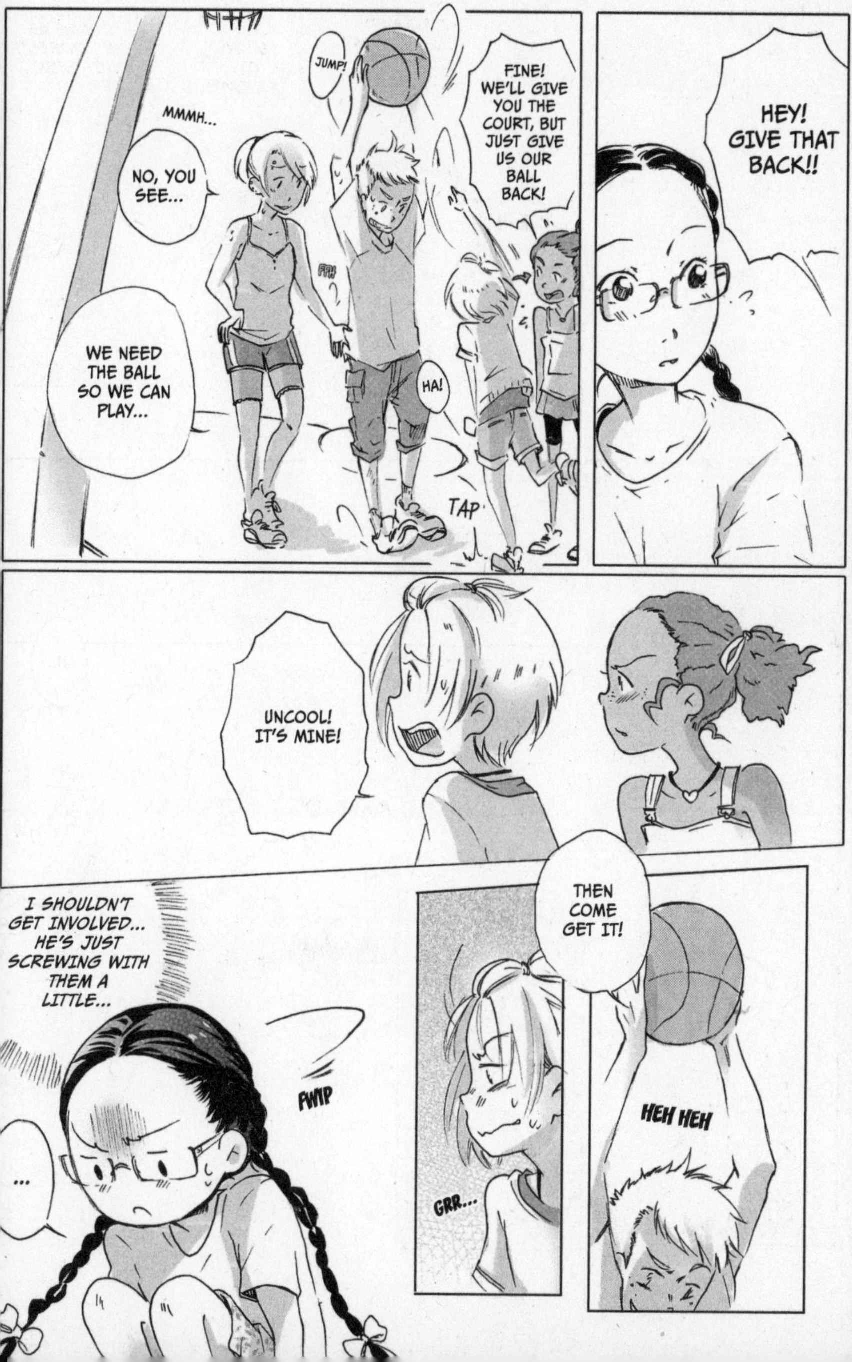
HEY! GIVE THAT BACK!!
FINE! WE'LL GIVE YOU THE COURT, BUT JUST GIVE US OUR BALL BACK!
JUMP!
MMMH...
NO, YOU SEE...
FFH
HA!
WE NEED THE BALL SO WE CAN PLAY...
TAP
UNCOOL! IT'S MINE!
THEN COME GET IT!
HEH HEH
GRR...
FWIP
I SHOULDN'T GET INVOLVED... HE'S JUST SCREWING WITH THEM A LITTLE...
...

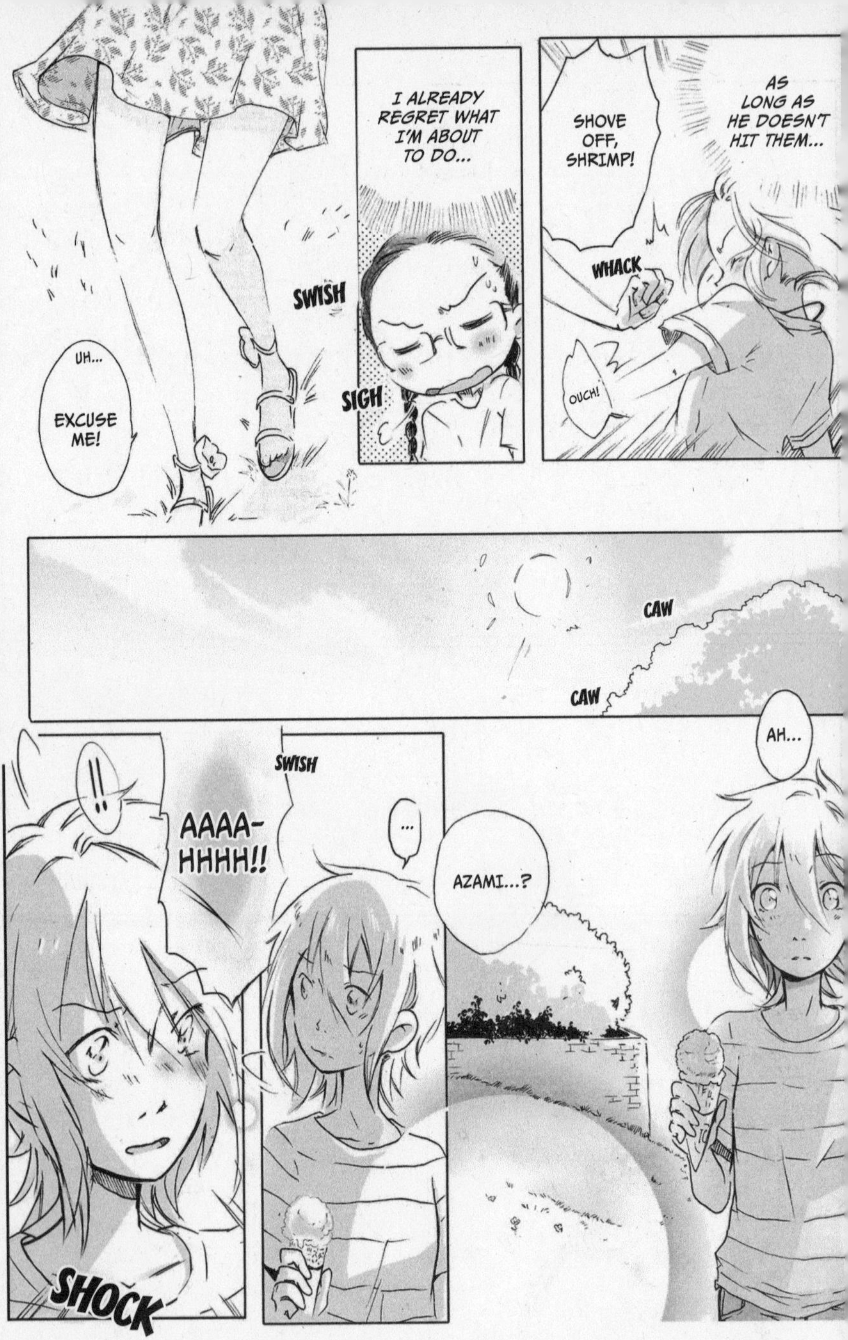
AS LONG AS HE DOESN'T HIT THEM...
SHOVE OFF, SHRIMP!
WHACK
OUCH!
I ALREADY REGRET WHAT I'M ABOUT TO DO...
SWISH
SIGH
UH...
EXCUSE ME!
CAW
CAW
AH...
SWISH
...
AZAMI...?
!!
AAAA-HHHH!!
SHOCK

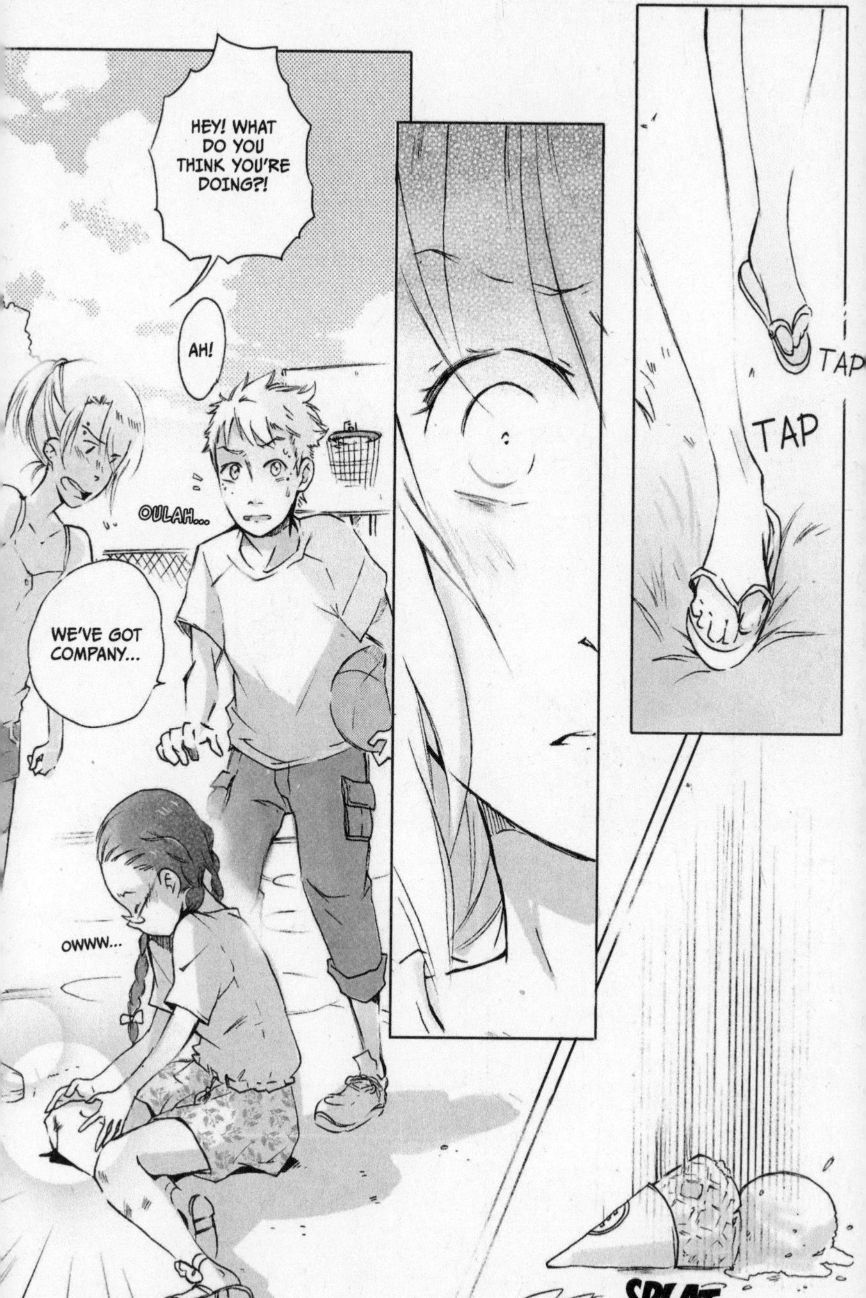
TAP
TAP
SPLAT
HEY! WHAT DO YOU THINK YOU'RE DOING?!
AH!
OULAH...
WE'VE GOT COMPANY...
OWWW...

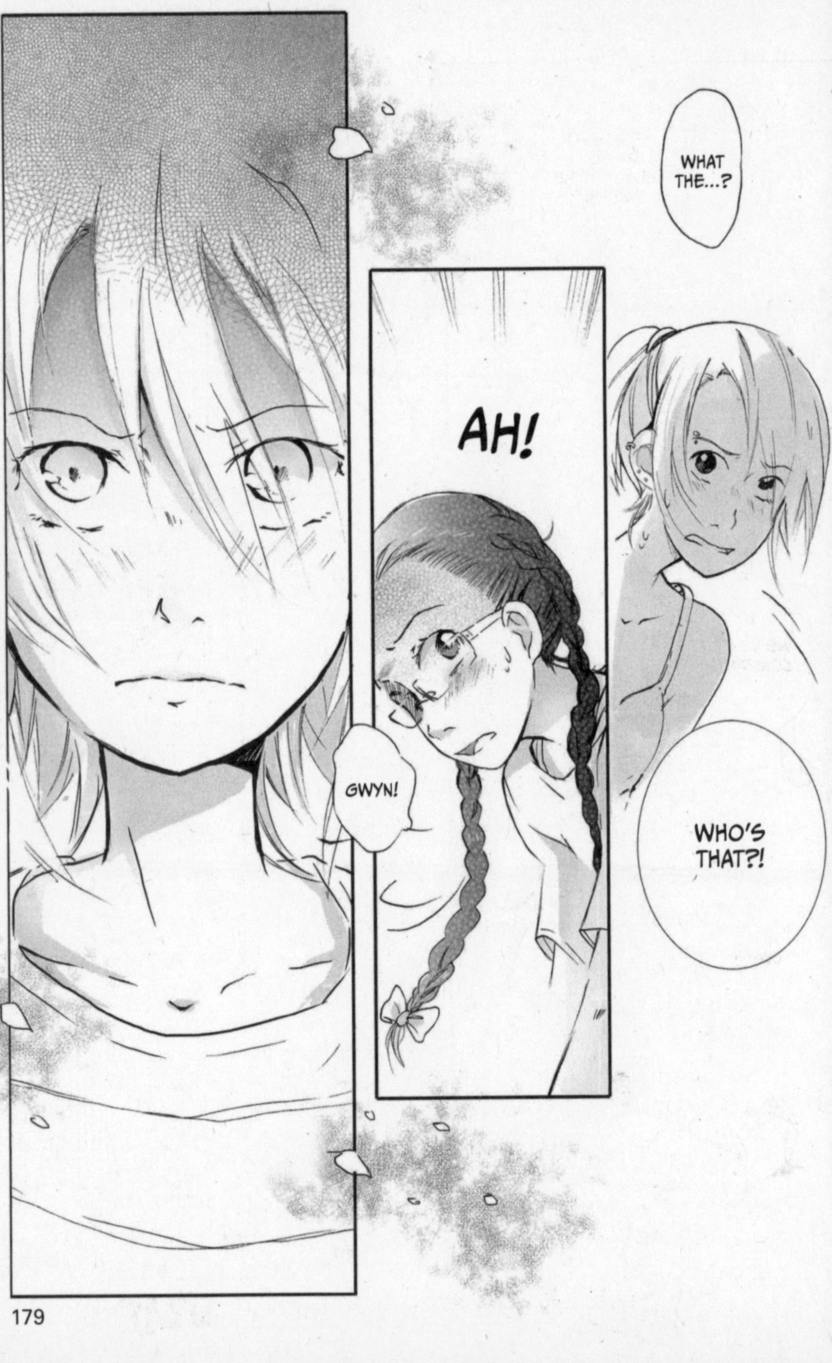
WHAT THE...?
WHO'S THAT?!
AH!
GWYN!

I FELL...!

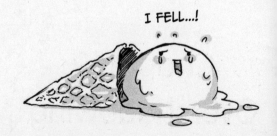

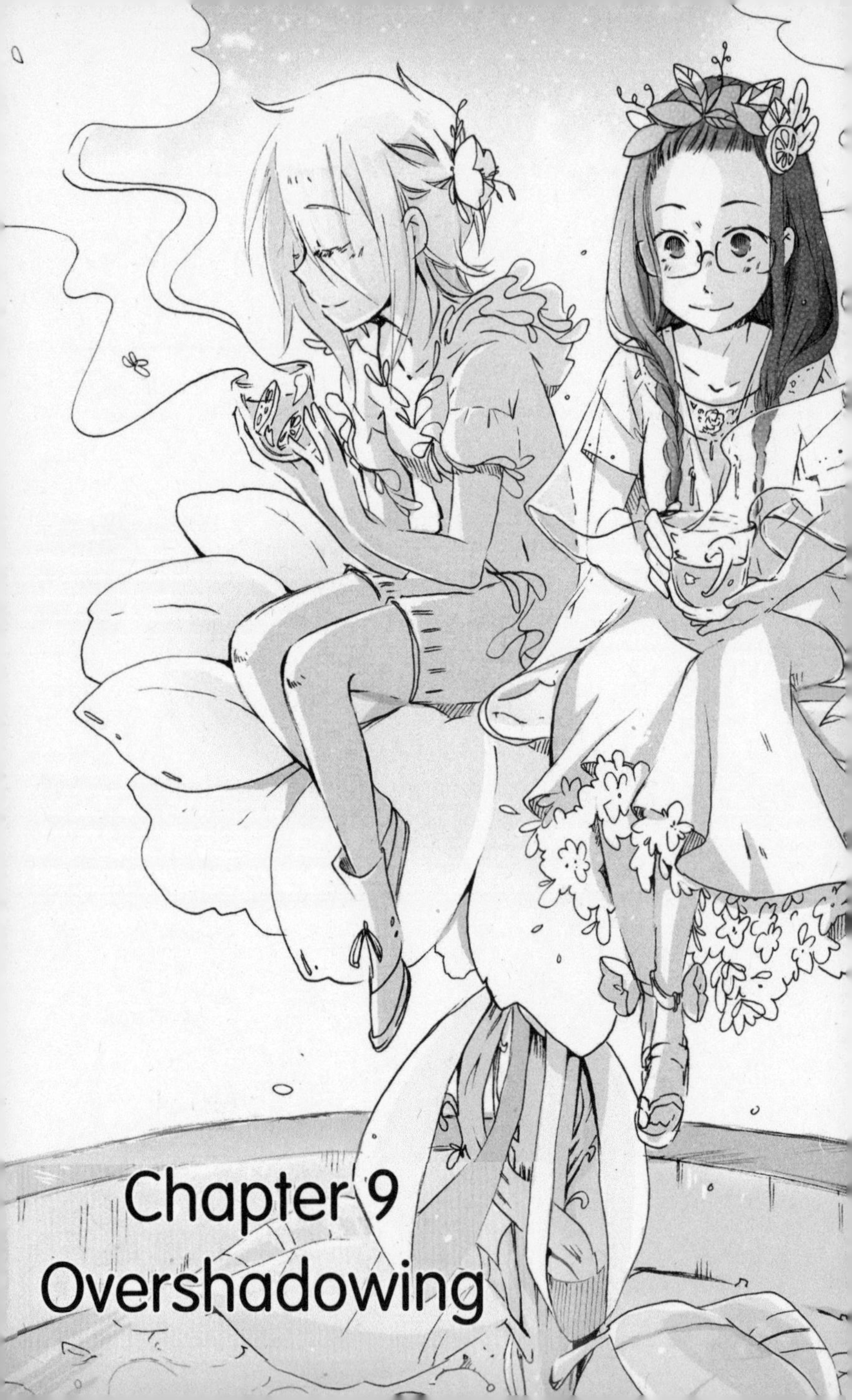
Chapter 9
Overshadowing

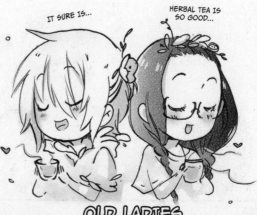

IT SURE IS...

HERBAL TEA IS SO GOOD...

OLD LADIES

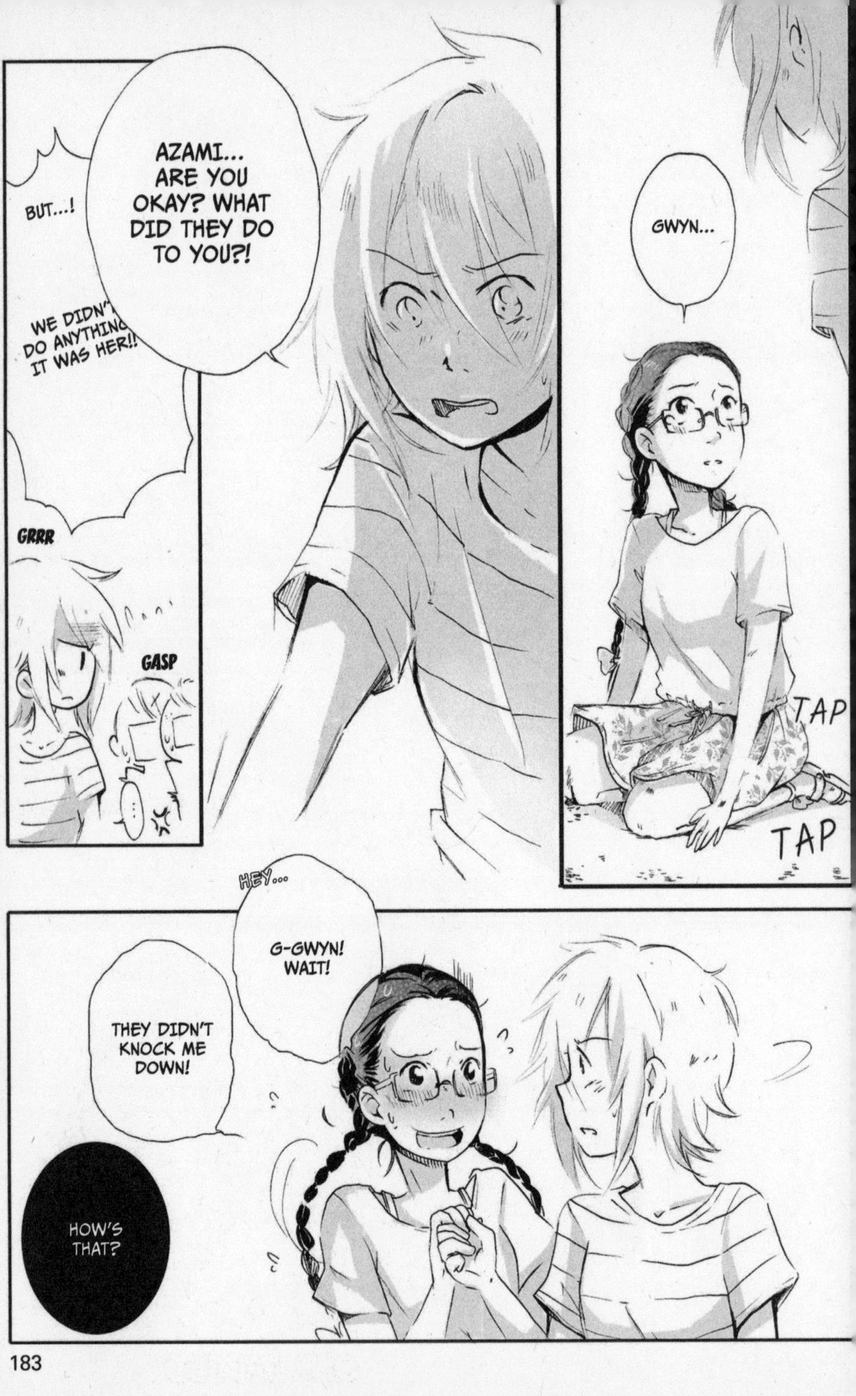
GWYN...
TAP
TAP
AZAMI... ARE YOU OKAY? WHAT DID THEY DO TO YOU?!
BUT...!
WE DIDN'T DO ANYTHING IT WAS HER!!
GRRR
GASP
...
HEY...
G-GWYN! WAIT!
THEY DIDN'T KNOCK ME DOWN!
HOW'S THAT?

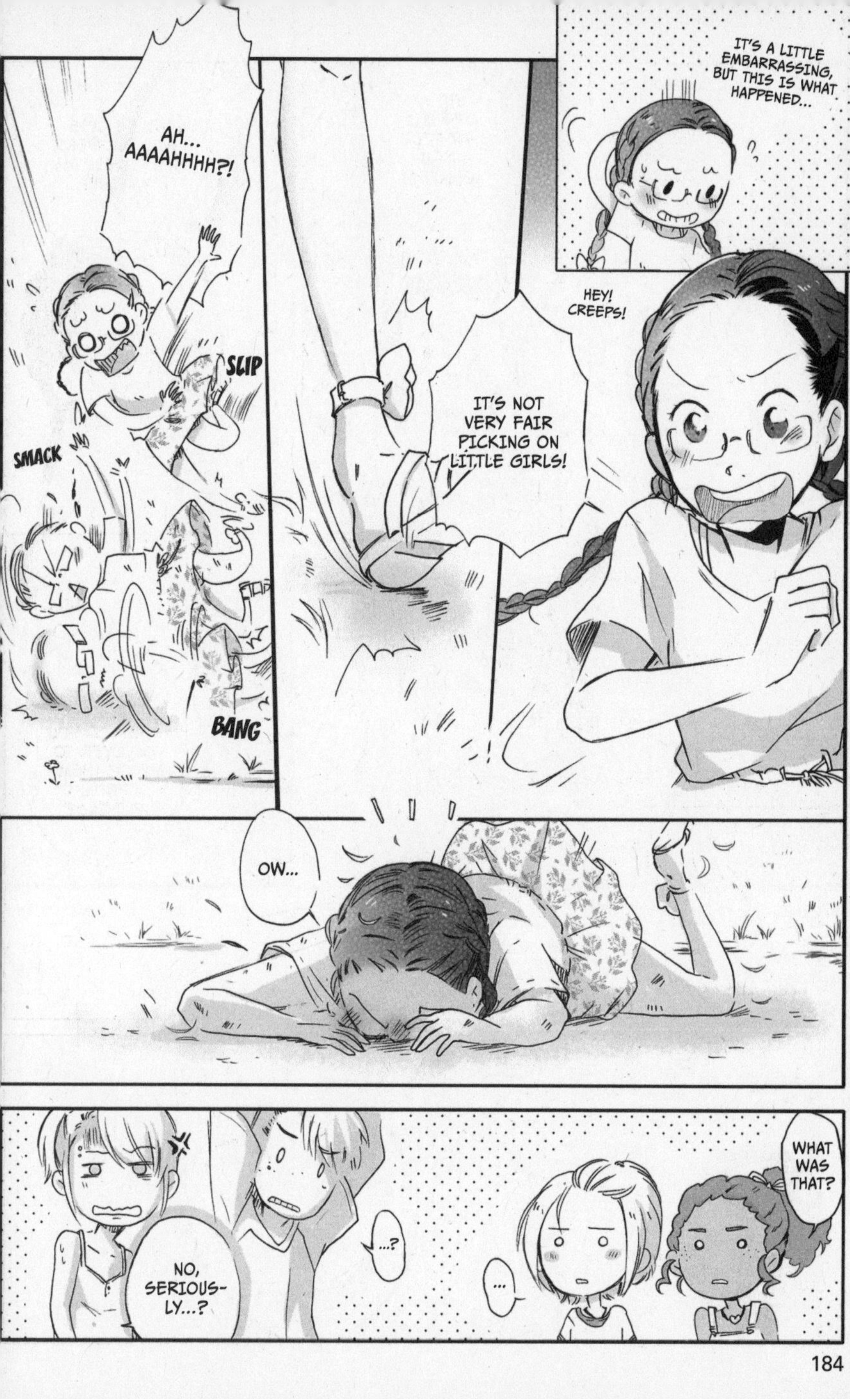
IT'S A LITTLE EMBARRASSING, BUT THIS IS WHAT HAPPENED...
HEY! CREEPS!
IT'S NOT VERY FAIR PICKING ON LITTLE GIRLS!
AH... AAAAHHHH?!
SLIP
SMACK
BANG
OW...
WHAT WAS THAT?
...
...?
NO, SERIOUSLY...?

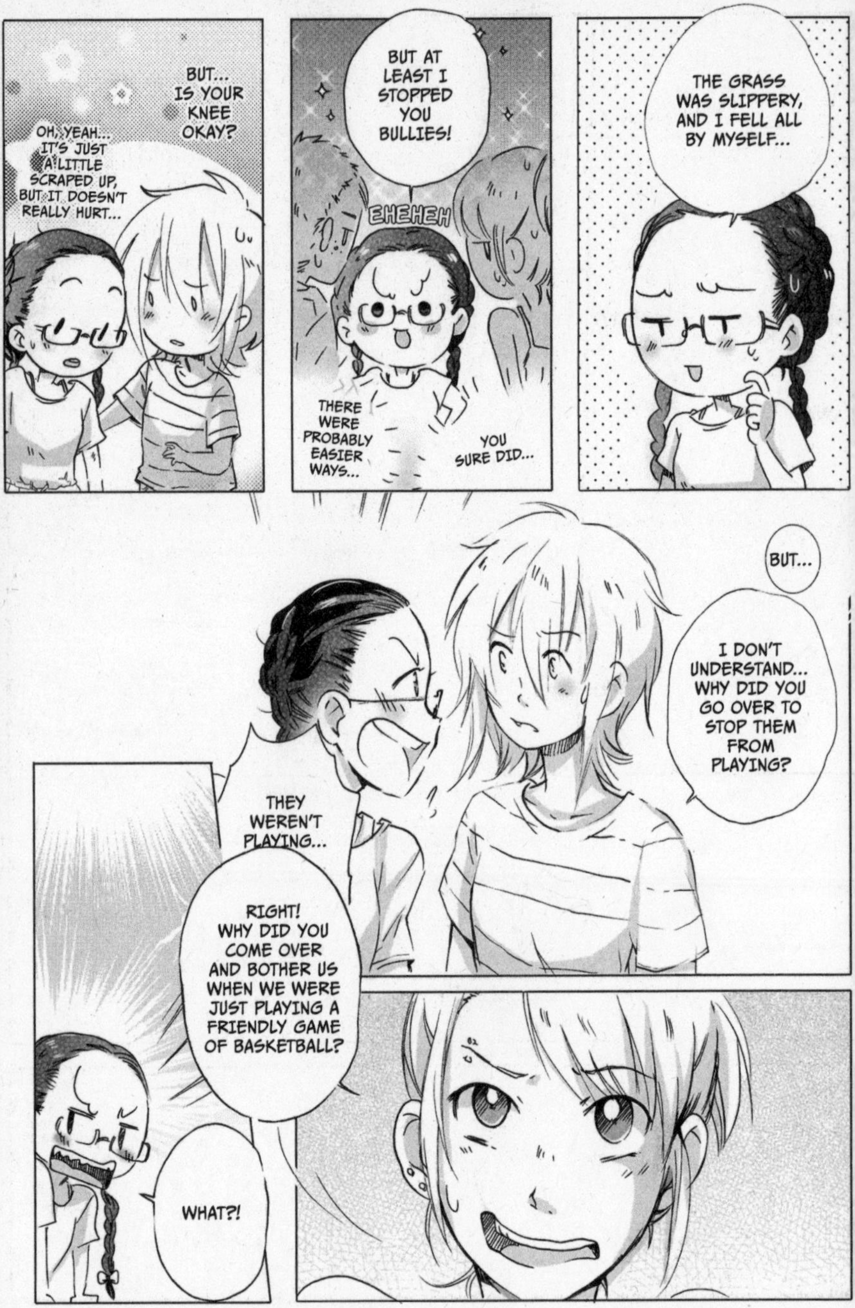
THE GRASS WAS SLIPPERY, AND I FELL ALL BY MYSELF...
BUT AT LEAST I STOPPED YOU BULLIES!
EHEHEH
YOU SURE DID...
THERE WERE PROBABLY EASIER WAYS...
BUT... IS YOUR KNEE OKAY?
OH, YEAH... IT'S JUST A LITTLE SCRAPED UP, BUT IT DOESN'T REALLY HURT...
BUT...
I DON'T UNDERSTAND... WHY DID YOU GO OVER TO STOP THEM FROM PLAYING?
THEY WEREN'T PLAYING...
RIGHT! WHY DID YOU COME OVER AND BOTHER US WHEN WE WERE JUST PLAYING A FRIENDLY GAME OF BASKETBALL?
WHAT?!

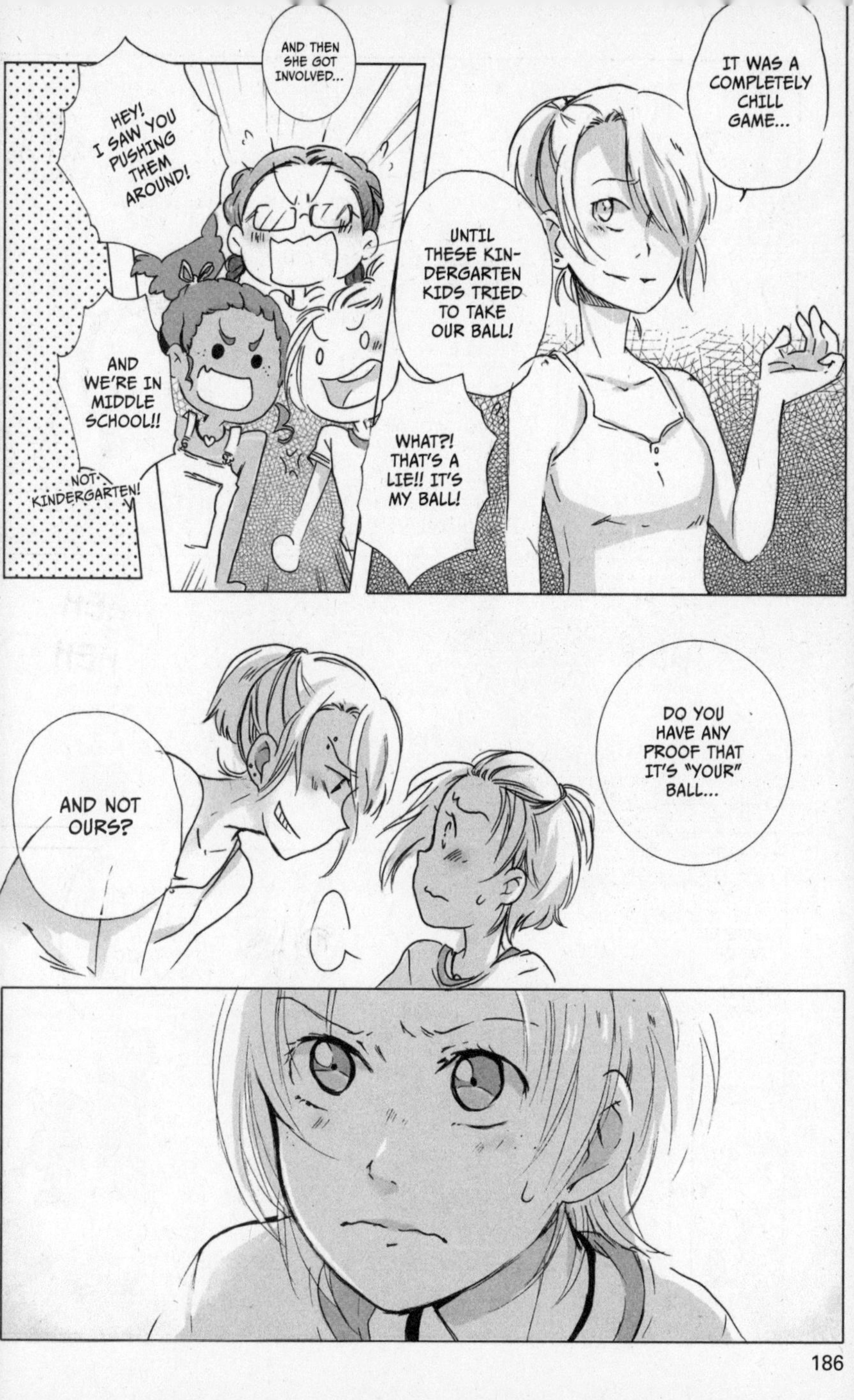
IT WAS A COMPLETELY CHILL GAME...
UNTIL THESE KIN-DERGARTEN KIDS TRIED TO TAKE OUR BALL!
WHAT?! THAT'S A LIE!! IT'S MY BALL!
AND THEN SHE GOT INVOLVED...
HEY! I SAW YOU PUSHING THEM AROUND!
AND WE'RE IN MIDDLE SCHOOL!!
NOT KINDERGARTEN!
DO YOU HAVE ANY PROOF THAT IT'S "YOUR" BALL...
AND NOT OURS?

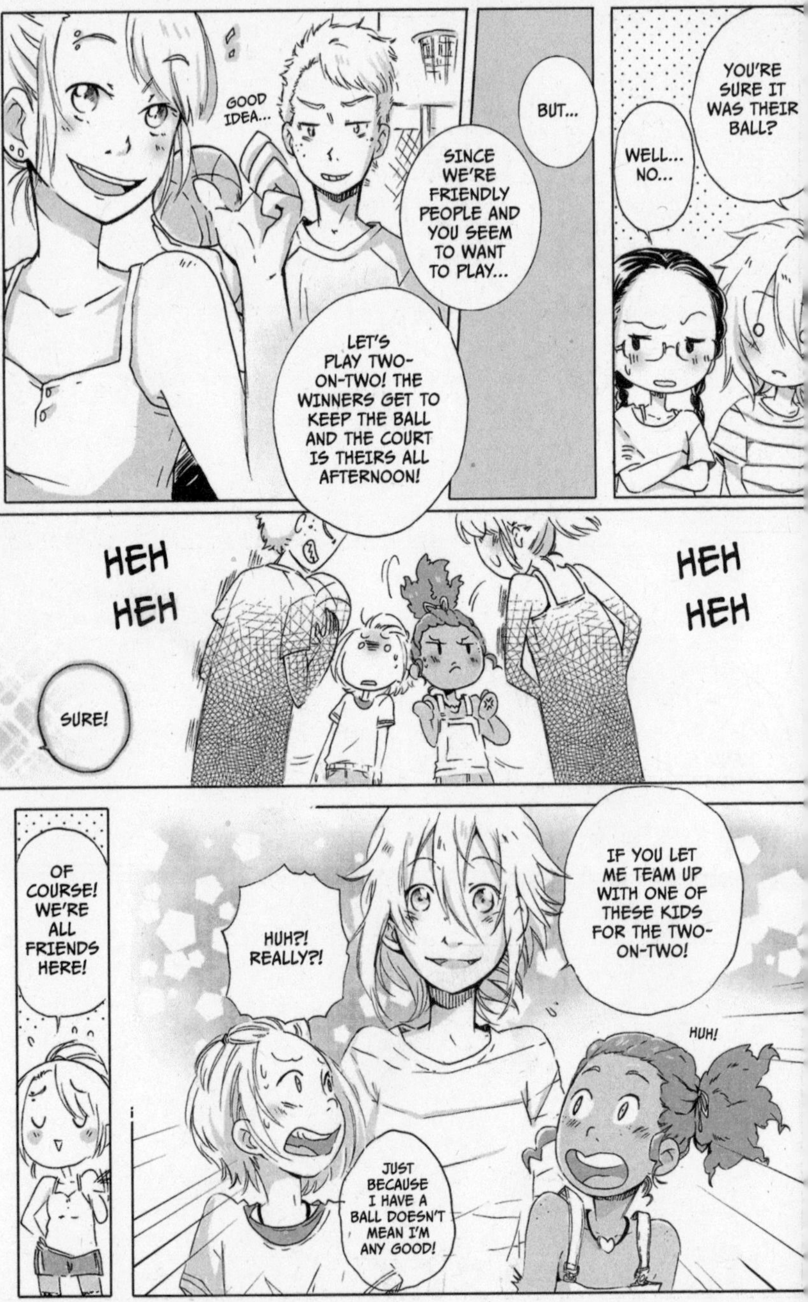
YOU'RE SURE IT WAS THEIR BALL?
WELL... NO...
BUT...
SINCE WE'RE FRIENDLY PEOPLE AND YOU SEEM TO WANT TO PLAY...
LET'S PLAY TWO-ON-TWO! THE WINNERS GET TO KEEP THE BALL AND THE COURT IS THEIRS ALL AFTERNOON!
GOOD IDEA...
HEH HEH
HEH HEH
SURE!
IF YOU LET ME TEAM UP WITH ONE OF THESE KIDS FOR THE TWO-ON-TWO!
HUH!
HUH?! REALLY?!
JUST BECAUSE I HAVE A BALL DOESN'T MEAN I'M ANY GOOD!
OF COURSE! WE'RE ALL FRIENDS HERE!

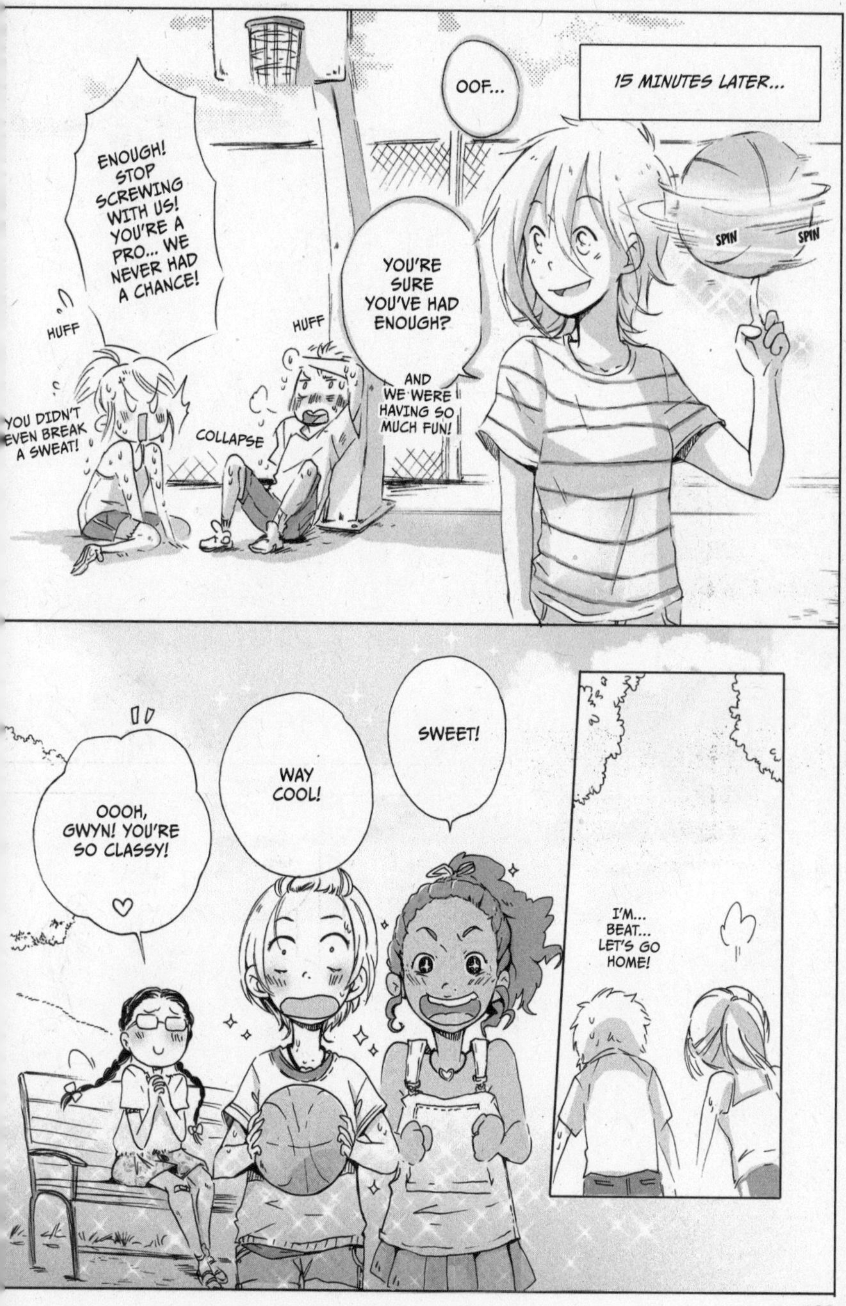
15 MINUTES LATER...
OOF...
SPIN
SPIN
YOU'RE SURE YOU'VE HAD ENOUGH?
AND WE WERE HAVING SO MUCH FUN!
ENOUGH! STOP SCREWING WITH US! YOU'RE A PRO... WE NEVER HAD A CHANCE!
HUFF
HUFF
COLLAPSE
YOU DIDN'T EVEN BREAK A SWEAT!
I'M... BEAT... LET'S GO HOME!
SWEET!
WAY COOL!
OOOH, GWYN! YOU'RE SO CLASSY!

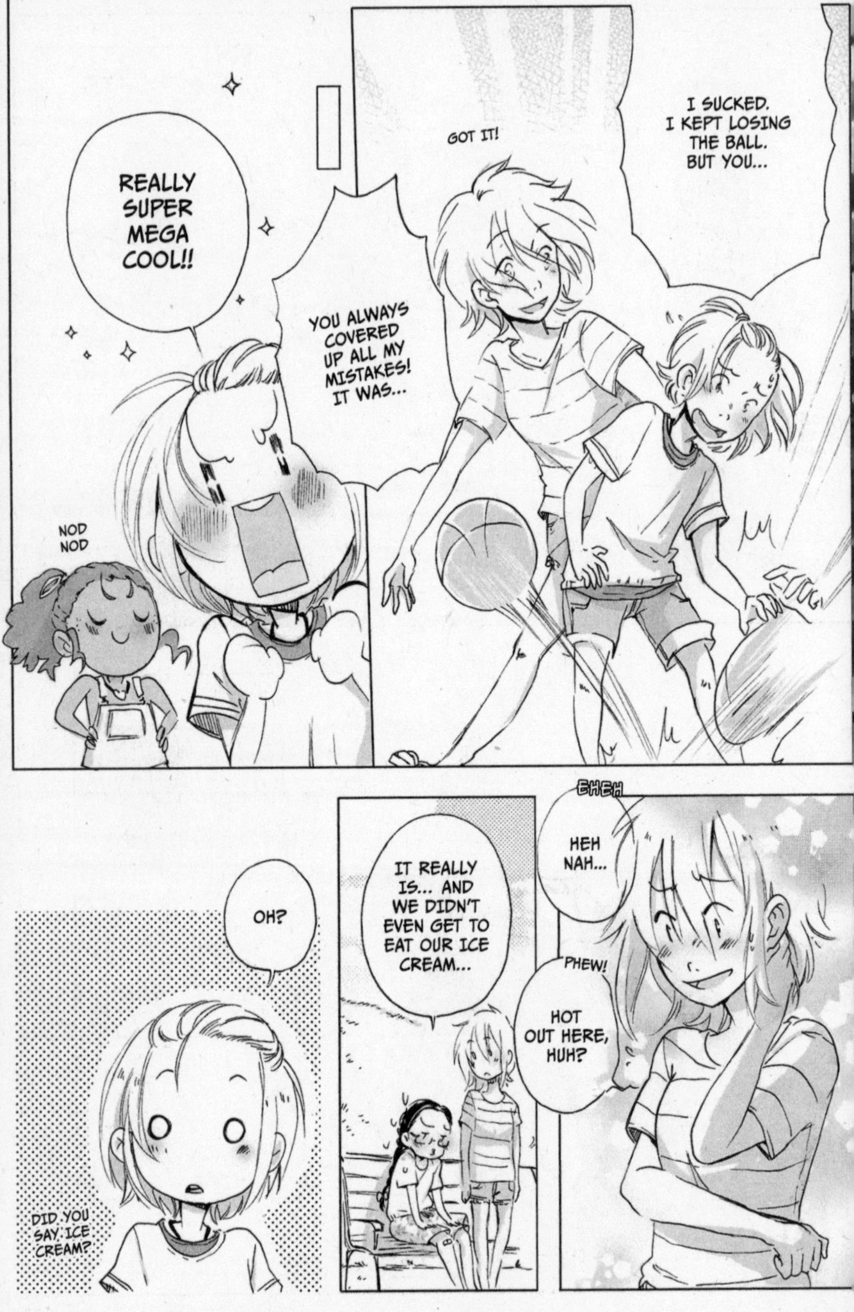

I SUCKED. I KEPT LOSING THE BALL. BUT YOU...
GOT IT!
YOU ALWAYS COVERED UP ALL MY MISTAKES! IT WAS...
REALLY SUPER MEGA COOL!!
NOD NOD
EHEH
HEH NAH...
PHEW!
HOT OUT HERE, HUH?
IT REALLY IS... AND WE DIDN'T EVEN GET TO EAT OUR ICE CREAM...
OH?
DID YOU SAY ICE CREAM?

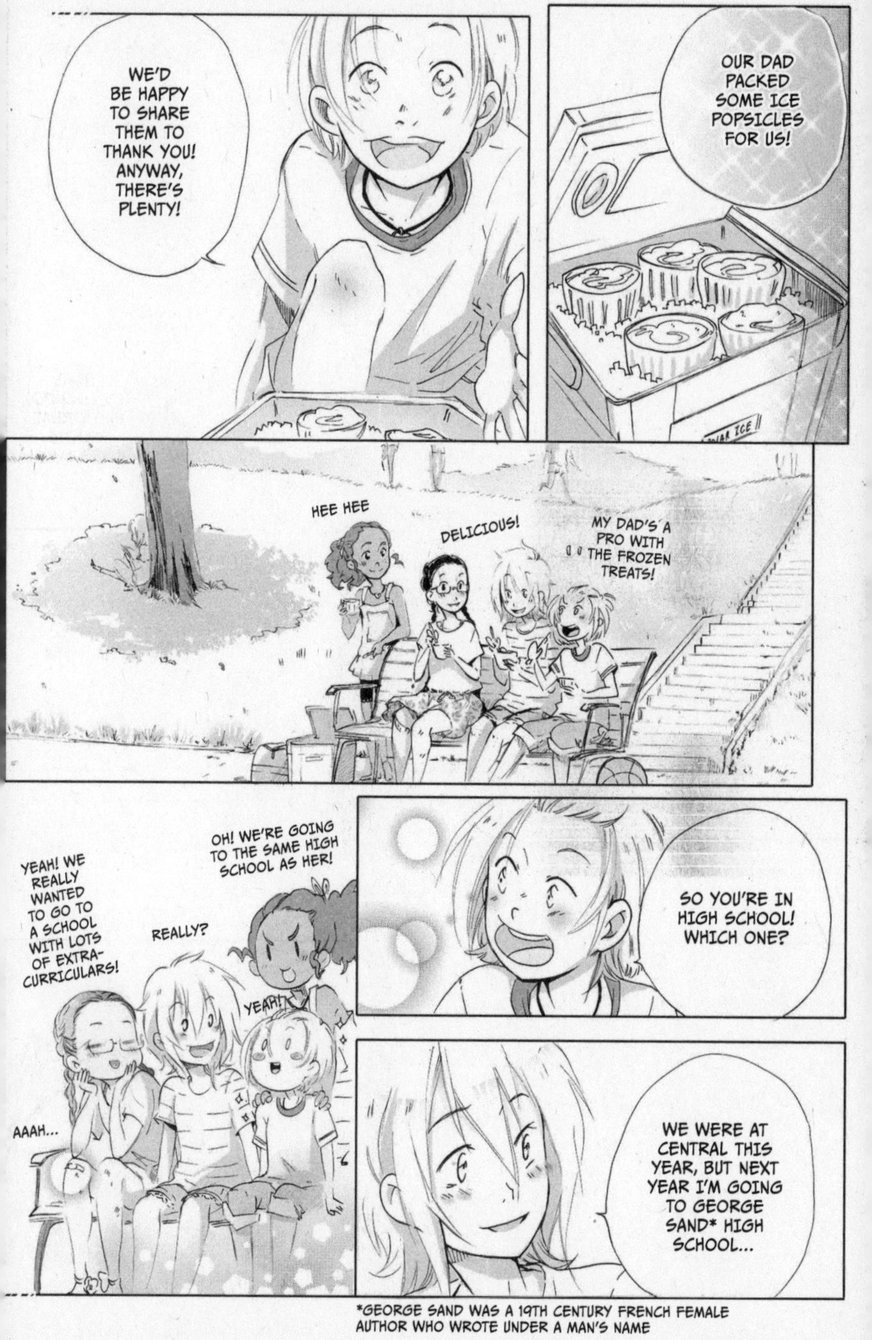
OUR DAD PACKED SOME ICE POPSICLES FOR US!
WE'D BE HAPPY TO SHARE THEM TO THANK YOU! ANYWAY, THERE'S PLENTY!
MY DAD'S A PRO WITH THE FROZEN TREATS!
DELICIOUS!
HEE HEE
SO YOU'RE IN HIGH SCHOOL! WHICH ONE?
WE WERE AT CENTRAL THIS YEAR, BUT NEXT YEAR I'M GOING TO GEORGE SAND* HIGH SCHOOL...
OH! WE'RE GOING TO THE SAME HIGH SCHOOL AS HER!
YEAH! WE REALLY WANTED TO GO TO A SCHOOL WITH LOTS OF EXTRA-CURRICULARS!
REALLY?
YEAH!
AAAH...

*GEORGE SAND WAS A 19TH CENTURY FRENCH FEMALE AUTHOR WHO WROTE UNDER A MAN'S NAME

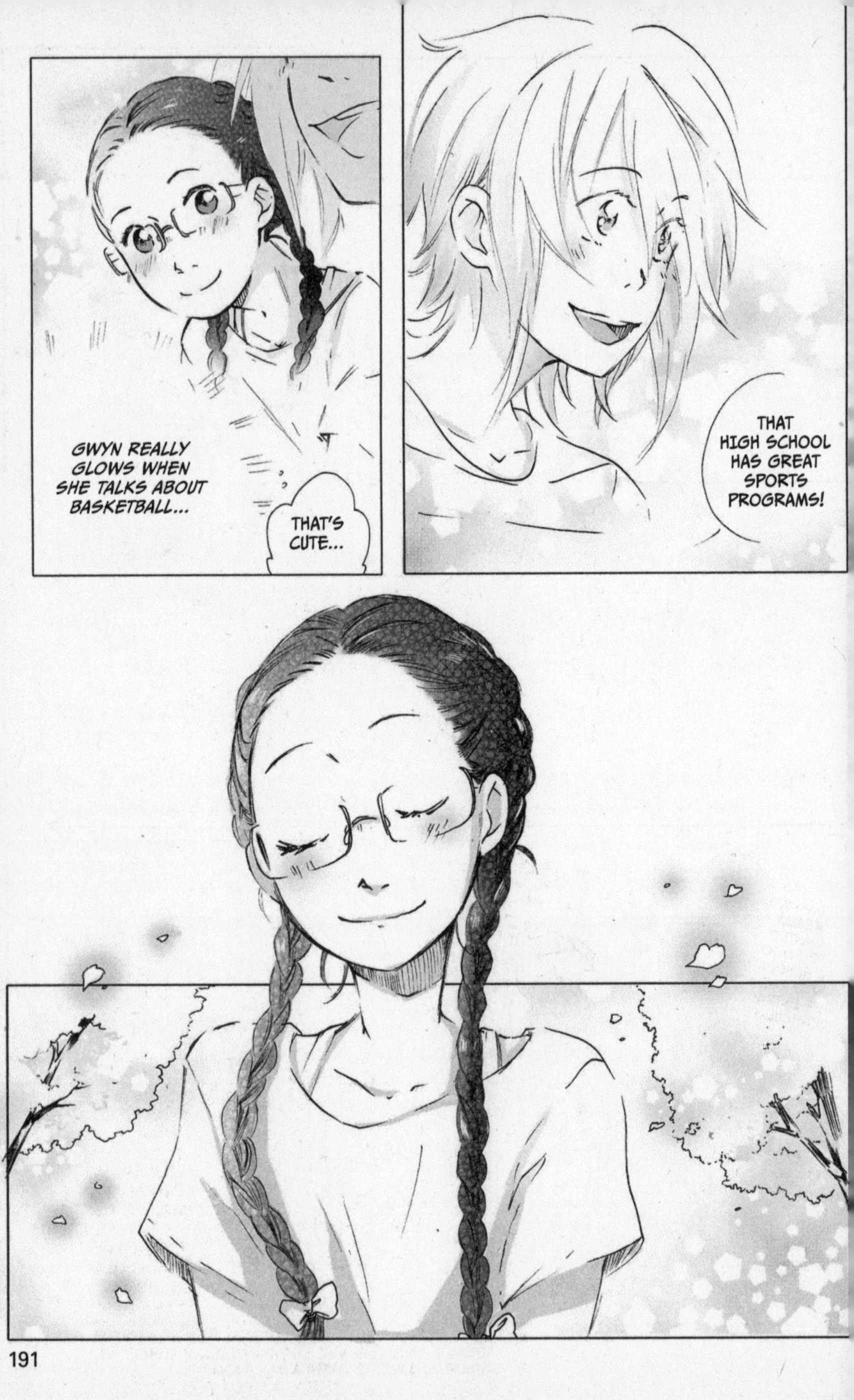
THAT HIGH SCHOOL HAS GREAT SPORTS PROGRAMS!
GWYN REALLY GLOWS WHEN SHE TALKS ABOUT BASKETBALL...
THAT'S CUTE...

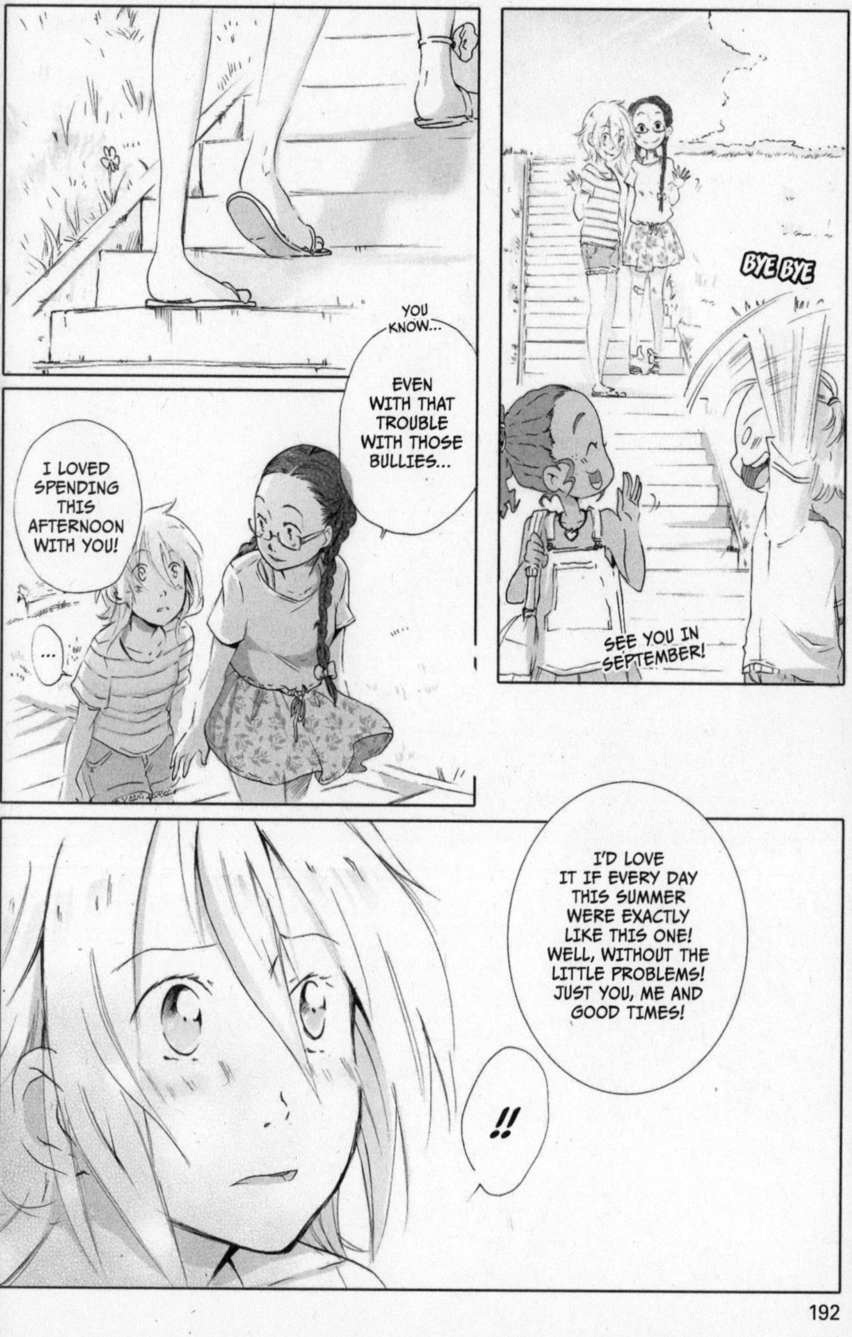
BYE BYE
SEE YOU IN SEPTEMBER!
YOU KNOW...
EVEN WITH THAT TROUBLE WITH THOSE BULLIES...
I LOVED SPENDING THIS AFTERNOON WITH YOU!
...
I'D LOVE IT IF EVERY DAY THIS SUMMER WERE EXACTLY LIKE THIS ONE! WELL, WITHOUT THE LITTLE PROBLEMS! JUST YOU, ME AND GOOD TIMES!
!!

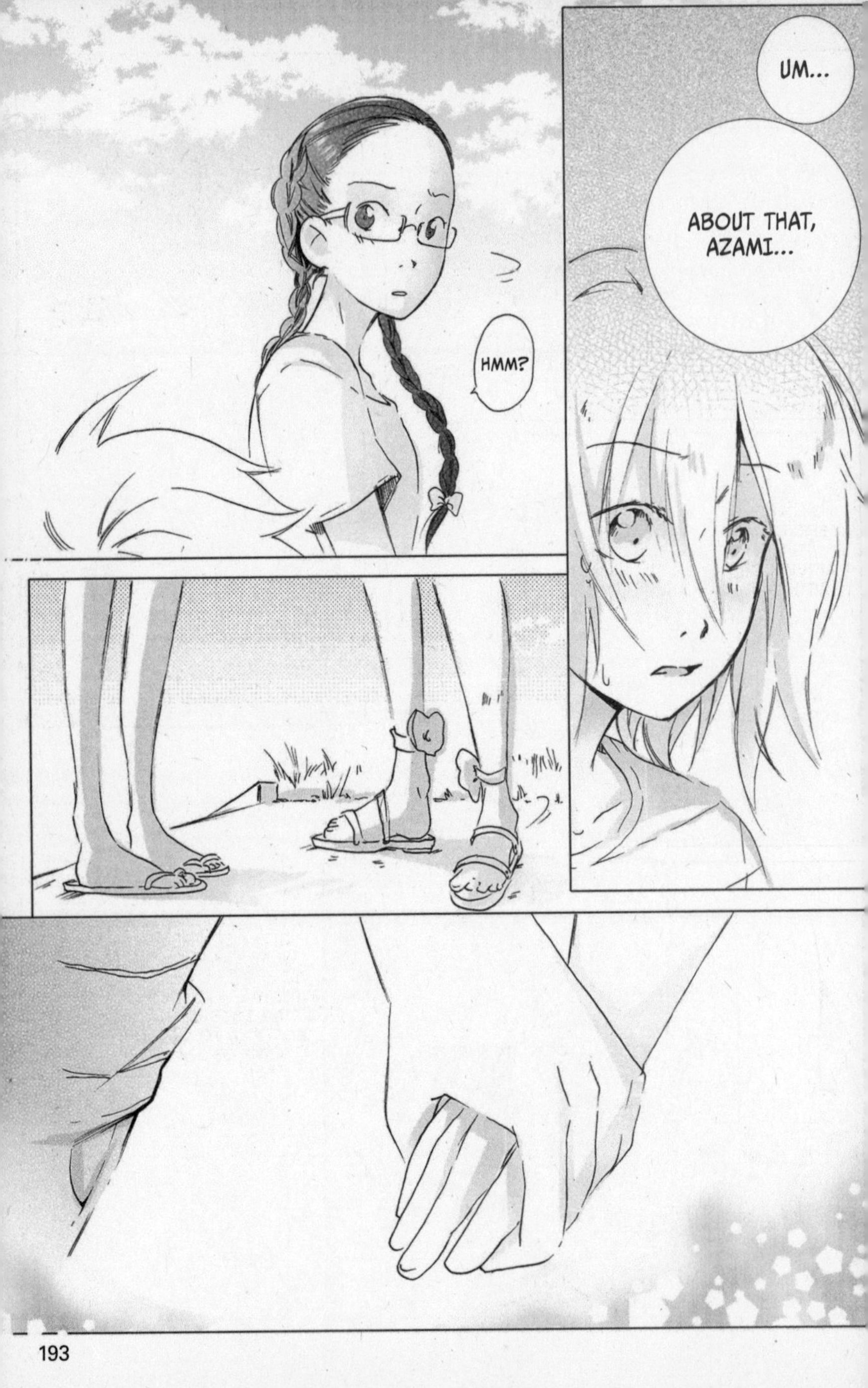
UM...
ABOUT THAT, AZAMI...
HMM?

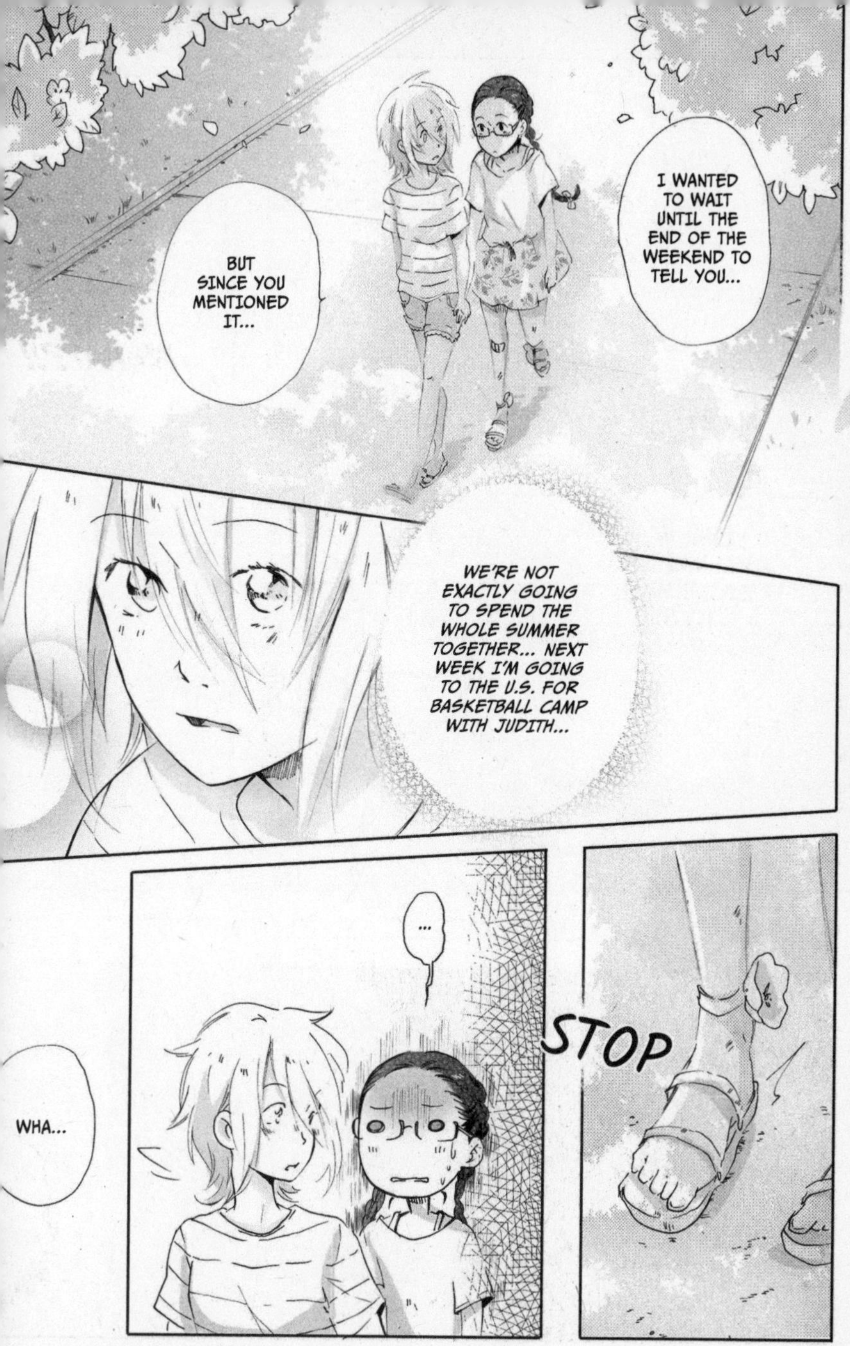
I WANTED TO WAIT UNTIL THE END OF THE WEEKEND TO TELL YOU...
BUT SINCE YOU MENTIONED IT...
WE'RE NOT EXACTLY GOING TO SPEND THE WHOLE SUMMER TOGETHER... NEXT WEEK I'M GOING TO THE U.S. FOR BASKETBALL CAMP WITH JUDITH...
STOP
...
WHA...

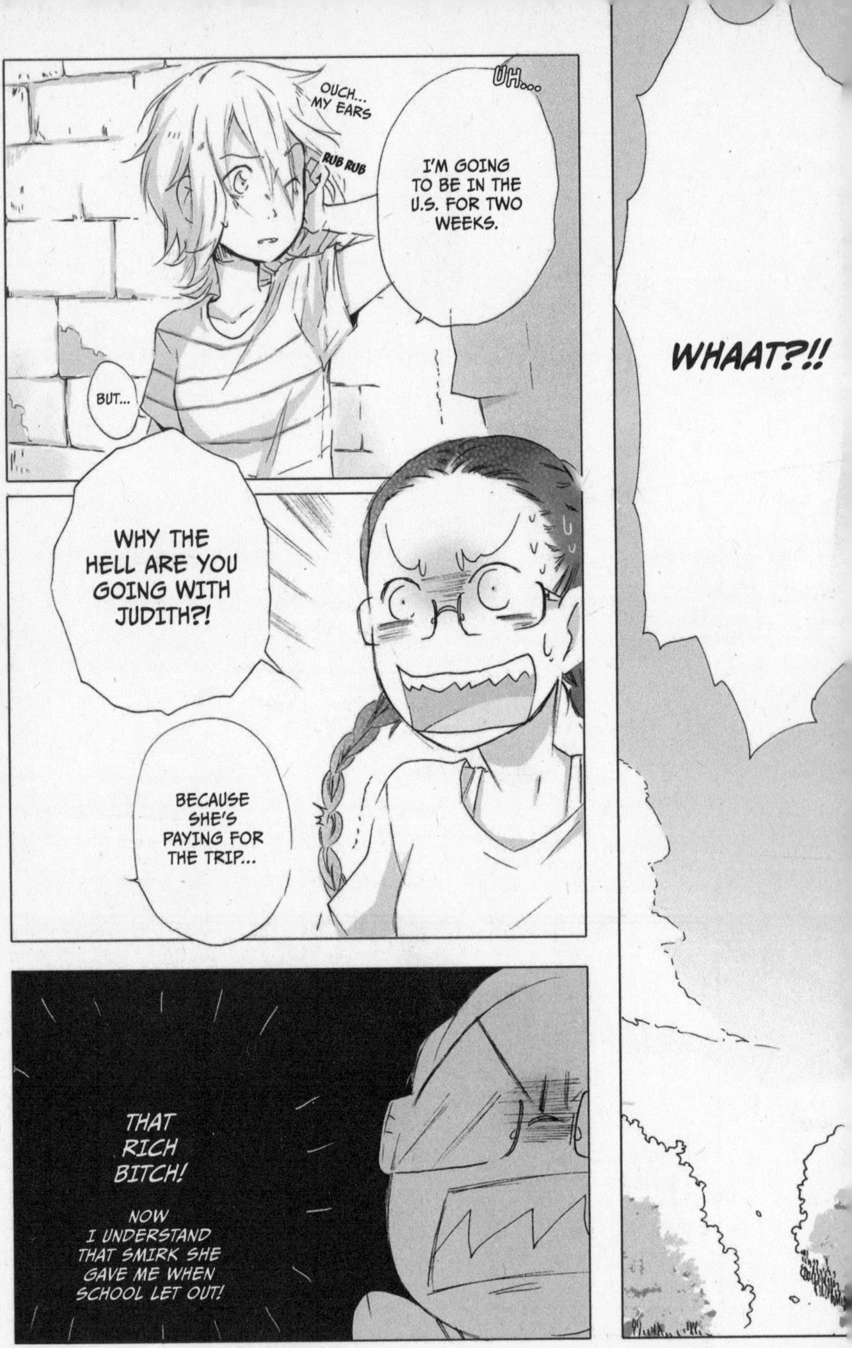
WHAAT?!!
UH...
I'M GOING TO BE IN THE U.S. FOR TWO WEEKS.
OUCH... MY EARS
RUB RUB
BUT...
WHY THE HELL ARE YOU GOING WITH JUDITH?!
BECAUSE SHE'S PAYING FOR THE TRIP...
THAT RICH BITCH!
NOW I UNDERSTAND THAT SMIRK SHE GAVE ME WHEN SCHOOL LET OUT!

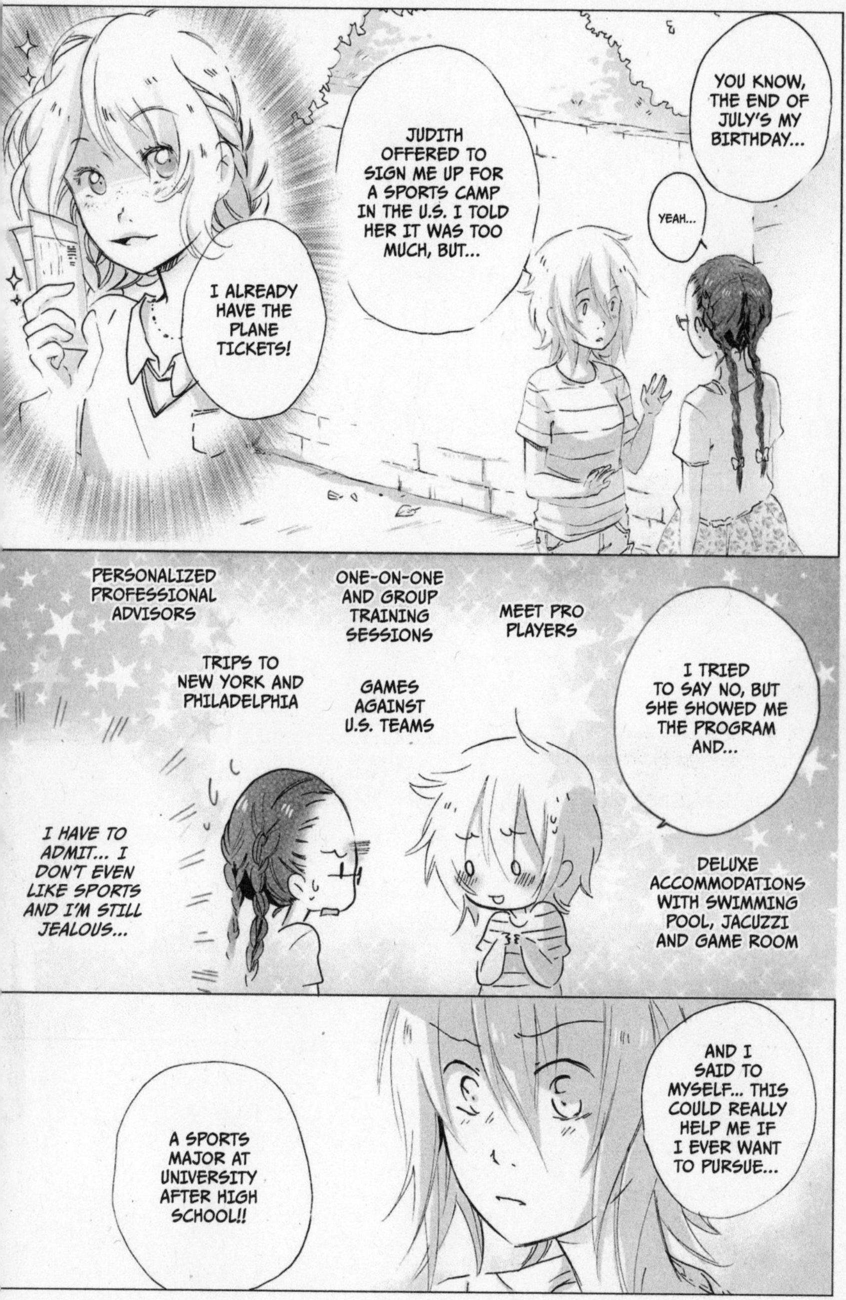
YOU KNOW, THE END OF JULY'S MY BIRTHDAY...
YEAH...
JUDITH OFFERED TO SIGN ME UP FOR A SPORTS CAMP IN THE U.S. I TOLD HER IT WAS TOO MUCH, BUT...
I ALREADY HAVE THE PLANE TICKETS!
I TRIED TO SAY NO, BUT SHE SHOWED ME THE PROGRAM AND...
MEET PRO PLAYERS
ONE-ON-ONE AND GROUP TRAINING SESSIONS
PERSONALIZED PROFESSIONAL ADVISORS
TRIPS TO NEW YORK AND PHILADELPHIA
GAMES AGAINST U.S. TEAMS
DELUXE ACCOMMODATIONS WITH SWIMMING POOL, JACUZZI AND GAME ROOM
I HAVE TO ADMIT... I DON'T EVEN LIKE SPORTS AND I'M STILL JEALOUS...
AND I SAID TO MYSELF... THIS COULD REALLY HELP ME IF I EVER WANT TO PURSUE...
A SPORTS MAJOR AT UNIVERSITY AFTER HIGH SCHOOL!!

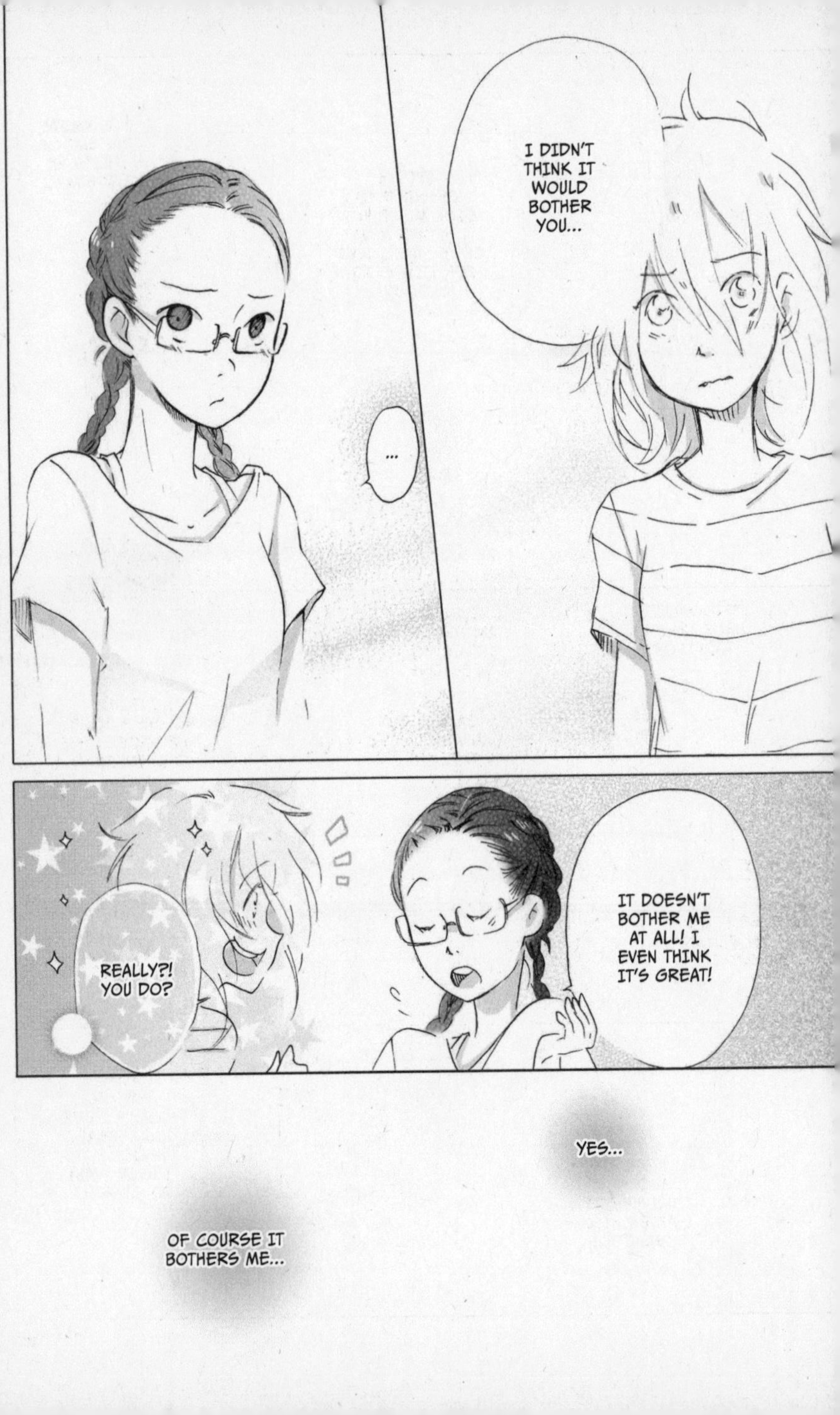
I DIDN'T THINK IT WOULD BOTHER YOU...
...
IT DOESN'T BOTHER ME AT ALL! I EVEN THINK IT'S GREAT!
REALLY?! YOU DO?
YES...
OF COURSE IT BOTHERS ME...

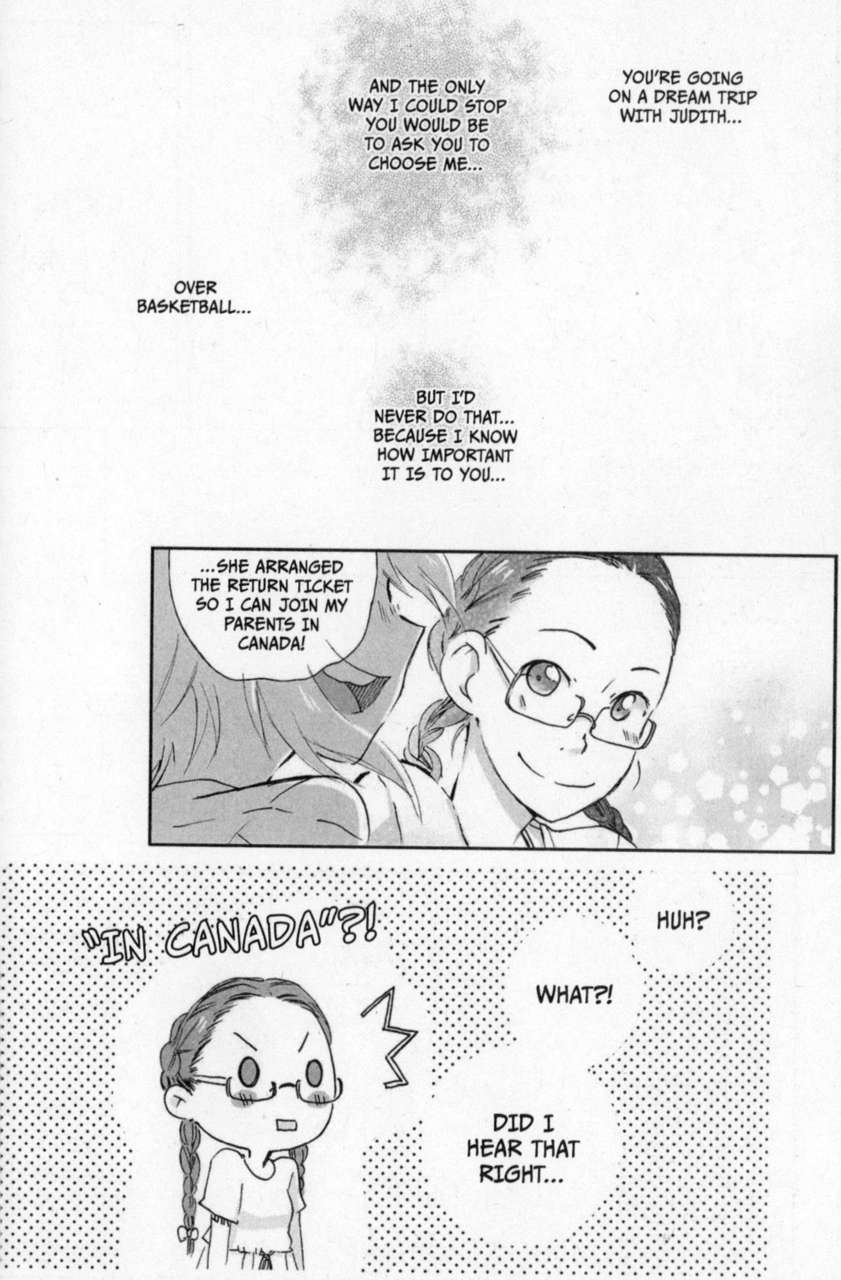
YOU'RE GOING ON A DREAM TRIP WITH JUDITH...
AND THE ONLY WAY I COULD STOP YOU WOULD BE TO ASK YOU TO CHOOSE ME...
OVER BASKETBALL...
BUT I'D NEVER DO THAT... BECAUSE I KNOW HOW IMPORTANT IT IS TO YOU...
...SHE ARRANGED THE RETURN TICKET SO I CAN JOIN MY PARENTS IN CANADA!
HUH?
WHAT?!
DID I HEAR THAT RIGHT...
"IN CANADA"?!

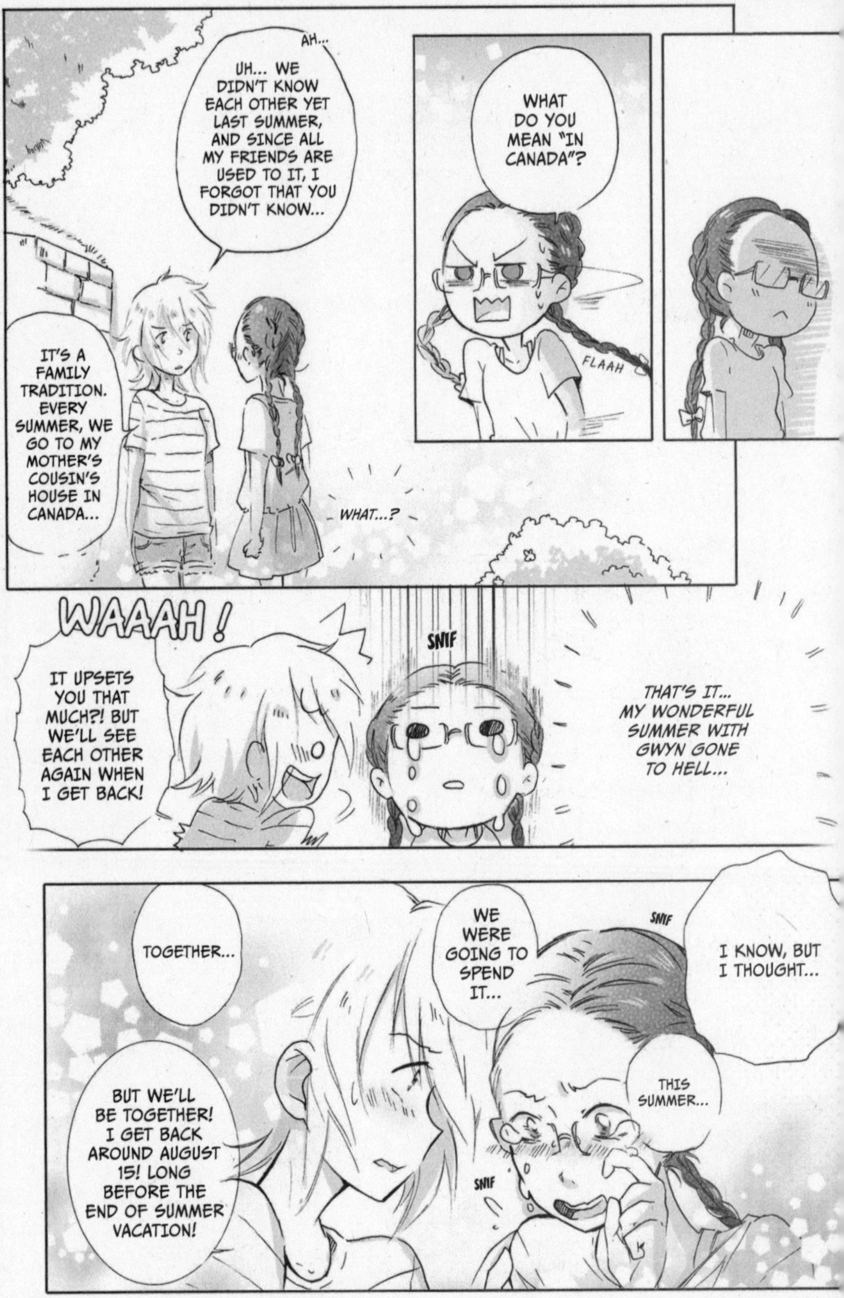
WHAT DO YOU MEAN "IN CANADA"?
FLAAH
AH...
UH... WE DIDN'T KNOW EACH OTHER YET LAST SUMMER, AND SINCE ALL MY FRIENDS ARE USED TO IT, I FORGOT THAT YOU DIDN'T KNOW...
IT'S A FAMILY TRADITION. EVERY SUMMER, WE GO TO MY MOTHER'S COUSIN'S HOUSE IN CANADA...
WHAT...?
THAT'S IT... MY WONDERFUL SUMMER WITH GWYN GONE TO HELL...
SNIF
IT UPSETS YOU THAT MUCH?! BUT WE'LL SEE EACH OTHER AGAIN WHEN I GET BACK!
WAAAH!
I KNOW, BUT I THOUGHT...
SNIF
WE WERE GOING TO SPEND IT...
TOGETHER...
THIS SUMMER...
SNIF
BUT WE'LL BE TOGETHER! I GET BACK AROUND AUGUST 15! LONG BEFORE THE END OF SUMMER VACATION!

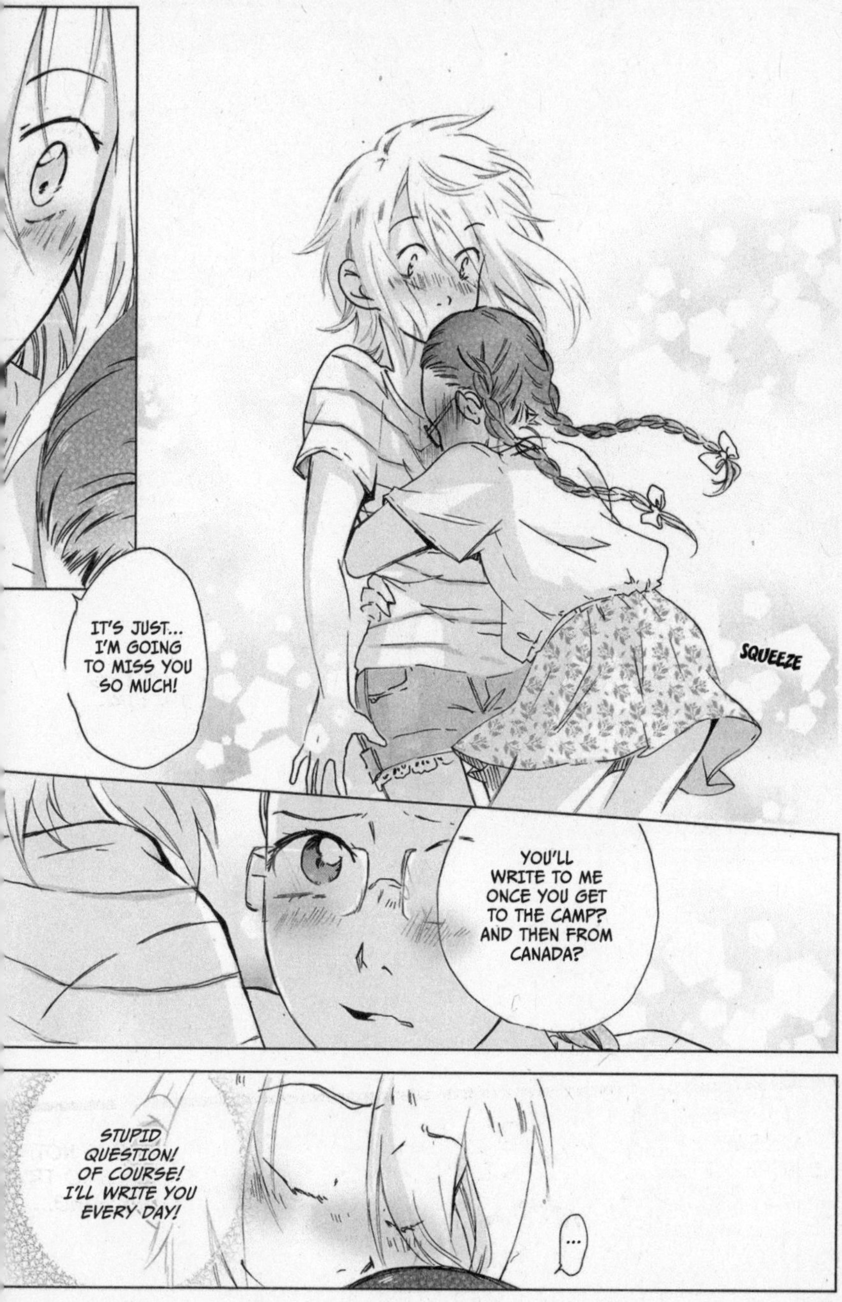
IT'S JUST... I'M GOING TO MISS YOU SO MUCH!
SQUEEZE
YOU'LL WRITE TO ME ONCE YOU GET TO THE CAMP? AND THEN FROM CANADA?
STUPID QUESTION! OF COURSE! I'LL WRITE YOU EVERY DAY!
...

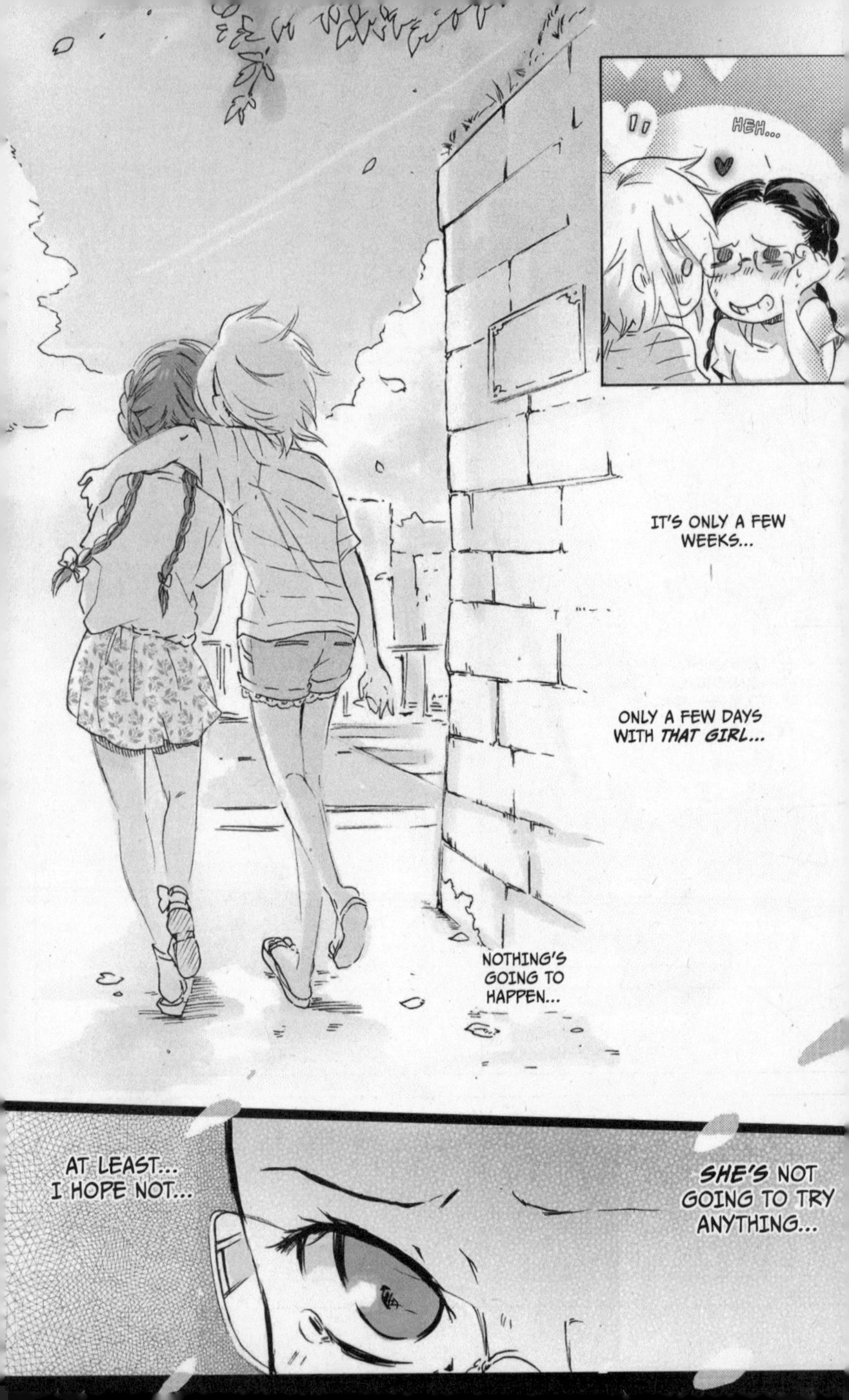
HEH...
IT'S ONLY A FEW WEEKS...
ONLY A FEW DAYS WITH *THAT GIRL*...
NOTHING'S GOING TO HAPPEN...
SHE'S NOT GOING TO TRY ANYTHING...
AT LEAST... I HOPE NOT...

SUPERHERO!

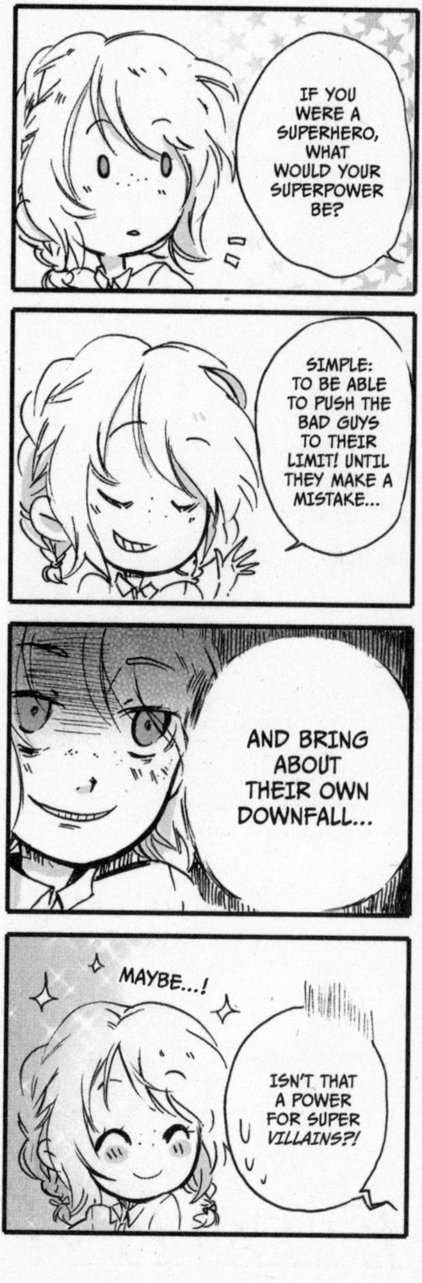
IF YOU WERE A SUPERHERO, WHAT WOULD YOUR SUPERPOWER BE?
SIMPLE: TO BE ABLE TO PUSH THE BAD GUYS TO THEIR LIMIT! UNTIL THEY MAKE A MISTAKE...
AND BRING ABOUT THEIR OWN DOWNFALL...
ISN'T THAT A POWER FOR SUPER VILLAINS?!
MAYBE...!

THE HAIR!

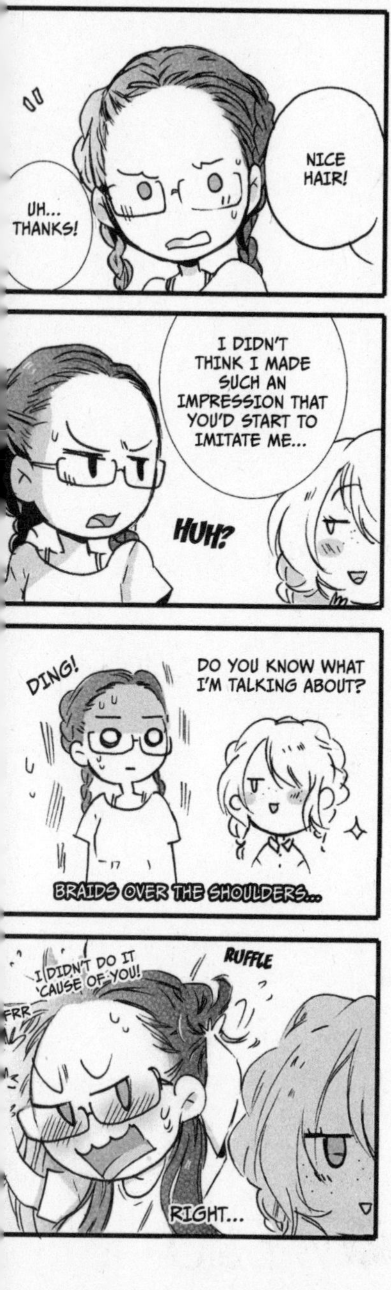
NICE HAIR!
UH... THANKS!
I DIDN'T THINK I MADE SUCH AN IMPRESSION THAT YOU'D START TO IMITATE ME...
HUH?
DO YOU KNOW WHAT I'M TALKING ABOUT?
DING!
BRAIDS OVER THE SHOULDERS...
RUFFLE
I DIDN'T DO IT 'CAUSE OF YOU!
FRR
RIGHT...

BREATH OF FLOWERS

BREATH OF FLOWERS

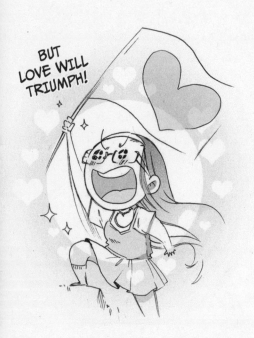

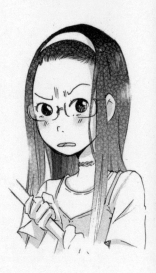

THE GUY WHO SAID "LOVE CONQUERS ALL" NEVER MET JUDITH...

BUT LOVE WILL TRIUMPH!

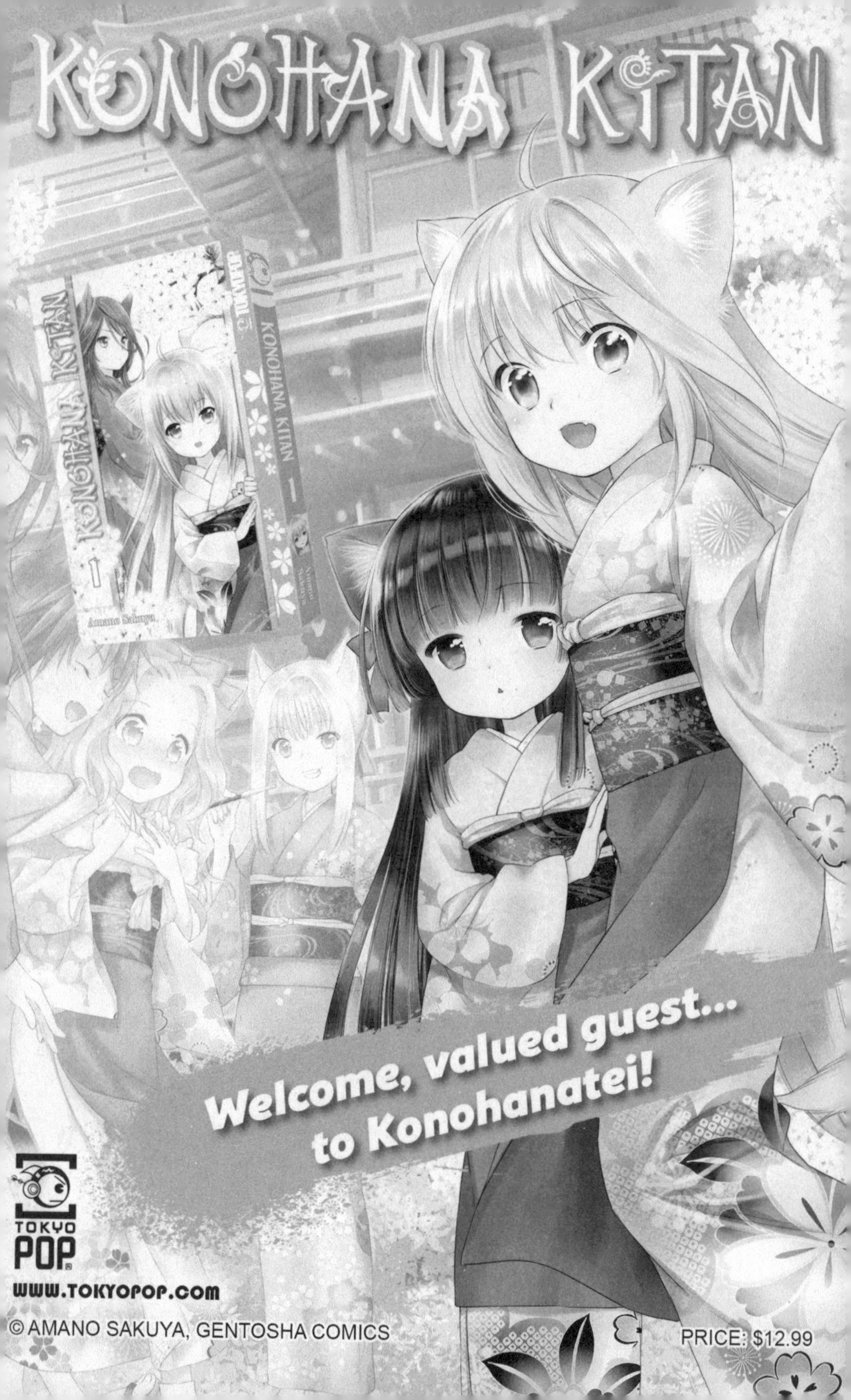
KONOHANA KITAN
KONOHANA KITAN 1
Amano Sakuya
Welcome, valued guest...
to Konohanatei!
TOKYO POP
WWW.TOKYOPOP.COM
© AMANO SAKUYA, GENTOSHA COMICS
PRICE: $12.99

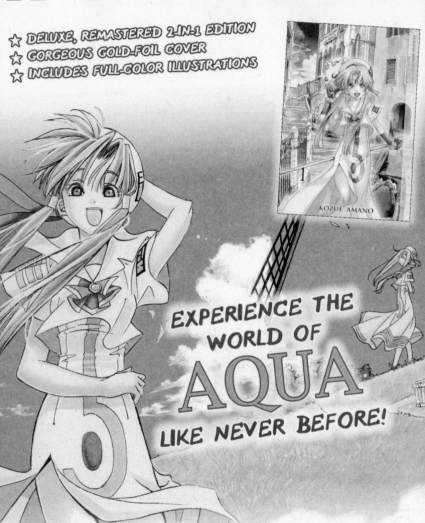

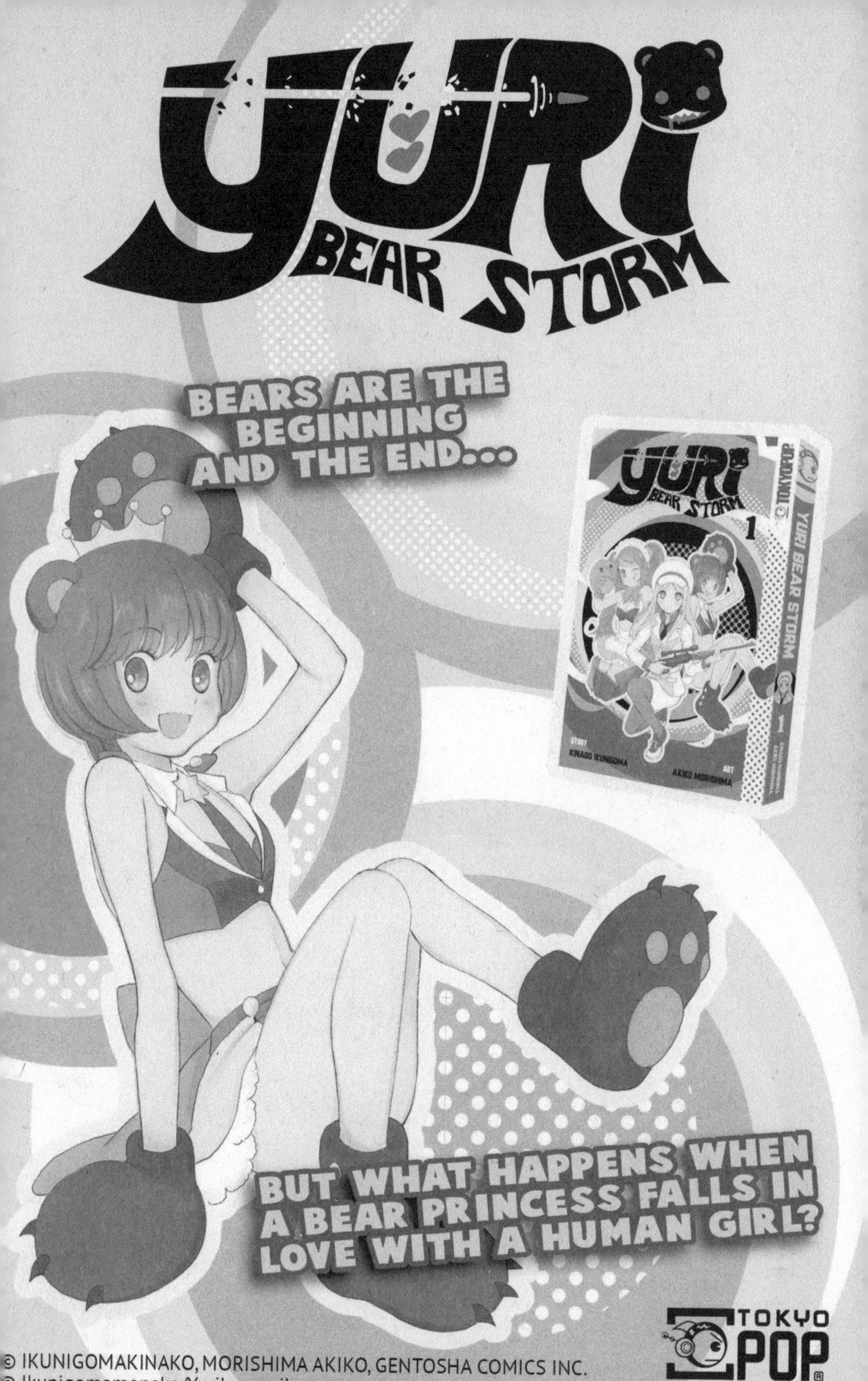
YURI BEAR STORM
BEARS ARE THE BEGINNING AND THE END...
YURI BEAR STORM 1
STORY KINAGO IKUNIGOMA
ART AKIKO MORISHIMA
TOKYOPOP
BUT WHAT HAPPENS WHEN A BEAR PRINCESS FALLS IN LOVE WITH A HUMAN GIRL?
TOKYO POP

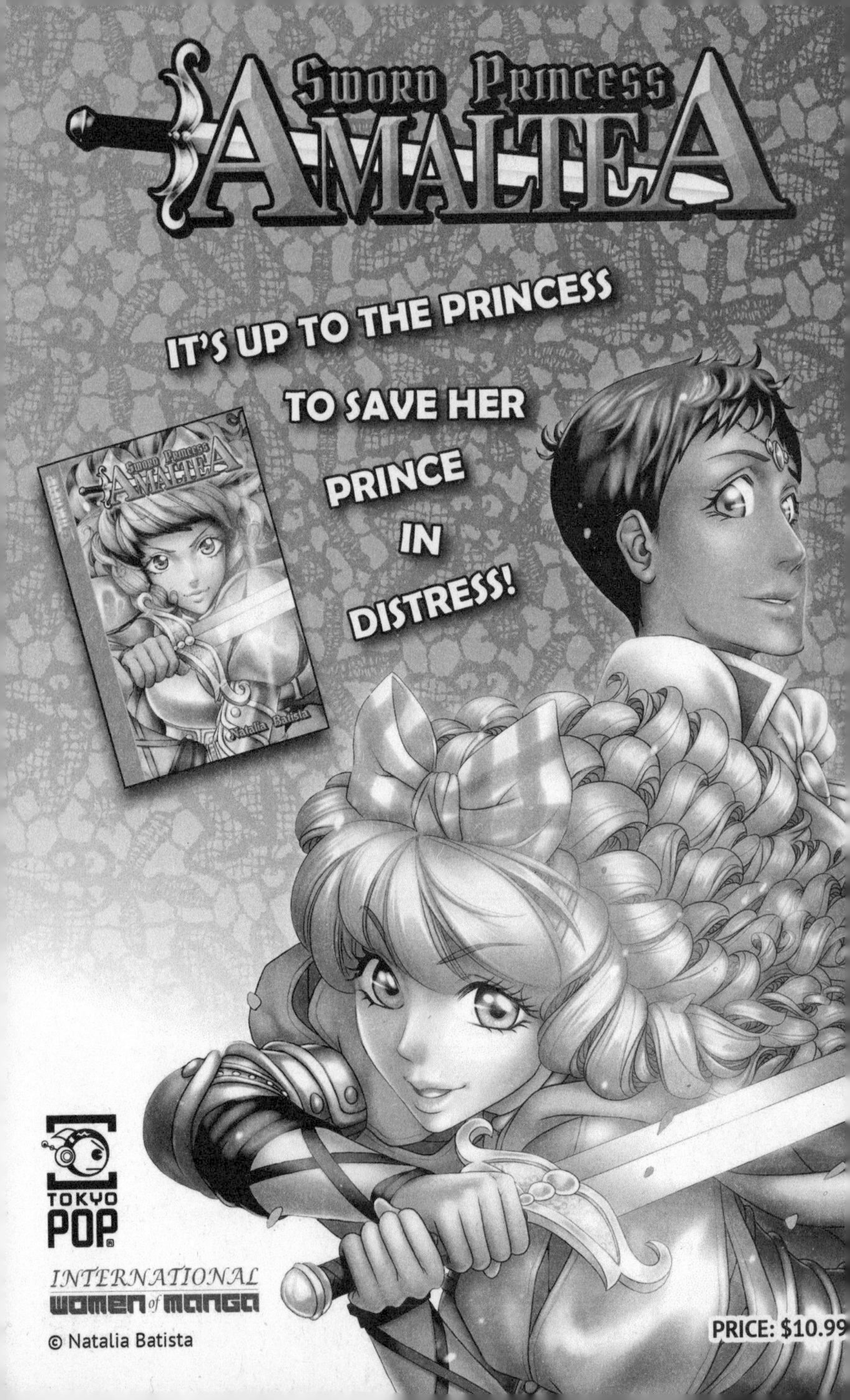

SWORD PRINCESS
AMALTEA
IT'S UP TO THE PRINCESS
TO SAVE HER
PRINCE
IN
DISTRESS!
Natalia Batista
TOKYO POP
INTERNATIONAL
WOMEN of MANGA
© Natalia Batista
PRICE: $10.99

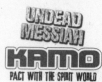

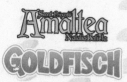

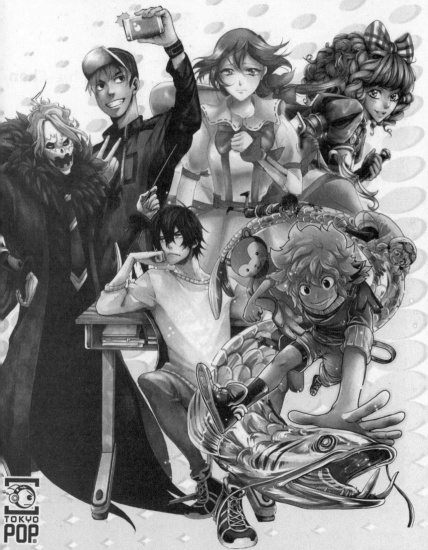

TOKYOPOP GmbH / *Goldfisch* - NANA YAA / *Kamo* - BAN ZARBO / *Undead Messiah* - GIN ZARBO / *Ocean of Secrets* - SOPHIE-CHAN / *Sword Princess Amaltea* - NATALIA BATISTA

TOKYOPOP
· PRESENTS ·

INTERNATIONAL
WOMEN of MANGA

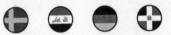

Nana Yaa

GOLDFISCH

An award-winning German manga artist with a large following for her free webcomic, ***CRUSHED!!***

Sophie-Chan

Ocean of Secrets

A self-taught manga artist from the Middle East, with a huge YouTube following!

Ban Zarbo

KAMO
PACT WITH THE SPIRIT WORLD

A lifelong manga fan from Switzerland, she and her twin sister take inspiration from their Dominican roots!

Gin Zarbo

UNDEAD MESSIAH

An aspiring manga artist since she wa a child, along with her twin sister she releasing her debut title!

Natalia Batista

Sword Princess Amaltea
Natalia Batista

A Swedish creator whose popular manga has already been published in Sweden, Italy and the Czech Republic!

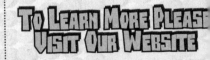

To Learn More Please Visit Our Website

www.TOKYOPOP.com

STAR COLLECTOR

By Anna B. & Sophie Schönhammer

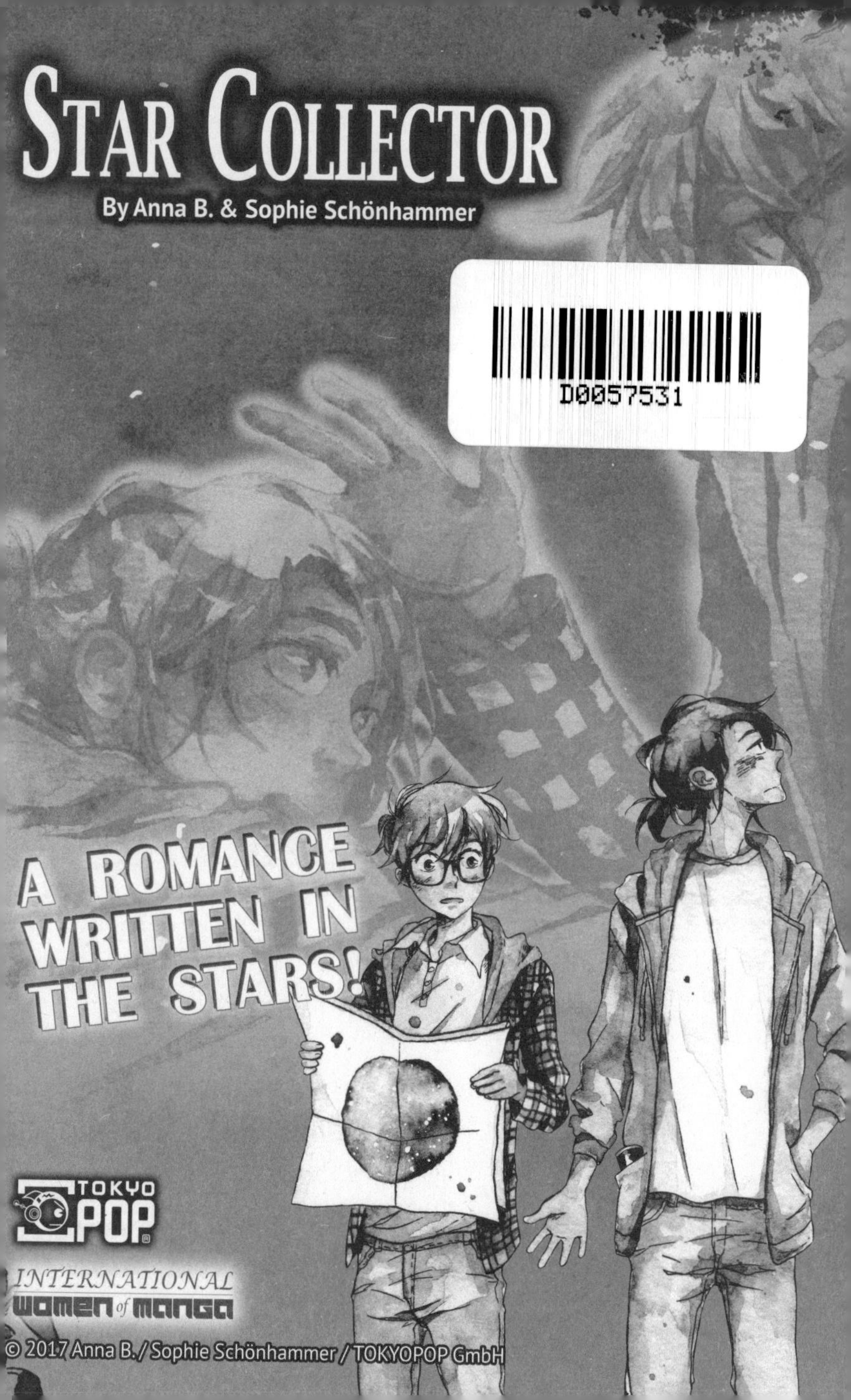
A ROMANCE WRITTEN IN THE STARS!

TOKYOPOP

INTERNATIONAL women of manga